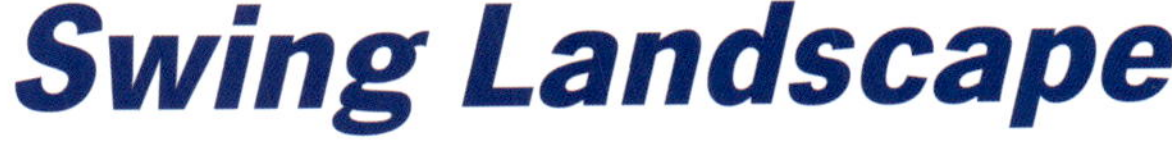
Swing Landscape

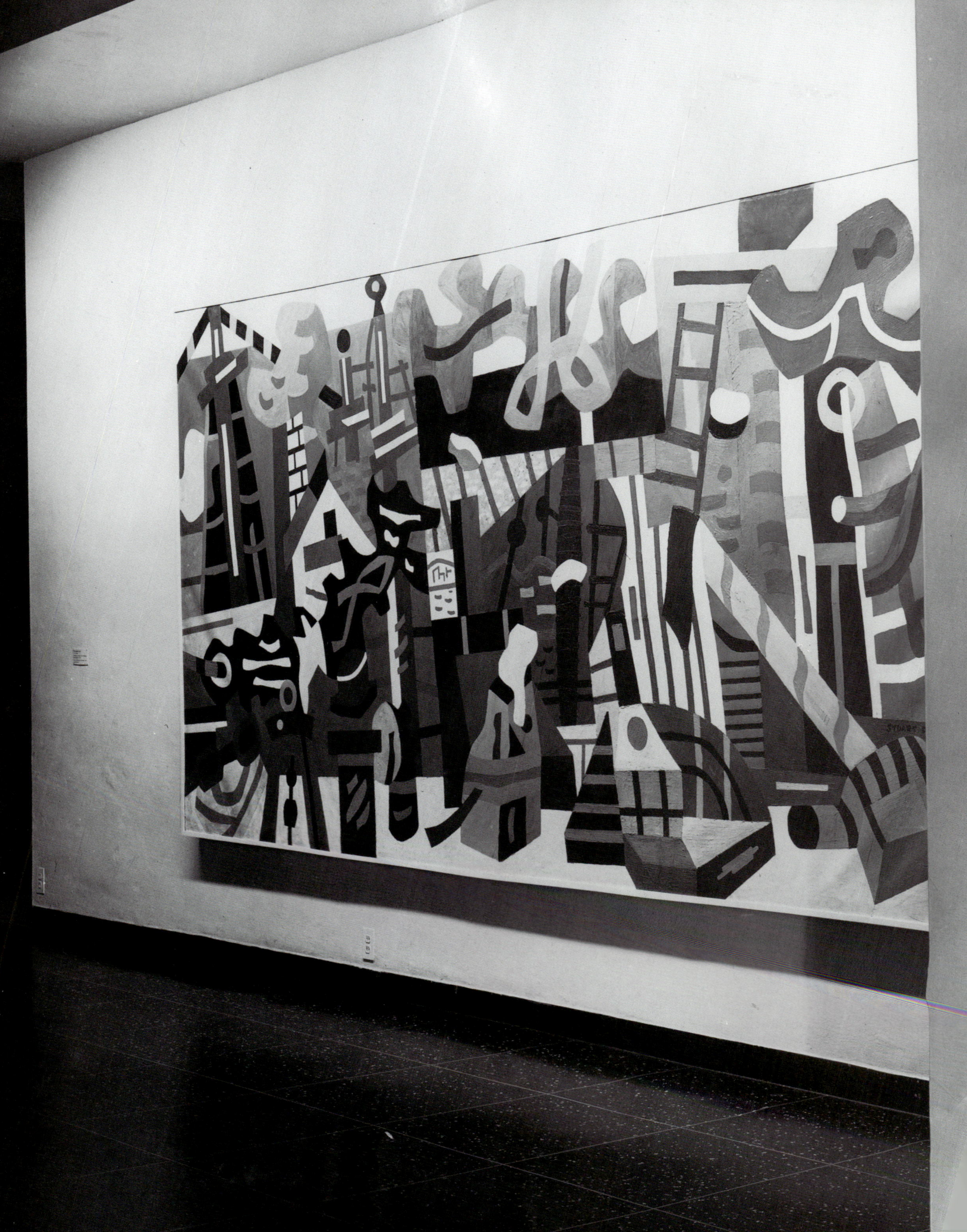

Swing Landscape

Stuart Davis and the Modernist Mural

Jennifer McComas

With an essay by
Jody Patterson

Sidney and Lois Eskenazi Museum of Art
Indiana University, Bloomington

Yale University Press
New Haven and London

Published to accompany the exhibition *Swing Landscape: Stuart Davis and the Modernist Mural*, organized by the Sidney and Lois Eskenazi Museum of Art, Indiana University, Bloomington. The exhibition, planned for fall 2020, was postponed for public health reasons related to the COVID-19 pandemic. The Checklist of the Exhibition reflects the works secured as of April 2020.

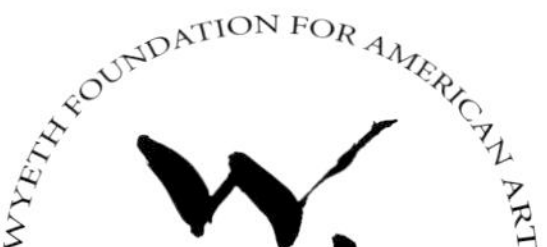

Generous support for this exhibition has been provided by Indiana University's New Frontiers in the Arts and Humanities Program, the Art Dealers Association of America Foundation, Susan Thrasher, David Jacobs, Ann Sanderson, and Paula Sunderman. Support for the catalogue was provided by the Wyeth Foundation for American Art. Research for this exhibition was supported by the Terra Foundation for American Art.

Sidney and Lois Eskenazi Museum of Art
Indiana University, Bloomington
1133 East Seventh Street
Bloomington, Indiana 47405-7509
https://artmuseum.indiana.edu

Yale University Press
302 Temple Street
PO Box 209040
New Haven, Connecticut 06520-9040
yalebooks.com/art

Designed and typeset by Katy Homans
Set in Century Expanded and News Gothic types
Printed in China by Regent Publishing Services Limited

Library of Congress Control Number: 2019957224
ISBN 9780300250671

A catalogue record for this book is available from the British Library.

The paper in this book meets the requirements of ANSI/NISO Z39.48-1992 (Permanence of Paper).

10 9 8 7 6 5 4 3 2 1

Cover: Stuart Davis, detail of *Swing Landscape* (page 2)

Frontispiece: Soichi Sunami, installation view of the exhibition *Stuart Davis* (page 138)

Page xii: Stuart Davis, detail of *Swing Landscape* (page 2)

Page 44: Lee Krasner, detail of *Untitled Mural Study* (page 57)

Page 66: Francis Criss (page 80)

Page 124: Stuart Davis, detail of *From Sketchbook 3, Drawing for "Landscape with Drying Sails"* (page 126)

Page 133: Stuart Davis, detail of *Wheel House* (page 127)

Page 134: Auction of student artwork at Indiana University, with *Swing Landscape* hanging on the back wall, June 8, 1946 (page 138)

Contents

Director’s Foreword

The Eskenazi Museum of Art at Indiana University is fortunate to be home to Stuart Davis’s stunning 1938 mural *Swing Landscape*, one of the most groundbreaking works of twentieth-century American art. We are forever grateful to the museum’s founding director, Henry Radford Hope, who had the foresight to negotiate with the Works Progress Administration for the mural’s allocation to Indiana University in 1941. *Swing Landscape* has been a cornerstone of the museum’s collection ever since, its vibrant colors and composition delighting our visitors over the decades. Stuart Davis (1892–1964), one of the towering figures of twentieth-century American art, has been the subject of much scholarship and many exhibitions. But scholars have not probed as deeply as one might expect into the interpretation of *Swing Landscape* or examined the context of its production in any detail.

We are proud to present *Swing Landscape: Stuart Davis and the Modernist Mural*, the first exhibition project to explore the mural’s aesthetics and history in depth. The exhibition and catalogue exemplify the type of serious research, inspired by the museum’s collection, which should be undertaken by a teaching museum located within a major research university. The project advances scholarship on *Swing Landscape*, examining its place in Davis’s larger oeuvre, its relationship to other abstract murals painted in the 1930s, and its commission for the Williamsburg Housing Project in Brooklyn. Considering *Swing Landscape*’s status as the Eskenazi Museum’s first major acquisition, it is fitting that the exhibition is one of the first to be presented in our newly refreshed galleries, following a two-and-a-half-year renovation (2017–19) of the museum’s I. M. Pei–designed building, and coinciding with the university’s bicentennial.

I want to particularly recognize the efforts of Dr. Jennifer McComas in conceiving, researching, and organizing this important exhibition and its accompanying catalogue. Dr. McComas recognized the need and opportunity to closely examine this major masterpiece in our collection, and I extend my gratitude to her for taking the initiative on this groundbreaking project.

Equally critical to the exhibition's success is the support of Indiana University's New Frontiers in the Arts and Humanities Program, the Art Dealers Association of America Foundation, the Wyeth Foundation for American Art, the Terra Foundation for American Art, David Jacobs, Ann Sanderson, Paula Sunderman, and our National Advisory Board member Susan Thrasher, who not only stepped forward with the first gift for this exhibition but recently established the museum's first exhibitions endowment. This exhibition is dedicated to her.

David A. Brenneman

Wilma E. Kelley Director, Eskenazi Museum of Art

Dedicated to Susan Thrasher

Acknowledgments

Swing Landscape: Stuart Davis and the Modernist Mural has been many years in the making, and its realization was made possible through the help of numerous individuals. First and foremost, I wish to thank Adelheid M. Gealt, Director Emerita, and David Brenneman, the Wilma E. Kelley Director of the Eskenazi Museum of Art, for their support of this project as it developed over the past years. Additionally, Diane Pelrine, Chief Curator Emerita, supported and encouraged my research for this exhibition in its earliest stages.

The exhibition's success is due to the generosity of our lenders, and especially to the directors, curators, registrars, and photographers at the following museums and archives whose works are included in this exhibition: the Addison Gallery of American Art at Phillips Academy; the Archives of American Art, Smithsonian Institution; the Art Institute of Chicago; the Columbus Museum of Art; Crystal Bridges Museum of Art; Davis Museum of Art at Wellesley College; the Harvard Art Museums; the High Museum of Art; the Hirshhorn Museum and Sculpture Garden, Smithsonian Institution; the Menil Collection; the Museum of Modern Art; the National Gallery of Art; the Pennsylvania Academy of the Fine Arts; the Sheldon Museum of Art, University of Nebraska; the Whitney Museum of American Art; and Yale University Art Gallery. I also wish to thank the art dealers and representatives of artists' estates who lent works from their collections or assisted me in locating other works, images, and documents: David Cowan, formerly of ACME Fine Art in Boston; Katherine Criss; Helen McNeil-Ashton; the Michael Rosenfeld Gallery LLC; and the Kasmin Gallery. I extend particular thanks to Earl Davis, the artist's son, for his support of the exhibition and for his great generosity as a lender.

Much scholarship on Stuart Davis precedes this publication. My own research was inspired and assisted by the writings and personal encouragement of many art historians and curators in the field, including: Katia Baudin, Director, Kunstmuseum, Krefeld, Germany; Greta Berman, Professor of Art History, The Julliard School; Harry Cooper, Curator and Head of Modern Art, National Gallery of Art; Judith F. Dolkart, Deputy Director, Detroit Institute of Arts; Nancy E. Green, Gale and Ira Drukier Curator of European and American Art, Prints & Drawings, 1800–1945, Herbert F. Johnson Museum of Art, Cornell University; Randall Griffey, Associate Curator, Modern and Contemporary Art, The Metropolitan Museum of Art; Barbara Haskell, Curator, Whitney Museum of American Art; Sarah Kianovsky, Curator of the Collection, Division of Modern and Contemporary Art, Harvard Art Museums; Kimberly Orcutt, formerly Andrew W. Mellon Curator of American Art, The Brooklyn Museum; and Nancy J. Troy, Victoria and Roger Sant Professor in Art, Department of Art and Art History, Stanford University.

As I developed and refined my arguments and theories about the history and interpretation of *Swing Landscape*, I presented my work at two conferences and published a scholarly article on the subject. For these opportunities to share my research with colleagues in academia, I am grateful to Rachel Stephens, Assistant Professor of Art History, University of Alabama, and chair of the "American Art: Building a National Identity" session at the 2016 Southeast College Art Conference; and to Gregor Langfeld, Assistant Professor at the University of Amsterdam, and art historian Tessel M. Bauduin, organizers of the 2017 *Canonizing Modernism* symposium at the University of Amsterdam and editors of the December 2018 issue of the *Journal of Art Historiography*, devoted to the same topic.

This project required me to conduct many hours of research at archives and museums. For facilitating my research, making materials available, and answering my questions, I am very grateful to the staffs of the Archives of American Art, Smithsonian Institution; The Brooklyn Museum; the former Corcoran Gallery of Art; the Houghton Library, Harvard University; the LaGuardia & Wagner Archives at the City University of New York; The Museum of Modern Art's Archives and its Painting and Sculpture Study Center; the National Archives and Records Administration in College Park; the Smithsonian American Art Museum; and the Syracuse University Libraries.

The dedicated and talented staff at the Eskenazi Museum of Art devoted a great deal of time and effort toward the realization of the exhibition, much of it during an unusually busy time when the museum was undergoing major renovations. The following colleagues provided research assistance, cleared image rights, managed the logistics of packing and shipping loans, raised funds, edited texts, managed publicity, helped conceptualize the installation, kept an eye on *Swing Landscape*'s fragile condition, and much more: Bill Bass, Art Handler and 3-D Visualizations; Janelle Beasley, Works on Paper Preparator; Anita Bracalente, Registrar; Nanette Brewer, Lucienne M. Glaubinger Curator of Works on Paper; Margaret Contompasis, Paintings Conservator Emerita; Heidi Davis-Soylu, Lucienne M. Glaubinger Director of Education; Carol Dell, Director of Administration; Heather Hales, Associate Registrar; Mariah Keller, Editor and Director of Creative Services; Shanti Knight, Photographer; Maggie Kroh, Assistant to the Director; Kristin Londergan, Marketing and Communications Coordinator; Ellen Lyon, Paintings Conservation Technician; Michelle Mandarino, Graduate Curatorial Assistant; Pete Nelson, Chief Preparator; Galina Olmsted, Assistant Curator, European and American Art; Julie Ribits, Beverly and Gayl W. Doster Paintings Conservator; Laura Scheper, Interpretation and Public Experiences Manager; Cassi Tucker, Manager of Museum Technology; Richard Valdez, Finance Manager; Andrew Wang, Graduate Curatorial Assistant; Jessie Waymire, Graphic Designer; and Patricia Winterton, Director of Development.

Also at Indiana University, I received important assistance from Faith Kirkham Hawkins, Associate Vice President, Office of the Vice President for Research; Cory Rutz, Director of Foundation Relations, Office of the Vice President for Research; Carrie Schwier, Outreach and Public Services Archivist, University Archives; and the staff of the Office of Research Administration.

It has also been a privilege to work with the enthusiastic and very capable staff at Yale University Press on the editing, design, and production of this publication: Amy Canonico, Laura Jones Dooley, Heidi Downey, Katy Homans, and Raychel Rapazza. I would also like to extend my sincere thanks to Jody Patterson, Associate Professor and Roy Lichtenstein Foundation Chair of Art History at Ohio State University, not only for the insightful essay she contributed to this catalogue, but for her pathbreaking work on Stuart Davis and murals of the 1930s.

Finally, I am honored that Indiana University's New Frontiers in the Arts and Humanities Program, the Art Dealers Association of America Foundation, the Wyeth Foundation for American Art, and the Terra Foundation for American Art recognized the project's advancement of scholarship on Stuart Davis and American art, and chose to award grants for this exhibition. I am also grateful to Susan Thrasher, David Jacobs, Ann Sanderson, and Paula Sunderman, who generously supported this exhibition.

Jennifer McComas

Curator of European and American Art
Eskenazi Museum of Art

Lenders to the Exhibition

Addison Gallery of American Art
at Phillips Academy, Andover

Archives of American Art,
Smithsonian Institution, Washington

Art Institute of Chicago

Columbus Museum of Art

Davis Museum of Art at Wellesley College

Earl Davis

Harvard Art Museums, Cambridge

High Museum of Art, Atlanta

Hirshhorn Museum and Sculpture Garden,
Smithsonian Institution, Washington

Kasmin Gallery, New York

Helen McNeil-Ashton

The Menil Collection, Houston

Michael Rosenfeld Gallery, LLC, New York

Museum of Modern Art, New York

National Gallery of Art, Washington

Pennsylvania Academy of the Fine Arts,
Philadelphia

Private Collection

Sheldon Museum of Art,
University of Nebraska, Lincoln

Whitney Museum of American Art, New York

Yale University Art Gallery, New Haven

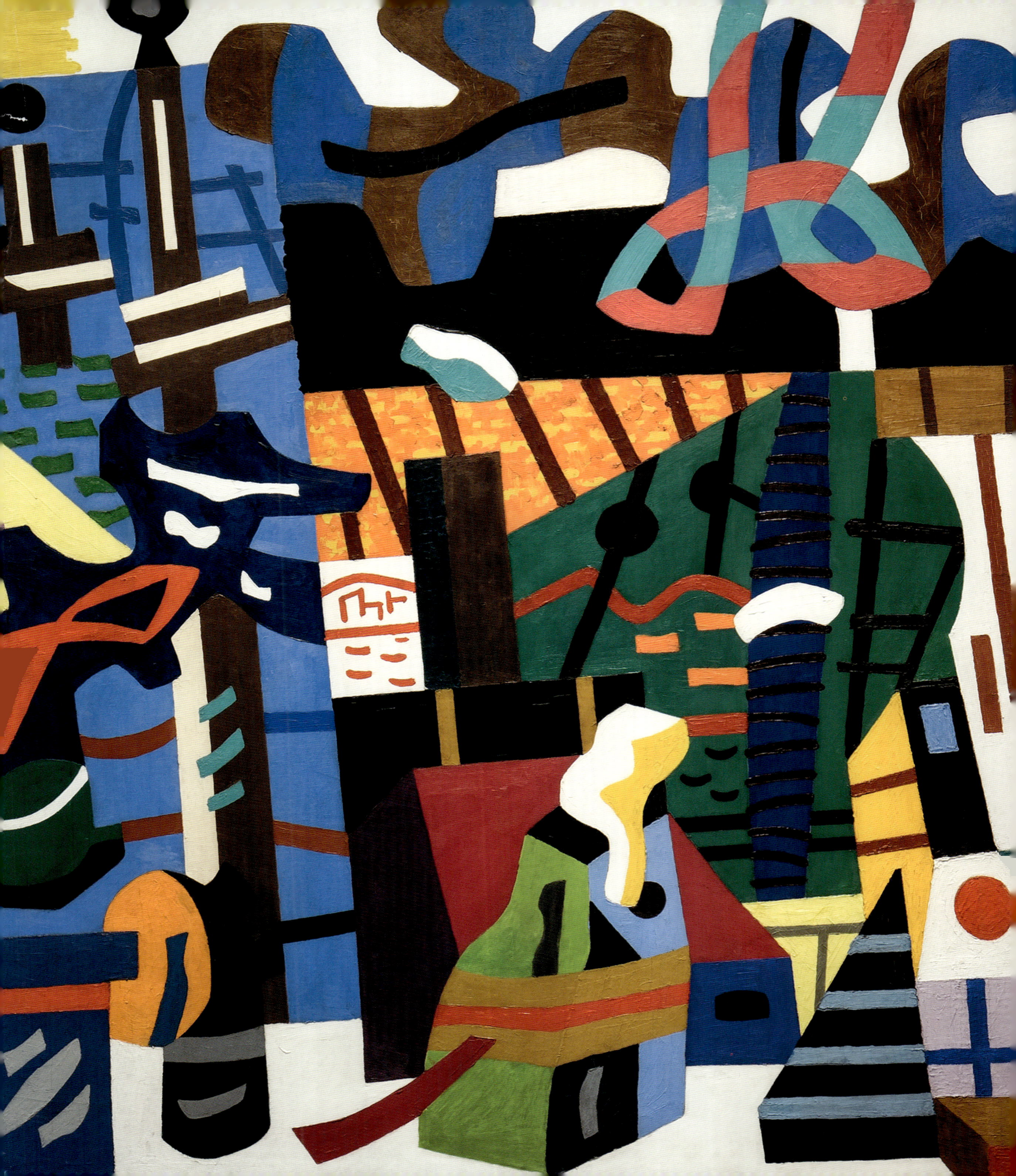

Swing Landscape in Context

Rediscovering Radical Meaning in Stuart Davis's Williamsburg Mural

Jennifer McComas

Stuart Davis's mural *Swing Landscape*, lauded as the "greatest American painting" of the first half of the twentieth century, was commissioned in 1936 by the Works Progress Administration's Federal Art Project (FAP).[1] Measuring seven by fourteen feet, the mural visually and physically dominates its surroundings. Its vibrant palette and frenetic composition embody Davis's distinctive response to Cubism and foreshadow the "allover" compositional strategies taken up in the next decade by the Abstract Expressionists (and seen, as well, in Davis's subsequent paintings such as *Ultra-Marine*). It is not surprising, then, that its formal qualities—notably its allusions to the rhythms of swing music—form the basis for its analysis in the literature on Stuart Davis. What is surprising, especially considering its intended installation in the Williamsburg Housing Project in Brooklyn, New York, is how little has been said about *Swing Landscape*'s intersection with progressive social ideals and leftist politics. Nor have most scholars examined its aesthetic relationship to other murals painted for the Williamsburg site or considered the audience for whom Davis presumed he was painting.[2] Why is this the case? Perhaps the simplest explanation is that *Swing Landscape* was never installed in the Williamsburg Houses. Since early 1942, it has instead been held at Indiana University, far removed geographically and culturally from its intended home and audience. Why was the mural rejected from the site for which it was commissioned? To date, no satisfactory answers to this question have been proposed. Some have suggested that it was "too modern" for a mass audience, but this theory fails to recognize that the Williamsburg Houses' architects and administrators *wanted* to create a modernist environment.[3] Unfortunately, the scattered

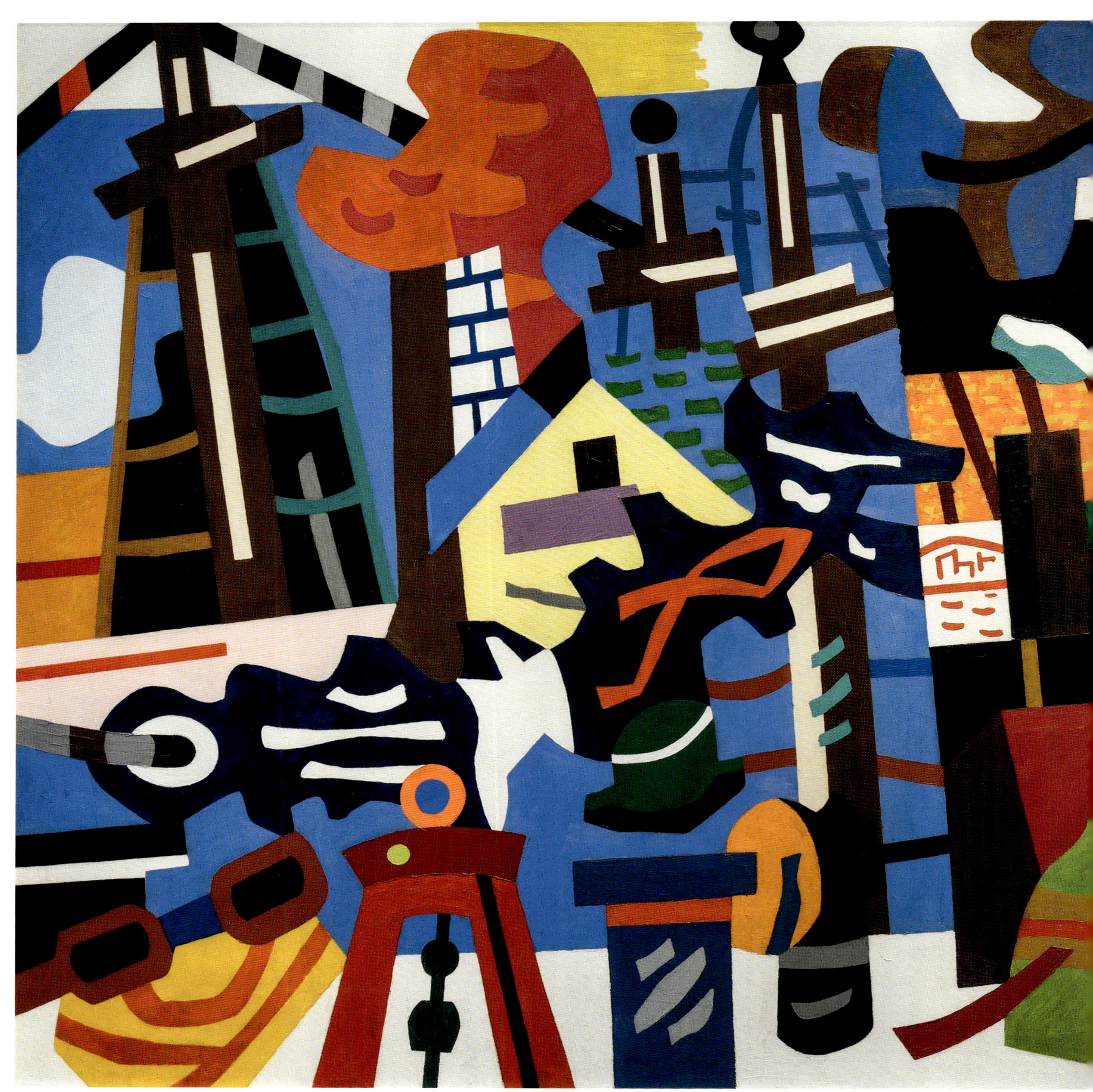

Stuart Davis, *Swing Landscape,* 1938
Oil on canvas, 86¾ × 173⅛ in. (220.3 × 439.7 cm). Allocated by the U.S. Government, Commissioned through the New Deal Art Projects, Eskenazi Museum of Art, Indiana University, 42.1.

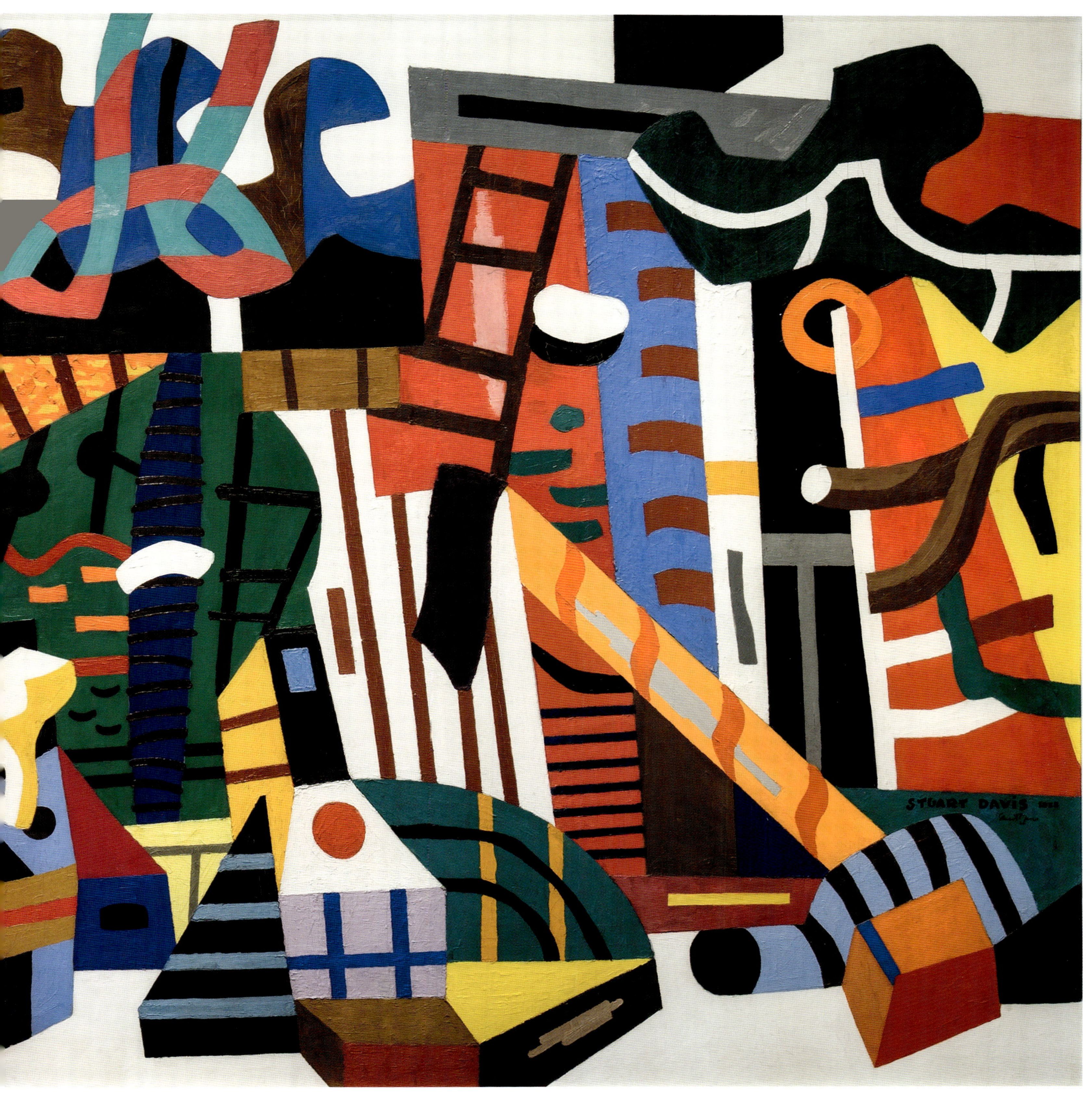
STUART DAVIS

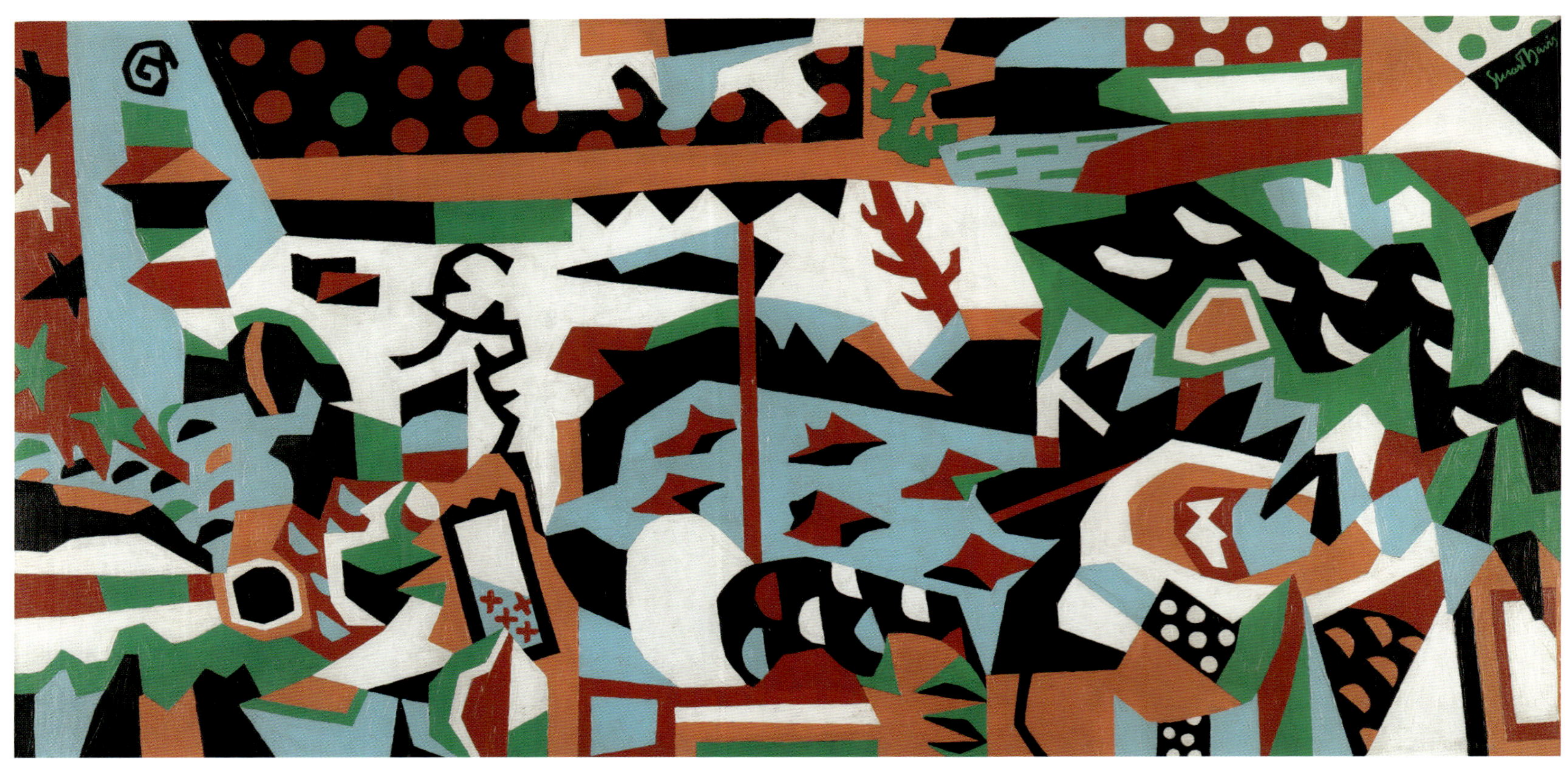

Stuart Davis, *Ultra-Marine,* 1943
Oil on canvas, 20 × 40⅛ in. (50.8 × 101.9 cm). Pennsylvania Academy of the Fine Arts, Joseph E. Temple Fund, 1952.11.

and incomplete nature of the archival documentation pertaining to *Swing Landscape*'s commission, production, and early history mean that the answers I propose are necessarily of a speculative nature, although they are grounded in a careful analysis of the larger social and aesthetic goals of the Williamsburg project.

Perhaps more critical to shaping prevailing readings of *Swing Landscape* is the remarkably persistent notion that Stuart Davis drew a line between his activist activities and his artistic pursuits. As recently as 2011, the respected Davis scholar William Agee stated that "Davis was more committed to radical politics, artists' rights, and social and artistic justice than any artist of the time, yet with the exception of two or three minor examples, it never showed in his art."[4] This essay argues the opposite. *Swing Landscape* may not be an *overtly* political work of art, but it indeed conveys a strong political message—if we only know how to find it. Unfortunately, the lack of any statements about *Swing Landscape* from Davis himself hinders any attempt to arrive at a nuanced and politically informed interpretation of the mural. To tease out its veiled meanings, I reconsider its relation to the architectural site for which it was commissioned, the expectations and interests of its patrons and audience, and, most important, how it illustrates Davis's conviction that abstract public art embodied socially and politically progressive values.

Public Housing in New York and Europe, 1919–39

That Davis painted *Swing Landscape* specifically for the residents of a public housing project—the only one to pair vanguard painting with modernist architecture—is far more significant than most scholars have acknowledged and is key to interpreting its composition. The Williamsburg Housing Project's significance vis-à-vis *Swing Landscape* is not merely a matter of aesthetics, however. It lies, instead, in cultural democratization—that is, by facilitating broader public access to modernist art. For, as Davis recognized, "a people's art can only come through the establishment of Federal support of art, better wages and hours legislation, and better housing conditions. In other words the establishment of the political, social, and economic conditions whereby the people have the time, the place, and the money to participate in artistic culture."[5] Before turning to the art, architecture, and social planning that distinguished the Williamsburg Houses, let us consider the historical, economic, and cultural issues that led to the establishment of federally subsidized housing in the United States, and specifically in New York City.

Even before the Great Depression, New Yorkers faced a severe shortage of affordable housing, a problem exacerbated by mass immigration to the city starting in the 1880s and continuing until 1924, when the passage of the Johnson-Reed Act implemented stringent immigration quotas. In the early twentieth century, Manhattan's Lower East Side was one of the most densely inhabited urban spaces in the world. Much of this population lived in nineteenth-century tenement buildings with substandard sanitation facilities, poor ventilation, and little fire protection. By the time of World War I, many

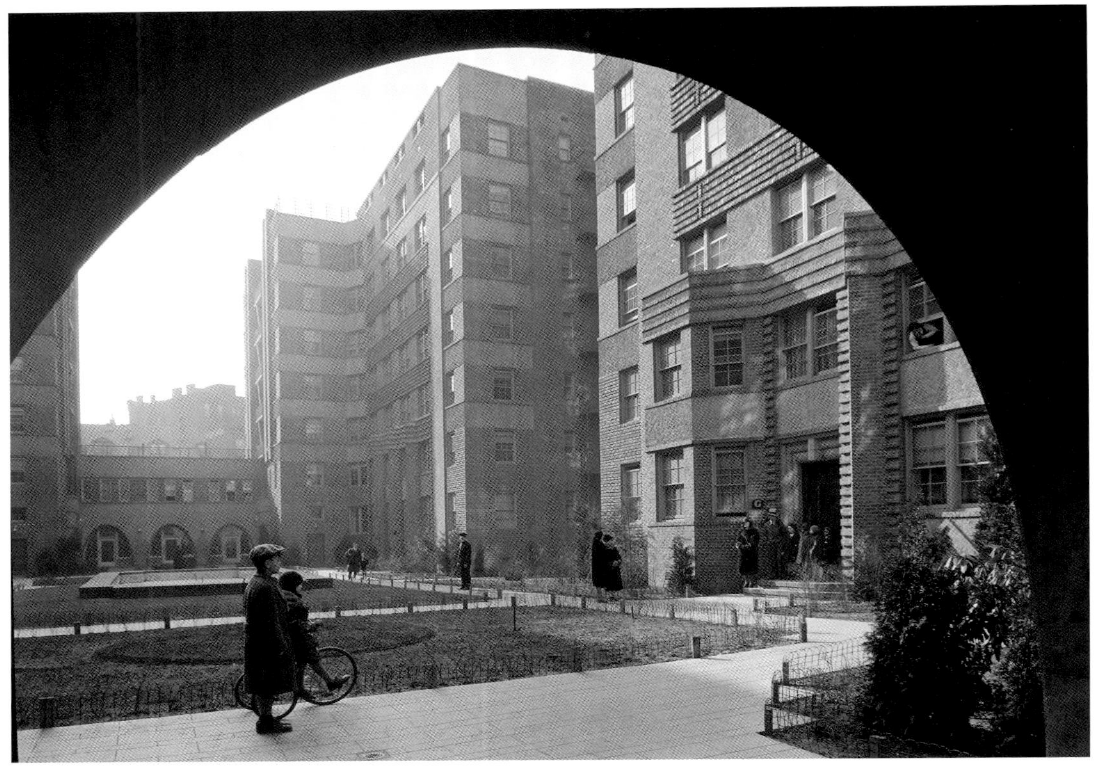

Samuel H. Gottscho, Amalgamated Housing, Inc. Through entrance arch 2, located at Grand and Columbia Streets, New York, January 10, 1931.

of the area's residents were moving to New York's outer boroughs in search of more space and higher-quality housing. But the outer boroughs were no more prepared than Manhattan to handle this population influx. In Williamsburg, Brooklyn, situated just across the East River from the Lower East Side, similarly inadequate and overcrowded housing conditions soon prevailed. In 1926, New York governor Al Smith attempted to address these problems with the passage of the New York State Housing Act, which granted tax incentives for the construction of limited-dividend housing for lower-income residents. But because this scheme required setting rents at below-market rates, corporate interest in the program was marginal, apart from the trade unions that primarily represented Jewish garment workers. Immediately following the passage of the Housing Act, for example, the Amalgamated Clothing Workers of America established a housing corporation to oversee the construction of cooperative housing for its members in the Bronx and on the Lower East Side. Other unions followed suit, but because there was little investment on the federal level, cooperative housing remained a risky financial endeavor in the United States. The Amalgamated's cooperatives were relatively successful only because the union received significant private backing from Abraham Cahan, editor of the *Forverts*, New York's major Yiddish newspaper.[6]

New York's cooperative housing ventures took their social and aesthetic cues from similar ventures in Europe, which faced its own housing crisis after World

War I. Approximately six million new homes were constructed in Europe between 1919 and 1933.[7] The limited-dividend model, in which low-rent housing was sponsored by labor unions and subsidized through tax incentives, was already common in some European cities by the time it was proposed in the United States. By the late 1920s, for example, over 70 percent of Berlin's new housing units were constructed under the auspices of the Gemeinnützige Heimstätten-Aktiengesellschaft (GEHAG), a building society that received most of its capital from socialist trade unions.[8] Elsewhere in postwar Europe, the threat of civil unrest, along with the rise of socialist political parties, incentivized city governments to make direct investments in affordable housing. In Vienna, the former imperial capital of the Habsburg Empire, a new socialist government pioneered one of Europe's most ambitious housing programs, subsidizing the construction of dozens of low-rent housing developments. Urban planners in the United States took note, with the Brookings Institution producing a study of Viennese mass housing in 1934.[9] Although the study determined that the Viennese model would not translate well to the American context, the residential architecture of so-called Red Vienna nevertheless exerted an influence—though not one that has been widely recognized—in New York. For example, the sites chosen for affordable housing developments in New York were, like their Viennese counterparts, well integrated into the existing urban fabric. In Germany (and less dense American cities), by contrast, low-rent housing estates were often constructed on large suburban plots far from city centers. Americans, like the Viennese, were also slower to embrace the streamlined, Bauhaus-influenced architectural style that characterized most German housing estates of the 1920s. For example, the Rabenhof, constructed in Vienna in the mid-1920s, contains an idiosyncratic blend of expressionist and art deco features, including pointed archways and chevron-patterned brick ornamentation. A similar expressionist aesthetic is evident in the patterned brick and stucco facade of the Amalgamated's cooperative building in Manhattan, known as the Grand Street Houses. Designed by the firm of Springsteen & Goldhammer, the building also follows Viennese models in its arrangement of buildings around a central courtyard, accessible through an arched passageway.[10] Most significant, however, was the European-style integration of medical, educational, and recreational facilities into this residential site.

European mass housing of the 1920s presented a living environment altogether different from that of the neighborhoods where most of its tenants previously resided. Developers broadly defined "housing" to encompass all aspects of life. Access to green space characterized the new developments across the continent, as did the integration of such amenities as shops, libraries, kindergartens, playgrounds, and even dental clinics. In her influential 1934 book *Modern Housing*, the housing reformer Catherine Bauer wrote that the United States had "almost no dwellings which can be said to measure up to the minimum working standard of modern housing as it has been accepted in European practice." She singled out the Amalgamated cooperatives for praise but in general dismissed limited-dividend housing ventures for failing to meet "the ordinary accepted European standard of light, air, and space," not to mention affordability.[11] For this state of affairs, she blamed the (unrealistic) American ideal of individual home ownership, which contributed to the American

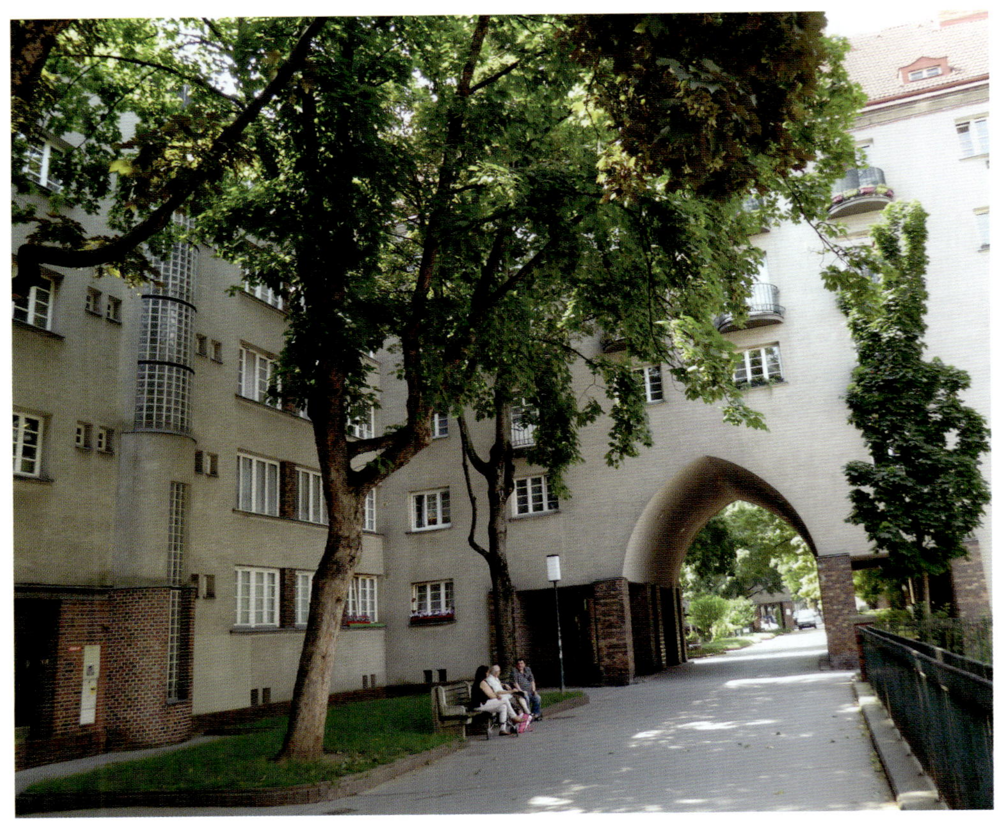

Hermann Aichinger and Heinrich Schmid, architects, Rabenhof, Vienna, 1925–28.

government's reluctance to directly aid the construction of high-quality affordable housing. Yet, prompted by the stock market collapse of 1929, change was on the horizon by the time Bauer's book was published. When Franklin Delano Roosevelt took office as president in 1933, half of all home mortgages were in default and the development of new housing was at a standstill. Following his inauguration, Roosevelt implemented a series of large-scale social programs and economic interventions—now known collectively as the New Deal—to counter the effects of the Depression. Public housing has been called "the most radical aspect of the New Deal" because it relied on direct government ownership and management, as opposed to indirect economic intervention.[12] In June 1933, following the passage of the National Industrial Recovery Act, the Public Works Administration (PWA) was established; it remained in existence until 1937, when it was replaced by the United States Housing Authority. The United States' first experimental public housing developments were constructed under the auspices of the PWA's Housing Division. In New York, the New York City Housing Authority (NYCHA), established in 1934, augmented the efforts of the PWA. In May 1934, NYCHA announced plans to construct an affordable housing project on a twenty-five-acre site in the Williamsburg section of Brooklyn. In addition to the housing units themselves, the site was to feature a nursery school, a health center, and communal social rooms.[13] The site was located within a densely populated neighborhood not far from the East River and the bridges to

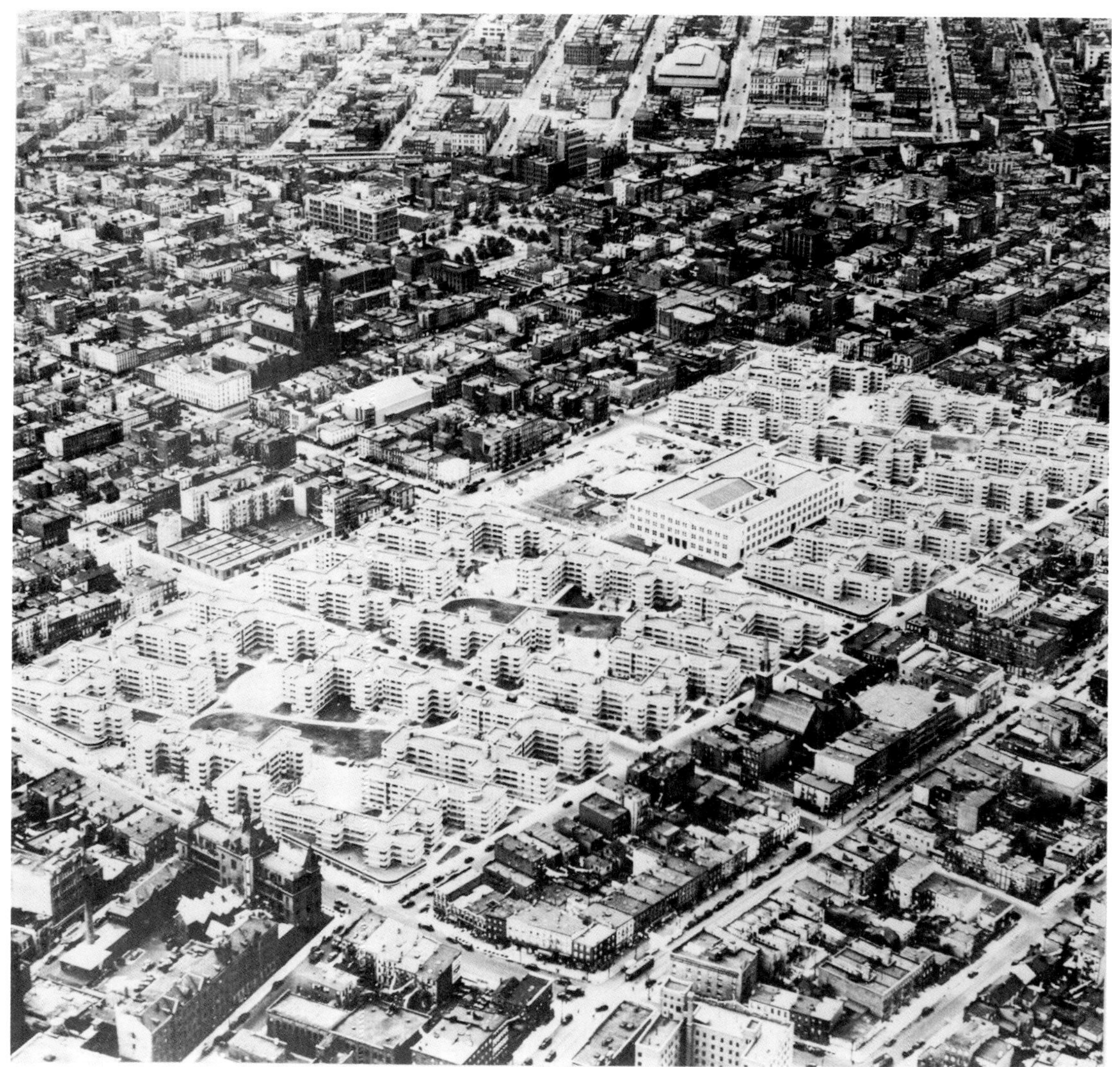

United States Public Works Administration and United States Committee on Architectural Surveys, *Williamsburg Houses, Brooklyn, New York City* (New York, 1939).

Manhattan. Invoking the right of eminent domain, the city razed twelve blocks of tenement housing described at the time as "virtually unrelieved slums."[14] Four years later, the Williamsburg Houses were complete and ready for occupancy.

The Williamsburg Housing Project

With 1,622 apartment units, the Williamsburg Houses was one of the largest public housing projects built in the United States before World War II. Costing approximately $13.5 million, it was six times more expensive than any similar project developed by the PWA. This investment enabled the development of a site recognized from its inception as a landmark of American modernist architecture.[15] Although a group of ten architects, the

Williamsburg Associated Architects, officially oversaw the design and planning for the Williamsburg Houses, the architect chiefly responsible for its design was William Lescaze (1896–1969). Born in Switzerland, Lescaze immigrated to the United States in 1920 but remained closely attuned to developments in European modernist architecture, traveling frequently to Berlin, Stuttgart, and other centers of architectural innovation. In fact, he was the only American architect in attendance at the founding conference of the Congrès Internationaux d'Architecture (CIAM) in La Sarraz, Switzerland, in June 1928. In an era when modernist homes were typically accessible only to the moneyed classes, CIAM's founding members were committed to the expansion of affordable housing that conformed to modernist aesthetic principles. One CIAM founder, Josef Frank, oversaw the construction of Vienna's Werkbundsiedlung, a suburban development of modernist—but modest—homes that offered an affordable alternative to urban apartment blocks.[16] Another, Ernst May, planned large-scale developments for working-class residents in Frankfurt. Lescaze shared with these architects an interest in modernist housing that reconciled affordability with good design and high-quality construction. Already in 1931, he had submitted a design for a proposed (but never realized) housing project on New York's Lower East Side.[17]

Lescaze's final design for the Williamsburg Houses consisted of twenty four-story, brick apartment blocks, each situated at a fifteen-degree angle to the street grid, a placement thought to maximize light and air circulation in the units. Art deco storefronts facing the perimeter streets helped integrate the site into the surrounding neighborhood. Nevertheless, the development bore little resemblance to the traditional New York streetscape. Two streets running through the site were, in fact, closed off to create four superblocks. Arranged around the perimeter of each block, the buildings surrounded landscaped courts featuring gardens, meandering paths, and playgrounds. Lescaze's positioning of free-standing apartment blocks in open spaces referenced a planning concept known as *Zeilenbau*, which characterized many of the German modernist housing developments of the 1920s. He appears to have been particularly attracted to the work of the GEHAG's chief architect, Bruno Taut, who designed numerous housing estates in Berlin between 1924 and 1933.[18] Taut's style is characterized by the use of color in the facades (most often demarcating doorways and stairwells) and simple geometric massing. In his design for the Williamsburg Houses, Lescaze likewise emphasized the buildings' horizontality with concrete bands that visually break up the tan brick facades and used stainless steel and blue tilework to articulate doorways, windows, and stairwells. German émigré architect Walter Gropius looked favorably on Lescaze's Williamsburg design, particularly praising his approach to space and light.[19] Space and light, so integral to modernist housing, informed Lescaze's advocacy for the installation of abstract murals in the housing project's communal social rooms. "By means of colors and forms, [these murals] would," he wrote, "continue the message of light, open air and imagination, which we have tried to embody in the buildings themselves."[20] This brings us to another of the New Deal's radical experiments—the federal patronage of public art.

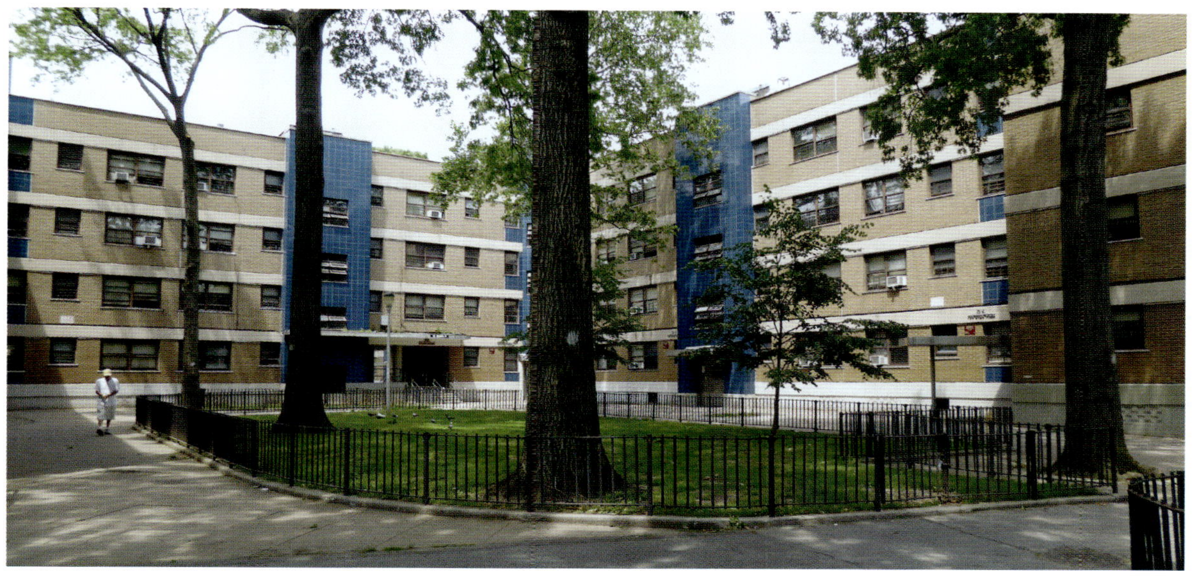

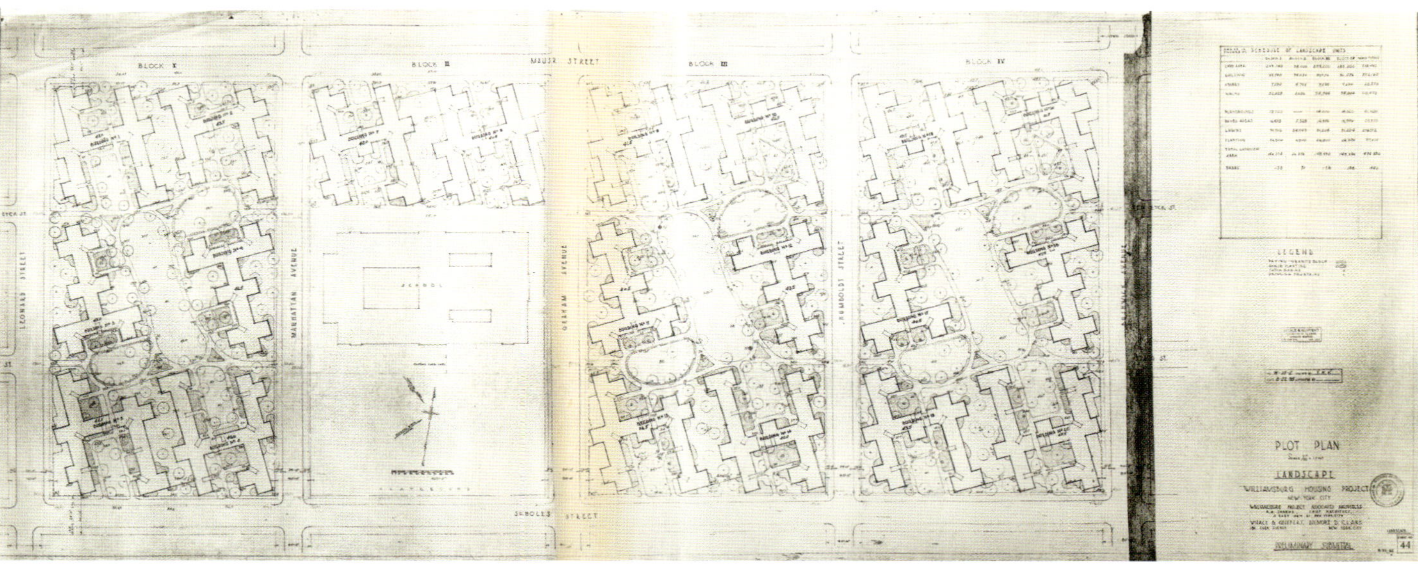

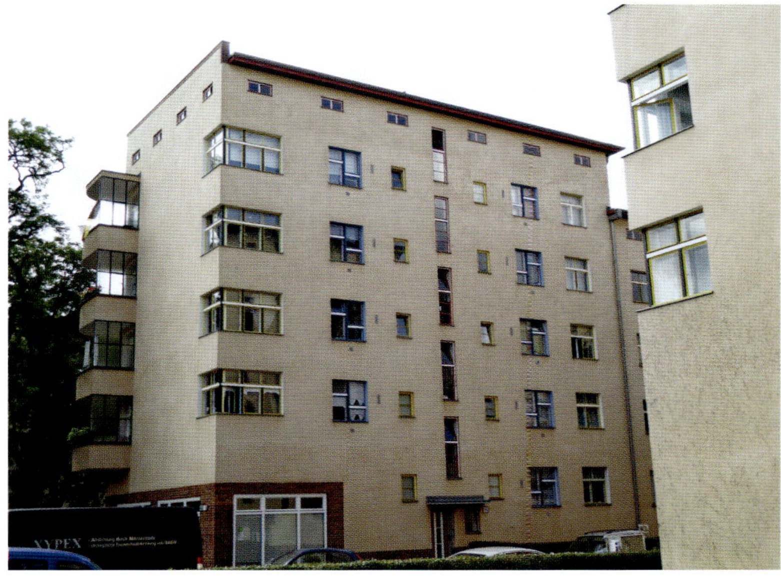

William Lescaze, architect, Williamsburg Houses, Brooklyn, 1938.

Williamsburg Associated Architects, plot plan for Williamsburg Housing Project, August 22, 1935.

Bruno Taut and Franz Hillinger, architects, Wohnstadt Carl Legien, Berlin, 1925–30.

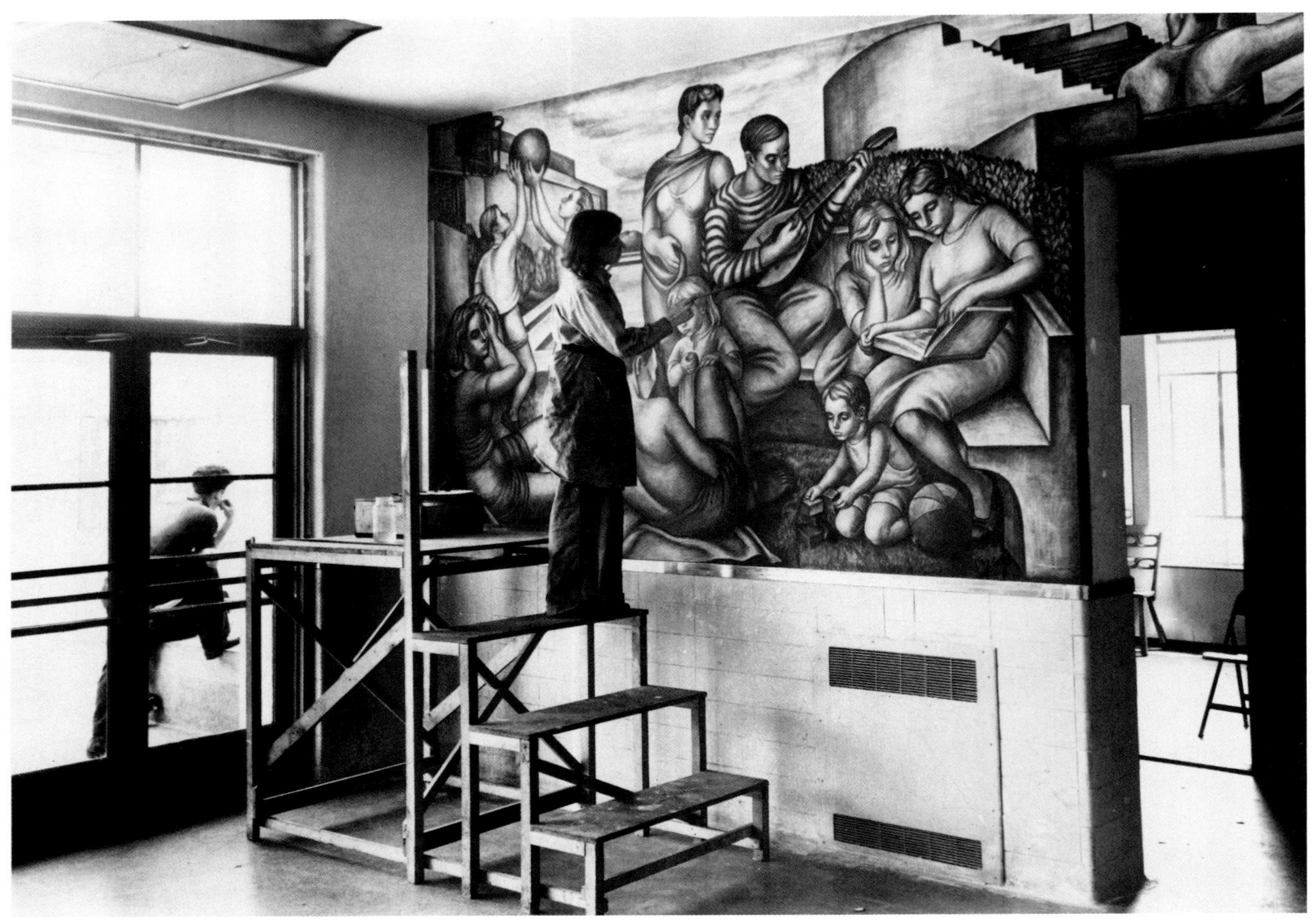

Marion Greenwood working on a fresco for the Red Hook Houses, New York, June 4, 1940. Photo: Shalat.

The Williamsburg Mural Project

What set American public housing of the 1930s—especially in New York—apart from its European models was the incorporation of public art on a large scale. As part of the federal effort to employ artists, several New Deal programs facilitated the creation of public art. These included the Public Works of Art Program (PWAP), which lasted only from December 1933 to June 1934; the Treasury Relief Art Project (TRAP), in existence from 1935 to 1938; and the Federal Art Project (FAP). The largest and longest lasting (1935–43) of these programs, the FAP was organized into multiple divisions. The Mural Division, headed by artist Burgoyne Diller, oversaw commissions for painted murals and frescos, stained glass, and mosaics.[21] Because it was funded by the government, public art commissioned through the PWAP, TRAP, or FAP was installed only in tax-supported, public institutions, including the new subsidized housing projects. Stylistically and thematically, most of the murals commissioned under the auspices of these programs evoked the work of Mexican muralists such as Diego Rivera and José Clemente Orozco. That is, they generally featured legible pictorial styles and uplifting social messages. This was especially true of murals designed for public housing, which Jonathan Harris contends "physically represented the intervention of the federal state into [the] lives" of demographic sectors seen as potentially disaffected or delinquent.[22] But placing murals in public housing also constituted a radical statement that all classes of society deserved access to art—and further emphasized that the government did not define quality of life by practicalities alone. However, the social and moral goals governing the creation of public housing indeed favored the placement of didactic murals—meant to convey messages about good citizenship and proper social behavior—in those settings. For example, the Red Hook Houses, constructed in Brooklyn at the same time as the Williamsburg Houses, contained a fresco titled *Blueprint for Living* in its community center. Painted by Marion Greenwood, whose training in mural painting in Mexico City is readily apparent, the mural clearly provides instruction for the housing project's residents. Its left-hand panel depicts a group of young people who engage in such wholesome activities as sports, reading, and music. They are, in Greenwood's words, "profiting from clean living."[23] Similar murals, emphasizing themes of good citizenship, family life, and hard work, were painted by Greenwood and her sister Grace Ames for the Westfield Acres housing project in Camden, New Jersey, and by Philip Guston for the Queensbridge Houses in New York City. By comparison, the mural program envisioned for Williamsburg was unprecedented not just aesthetically but socially.

The Williamsburg murals rank among the first abstract murals produced in the United States. Although we rarely associate abstraction with WPA murals, approximately forty were painted for sites in New York City. Thanks largely to the advocacy of Burgoyne Diller, the FAP's Mural Division encouraged artistic experimentation. Because abstract or non-objective art was perceived as therapeutic, the most receptive clients for abstract murals were hospitals. For example, a suite of abstract murals by Ilya Bolotowsky, Albert Swinden, Joseph Rugolo, and Dane Chanase was commissioned in 1937 for the Hospital for Chronic Diseases on Roosevelt Island.[24] Abstraction, with its connotations of modernity, was also deemed appropriate for sites with technological and transportation-related functions. These included Newark Airport, where Arshile Gorky painted a series of abstract murals on the subject of aviation, and Radio Station WNYC, for which Stuart Davis, Lee Krasner, John von Wicht, Byron Browne, and Louis Schanker designed murals.[25] But Williamsburg was the only public housing project to receive abstract murals. In 1936, just as construction was getting under way, Diller selected twelve painters (Ilya Bolotowsky, Harry Bowden, Byron Browne, Francis Criss, Stuart Davis, Willem de Kooning, Balcomb Greene, Paul Kelpe, Jan Matulka, George McNeil, Eugene Morley, and Albert Swinden) to create seventeen murals for installation in communal social rooms located in several of the buildings.[26] Documentation shows that at least one sculptor, Martin Craig, also received a commission to design relief sculptures for the site. It is also possible that José Ruiz de Rivera carved a marble sculpture for installation on the Williamsburg grounds. These works count among the few abstract sculpture designs produced under the auspices of the FAP.[27]

As federal employees hired to produce public art, the Williamsburg artists did not enjoy complete artistic freedom, even given the project's vanguard orientation and the FAP's general openness to its artists' stylistic independence. According to the FAP's

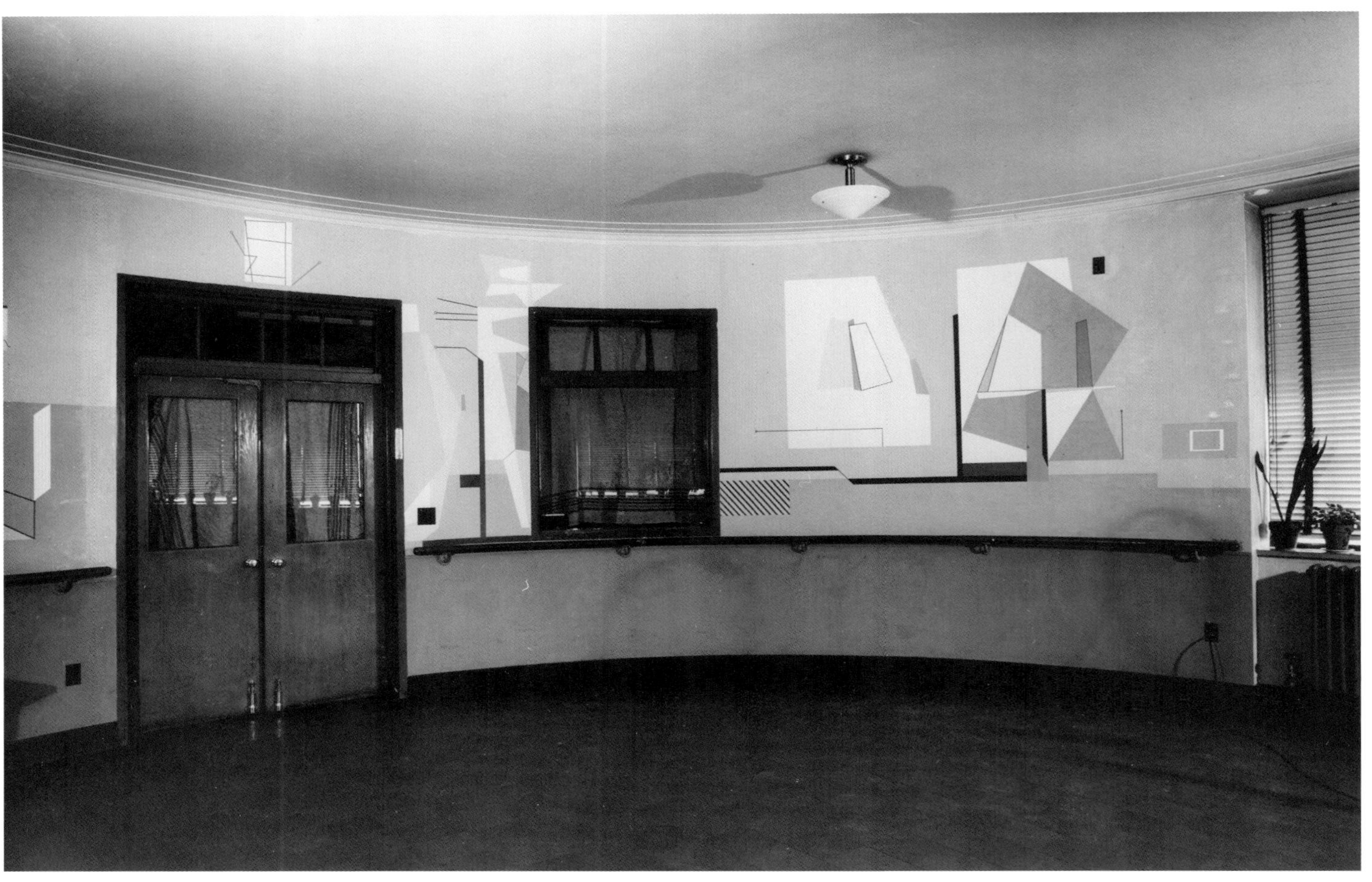

Mural by Ilya Bolotowsky at the Hospital for Chronic Diseases, Roosevelt Island, New York.

procedures, the specifications for murals—including their content, medium, and size—were to be developed collaboratively by the Mural Division and a representative of the site where the mural would be installed. Following these initial decisions, the individual mural designs were subject to a lengthy approval process involving the submission of multiple studies. Artists first submitted a black-and-white sketch, then a color sketch and a full-scale color detail in the same medium in which the mural would be painted, and finally a full-size cartoon. Work on the mural itself commenced only after approval of the cartoon by the Mural Division head, the Subject and Approvals committee, and New York's Municipal Art Commission. Representatives of those agencies viewed the finished mural in situ and only then granted permission for its installation.[28] Given the preference for didactic imagery in housing projects, convincing all these administrators that abstract murals were appropriate for the Williamsburg Houses must have been challenging. Indeed, one wonders if such a radical aesthetic orientation would have been possible at all had the Williamsburg Houses not been planned for white tenants.[29] A comparison of the Williamsburg abstractions with Heinz Warneke's sculptures for the Harlem River Houses, a housing project designated for African Americans, is telling. One of Warneke's sculptures depicts a mother holding an infant, and the other portrays a male laborer in a docile, kneeling pose. Both works apparently reinforce NYCHA's behavioral expectations for African American tenants.[30]

To make his case for abstraction, Burgoyne Diller likened the proposed Williamsburg murals to the therapeutic abstractions designed for hospitals: "The decision to place abstract murals in these rooms was made because these areas were intended to provide a place of relaxation and entertainment for the tenants. The more arbitrary color, possible when not determined by the description of objects, enables the artist to place an emphasis on its psychological potential to stimulate relaxation."[31] Perhaps in response to a criticism made by Austrian émigré architect Frederick Kiesler that most WPA murals were poorly integrated into their architectural surroundings, Diller also argued that "the arbitrary use of shapes provides an opportunity to create color patterns clearly related to the interior architecture and complementing the architects' intentions."[32] Diller's argument recalls that of French painter Fernand Léger, perhaps the most influential abstract muralist—especially for American artists—of the interwar period. Beginning in 1920, Léger had collaborated with the architect Le Corbusier, whose starkly geometric buildings and unornamented white walls suggested new opportunities for modernist artists to invent a new form of "architectural painting." Léger's abstract "mural paintings" of the mid-1920s are meant to complement the forms and volumes of modernist architecture, but he emphasized that they were not merely decorative. Recognizing that the austerity of modernist housing might be psychologically challenging for its inhabitants, he stressed the therapeutic effects of color, which he called a "vital necessity" to maintaining psychological and physical health.[33]

In October 1936, the initial sketches for the Williamsburg murals received a positive critique from a WPA administrator, David Comstock, who felt that "the sketches, as a whole, show that the artists have been well selected and that their work has been carefully guided by both the FAP and the architects. The color and scale are excellent in all the sketches and the style is well divided between the more traditional and the abstract modern. I see no objection to the abstract designs . . . if color and composition are good."[34] Despite Comstock's characterization of the murals' styles, only two artists submitted designs that we might classify as traditional, that is, representational. Francis Criss, using a brightly colored precisionist style, submitted four designs featuring New York street scenes. Eugene Morley prepared four studies that depicted scenes of workers engaged in construction, factory work, and other labor (see pages 80–85, 112–15). In their subject and their social realist style, Morley's studies depart dramatically from those of the other Williamsburg artists. They clearly did not meet the aesthetic criteria of Lescaze and Diller, who had argued that after an eight-hour factory shift, the Williamsburg tenants would find painted images of more machines "neither interesting nor stimulating." NYCHA head Langdon Post also expressed concern that "the sketch depicting certain scenes in New York City was perhaps bringing the tenants' ordinary life too closely into the home."[35] When studies for the Williamsburg murals were displayed in the Museum of Modern Art's 1936 exhibition *New Horizons in American Art*, promoting the work of the FAP, Morley's sketches, unsurprisingly, were not among them.[36] Abstraction dominated the

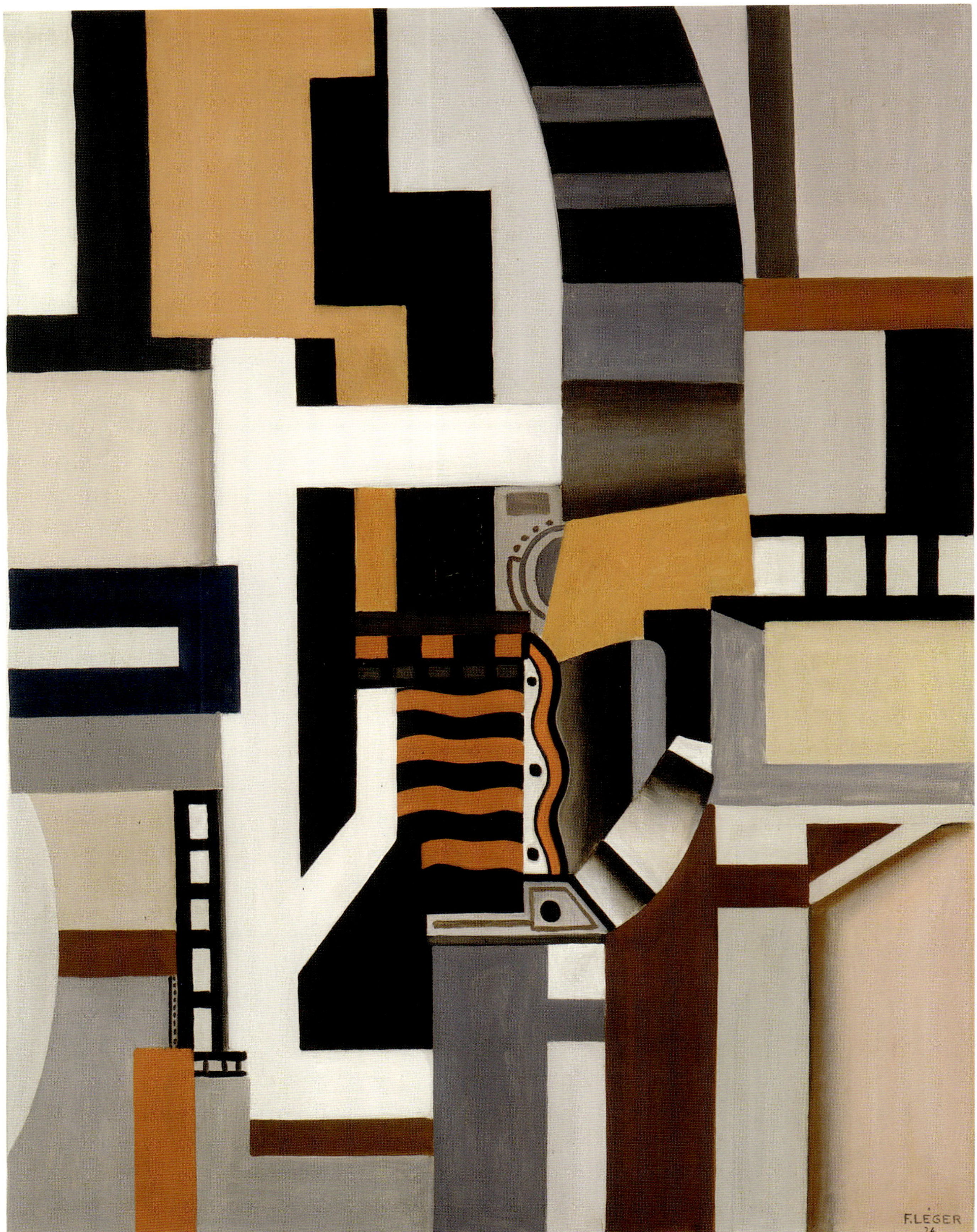
F.LÉGER
24

remaining Williamsburg mural designs. Ilya Bolotowsky, Harry Bowden, Byron Browne, and Jan Matulka produced compositions blending surrealist-inspired biomorphic and hard-edge geometric forms, while Balcomb Greene, Paul Kelpe, and Albert Swinden favored a purer approach to geometric abstraction. Stylistically, the studies by Willem de Kooning and George McNeil fall somewhere between these two poles but are likewise devoid of obvious references to the natural world (for images, see "The Williamsburg Public Art Project: A Visual Compendium," in this volume). Davis's mural is the most difficult to classify, being neither completely abstract nor clearly representational. Although all the murals designed for the Williamsburg Houses were aesthetically groundbreaking, many scholars have singled out *Swing Landscape* for praise. Indeed, it is the only Williamsburg mural to have achieved canonical status.[37] Art historians have analyzed *Swing Landscape*'s iconography and composition, but to gain a comprehensive perspective on this mural's unique role in Davis's oeuvre—and, indeed, within the broader history of American mural painting—we must also examine the social function that Davis himself saw as intertwined with its aesthetic innovations. We begin with a reconsideration of *Swing Landscape*'s geographic associations.

Fernand Léger, *Composition,* 1924
Oil on canvas, 51½ × 39¾ in. (130.8 × 101 cm). Jane and Roger Wolcott Memorial, Gift of Thomas T. Solley, Eskenazi Museum of Art, Indiana University, 75.41.1. © 2019 Artists Rights Society (ARS), NY / ADAGP, Paris.

Gloucester and New York

Swing Landscape's ostensible subject matter—the Gloucester, Massachusetts, waterfront—has encouraged many scholars to analyze the composition independently of its presumptive audience of working-class New Yorkers. Formally, the mural indeed relates closely to a body of work Davis produced in the 1930s focusing on Gloucester. Its overall composition closely echoes that of *Red Cart* of 1932, while the placement of the sail, buoy, and oil derrick at the left has close parallels with his 1931–32 *Landscape with Drying Sails.* Lowery Stokes Sims further notes that the center and right sections are based directly on the 1934 painting *American Waterfront, Analogical Emblem.*[38] Highly abstracted maritime images, including lobster traps, masts, rigging, and water, are embedded throughout the composition. Although the abstract nature of the mural suggests a generic view—perhaps only an idea—of Gloucester, Karen Wilkin identifies the scene more specifically as "a fragmented, conflated view of Smith's Cove, an inlet at the foot of Gloucester's hills." Wilkin also finds it difficult to reconcile the mural's Gloucester iconography with its proposed installation in a housing project for low-income New Yorkers.[39] Given that most Williamsburg residents had no connection with Gloucester and would never visit the town, this is an understandable dilemma. What possible meaning could the tenants find in this mural's subject? But this question begs the question, would the Williamsburg audience *know* that the mural depicted an abstracted view of a New England seaside town? Certainly, the *New York Times* art critic Edward Alden Jewell (who was familiar with Davis's work), made no connection between *Swing Landscape* and Gloucester in his 1938 critique of the mural, referring to it as a "non-objective inebriant."[40]

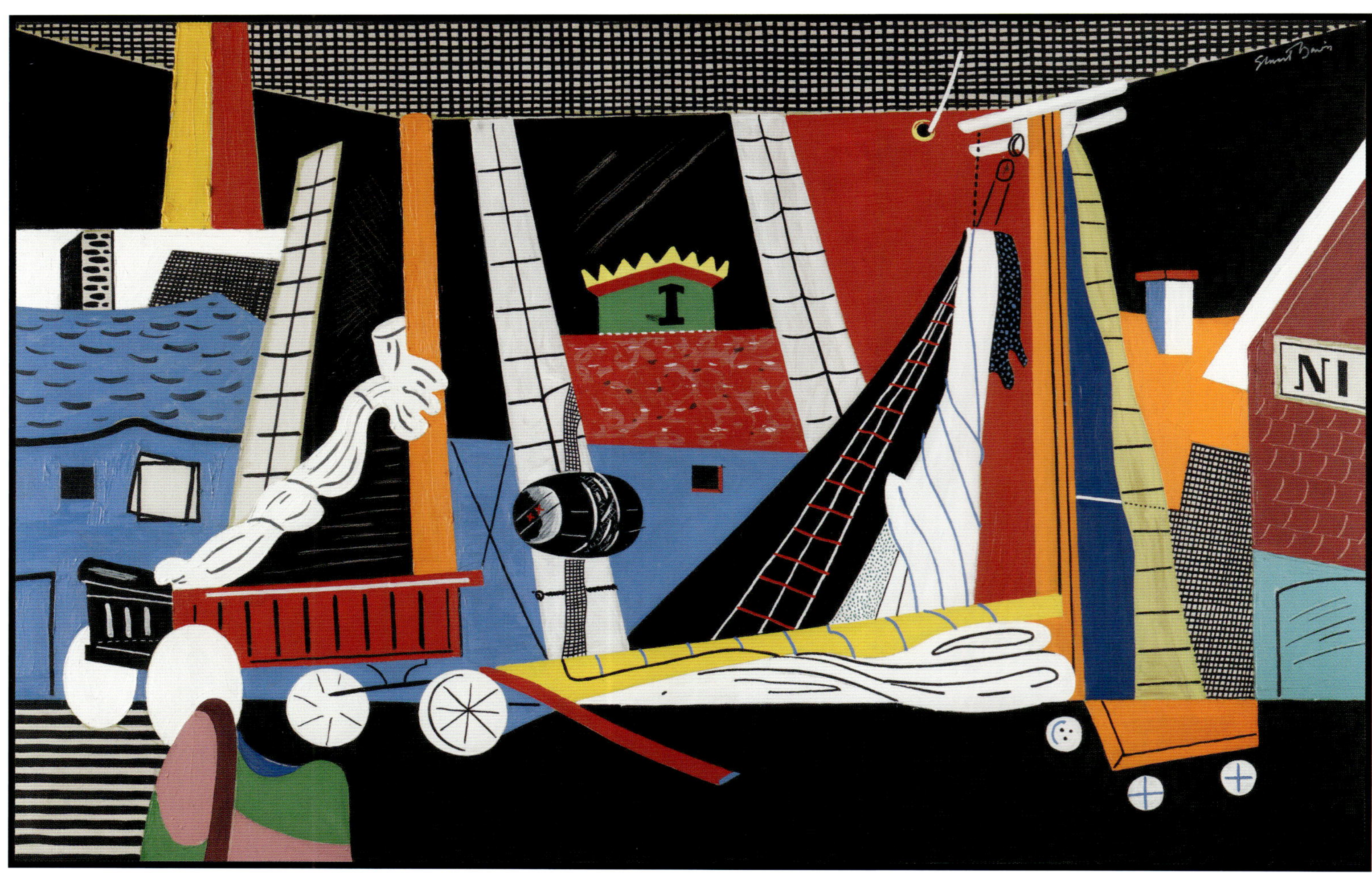

Stuart Davis, *Red Cart,* 1932
Oil on canvas, 32¼ × 50 in. (81.9 × 127 cm). Addison Gallery of American Art at Phillips Academy, Andover, Massachusetts, museum purchase, 1946.15. © 2019 Estate of Stuart Davis / Licensed by VAGA at Artists Rights Society (ARS), NY.

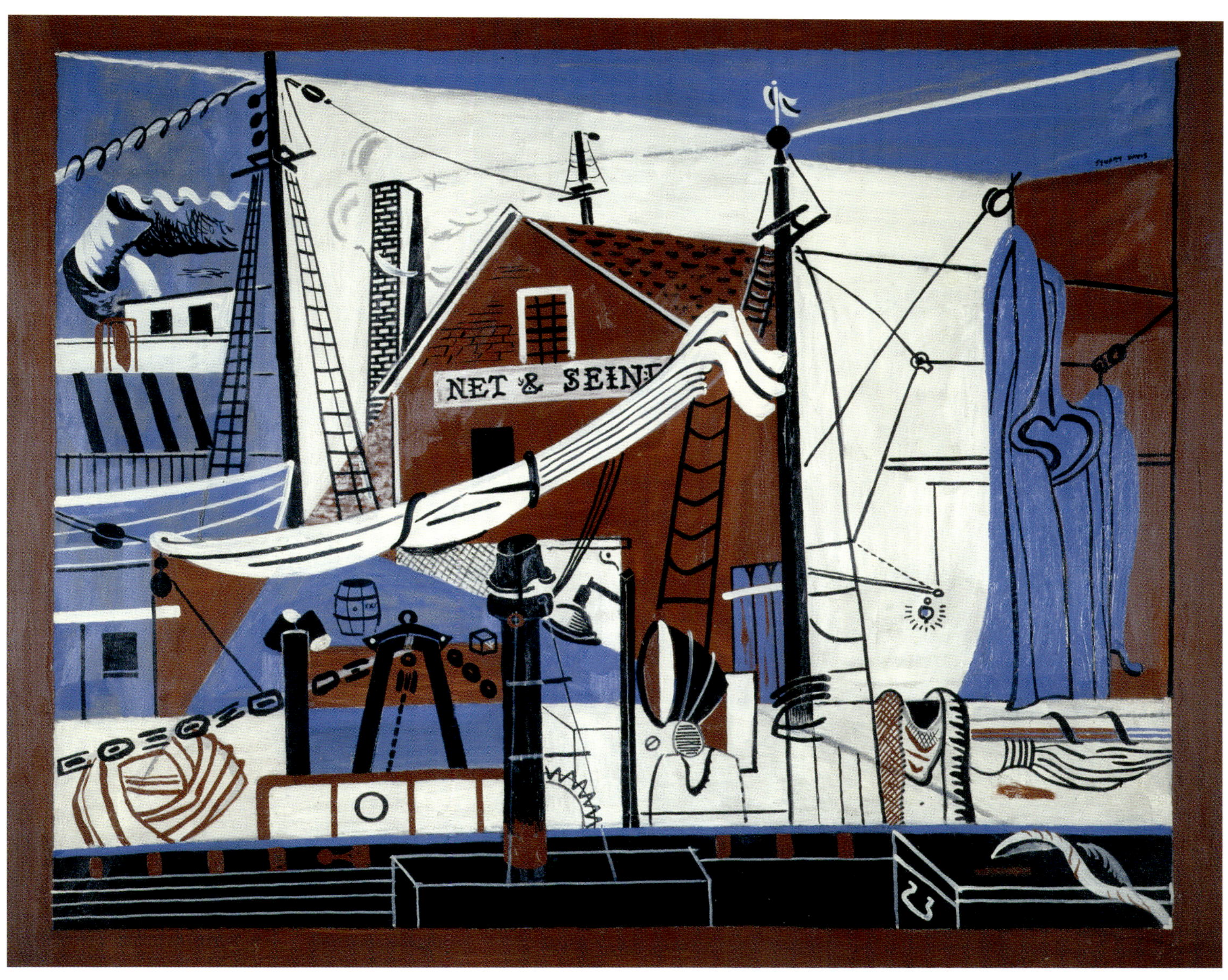

Stuart Davis, *Landscape with Drying Sails,* 1931–32
Oil on canvas, 32 × 40 in. (81.3 × 101.6 cm). Columbus Museum of Art, Ohio: Museum Purchase, Howald Fund II, 1981.012.

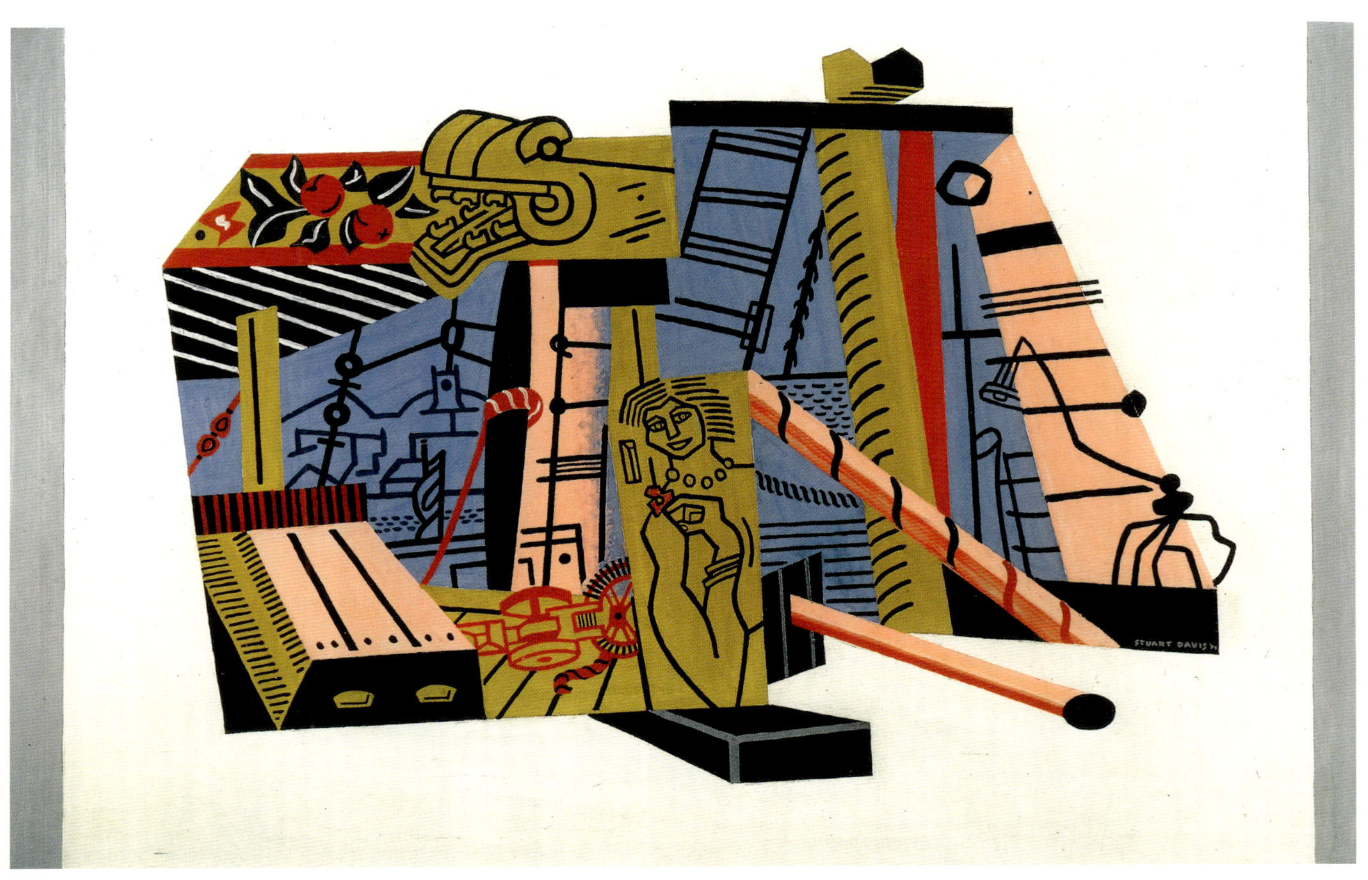

Stuart Davis, *American Waterfront, Analogical Emblem*, 1934
Oil on canvas, 32 × 50 in. (81.3 × 127 cm). Private collection.

We find hints to how the Williamsburg tenants might have understood *Swing Landscape* in the many misinterpretations of the mural that have found their way into print. A number of art historians—evidently unfamiliar with Davis's large Gloucester oeuvre—have asserted that *Swing Landscape* portrays an abstracted view of New York City, misidentifying its harbor motifs as playgrounds, roads, and apartment buildings. Some have recognized maritime imagery in the work but have associated it with the Port of New York or the East River. For example, the oil derrick pictured in the upper left of the composition has been misread as a fragment of the Williamsburg Bridge.[41] William Agee, complaining of these "egregious misreadings," implies that the mural's commission for a Brooklyn housing project is a mere annoyance, a roadblock preventing us from arriving at the proper recognition of its Gloucester subject.[42] On the contrary, these misinterpretations are valuable, for they suggest that the Williamsburg tenants might, in fact, have perceived in *Swing Landscape* an abstracted New York scene reminiscent on some level of their surroundings. Might Davis have, in fact, intended such a reading—or at least anticipated the possibility?

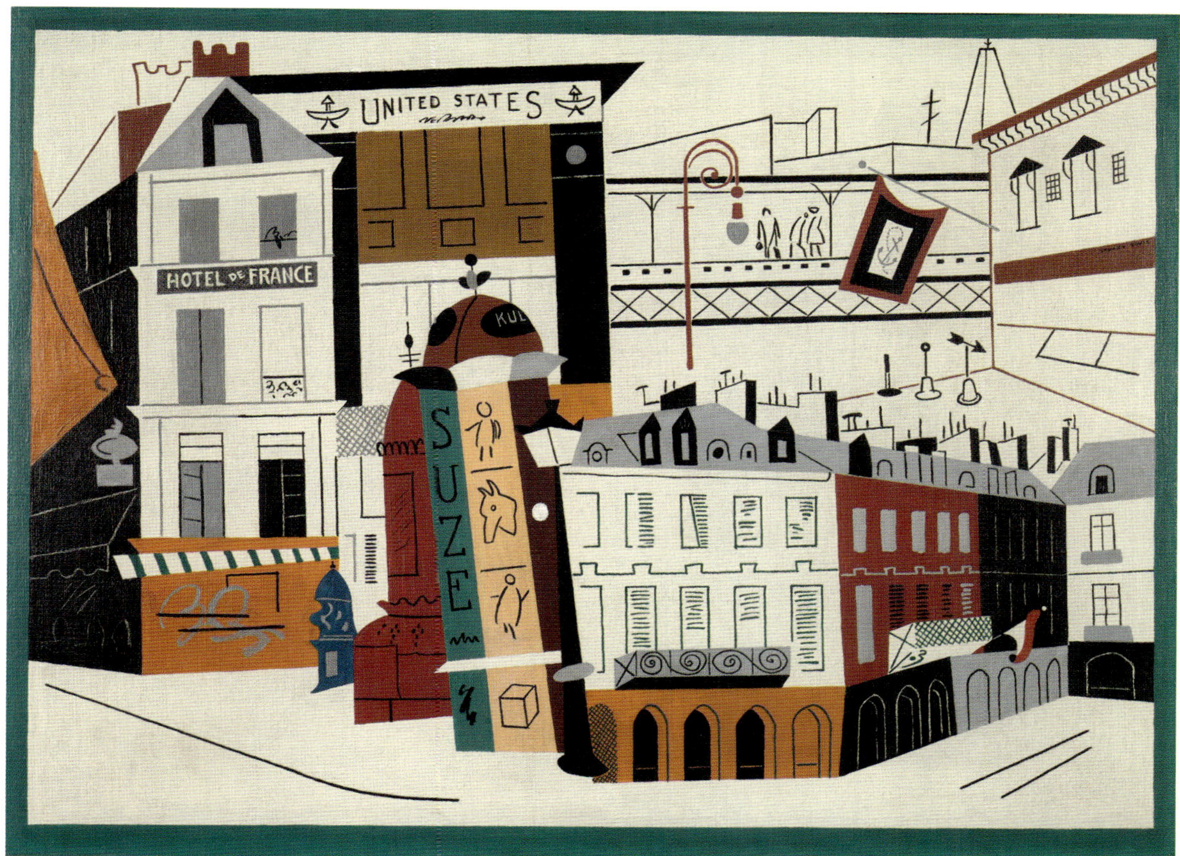

Stuart Davis, *New York—Paris No. 2,* 1931
Oil on canvas, 30¼ × 40¾ in. (76.9 × 102.2 cm). Portland Museum of Art, Portland, Maine: Hamilton Easter Field Art Foundation Collection, Gift of Barn Gallery Associates, Inc., Ogunquit, Maine (1979.13.10). © 2019 Estate of Stuart Davis / Licensed by VAGA at Artists Rights Society (ARS), NY.

Much about *Swing Landscape* raises the possibility of geographical ambiguity, beginning with its title. Many of Davis's Gloucester paintings include references in their titles to specific regional locales, such as Cape Ann or Smith's Cove. However, both of the titles associated with his Williamsburg mural—*Swing Landscape* as well as the earlier *Waterfront Forms*—seem almost intentionally vague about the scene's geography.[43] Despite *Swing Landscape*'s many references to Gloucester, does its title, in fact, allude to a secondary geographical association? Swing music, which was closely associated with Harlem nightlife, had distinctly urban connotations in the 1930s. Its syncopated rhythms and frenetic energy—so perfectly captured in *Swing Landscape*'s vibrant composition—paralleled the fast pace of urban life, and especially life in a densely built and rapidly modernizing city such as New York. Although Davis modeled his composition on earlier Gloucester paintings, he paid at least one visit to the area around the Williamsburg site seeking additional inspiration for the mural.[44] The hypothesis that *Swing Landscape* might simultaneously portray Gloucester and—at least in a conceptual sense—New York, is further supported by Davis's own discussion of geographical representation in his painting *Landscape with Drying Sails:*

> *I spent a great many years in Gloucester, Mass., always found it visually exciting, and eventually learned to organize some of this response in terms of Color-Space configurations. The picture "Drying Sails," along with others of the same years after my return from one year in Paris, objectifies my intuitive preferences for certain aspects of that then exciting panorama. What is communicated of course has little or no factual content but is nevertheless directly referential to the Gloucester locale. The method or expression, the colors and shapes, were products of experiences in my life and art that were not confined to my Gloucester residence. In that sense the painting is not a "Gloucester" painting. But although the "Idea" in this painting is non-local in character, its application is realized in relation to a specific Gloucester subject matter. It has New York, Philadelphia, and Paris in it too, but remains Gloucester.*[45]

Precedent is also set by Davis's three *New York–Paris* paintings of 1931. In these works (perhaps most successfully in *New York–Paris No. 2*), he seamlessly blends motifs from the two cities into one painted environment. Could he not perhaps have had a similar intention in *Swing Landscape*?

Urban Allusions

Presumably convinced by Burgoyne Diller's arguments, NYCHA administrators believed that the Williamsburg murals should offer the housing project tenants a break from the cares of their everyday lives. In painting an abstracted landscape inspired by Gloucester, Davis could have fulfilled NYCHA's request that the muralists avoid depictions of urban life, instead focusing on "more rural" scenes.[46] Instead, he designed a mural that abstractly—but unmistakably—reflects the urban experience. A comparison of *Swing Landscape* with Fernand Léger's painting *The City* supports this interpretation. *The City,* a mural-scale work painted in 1919, confronts us with the dynamism of the modern urban environment—thanks in part to Léger's appropriation of the aesthetics of modern advertising. Léger was fascinated by billboards, which visually fragmented the urban landscape and introduced a new pictorial language dependent upon simplified forms and bright colors.[47] One of the French painter's prime attractions for Davis was this fascination with the urban environment, including its advertising, machinery, and commercial products. As early as 1913, Léger had remarked (in words Davis echoed in his own writings) that "present-day life, more fragmented and faster moving than life in previous eras, has had to accept as its means of expression an art of dynamic divisionism. . . . The modern conception is not simply a passing abstraction, valid only for a few minutes; it is the total experience of a new generation whose needs it shares and whose aspirations it answers."[48] Davis had ample opportunity to view and study *The City,* which was exhibited in Léger's first solo exhibition at New York's Anderson Galleries in 1925, and again in 1927 in the *Machine Age Exposition,* held in a commercial space on West Fifty-Seventh Street. At that time, the painting had just been acquired by the collector and artist William Gallatin, who subsequently displayed it in his Gallery of Living Art at New York University. By the time of Léger's 1935 retrospective at MoMA—in which a large-scale study for *The City* was featured—Davis had become acquainted with the French artist and was an enthusiastic promoter of his theories.[49]

Swing Landscape's striking visual affinity with *The City* has been noted by numerous scholars.[50] Both

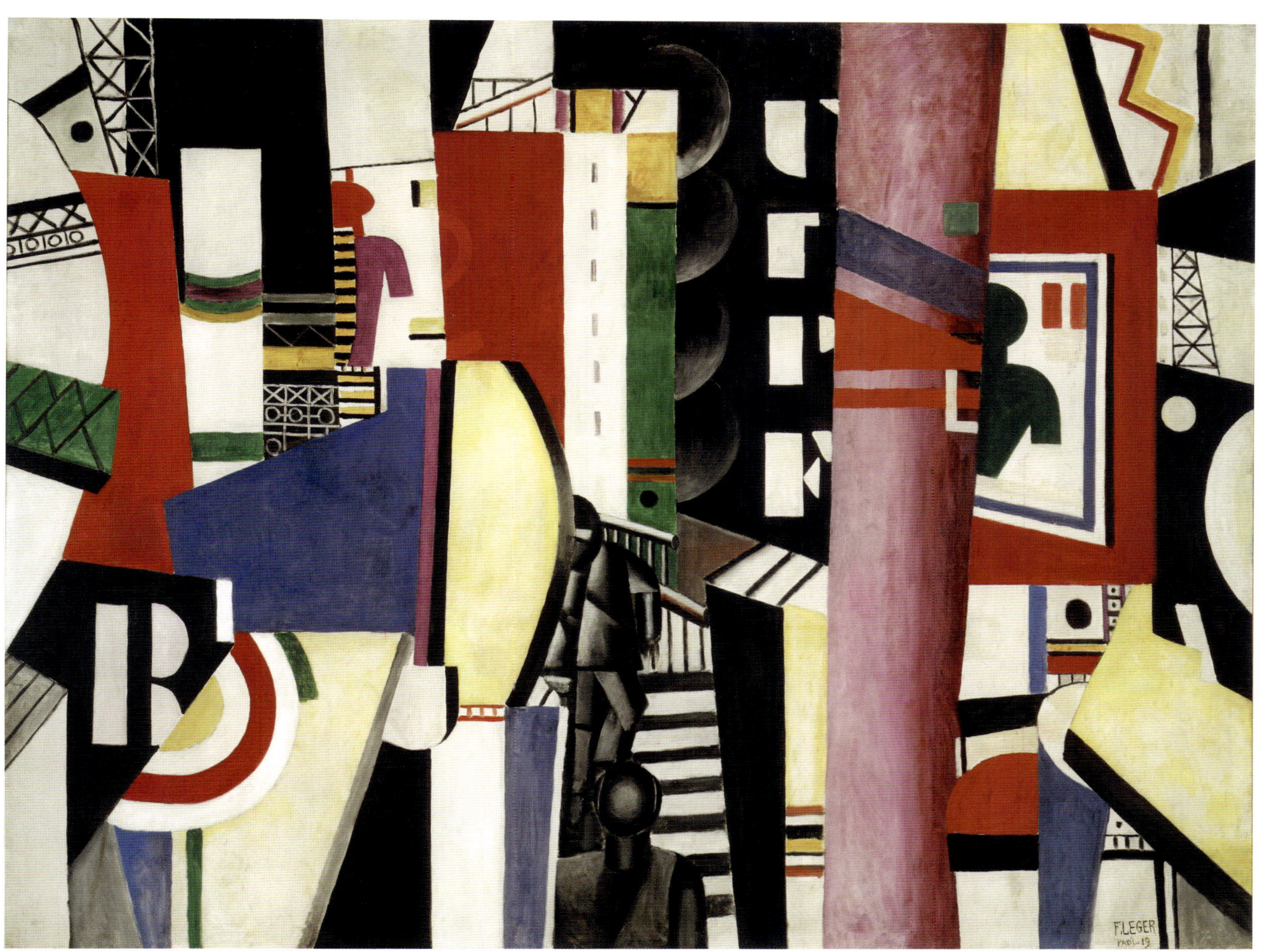

Fernand Léger, *The City,* 1919
Oil on canvas, 91 × 117½ in. (231.1 × 298.4 cm). Philadelphia Museum of Art, A. E. Gallatin Collection, 1952, 1952-61-58.

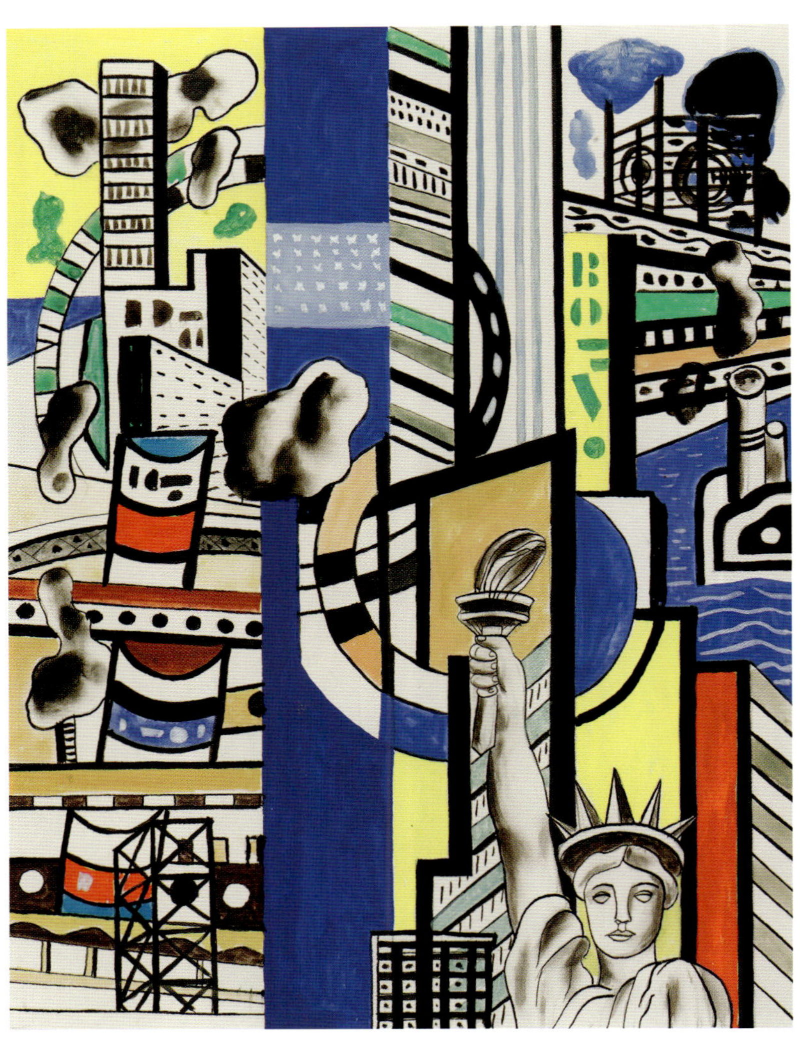

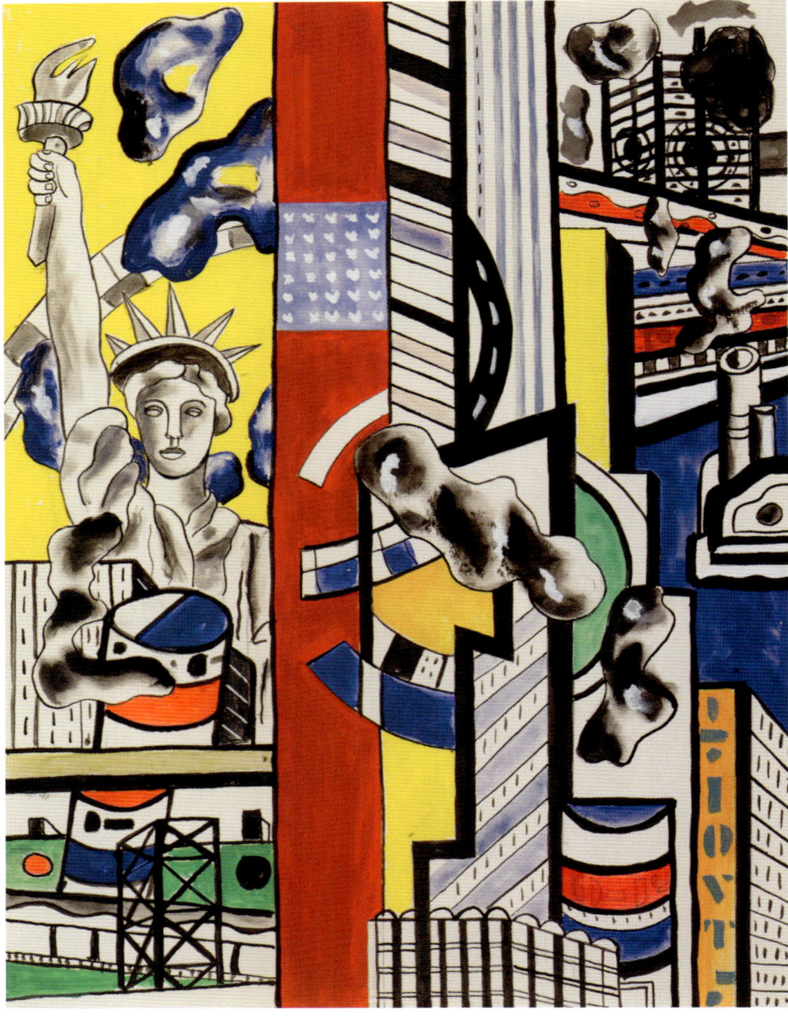

Fernand Léger, *Studies for a Cinematic Mural I–IV,* 1938–39
Gouache, ink, pencil, and wash on cardboard, each approx. 20 × 16 in. (50.7 × 40.5 cm). Museum of Modern Art, Given anonymously, 738.1966; 741.1966; 743.1966; 737.1966. © Artists Rights Society (ARS), NY / ADAGP, Paris.

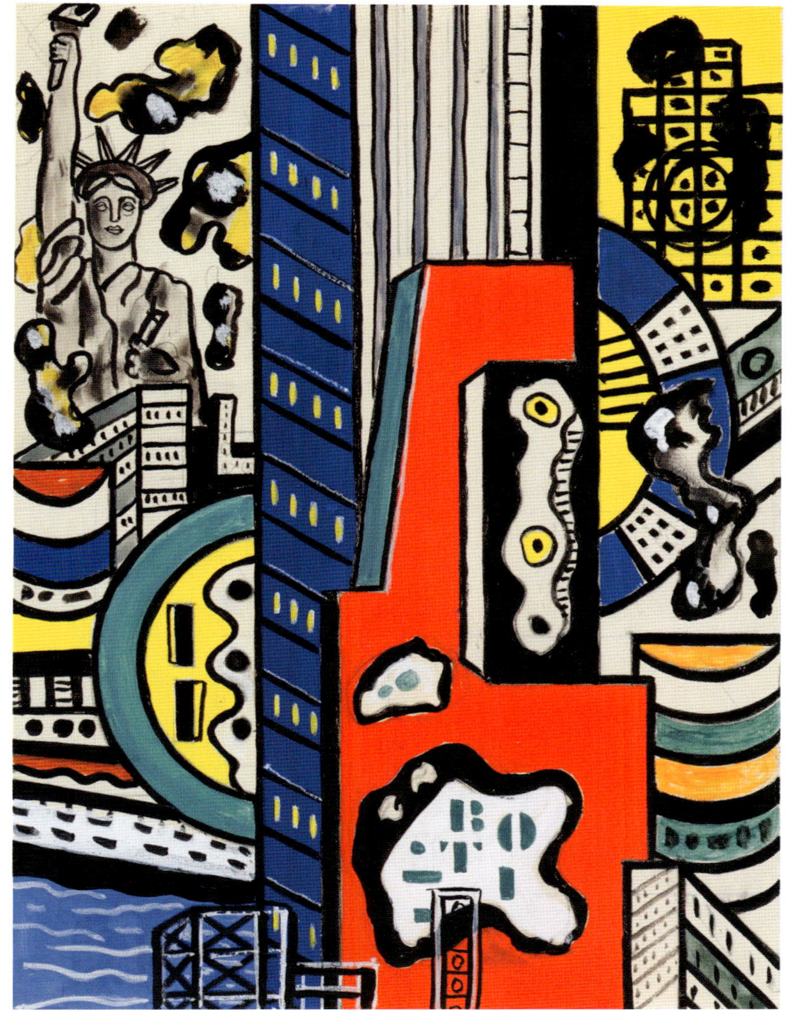

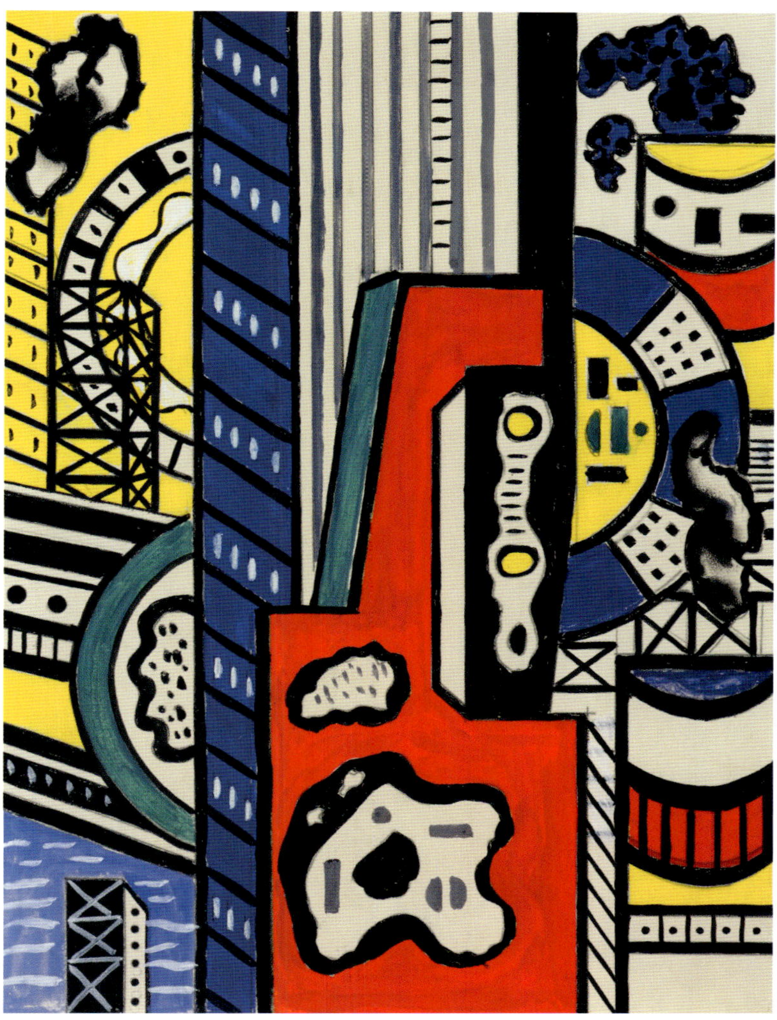

works are characterized by vibrant, kaleidoscopic palettes and collage-like compositions resulting from the interplay of fragmented and overlapping forms. Lacking a central focus, the eye darts around continuously without rest. In both paintings, these elements—enhanced by the works' large scale—evoke the visual overstimulation of modern urban life. This is accomplished in part through the artists' adoption of the cinematic technique of montage, in which disparate images are spliced and juxtaposed together for dramatic or narrative effect. During his 1938–39 visit to New York, Léger even more explicitly embraced filmic strategies (employing them to illustrate urban experience) in his proposal for a *Cinematic Mural* to be projected on the walls of Rockefeller Center's International Building. The architect, Wallace K. Harrison, explained that the "moving mural . . . would have gone at the same rate that the escalators went up."[51] The project was never realized, but Léger produced seven watercolor studies, which together read as a series of animated film stills evoking the experience of arriving by ship in New York harbor, watching the skyscrapers and the Statue of Liberty come into view. Perhaps not coincidentally—and, as we shall see, relevant to understanding *Swing Landscape*—this was a watery vista desired by a growing number of would-be immigrants who, in the late 1930s, sought refuge from European fascism.

It is also worth comparing *Swing Landscape* with Davis's own *New York Mural*, painted in 1932 for MoMA's exhibition *Murals by American Painters and Photographers* and displayed there with the title *Abstract Vision of New York: a building, a derby hat, a tiger's head, and other symbols.*[52] *New York Mural* presents a conglomeration of stylized, yet easily recognizable, New York City symbols and landmarks. Although the maritime forms embedded within *Swing Landscape*'s composition are much more stylized, both murals rank among Davis's most successful applications of montage. In these works, he created geographic portraits by shuffling, rearranging, and abstracting symbols and motifs associated with particular places. And there are further visual continuities between Davis's two murals. The most prominent motif in *New York Mural* is architecture. Dominating the central portion of the composition is the recently completed Empire State Building. Just to its right is a geometric red-and-white form possibly portraying Tudor City, an apartment complex constructed on Manhattan's east side in 1926.[53] The incorporation of these elements into *New York Mural* reveals Davis's interest in modernist architecture, including housing, before his involvement with the Williamsburg project. More significant, however, are *New York Mural*'s clear references (at least to a viewer in 1932) to New York politics. In particular, the composition contains numerous allusions to Al Smith, New York's Democratic governor, who ran unsuccessfully for president in 1928. Among other references, Davis invokes the governor through two brown derby hats, Smith's signature accessory.[54] But what does this have to do with *Swing Landscape*?

In the lower left section of *Swing Landscape*, positioned directly above a blue pipelike form, floats a shape in the form of a green bowler hat. The resemblance to the brown derby hats of *New York Mural* is

Stuart Davis, *New York Mural*, 1932
Oil on canvas, 84 × 48 in. (213.4 × 121.9 cm). Norton Museum of Art, West Palm Beach, FL, Purchase, R. H. Norton Trust, 64.17.

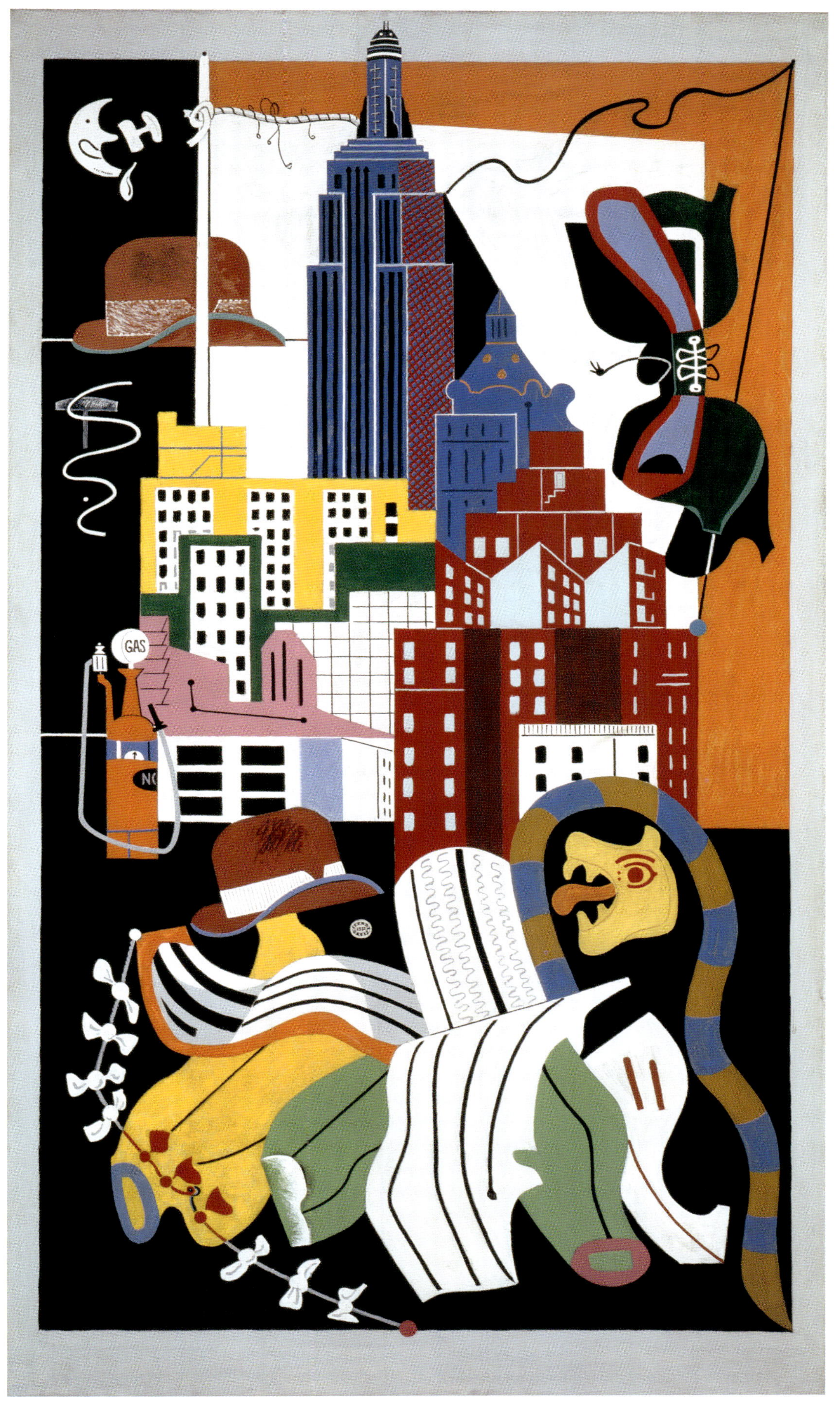
GAS

unmistakable. What is this hat—a probable reference to Al Smith—doing in this supposed homage to the Gloucester waterfront? The working-class audience for whom Davis painted *Swing Landscape* may provide the answer. Smith championed many progressive causes of concern to the urban working classes. These included the improvement of safety regulations in factories and—of direct relevance to housing project tenants—affordable housing (recall that he signed the 1926 New York State Housing Act into law). The inclusion of the hat is significant yet, on its own, might be considered an eccentric detail, a quirky nod to Davis's voting inclinations and those of his presumptive audience. Does *Swing Landscape* hide more allusions to Davis's social and political interests, interests that certainly also concerned the audience for whom he was painting?

Abstract Activism

Stuart Davis's role from January 1935 to December 1937 as editor of the Artists Union's magazine *Art Front* gave him a unique platform for his activism on behalf of artists and against fascism, issues he viewed as intertwined. But because his paintings from this era look "upbeat" and appear to refer "more to jazz and technology than to pressing social or political issues," the contention that he "scrupulously separate[d] his painting and his political activism" recurs throughout the literature.[55] However, such an assertion does not square with his support for public art and his admiration for murals—notably Pablo Picasso's powerful *Guernica*, painted in the same year as *Swing Landscape*—that seamlessly blended vanguard aesthetics and political messages.[56] Davis frequently argued that abstraction was a "direct progressive social force," and the Williamsburg Housing Project—with its progressive aesthetic and social orientation—offered the perfect environment for him to put his advocacy for modernist public art into practice.[57] Again, *Swing Landscape*'s title offers critical insight into the social meaning inscribed within this modernist public artwork. With few exceptions, *Swing Landscape*'s relation to swing music has been understood on purely aesthetic terms. But in 1960, Rudi Blesh, in one of the first monographs published on Davis, commented that the artist "thought of swing as 'an expression of social forces that was in itself a social force.'"[58] Blesh elaborated no further, leaving us to wonder what this statement means. If we are unaware of swing music's political connotations, we find it hard to appreciate the radical messages to which *Swing Landscape*'s title alerts us.

During its Depression-era heyday, swing was regularly promoted on the political left as a democratic musical form, in part because it subverted segregationist norms. Commentators for the communist press emphasized swing's roots in African American musical forms, underscoring the diverse traditions on which American culture rested for the white jazz enthusiasts who patronized Harlem clubs.[59] But more radical was the integration of some swing bands themselves, for example those led by Count Basie, who was black, and Benny Goodman, who was Jewish. Pianist Teddy Wilson, an African American member of Goodman's band, observed that "audiences don't draw color lines when they're listening to music. When we go out to play, nobody cares what colors or races are represented just so long as we play good music."[60] As much (or more) than its modern sound, such racial mixing (along with swing's general associations with African Americans and Jews) contributed to its condemnation as "degenerate" in Nazi Germany.

Davis, of course, loved the sound of swing. He even hired Duke Ellington to play at a 1943 exhibition opening, so guests would better see how his paintings "echo the rhythms and tempo of swing."[61] But he was also sympathetic to the leftist and antisegregationist ideals associated with this musical genre, and he applied those ideals to visual art. At a time when many subscribed to biologically determined notions of creativity—assuming that an artist's racial or ethnic background informed the essential nature of his or her art—Davis published "Race, Nationality, and Art," the Marxist art critic Meyer Schapiro's refutation of such notions, in the March 1936 issue of *Art Front*. Like Schapiro, who points out that the racial classification of artists was integral to the fascist enterprise, Davis insisted that modernist art was "unrestricted by racial or national boundaries."[62] The Williamsburg muralists themselves—half of whom were immigrants—proved Davis's point.[63] In an era when American culture was troubled not only by tense race relations but by virulent antisemitic and anti-immigrant attitudes, could *Swing Landscape*'s particular musical allusions encode a call for the harmonious coexistence of New York's ethnically and religiously diverse population? Although we can only speculate about this, it is useful to consider some of the social and political issues that were on Davis's mind—and the minds of many others on the left—between 1936 and 1938, the years of *Swing Landscape*'s execution.

Davis's readiness to blend political and artistic activities is illustrated, in part, through his involvement with An American Group, a leftist artists' cooperative that sought to raise awareness of humanitarian crises and social justice issues through its members' art. In the late 1930s, the group organized two exhibitions addressing such themes. In 1938, in collaboration with the FAP, An American Group sponsored *Housing: Roofs for Forty Million*, which called attention to the lack of adequate affordable housing in the United States. In February 1937, Davis participated in the group's *Waterfront Art Show*, cosponsored by the Marine Workers Committee and exhibited at the New School for Social Research.[64] According to the *Daily Worker*, the *Waterfront Art Show*, which expressed the artists' solidarity with striking dockworkers, was "the first important mass art exhibition in this country with the definite aim of supporting the rank and file of labor."[65] Unquestionably, the relation between his Williamsburg mural's waterfront subject and the labor movement would have been on Davis's mind as he was painting *Swing Landscape*: his presumptive spectators lived only a short distance from the East River, and many were employed as dockworkers or at the Brooklyn Navy Yard in ship construction. An urban waterfront, in fact, is the subject of one of Davis's most overtly political works, *Waterfront Demonstration*, which he contributed to the *Waterfront Art Show*. The 1936 gouache depicts uniformed police officers brutally silencing a demonstrator. On the surface, the work expresses Davis's support for the labor movement and his alarm at police brutality in the United States. But the tangle of barbed wire behind the figures and the ominously dangling lightbulb above equally evoke the prisons of fascist Spain and Germany, where political prisoners were interrogated, often under torture.[66] An alternate title for this gouache—*Artists against War and Fascism*—seems to support this dual reading of the composition.

A supporter of the Popular Front, the coalition of leftist groups opposed to fascism, Davis was particularly concerned about the suppression of modern art

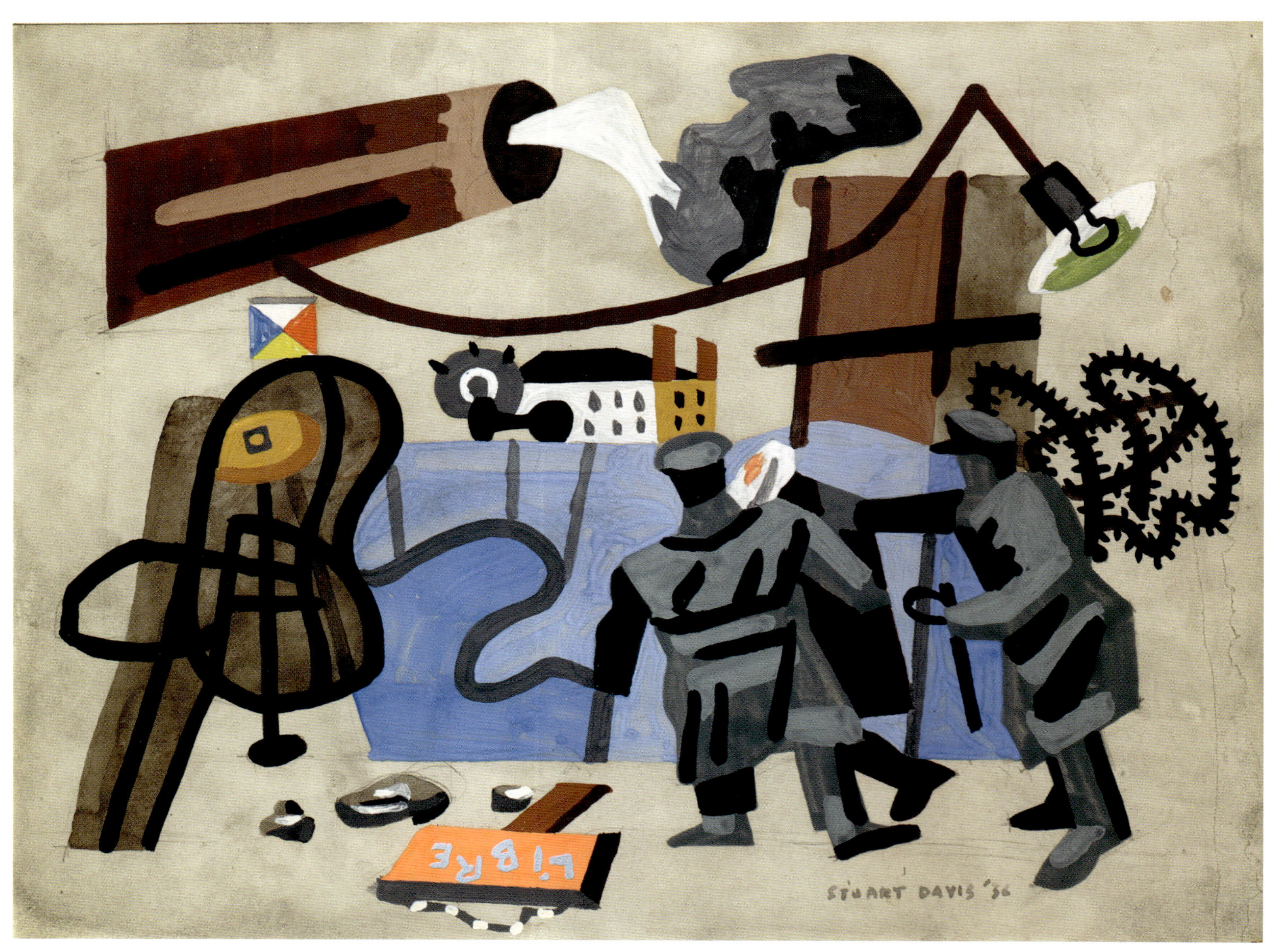

Stuart Davis, *Waterfront Demonstration,* 1936
Gouache and pencil on paper, 11⅜ × 15½ in. (28.9 × 39.4 cm). Collection of Fayez Sarofim. © 2019 Estate of Stuart Davis / Licensed by VAGA at Artists Rights Society (ARS), NY.

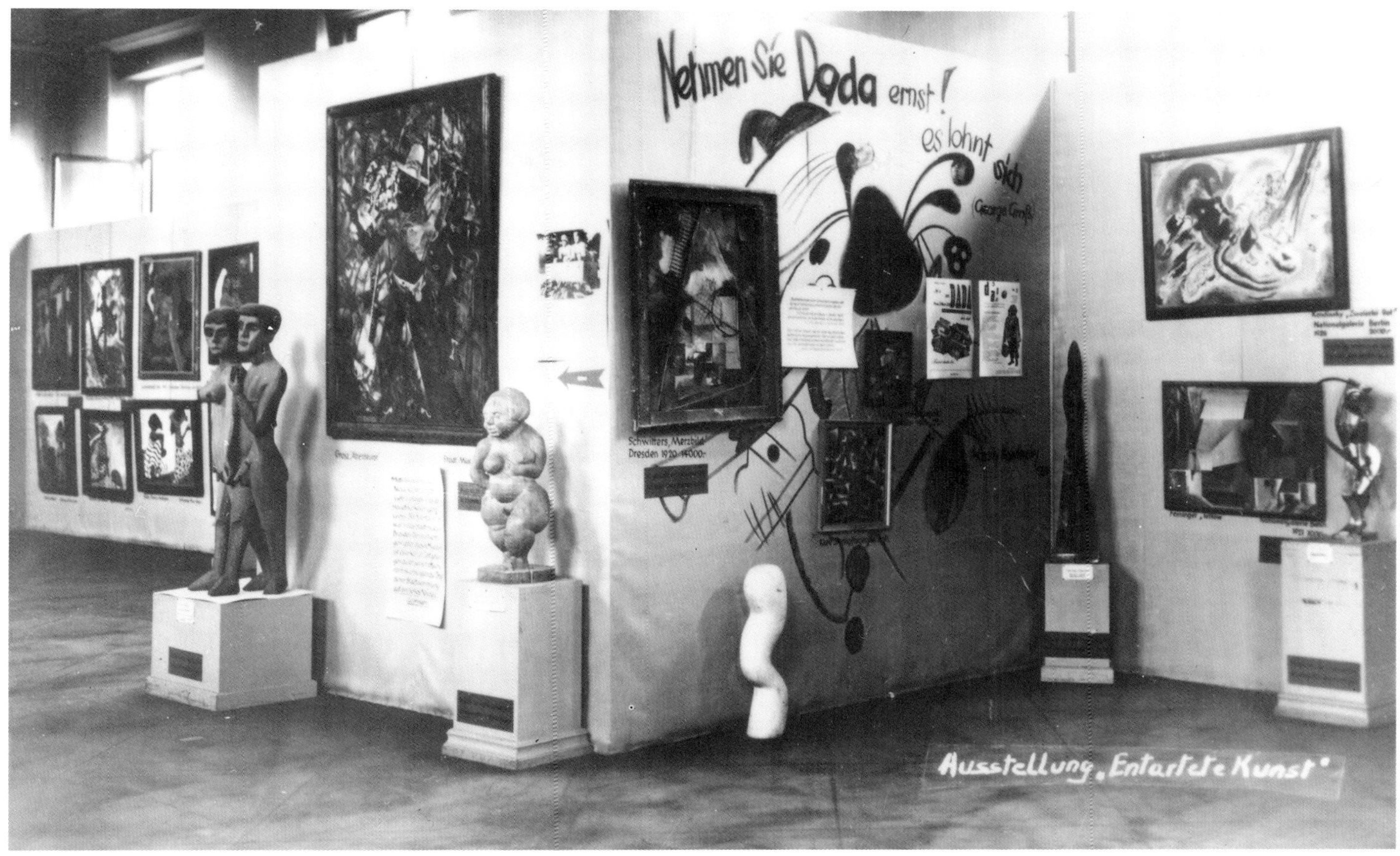

South wall in the third room of the exhibition *Entartete Kunst* (*Degenerate Art*) in the arcades of the Munich Hofgarten, opened on July 19, 1937.

(and music) in Nazi Germany and other fascist regimes. In late 1935, in his capacity as editor of *Art Front,* Davis sent out a call for an artists' congress to combat fascism and address its threats to democratic culture and artistic freedom.[67] He must have been appalled to see reports of the *Degenerate Art* exhibition, which opened in Munich in July 1937, as he was at work on *Swing Landscape.* Featuring more than six hundred works of modern art confiscated from German museums, the *Degenerate Art* exhibition was orchestrated by Joseph Goebbels, propaganda minister for the Third Reich. Not simply a defamation of modernist art and artists, the exhibition advanced antisemitic ideology, with slogans on the walls connecting modern art with Jews and others the Nazis considered inferior. The American press widely reported on the exhibition, with journalists and editorialists generally expressing shock and outrage.[68] One month after the opening of *Degenerate Art,* Davis penned one of his most incisive articulations of the democratic symbolism and social progressivism inherent in abstract art, arguing that if abstraction lacked such meaning, then "we would expect to find abstract art on the side of reaction and thriving under that patronage, because its supposed social neutralism would not make it a political issue. But . . . Hitler proclaims abstract art to be a product of Jewish degeneracy and advises sterilization of abstract artists as insane persons. He physically destroys abstract art just as he burned the books. Why does Hitler outlaw abstract art? Because Fascism denies democracy in culture just as it denies democracy in science and government."[69] In response to the cultural suppression and racial intolerance characterizing fascist regimes, modern art and swing music—two particular banes of Hitler—became symbols of democratic freedom in the United States during the late 1930s.[70]

Seen against this backdrop, *Swing Landscape* takes on a political significance rarely remarked upon. By virtue of its exuberantly "degenerate" style and—through its visual references to swing—its coded advocacy of racial tolerance and diversity, we can read the mural as a celebration of artistic and political freedom and as a visual indictment of fascism. Reading New York into *Swing Landscape* also supports this interpretation, particularly when we consider the mural's intended installation in a neighborhood heavily populated by immigrants and their children. Although less explicitly than in Léger's *Cinematic Mural* studies, the composition's waterfront setting recalls the city's status as the American port of entry not only for those immigrants but for most refugees fleeing Nazi Germany. Likewise, the green bowler hat is also significant in this context, for Al Smith was an outspoken opponent of fascism. Yet it was precisely by ascribing such powerful social and political power to abstract art that Davis clashed not only with many on the left, who advocated for didactic, legible artistic styles for public art, but also with FAP Mural Division director Burgoyne Diller.[71] To understand why, we must examine Davis's participation in the often acrimoniously polemical dialogue surrounding abstraction—and informing its application to public art—in the 1930s.

Public Art and the Politics of Abstraction

Stuart Davis has been called one of "the most prominent public artists of the interwar years."[72] Not only did he devote most of his own artistic energies toward the production of murals, but as a representative of the Artists Union and the American Artists' Congress, he lobbied for increased federal arts funding and an expanded role for public art. He strongly believed that the FAP's mural program, along with its exhibitions and community art centers, offered artists an unparalleled and unprecedented opportunity to engage a mass audience.[73] Davis rejected the prevailing view that traditional realist styles were best suited to public spaces, concurring instead with Fernand Léger, who asked the readers of *Art Front,* "What kind of representational art would you impose upon the masses, to compete with the daily allurements of the movies, the radio, large-scale photography and advertising?"[74] Further, Davis argued that "the painting of today, if it is alive, must be as different from that of previous epochs as our time is different, because art is one of the forms of social expression and must change as society changes."[75] For Davis, like Léger, abstraction functioned as a sort of "new realism," translating the experience of modernity into a new visual language, one that conveyed the altered sensory perceptions enabled by modern technologies: "An artist who has traveled on a steam train, driven an automobile, or flown in an airplane doesn't feel the same way about form and space as one who has not. An artist who has used a telegraph, telephone, and radio doesn't feel the same way about time and space as one who has not. And an artist who lives in a world of motion pictures, electricity, and synthetic chemistry doesn't feel the same way about light and color as one who has not."[76] Davis acknowledged that the future tenants of the Williamsburg Houses were likely unfamiliar with abstract painting because it was "too expensive," alluding to modernism's association with uptown museums, galleries, and collectors. But he was convinced of their receptivity to abstract murals because urban dwellers in the 1930s were, in fact, already familiar with the visual language of modernism through "the shape and color of clothes, autos, cameras, airplanes, trains [and] cooking utensils."[77]

While Davis championed abstract art—and strongly argued for its social relevance and political value, especially in the form of public art—he staunchly opposed non-objectivity, which formed a major strand of abstraction in the 1930s. Non-objective art—art without any visual references to the physical world—was promoted by the artist Hilla Rebay, who in 1939 became the first director of the Museum of Non-Objective Painting (now the Guggenheim Museum). A spiritualist interested in Christian mystical and Buddhist ideas, and influenced by Wassily Kandinsky's 1912 treatise *On the Spiritual in Art,* Rebay believed that non-objective art directly conveyed a pure state of spirituality by abandoning references to the material world.[78] At the same time, Rebay felt that non-objective art was, in essence, a universal aesthetic language that could help break down cultural and national boundaries. But Davis argued that only a "spiritualistic priesthood" could understand an art devoid of references to the natural world. Not only did he believe that non-objectivity "can have no meaning for the great masses of people," but he went so far as to equate it with the "political suppression of the masses" because it further entrenched the divide between them and a "cultural aristocracy."[79]

Burgoyne Diller, as we have seen, was also a staunch proponent of abstract public art, citing its therapeutic nature and its aesthetic complementarity with modern architecture. The muralists he selected for the Williamsburg project worked in a wide range of styles, and the site could have functioned as a showcase for abstract diversity. But of the seventeen murals originally commissioned, only seven (or perhaps eight) were completed. And of these, only five—one each by Ilya Bolotowsky, Albert Swinden, and Balcomb Greene and a pair by Paul Kelpe—were installed in 1938. Confusingly, extant correspondence reveals that one of Davis's mural studies, along with sketches by Bolotowsky and Swinden, was rejected—with no reason provided—in July 1937. Yet by that time, Davis had already begun painting *Swing Landscape,* and he evidently continued working on it until May 1938.[80] And as we know, the murals by Bolotowsky and Swinden were installed in the housing project the following year. George McNeil, too, seems to have completed his mural, as revealed by a documentary photograph, but it was not installed and has since been lost (see pages 72–73, 111, 122–23).[81] Francis Criss's mural *Sixth Avenue El* was also completed and, along with *Swing Landscape,* was displayed in the May 1938 exhibition *Murals for the Community* at the FAP's New York gallery. Because both murals were completed but neither was ever installed, they must have been rejected around this time. To date, no report or correspondence has surfaced to provide a clear reason for the final acceptance or rejection of specific murals commissioned for the Williamsburg project, but one factor in the overall reduction of the mural program was likely financial. As early as summer 1937, almost a year before the project was completed, concerns were raised over its high cost.

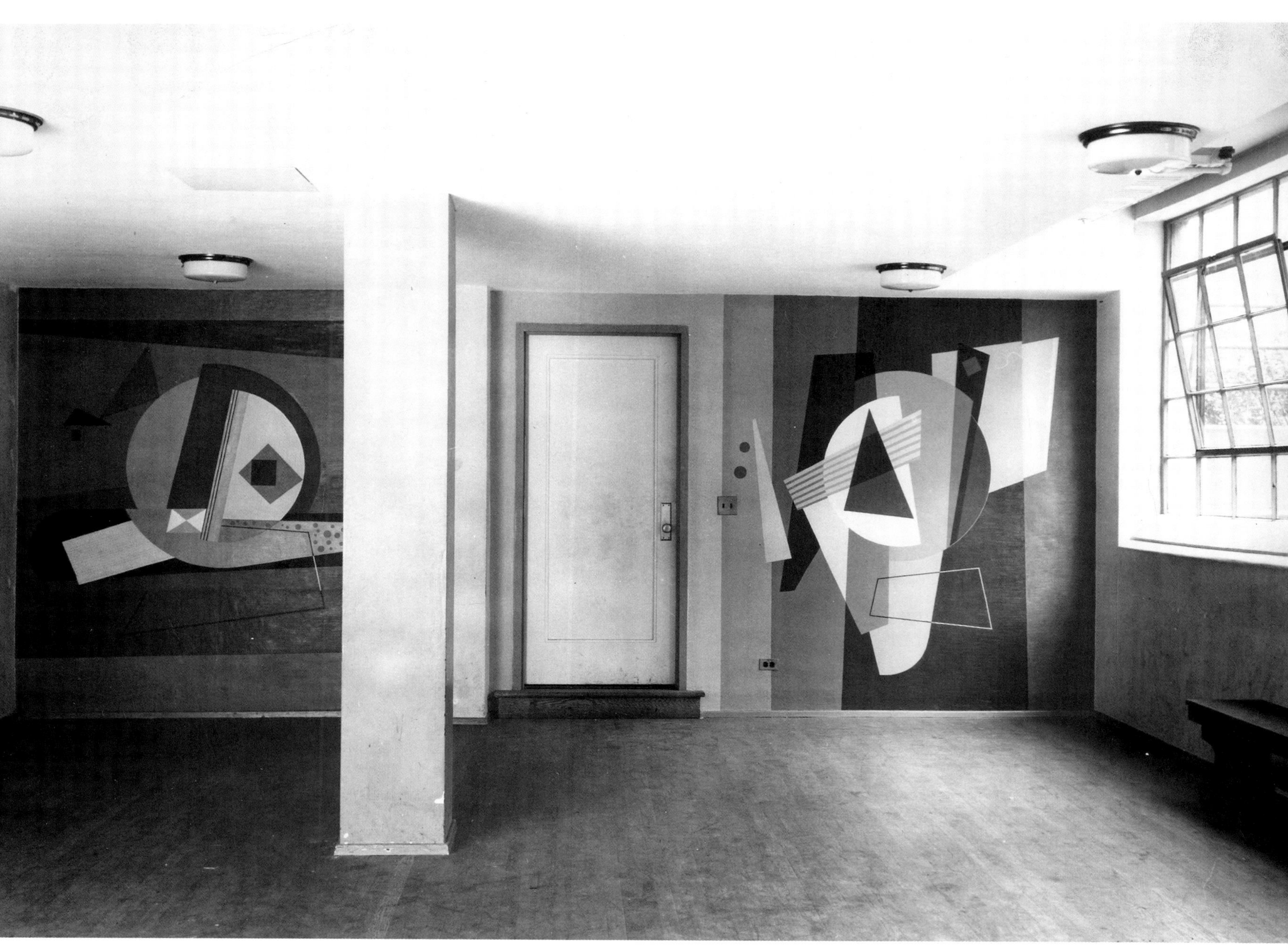

Paul Kelpe's murals in the Williamsburg Housing Project, ca. 1938.

Financial worries were likely also responsible for the elimination of carved relief sculptures for the site.[82] The decision to reject the finished murals by McNeil, Criss, and Davis was eased by their being, like most FAP murals, "portable murals," that is, large oil paintings on canvas, rather than frescoes painted in situ. Thus, NYCHA—which had made no financial investment in the project—had little to lose by rejecting finished murals.[83]

But why was *Swing Landscape,* a mural that Jody Patterson has argued was "tailor-made" for the Williamsburg residents, rejected?[84] While artist Carl Holty's assertion that *Swing Landscape* was "too good to hang in . . . a new housing project" certainly cannot be the reason, the most likely factor in its rejection indeed related to aesthetics. Archival sources reveal that Davis argued with fellow muralist Paul Kelpe—whose mural was originally to be installed in the same social room—on an aesthetic matter, no doubt concerning the issue of non-objectivity.[85] But an argument with Burgoyne Diller is even more illuminating. In June 1937, as Davis was at work on *Swing Landscape,* Diller informed him that he would be receiving a new studio assistant. Davis told Diller he would need one who "could understand my ideas and do necessary research with understanding." In reply, Diller—noting that he too was an abstract artist—retorted that Davis "[couldn't] tell him that a painting like that required research."[86] This exchange reveals a fundamental difference between Davis's and Diller's conceptions of the role and purpose of abstract art. Although both artists believed that abstraction could express democratic ideals, they interpreted this concept very differently. Davis, as we have seen, insisted that his abstracted compositions, by retaining elements of representation, embodied the sensory and material essence of contemporary American life. Diller, on the other hand, was more in tune with Rebay's philosophy of non-objectivity. Guided by the utopian and universalist ideals of the Dutch De Stijl movement, Diller adopted Piet Mondrian's austere geometric style (known as neoplasticism), avoiding allusions to the physical world. As Barbara Haskell has written, by "obliterat[ing] reminders of the social, political, and economic differences between people, [neoplasticism] accorded with the egalitarian tenets of democracy" in the eyes of its practitioners.[87]

The artistic divergence between Diller and Davis is pointedly illustrated by the conspicuous absence of Davis's name from the membership rolls of the American Abstract Artists (AAA), a group cofounded by Diller in 1936. Although the AAA promoted all forms of abstraction, its members expressed a general bias toward variants of geometric abstraction, constructivism, and neoplasticism. Although many rejected Rebay's esoteric views of non-objectivity, they generally perceived abstraction in universal—not socially or culturally specific—terms, as Davis did.[88] The murals ultimately selected for installation in the Williamsburg Houses were all by artists affiliated with the AAA and whose work was essentially non-objective in character. The same is true of most murals installed in other sites supervised by Diller, such as the Hospital for Chronic Diseases on Roosevelt Island in the East River.[89] The Williamsburg murals by Bolotowsky, Greene, and Swinden—and, to a lesser extent, by Kelpe—are serene, geometric compositions that visually aligned with Lescaze's architecture. Their palettes are limited to a range of complementary hues. None of these murals contain anything evocative of the natural world. Significantly, they also closely conform to the guidelines for public art set out by FAP director Holger Cahill in 1936: "The color, the scale, and the character of the painting must have clarity, largeness, carrying power, and a rhythmic order that leads the eye easily through the whole space. Mural art is suited to large simple forms, and its color schemes are much more severely limited than those of the easel painter."[90] In addition to the few extant photographs of the murals in situ in the Williamsburg Houses, we gain insight into the aesthetic effect of their installation from the artist Olin Dowes's survey of public art in the new housing projects: "Complete abstraction reigns in the Williamsburg housing project in Brooklyn. Here three of William Lescaze's rooms are painted with rather large geometrical symbols from ceiling to baseboard by Paul Kelpe, [Balcomb] Greene and Ilya Bolotowsky. In each room the same system is employed, alternating a decorated wall or panel with one painted a plain color, sometimes allowing a door to give the needed relief between two detailed passages. In one room a restrained harmony of blues, greys and deep brown, and well-chosen stylish shapes make particularly effective murals. If you like abstraction you will enjoy its skillful use in these carefully executed arrangements."[91] In short, the murals that ended up on the walls of the Williamsburg Houses were decorative panels that supported Lescaze's wish for a painted complement to his architectural design and Diller's desire to create a restful, harmonious environment—one based on neoplastic aesthetic principles.

By looking at the murals installed in the Williamsburg Houses in 1938, we can begin to understand why *Swing Landscape* was not among them. Davis's mural neither complements the other Williamsburg murals aesthetically nor fulfills the formal criteria of Cahill, Diller, or Lescaze. Although Karen Wilkin has asserted that *Swing Landscape* "admirably fulfill[ed its] mandate . . . to be public art," because it is appealing "even to the visually unsophisticated," this is not how it was perceived in 1938.[92] Notably, the *New York Times* art critic Edward Alden Jewell, despite his generally sympathetic attitude toward modernist innovation, pronounced *Swing Landscape* an unsuccessful example of public art. In his review of the Federal Art Gallery's May 1938 exhibition *Murals for the Community*, Jewell expressed a sense of being overwhelmed by the mural. Of its bold palette, he complained that "the color shrieks as if stricken with pain that cannot be less than acute," and he observed that Davis's *Egg Beater* paintings of the 1920s, with their simpler compositions and more subdued palettes, would have "magnified much more convincingly" as murals. His rather flippant remark that *Swing Landscape* "deserves a room of its own or an entire housing project" is reminiscent of the architect Paul Nelson's observation about the architectural paintings of Fernand Léger: "A painting of Léger's no longer wants a wall to hang on—it demands a room."[93] And Jewell's further comment that *Swing Landscape* "cancels everything else in range" adds insight into the mural's elimination from the housing project.[94] If *Swing Landscape* was "too modern" for a housing project, this is true only inasmuch as it, alone among the Williamsburg murals, celebrates the cultural diversity and chaos of modern American life. Whether its encoded social meanings or urban allusions offended its FAP or NYCHA patrons is hard to say. But what does seem clear is that they expected "architectural painting" to be subservient to the architecture.

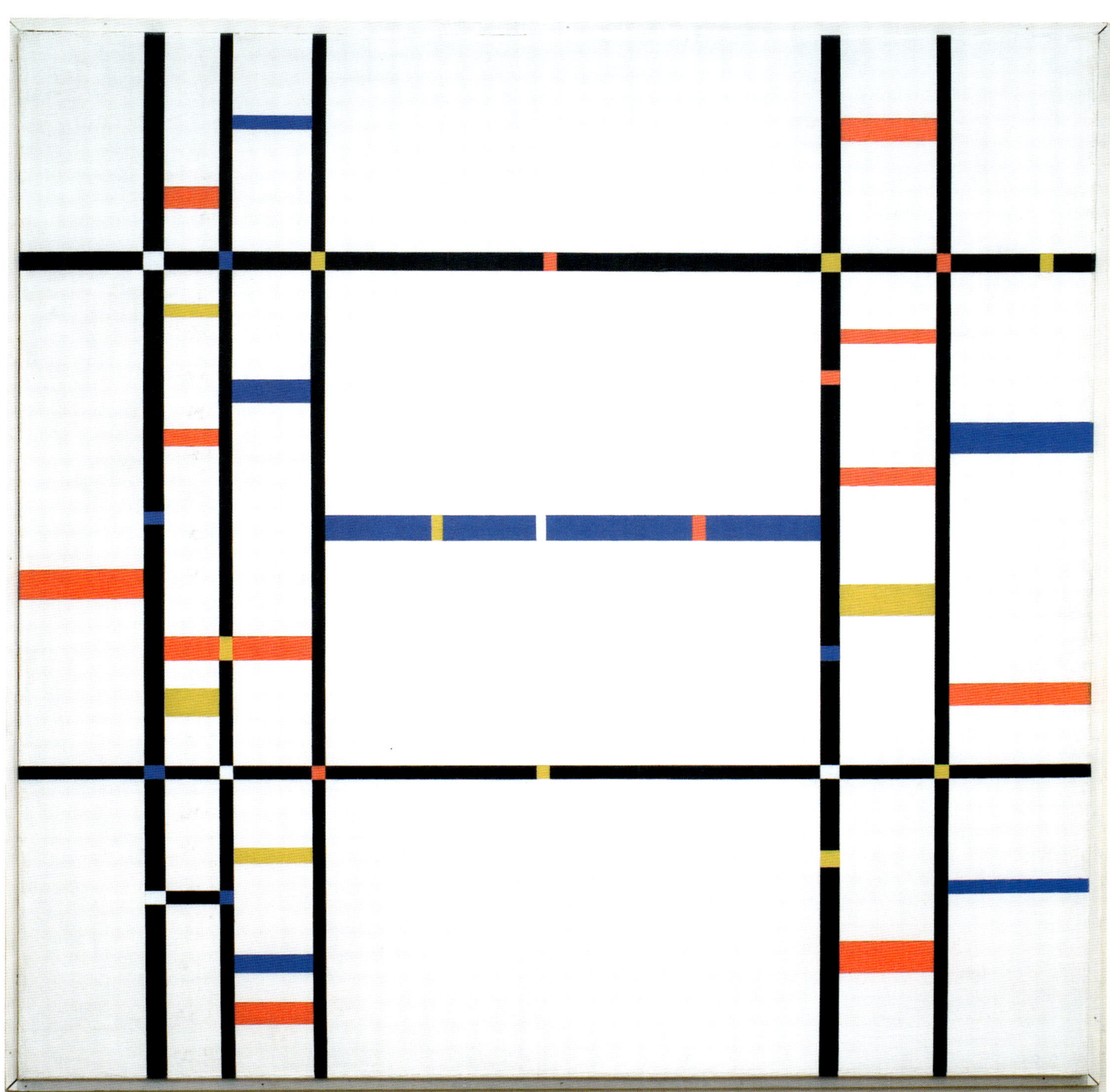

Burgoyne Diller, *Composition,* 1943–44
Oil on canvas, 42 × 42 in. (106.7 × 106.7 cm). Davis Museum at Wellesley College, Gift of Theodore Racoosin, 1959.13. © 2019 Estate of Burgoyne Diller / Licensed by VAGA at Artists Rights Society (ARS), NY.

From Brooklyn to Bloomington

The only public housing project to pair modernist architecture with vanguard art, the Williamsburg Housing Project and its murals constituted a unique experiment within the history of both housing and public art. Had the proposed artistic program been fully realized, the Brooklyn site would have contained the most extensive collection of abstract murals in the United States and perhaps in the world. Unfortunately, the Williamsburg project was too visionary to serve as a sustainable model for American public housing. In 1935, Lescaze optimistically anticipated that the Williamsburg Houses would be "the best demonstration of intelligent and successful modern, low-cost housing in America."[95] But the construction costs associated with the buildings' modernist design and high-quality materials could not be adequately offset by the low rents paid by tenants, rents that already had to be supplemented by government subsidies to cover maintenance costs.[96] Williamsburg's ambitious artistic program, likewise, was conceived under conditions that prevailed in the United States for barely a decade—an era that remains unique in American cultural history. At no other time has the federal government made such a massive investment in the arts, enabling artists to pursue even experimental projects at its expense. Yet the costs of producing and installing seventeen murals and a series of relief sculptures proved prohibitive. And ultimately, NYCHA was unable to care for even the five murals installed in 1938. In the following decades, the murals by Bolotowsky, Swinden, Greene, and Kelpe fell victim to neglect. The communal social rooms in which they were displayed were converted into offices and storerooms, and the murals, some of which had suffered from vandalism, were painted over.[97] Rediscovered under multiple coats of paint in the late 1970s, they were eventually removed, restored, and installed in the Brooklyn Museum. Similarly tragic fates befell many other murals—whether traditional or vanguard in style—produced under the auspices of the New Deal programs of the 1930s. In retrospect, then, we should be grateful that *Swing Landscape* never made it onto the walls of the Williamsburg Houses.

In 1939, Stuart Davis made one of his pithiest statements on aesthetics: "Anyone can appreciate abstract art just as anyone can appreciate music. Look at it and enjoy it."[98] As Davis tells us in his own words, it is not necessary to know anything about the social, political, or art historical context of *Swing Landscape* to enjoy its visual exuberance. It is not even necessary to know—although it arguably increases one's enjoyment of it—that the mural contains an abstracted tangle of forms based on the Gloucester waterfront, montaged into an energetic composition that draws on the rhythms of swing music and the pace of urban life. But a consideration of the mural's multivalent meanings—which are not so obvious on the surface—opens our eyes to *Swing Landscape*'s true complexity and artistic significance. Davis used this public commission to respond to the turbulent political and social crises of his day—labor strikes, racial segregation and antisemitism, and the growing fascist threat to artistic expression in Europe among them. Painting a mural for a public housing project also gave Davis the opportunity to fulfill a cherished goal: the democratization of modern art. And despite *Swing Landscape*'s failure to be installed in the Williamsburg Houses, it is important to recognize that Davis did not fail to meet this goal. Thanks to the federal allocation of the mural to Indiana University in early 1942, many

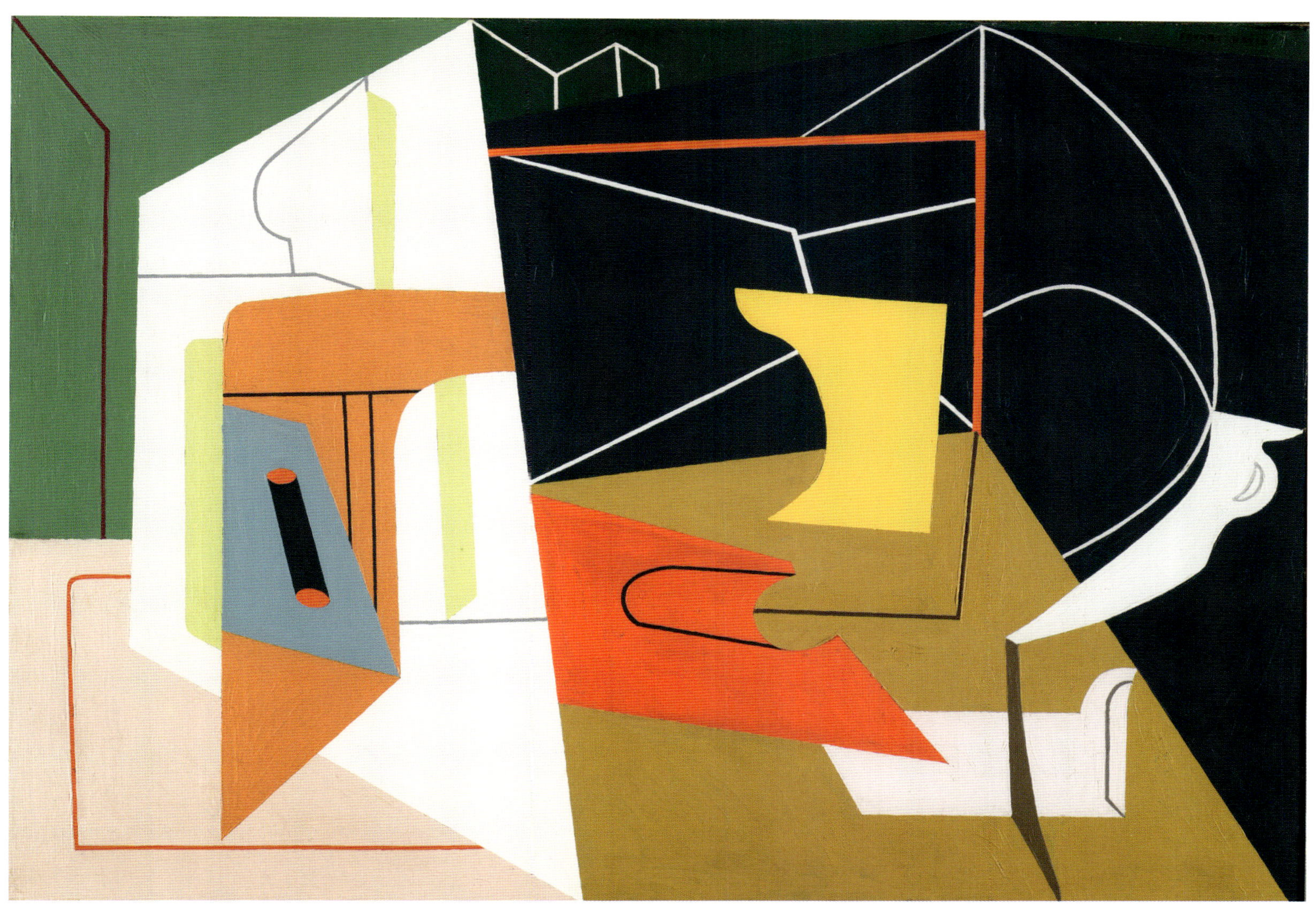

Stuart Davis, *Egg Beater No. 4,* 1928
Oil on canvas, 27⅛ × 38¼ in. (68.9 × 97.2 cm). The Phillips Collection, Washington, DC, Acquired 1939.

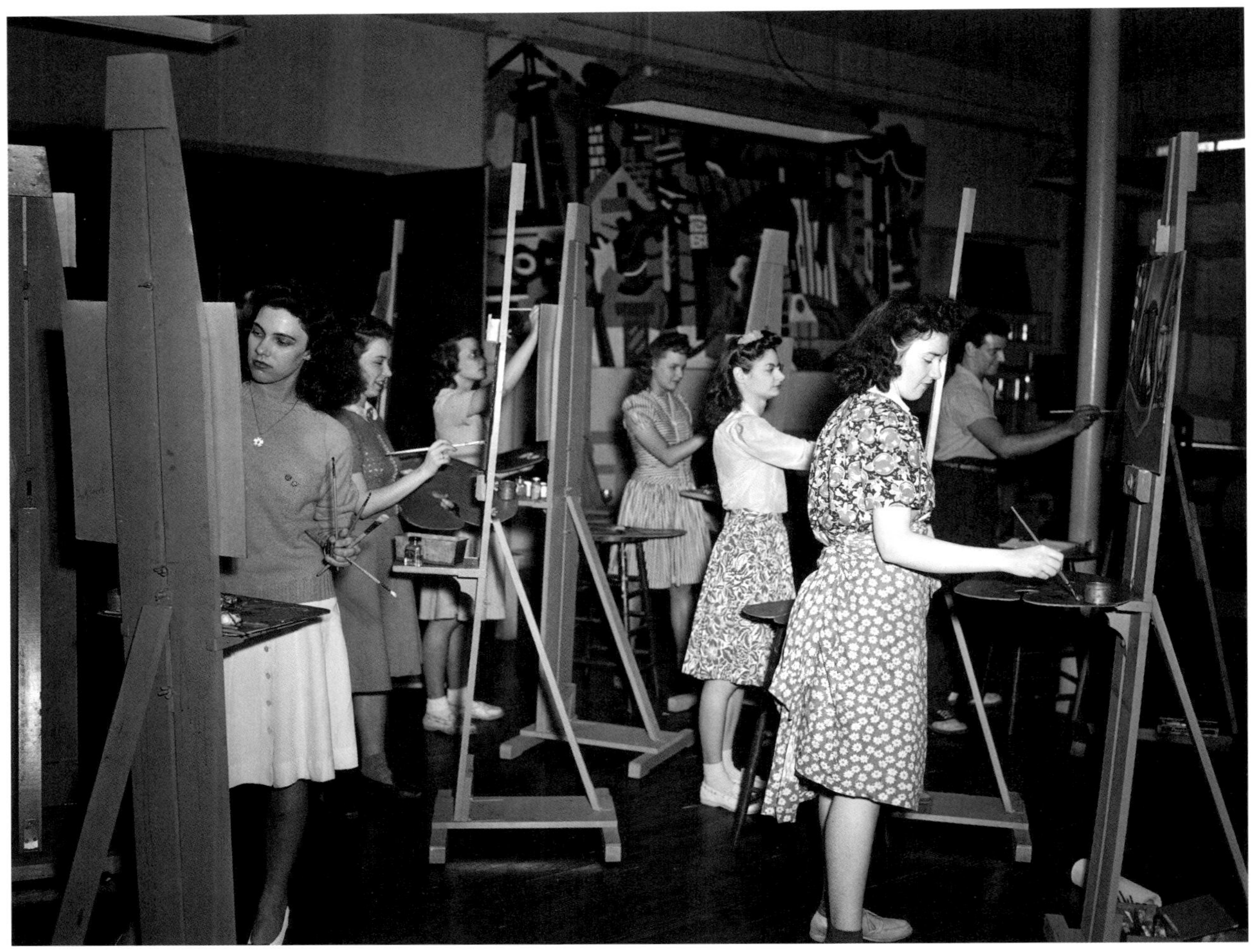

Painting class at Indiana University, April 29, 1942. *Swing Landscape* can be seen in the background.

university students and faculty encountered modern art for the first time.[99] In fact, in the two decades before the establishment of the university art museum in the early 1960s, the mural was perhaps more visible to more people than it would have been even in Brooklyn. Transformed into a backdrop for parties, student art auctions, painting classes, and even swing dances, *Swing Landscape* energized campus life and opened the eyes and minds of its midwestern spectators.[100] Sadly, however, the distance in space and time from the public housing projects of New Deal New York has resulted in the muting of *Swing Landscape*'s radicalism. Two decades into the twenty-first century, it is high time to recover the social and political messages embedded within the mural's vibrant modernist composition and to consider their relevance to contemporary viewers. As in the 1930s, the world of 2020 is challenged by income and housing inequalities, nationalist extremism, and threats to artistic expression. In helping us learn from the past, *Swing Landscape* offers vital lessons to today's spectators about democracy, tolerance, and artistic freedom—if only we will learn how to interpret its messages.

1. William Agee, "The Murals, 1921–1957," in Boyajian and Rutkowski, *Stuart Davis*, 1:83.

2. Exceptions include the following recent articles: Patterson, "Art of Swinging Left"; and McComas, "Public Art and the Perils of Canonization."

3. For example, in the wall texts and brochure for the 2005 exhibition *Stuart Davis and American Abstraction: A Masterpiece in Focus*, Philadelphia Museum of Art (copies in curatorial files, Eskenazi Museum of Art).

4. William Agee, "Introduction," in *American Vanguards*, 3.

5. Stuart Davis Papers, March 9, 1938, Harvard Art Museums Archives, cited in Patterson, "Modernism for the Masses," 197–98.

6. Radford, *Modern Housing for America*, 115–17.

7. Rodgers, *Atlantic Crossings*, 383.

8. Miller, *Architecture and Politics in Germany*, 104.

9. The Viennese housing projects included the Karl-Marx-Hof, Reumannhof, Herwegh-Hof, Matteoti-Hof, Julius Popp-Hof, Metzleinstaler-Hof, and Rabenhof. For more on Viennese housing of the era, see Blau, *Architecture of Red Vienna*. On the American response, see Hardy, *Housing Program of the City of Vienna*.

10. The influence of Viennese style is also noted in Stern, Gilmartin, and Mellins, *New York, 1930*, 421.

11. Bauer, *Modern Housing*, 237–38.

12. Radford, *Modern Housing for America*, 86–88, 91.

13. Postal, *Landmarks Preservation Designation Report*, 7.

14. Federal Writers' Project, *WPA Guide to New York City*, 455.

15. The Williamsburg Houses were featured in MoMA's 1936 exhibition *Architecture in Government Housing*.

16. The Werkbundsiedlung, constructed in 1932, was modeled on the Weissenhofsiedlung (1926–27) in Stuttgart, an experimental modernist suburb developed by the Deutscher Werkbund.

17. "Proposed Housing Development," 265–66.

18. Miller, *Architecture and Politics in Germany*, 104. Among Taut's Berlin housing estates are the Hufeisensiedlung, Siedlung Schillerpark, Zehlendorf, and Wohnstadt Carl Legien.

19. Brock, "Modernist Scans Our Skyline."

20. William Lescaze to Langdon Post, June 28, 1937, New York City Housing Authority (hereafter NYCHA) Papers, box 53D3, folder 10.

21. "Methodology," typescript, 1942, RG 69, box 63, entry 1030, National Archives and Records Administration (hereafter NARA), 36.

22. Harris, *Federal Art and National Culture*, 65.

23. Harris, *Federal Art and National Culture*, 70.

24. Green and Butler, *Revealed*, n.p.

25. On Gorky's murals, which are no longer extant, see Bowman, *Murals without Walls*.

26. According to the *Cumulative Monthly Progress Report, Federal Art Project of the Works Progress Administration, November 1, 1935 to May 1, 1936*, RG 69, box 64, NARA, "a series of 17 murals, all of them Abstractions," were in progress, though not yet approved, for the Williamsburg Housing Project.

27. Carr, "New Deal and Sculptor," 77. Carr describes Rivera's 1936 work, titled *Composition*, as a marble sculpture bearing the influence of Hans Arp. In an interview in 1968, Rivera recalls working on only one FAP commission—an aluminum sculpture titled *Flight* for Newark Airport (oral history interview with José de Rivera, February 24,1968, Archives of American Art). However, a photograph of a sculpture matching Carr's description of *Composition* is housed in the Federal Art Project Photographic Division collection at the Archives of American Art. Although it does not bear an inscription linking it with the Williamsburg Houses, the photograph's existence does suggest that he may, in fact, have worked on two FAP commissions.

28. *Methodology*, typescript, 1942, and *New York City Art Project, NYC Application #15004, Supplementary Data*, RG 69, box 63, entry 1030, NARA.

29. Radford, *Modern Housing for America*, 100; Bloom, *Public Housing That Worked*, 6. NYCHA segregated its housing as a concession to public opinion in order to build political support for public housing.

30. The sculptures are reproduced in Dowes, "Art for Housing Tenants," 620–21.

31. Burgoyne Diller, "Abstract Murals," in O'Connor, *Art for the Millions*, 69.

32. Frederick Kiesler to Holger Cahill, October 30, 1935, cited in Berman, "Lost Years," 42; Diller, "Abstract Murals," 69.

33. Fernand Léger, "Color in Life (Fragment of a Study on the New Plastic Values)," cited in Anna Vallye, "Between the Easel and the Mural: On the Social Ambitions of Painting in Space," in Baudin, *Fernand Léger: Painting in Space*, 52.

34. David C. Comstock, WPA Color Consultant, to H. A. Gray, Director of Housing, Washington, DC, October 1, 1936, NYCHA Papers, box 53B8, folder 11.

35. Berman, "Lost Years," 42; Langdon Post to Burgoyne Diller, October 30, 1936, NYCHA Papers, box 53C1, folder 4.

36. *New Horizons in American Art*, 143–44.

37. McComas, "Public Art and the Perils of Canonization."

38. Sims, *Stuart Davis: American Painter*, 238.

39. Wilkin, "Stuart Davis in Philadelphia," 43.

40. Jewell, "Commentary on Murals."

41. Berman, "Lost Years," 144–45; Scott and Rutkoff, *New York Modern*, 292; Hughes, *American Visions*, 437.

42. Agee, *Modern Art in America, 1908–1968*, 178.

43. The title *Waterfront Forms* was long thought to refer to a separate, lost mural. However, the authors of the 2007 catalogue raisonné

convincingly argue that it was simply an earlier title for *Swing Landscape*. See Boyajian and Rutkowski, *Stuart Davis*, 2:626.

44. Stuart Davis calendars, August 28, 1937, cited in Boyajian and Rutkowski, *Stuart Davis*, 3:293.

45. Stuart Davis to D. S. Defenbacher, October 18, 1946, cited in Boyajian and Rutkowski, *Stuart Davis*, 3:250. John X. Christ also downplays the importance of Gloucester in his analysis of the mural, writing that "the identifiable sites that figure so prominently in the early thirties are barely legible. . . . *Swing Landscape* does evoke modern experience, but less through its suggestion of a specific place or set of objects than by its formal analogies to jazz and evocation of the rhythm of contemporary life" ("Stuart Davis and the Politics of Experience," 60–61).

46. Langdon Post to Burgoyne Diller, October 30, 1936, NYCHA Records, box 53C1, folder 4.

47. Jodi Hauptman, "Imagining Cities," in Lanchner, *Fernand Léger*, 75.

48. Fernand Léger, "The Origins of Painting and Its Representational Value," in Fry, *Functions of Painting*, 8–10.

49. Master checklist for *Fernand Léger: Paintings and Drawings*, Museum of Modern Art, 1935: https://www.moma.org/documents/moma_master-checklist_387253.pdf. Davis and Léger met during Davis's year in Paris (1928–29). In 1935, Davis published a translation of Léger's speech "The New Realism" in *Art Front*.

50. These include: Lane, *Stuart Davis: Art and Art Theory*, 39; and Barbara Haskell, "Stuart Davis: A Chronicle," in Haskell and Cooper, *Stuart Davis: In Full Swing*, 183.

51. Cited in Katia Baudin, "Fernand Léger and Wallace K. Harrison: An American Dream Come True," in Baudin, *Fernand Léger: Painting in Space*, 187.

52. *Murals by American Painters and Photographers*, 22. Painted for a museum exhibition, *New York Mural* is perhaps a mural more in theory than in practice, but it served as Davis's introduction to the production of public art, complete with restrictions, such as size and orientation, set by the patron.

53. Sims, *Stuart Davis: American Painter*, 218.

54. Other Smith references include the martini glass in the upper right, an allusion to Smith's support for the repeal of Prohibition; and the foreground bananas, possibly referring to his reputation as "top banana" during the 1928 presidential campaign. More generally, the tiger's head symbolizes Tammany Hall, the association that controlled the Democratic Party in New York.

55. Whiting, *Antifascism in American Art*, 67; Karen Wilkin, "Stuart Davis and Drawing," in Wilkin and Kachur, *Amazing Continuity*, 25.

56. Lane, *Stuart Davis*, 39. *Guernica*, painted in response to the bombing of Basque civilians by the German Condor Legion at the behest of Francisco Franco, was displayed in the Spanish Republic's pavilion at the *Exposition Internationale* of 1937 in Paris.

57. Stuart Davis, "Abstract Painting Today," in O'Connor, *Art for the Millions*, 126.

58. Blesh, *Stuart Davis*, 55. *Swing Landscape*'s formal relationship with swing music was first analyzed in detail in Lucas, "Fine Art Jive of Stuart Davis," 33–36.

59. Bakan, "Jazz and the 'Popular Front,'"43.

60. Quoted in Erenberg, *Swingin' the Dream*, 129.

61. Cited in Patterson, "Modernism for the Masses," 214.

62. Schapiro, "Race, Nationality, and Art," 10–12; Davis, "Cube Root," 33–34.

63. Kelpe was born in Germany, de Kooning in the Netherlands, and Swinden in England. Matulka, born in the Austro-Hungarian Empire, was Czech, and Bolotowsky and Criss were Russian Jews (Criss was born in England while his parents were in the process of emigrating).

64. Brace, "American Group," 274–75; Langa, *Radical Art*, 35.

65. "Marine Art," *Daily Worker*, February 28, 1937, cited in Hemingway, *Artists on the Left*, 134.

66. Cécile Whiting also interprets the lamp as an "interrogation lamp," and further describes the scene as a battleground (*Antifascism in American Art*, 65).

67. Davis, "American Artists' Congress," 8.

68. The most comprehensive overview of the *Degenerate Art* exhibition is found in Barron, "*Degenerate Art.*"

69. Stuart Davis, "Notes on the Nature of Abstract Art," typescript, August 27, 1937, Stuart Davis Papers, Houghton Library, Harvard University, microfilm reel 1.

70. McComas, "Canonizing Hitler's 'Degenerate Art,'" 203–18.

71. Meyer Schapiro, the leading leftist art critic of the 1930s, felt that abstract artists were too concerned with formal problems to produce socially relevant art.

72. Christ, "Stuart Davis as Public Artist," 65.

73. His stance is apparent, for example, in the undated typescripts "For a Permanent Art Project: Expansion Program for Greater Public Use of Art" and "Federal Art Project and the Social Education of the Artist," Stuart Davis Papers, box 1/1, Archives of American Art.

74. Léger, "New Realism Goes On," 7–8.

75. Davis, "Abstract Painting Today," 127.

76. Stuart Davis, "Is There a Revolution in the Arts?" *Bulletin of American Town Meetings of the Air* (February 1940): 12, cited in Patterson, "Art of Swinging Left," 108.

77. Davis, "Synopsis on Abstract Art in Williamsburg Project," typescript, October 1937, Stuart Davis Papers, Harvard University, microfilm reel 1.

78. Lukach, *Hilla Rebay*, xii.

79. Davis, "Notes on the Nature of Abstract Art."

80. H. A. Gray to Langdon Post, July 27, 1937, NYCHA Papers, box 53D1, folder 15; Haskell, "Stuart Davis: A Chronicle," 182–83.

81. This photograph was brought to my attention in August 2019 by Helen McNeil-Ashton, the artist's daughter. It corroborates McNeil's recollection, in an oral history of 1968, of the then-lost mural (oral history interview with George McNeil, January 9–May 21, 1968, Archives of American Art). Despite McNeil's recollections in this interview, scholars have believed until now that McNeil's mural was never completed.

82. H. A. Gray to Harold Ickes, July 16, 1937, cited in Patterson, "Modernism for the Masses," 205; Carr, "New York Sculpture," 402.

83. Langdon Post to H. A. Gray, July 2, 13, 1937, NYCHA Papers, box 55B3, folder 4.

84. Patterson, "Art of Swinging Left," 115–17.

85. Oral history interview with Carl Holty, December 8, 1964, Archives of American Art; Patterson, "Modernism for the Masses," 100. The exhibition catalogue for *New Horizons in American Art* indicates that separate murals by Davis and Kelpe were to be installed in the same room (*New Horizons in American Art*, 143–44).

86. Memorandum, June 29, 1937, Stuart Davis Papers, box 1/1, Archives of American Art.

87. Haskell, *Burgoyne Diller*, 43.

88. Knott, *American Abstract Art of the 1930s and 1940s*, 22.

89. An exception is Radio Station WNYC. While the murals designed by John von Wicht, Byron Browne, and Lee Krasner were geometric abstractions, Louis Schanker's portrayed the recognizable forms of musical instruments, as does Davis's mural, which also contains stylized forms of radio and technological equipment.

90. Holger Cahill, "Introduction," in *New Horizons in American Art*, 32.

91. Dowes, "Art for Housing Tenants," 621.

92. Wilkin, *Stuart Davis*, 146–47.

93. Jewell, "Commentary on Murals"; Paul Nelson, "Peinture spatiale et architecture à propos des dernières oeuvres de Léger," *Cahiers d'Art* 12, no. 1–3 (1937): 86, translated and cited in Carolyn Lanchner, "Fernand Léger: American Connections," in Lanchner, *Fernand Léger*, 43–44.

94. Jewell, "Commentary on Murals."

95. William Lescaze to Mayor Fiorello La Guardia, July 29, 1935, NYCHA Papers, box 53B7, folder 10.

96. Bloom, *Public Housing That Worked*, 32.

97. London, *Legacy Regained*, 3; Gallati, *Williamsburg Murals*, n.p.

98. Stuart Davis, typescript of radio broadcast, "Dedication of W.P.A. Federal Art Project Murals at Broadcasting Station WNYC, August 2, 1939, 8 p.m. Stuart Davis," Stuart Davis Papers, folder: "Writings, re. American Artists Congress," Federal Art Project, Archives of American Art.

99. Hope commented on the overall ignorance of the fine arts he found among Indiana University students and faculty to Paul J. Sachs, his mentor at Harvard (Henry Radford Hope to Paul J. Sachs, November 26, 1945, Harvard University Art Museum Archives, HC 3, box 45, file 881 [2 of 2]). Details about the mural's allocation to Indiana University are found in the Papers of the Cincinnati Modern Art Society, Archives and Rare Books Department, University Libraries, University of Cincinnati (copies in curatorial files, Eskenazi Museum of Art).

100. At least once, the mural served as the backdrop for a dance accompanied by Tommy Dorsey's swing orchestra. See Boyajian and Rutkowski, *Stuart Davis*, 3:293. Historic photographs showing other placements of *Swing Landscape* around campus in the 1940s are reproduced in the "*Swing Landscape:* A History" section of this catalogue.

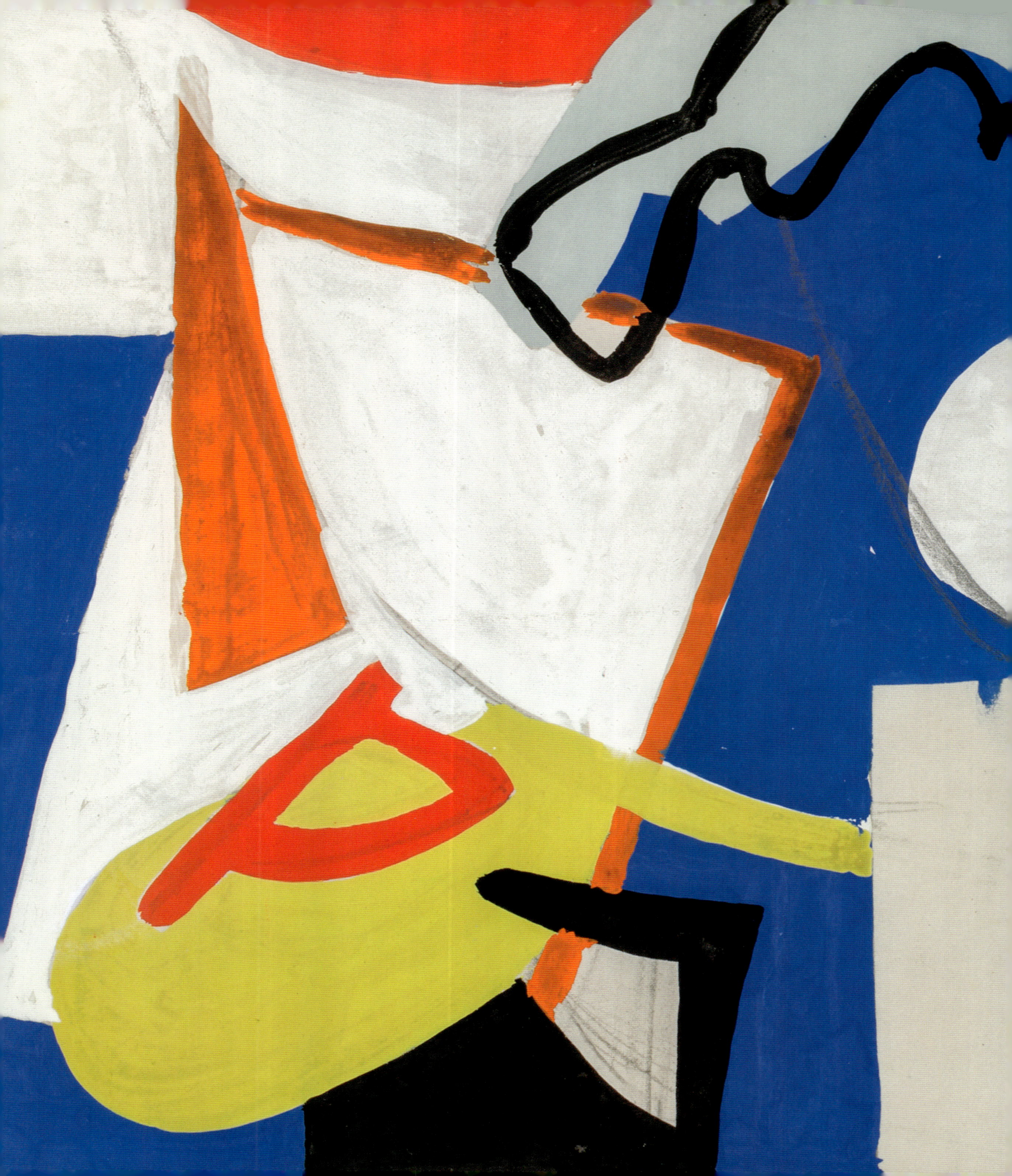

The Broad and Open Way

American Modernisms of the Thirties

Jody Patterson

It was at the end of the 1930s that Stuart Davis completed *Swing Landscape*, a monumental tour-de-force of abstract form and color whose aesthetic achievements fixed the artist's place within histories of twentieth-century American modernism. As scholarly accounts concur, Davis was a virtuoso artist who assimilated the lessons of European modernism to forge a distinctive approach to painting whose legacy remains unassailable; equally, his views on art, both published and personal, were culturally sophisticated and characterized by intellectually exacting argument. It seems to me, however, that perhaps more so than any other modernist artwork of the period, *Swing Landscape* points to "what we have lost" in the ensuing development of modernism. The painting was commissioned in 1936 by the New York Mural Division of the Works Progress Administration's Federal Art Project (WPA/FAP). A return to the historical conditions that brought the mural into existence—broaching an inquiry into what was necessary to produce a federally funded large-scale modernist painting created for a popular audience—invites engagement with some unruly historical particulars. Assessments of the contributions made by American modernists during the New Deal era have been dogged by a constellation of overlapping and intertwined issues related to patronage, audience, and formal innovation. By 1939, New Deal administrator Forbes Watson, who had been a supporter of modern art, albeit of a moderate type, since the 1920s, was already wary of the judgments of posterity. Watson served as technical director of the short-lived Public Works of Art Project (PWAP), the first of the New Deal cultural initiatives in operation from 1933 to 1934, and subsequently as chief adviser to the Treasury Department's Section of Painting and Sculpture (later renamed the Section of Fine Arts), which ran from 1934 to 1943. "Let us remember," cautioned Watson, "that in estimating the work that is being done today in our midst we might as well realize that the future may arrive at conclusions entirely different from ours." He feared—with good reason—that cultural ideologues seeking to preserve the independent identity of the artist and the autonomy of art itself would find little to recommend in the public art of the period, modernist or otherwise. These issues emerged during the 1930s and were subsequently exacerbated by the shifting character and priorities of modern art in the decades that followed. Abstract painter George McNeil, who studied under Jan Matulka and Hans Hofmann at the Art Students League in New York and helped to found the American Abstract Artists' (AAA) group in 1936, later commented on how the narrow formalist rubric associated with postwar American painting does not adequately capture the broader aspirations of many modernists who were employed by the arts projects. As McNeil observes, the designation "modern art" is "meaningless" today in relation to the abstract murals of the 1930s.[1]

The "muralizing" of easel painting during the New Deal era has also vexed evaluations of modernist muralism, both during the 1930s and in subsequent historical assessments. What I mean by this is that the majority of modernist murals surviving from this period—most, like *Swing Landscape*, commissioned under the FAP—are now hung on the walls of museums, and this points to their uncertain status *as murals*. Financial and technical restraints meant that the bulk of FAP murals were painted in oil on canvas in a studio and later glued to the wall on site. Some murals were painted independently of a specific destination and were instead commissioned to fulfill the relief aspect of the WPA's mission. The portability of these "murals without walls" meant that they could be installed wherever a public wall became available, though unlike other artworks created on the project, mural designs needed the approval of a cosponsor with public walls to decorate. For some critics and administrators, the final disposition of FAP murals was generally less relevant than providing paychecks to painters; for others, however, the impermanence of the murals and their execution in isolation from the dynamics of site specificity meant that these works were not murals at all but large-scale easel paintings. I will not unravel the semantics of muralism here, but the point should be made that this was hardly a new phenomenon in the history of Western wall painting: a preponderance of murals commissioned in Europe during the nineteenth century were executed in this fashion, and the most iconic of all twentieth-century modernist murals, *Guernica*—which Davis hailed after its unveiling in 1937 as "one of the greatest formal syntheses in the history of art"—was not completed in situ; instead, it was painted in oil on canvas in Pablo Picasso's studio in Paris, which has done little to detract from the power of its public mode of address *as a mural* (though *Guernica* ultimately met the same fate as the modernist murals under consideration here and now hangs on the wall of a museum). Moreover, modernist murals of the 1930s were not *simply* precursors to the large-scale paintings of the New York School. The precise ways in which the murals of the 1930s exceed the circumscribed demands conventionally placed on modernist painting are the subject of what follows.[2]

The Long Shadow of Figuration

American art of the 1930s is customarily and correctly associated with the dominance of figuration. Whether realist or naturalist, radical or reactionary, most Depression-era painting tends toward a focus on readily legible narratives set within a recognizably American context. This may have been the decade when the American Dream was called into question, but it was also when, as cultural historian Warren Susman notes, phrases such as "the American Way of Life" came into common usage.[3] As the "national character" turned inward and aspects of the "usable past" were invoked with increasing frequency, Americans were urged to reimagine their communal values and shared beliefs. The nation was encouraged to steel itself against economic uncertainty and fend off political incursions against democracy. Artists associated with the American Scene and social realism responded by capturing differing aspects of contemporary experience in the world's foremost urban-industrial nation, while regionalists offered paeans to the rural heartland in naturalist idioms that either rejected the lessons of modernism outright or assimilated modernist means to serve more conventional ends. Although figuration was not monolithic or necessarily antimodern, claims for the hegemony of nostalgic agrarian idylls with midwestern motifs effectively served as a foil against which abstract painting developed. In December 1934, a self-portrait of Missouri-born Thomas Hart Benton was featured on the cover of *Time* magazine, which ran a long article on regionalist painters as the new heroes of American art who were "destined to turn the tide of artistic taste in the United States." Modernist rejoinders to popular endorsements of "domestic naturalism"—a phrase Davis used to express his contempt for the art of Benton and his ilk—countered such "chauvinistic ballyhoo" by further refining their aesthetic and theoretical justifications for the turn to advanced modernism.[4]

The Mural, Yes

Despite the widespread miseries endured during the Depression, the New Deal arts projects generated a degree of optimism and excitement within the cultural milieu that was seldom found in other spheres of American life. Leftist artist and critic Charmion von Wiegand suggested that "bread, pigment, walls, and freedom of expression" were all that was required for a cultural revolution.[5] The gravity of the economic crisis had something of an equalizing effect on the nation's labor force, regardless of workers' particular skill sets, and acted as a spur to collective action. The Roosevelt administration was acutely aware that the massive contraction of the economy and the resultant spike in unemployment was accompanied—at least among liberals and leftists—by the expectation of sweeping state intervention. Millions of Americans, artists among them, were jobless and fractious, so the federal government put them to work. The New Deal projects offered an alternative to the elitism of the failing market and the caprices of private patronage, instead enfranchising artists within a broad-based democratization of culture.[6] Like so many New Deal initiatives, the arts projects were an ad hoc attempt to ameliorate the worst effects of the Depression. Nevertheless, the sheer volume and diversity of art produced during the 1930s was a direct result of federal support. The FAP was the most extensive and influential of the visual arts programs. It was under the direction of Holger Cahill, who sought to implement the aesthetic philosophy set out by John Dewey in his *Art as Experience* (1934) and restore to art its continuity with everyday experience. Cahill's commitment to community participation in the arts meant that he championed muralism; as he asserted, "The contemporary emphasis upon human significance in art" found its "strongest expression" in public wall painting.[7] He was also a champion of American modernism. Although the FAP favored conventionally realist images of recognizable subjects, with regional directors tolerating various degrees of experimentation, the project was not inimical to modernist painting, and its output was marked by a stylistic heterogeneity that far outpaced work sponsored by the Section of Painting and Sculpture. Furthermore, during a period when freedom of expression was sharply restricted under totalitarian regimes, the FAP's openness to stylistic pluralism extended the state's ideological reach by demonstrating a democratic inclusivity. Though modernism remained marginal to overarching critical and institutional biases toward figurative styles, *Swing Landscape* stands as a testament to the benefits that accrued to modernist painting through public support for the arts.

The WPA's support for artists was matched by the Roosevelt administration's mandate to cultivate new audiences for art. An aspirational estimation of the American public as a nation of potential cultural consumers brought renewed interest in large-scale painting, an artform that resisted—it was claimed—commodification as a luxury good traded among wealthy collectors. The improvisatory character of New Deal programs meant that the FAP evolved as a series of negotiations between artists and administrators. Ongoing dialogue, and the sense of artistic agency and community it fostered, was an important aspect of the project, as well as a clear marker of what set the public art of the 1930s apart from the contemporary art trade and modernist gallery scene. Davis confirmed that "there was a fair approximation to democratic procedure" on the FAP, "and the artists gained considerable voice in the determination of the Art Project's policies." The public nature of wall painting, and the press attendant on evaluating how taxpayers' money was spent, ensured that the murals connected with a national audience on a level not previously possible—or even conceivable.[8]

From the outset, the Mexican mural renaissance set the benchmark for public muralism in America. Although the Mexican model was compromised by certain discrepancies between rhetoric and actuality—namely, the revolutionary potential of artworks aligned with what many deemed a counterrevolutionary state—it established the mural's credentials as a mode of painting geared toward a popular audience. The most prominent exemplars of the Mexican movement, Diego Rivera, José Clemente Orozco, and David Alfaro Siqueiros, undertook commissions in the United States during the early 1930s, thereby augmenting the prominence and accessibility of wall painting. While in New York in 1934, Siqueiros expressed his belief that murals constituted "the effective daily expression of art for the masses." As the most technically experimental of the Mexican muralists, he also pressed for an approach to wall painting that would "make use of all the *modern tools and materials* which serve the purpose of our art." The establishment of the FAP meant that artists employed on the rolls could follow the lead of their Mexican counterparts. American muralism lacked much of the radical cachet of Mexican murals because the project did not permit work with immediate political content, but artists similarly

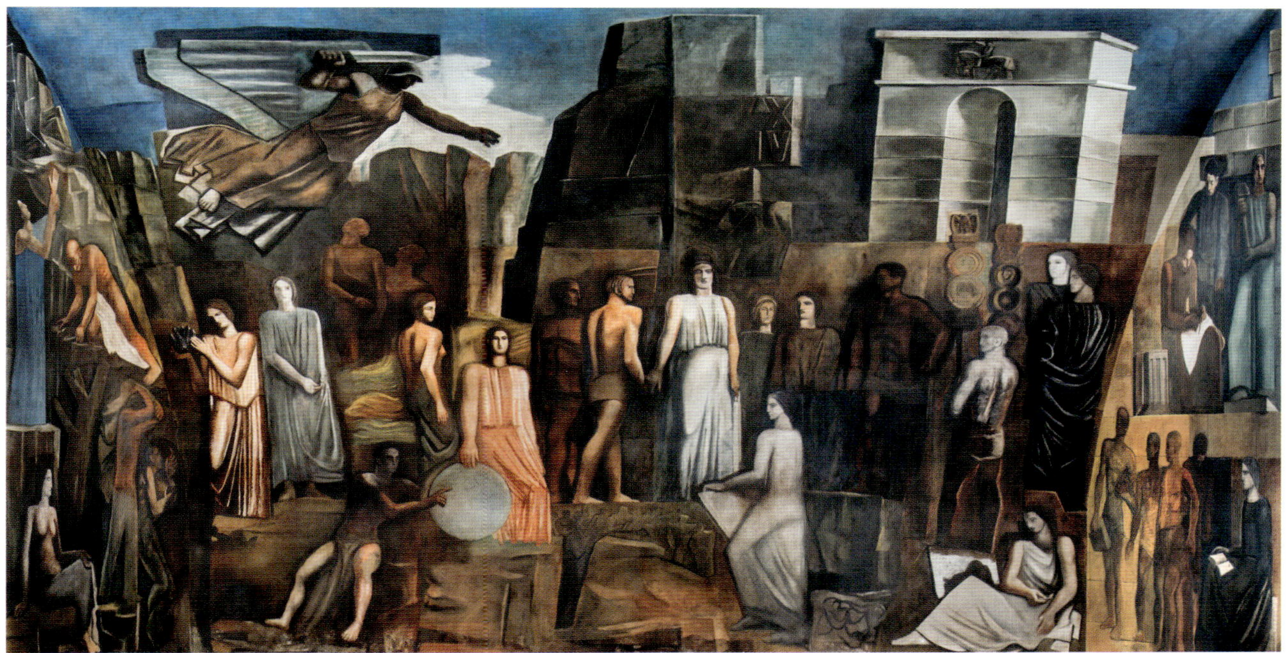

Mario Sironi, *Italy among the Arts and Sciences* (detail), 1950 restoration of the 1935 original
Sapienza University of Rome. © 2019 Artists Rights Society (ARS), New York / SIAE, Rome.

accepted the state's role as patron and administrator in exchange for financial support and an opportunity to paint for a broad audience.[9]

A popular mural program enabled the Roosevelt administration to take advantage of public culture to shore up its legitimacy. Although the FAP was lauded for recognizing artists as workers whose professional skills were valued and deserving of a living wage, critics of public art denounced the projects as strategic measures contrived to divert attention temporarily from the current crisis. Addressing members of the Artists Union in 1936, art historian and independent leftist Meyer Schapiro warned: "Artistic display is a familiar demagogic means; the regime that patronizes art confirms its avowals of peace and unprejudiced concern with the good of the people as a whole." Although I would argue that the instrumentalization of wall painting in the interest of "governmental demagogy" was ancillary to the more expedient objectives of the FAP to provide opportunities for paid work, the New Deal administration was aware of the mural's "power to move and to direct," and it was not alone in doing so. As Romy Golan observes, "Populism and the potential of the mural and photomural to build consensus played straight into the hands of totalitarian regimes." Enthusiasm for wall painting was no less fervent, for example, in Benito Mussolini's Italy, where leading futurist artist Mario Sironi assimilated neoclassical elements into monumental paintings such as *Italy among the Arts and Sciences* (1935). "In the Fascist state art requires a social function," intoned Sironi in his "Manifesto of Mural Painting," published

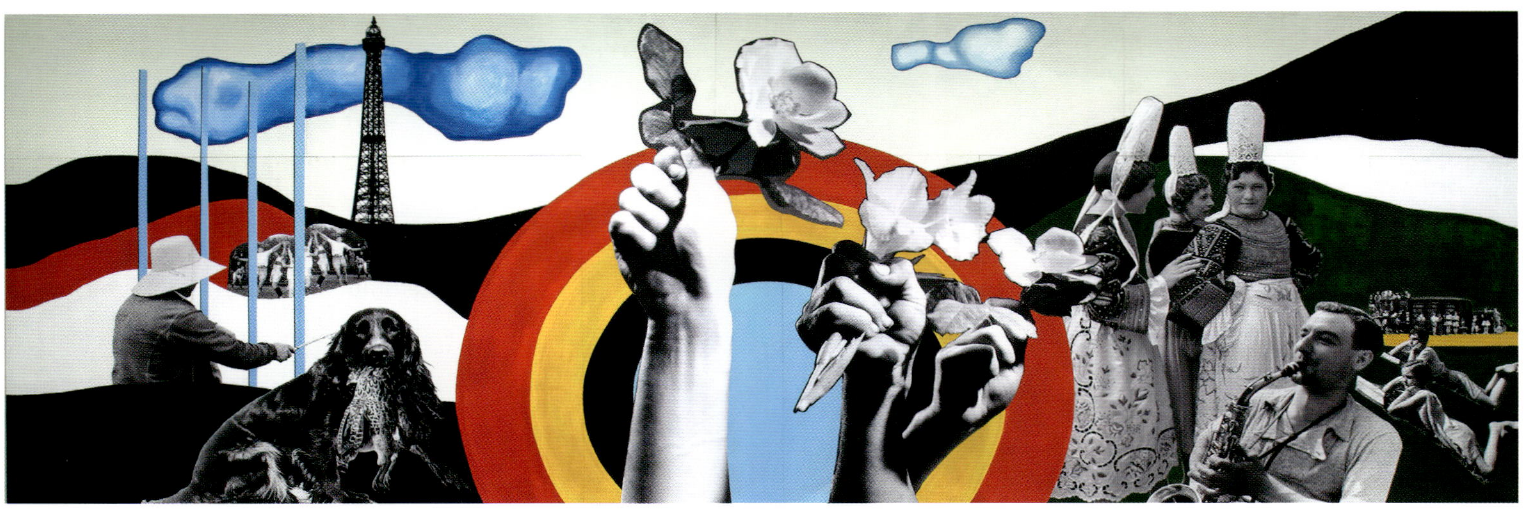

Fernand Léger and Charlotte Perriand, *Essential Happiness, New Pleasures,* Pavilion of Agriculture, International Exposition, Paris, 1937
Museo Nacional Centro de Arte Reina Sofia, Madrid. © 2019 Artists Rights Society (ARS), NY / ADAGP, Paris.

in 1933 as the first of Roosevelt's public art projects got under way. Using rhetoric indistinguishable from that issued by champions of the New Deal projects, Sironi continued: "The individualist conception of 'art for art's sake' is dead . . . mural painting is social painting par excellence." By mid-decade the newly elected Popular Front government in France also embraced muralism, most visibly in 1937 on the occasion of the Paris International Exposition. Artists such as Fernand Léger, who was already well known to American modernists as a vocal proponent of wall painting, were enlisted to create public artworks that pointed the way toward a new and inclusive socialist culture. Among the monumental panels he designed for five of the French pavilions at the exposition, *Essential Happiness, New Pleasures* served as an example of the renewed vibrancy of muralism. Designed in collaboration with Charlotte Perriand, the photomural featured bold primary colors combined with collaged cutouts of workers enjoying their well-deserved leisure. The result, which successfully wed the techniques of montage to a communist political agenda, was an edifying modernist mural that wholly resisted the retardataire forms of socialist realism.[10]

Léger's calls for an international mural revival were accompanied by several trips to New York during the 1930s to secure commissions. Though his French citizenship precluded his participation on the FAP, he was enthusiastic about the project, principally its support for modern artists. Through the lobbying efforts of Burgoyne Diller, head of the New York Mural Division and an abstract painter in his own right, modernists benefitted from federal patronage. Williamsburg muralist Balcomb Greene, who worked in a non-objective idiom, confirmed that despite the prevalence of commissions executed in conventionally realist styles the FAP was "able to place many abstract murals, and without the expected indignation." To those detractors who continued to question the ability of formally sophisticated art to appeal to a popular audience, modernists countered that the public had been coerced into complacency and was, as Davis argued, "preconditioned to look with suspicion on anything beyond the literal, the sentimental, or the academic." Adopting a Deweyan stance, Davis believed that modern art offered an aesthetically significant experience and could contribute to the development of a participatory democracy, provided that such art did not remain sequestered in museums and private collections or confined to the leisure pursuits of a privileged few. "Modern Art will become part of the common art language of the masses," Davis asserted, "as opportunity for participation in authentic art experience is made available to them." Léger agreed with his American counterparts: "If our works have not made their way among the people, the fault . . . is that of the social; it is not due to any lack of human quality on the part of the works in question." Modernism need not be divorced from everyday life, and its techniques were not remote from ordinary human environments, as many champions of an illustrative naturalism alleged. A broad-based mural movement should not be hindered by artistic anachronism but should progress in accordance with the new stylistic possibilities of the contemporary age; moreover, unlike naturalistic depictions of the world, which merely reflected current realities back to the masses in unchanged form, access to the most advanced modernism would rectify the enforced impoverishment of their understanding of art and, perhaps, challenge complacency in attitudes toward the status quo. Davis was optimistic about the future of American modernism, for now, since the establishment of the FAP, "sincere efforts were made to allocate and give it social currency."[11]

Modernism in the Streets

The development of American modernism during the 1930s advanced through artists' involvement in the leading political causes of the decade. Among the stimuli that energized modernist practices were those encountered through the influence of the Communist Party. This was a period when the politics of the left went mainstream and when, by extension, political commitment merged with public culture to foster a sense of social purpose. Artists attracted by the party's revolutionary rhetoric were empowered to pursue their rights collectively alongside fellow workers. They were drawn into the orbit of organizations such as the John Reed clubs, whose activities served as a focus for communist culture, and also the Artists Union, in which Davis assumed a prominent role from 1934 to 1937, serving as an editor of the union's publication *Art Front.* The union looked after the welfare of artists within the New Deal art programs, staging demonstrations, campaigning—not always successfully—for freedom of expression, and lobbying for permanent federal funding for the arts. Union members supported picket lines in New York and other cities and marched in May Day parades for which they provided banners and floats. This new militancy, as Davis observed, meant that "artists at last discovered that, like other workers, they could only protect their basic interests through powerful organizations."[12]

Political commitment did not limit artists to illustrative propaganda or the obsolete naturalism of the social realists, though work in this vein accounts for much of the art on the left during this period. There was an understanding, among modernists at least, that art was distinct from party politics and should operate with relative autonomy. Inscriptions of ideologies into modernist styles, and the tensions such inscriptions generated between the social and the aesthetic, was a central problem. Debate on the matter, within the United States and abroad, focused on the realism of modern form, as was highlighted at the Maison de la Culture in Paris, where communists and fellow travelers engaged in fiery polemics over the political viability and social efficacy of socialist realist, surrealist, and abstract idioms. Davis's paintings of the 1930s are often characterized as abstractions; despite the absence of illusionism in his work, he conceived of his approach to painting as realist. The dialectical interplay of colors and forms abstracted from nature was, in his estimation, more appropriate to representations of the conditions of modernity than straightforward transcription. Davis did not, however, forsake legibility for esoteric technical experimentation, and he distanced himself from non-objectivity. A case in point is the neoplasticism of widely respected international modernist Piet Mondrian, whose influence contributed to a proliferation of varieties of geometric abstraction within the AAA group. Davis rejected Mondrian's "pure plastic art" as idealist for its withdrawal from the world of material reality, instead espousing an abstract art that derived its subject matter from common experience. Davis's compositions consistently include vestigial naturalistic signs that encourage the viewer to identify specific motifs. His intractability on the realism of his formal lexicon was matched by a realist ideology. The modern artist's aesthetic choices–juxtaposition of contrasting elements, fragmentation of pictorial space, distortions of size and scale–demonstrated that superficial appearances are subject to radical transformation. The methods of modernism, according to Davis, suggested that a new synthesis in life, as in art, could be achieved through human perception and intervention. It is impossible to understand the vehemence and persistence of arguments over realism within the cultural crucible of the 1930s if one abides by the conventional formalist wisdom that realism is something from which modernism fully and finally liberated itself. Even Mondrian, with his circumscribed neoplastic vocabulary, alleged that his paintings revealed a "new reality." On the surface such pitched battles may seem a hermetic art world diversion during a period of crisis, but in a decade riven by ideological confusion, the issue of realism was freighted with competing definitions of reality itself.[13]

When it came to vital issues of style and form, modernists on the left enjoyed substantially more freedom in the United States than many of their international counterparts. The Communist Party's tactical move to the Democratic Front at mid-decade not only meant backing Roosevelt and the New Deal (and, by extension, the arts projects) but entailed an increasing openness to modernist culture. Writing for the *Daily Worker,* communist artist and critic Jacob Kainen observed that there was no "official" Marxist position to uphold in aesthetic matters. Although he continued to find abstract art, especially non-objectivity, "barely comprehensible," he maintained, "What plastic approach, what type of content and kindred questions are open to debate at all times."[14] Charmion von Wiegand used her art column in the *New Masses* to impress upon readers that artistic form is "the one and only true problem of Western art." As an abstract artist herself, she welcomed "the presence of so many young, capable, and articulate artists in the abstract field" and argued that "modern art functions efficiently and carries a message more adequately than the old-fashioned type of illustra-

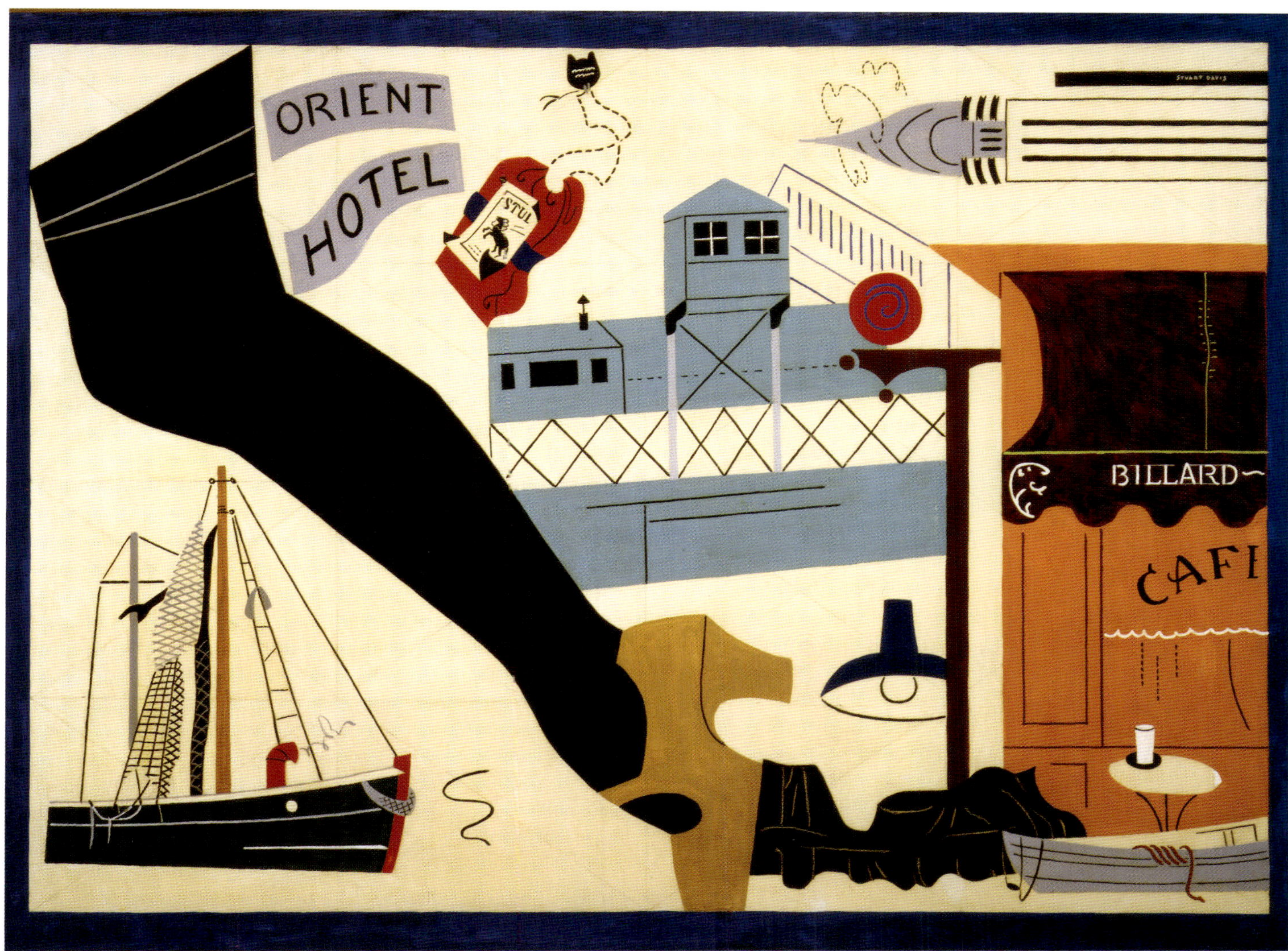

Stuart Davis, *New York–Paris No. 1*, 1931
Oil on canvas, 39 × 51¾ in. (99 × 131.4 cm). University of Iowa, Stanley Museum of Art, University Acquisition, 1955.5. © 2019. Estate of Stuart Davis / Licensed by VAGA at Artists Rights Society (ARS), NY.

tion."[15] The global aspirations of communism also meant that leftist culture remained attuned to transcontinental developments during the 1930s, further distinguishing it from the fully Americanized isolationism underpinning the promotion of regionalism and American Scene painting. Davis drew attention to the impact of French modernism on his practice in a series of three paintings synthesizing memories of his trip to Paris in 1928–29 with impressions of New York. In *New York–Paris No. 1* (1931), whose clean lines and saturated colors recall the look of contemporary advertising, he set the scene by placing a Parisian café next to a New York El station, both of which appear below a stylized rendering of the recently completed Chrysler Building. Davis has rotated the Chrysler Building onto its side so that it doubles as a fountain pen. A Gloucester schooner and pouch of Stud tobacco are separated by a fashionable woman's leg clad in stockings, garter, and heeled shoe. The abstracted leg, which dominates the composition and bisects it diagonally, may have been a nod to the imagery of women's legs that appear in the concluding shots of Léger's *Ballet Mécanique* (1921), an experimental film made in collaboration with American artists Dudley Murphy and Man Ray.

The roots of Davis's modernism lay in the aesthetics of synthetic cubism and collage. Cubism was the cornerstone of Albert E. Gallatin's collection, the Museum of Living Art on Washington Square, which included paintings by Georges Braque, Juan Gris, Léger, and Picasso, alongside those by important European modernists such as Jean Arp, Jean Hélion, Joan Miró, and Mondrian. Unlike the Museum of Modern Art, which showed little interest in American abstraction during the 1930s, Gallatin hung European and American artists together, thereby fostering a transatlantic dialogue on the development of modern art. Among the fourteen works on view by Léger was *The City* (1919), a mural-sized oil on canvas that was particularly influential among New York modernists for its abstract treatment of forms derived from mass industrial culture (see page 23). Davis's *Swing Landscape* owes clear formal debts to Léger's monumental canvas, as does *Aviation: Evolution of Forms under Aerodynamic Limitations* (1936–37), the suite of FAP murals created by Arshile Gorky for the new Administration Building at Newark Airport. Gorky also made claims for the realism of his murals; he, too, transposed recognizable objects into an abstract idiom, arraying them across the two-dimensional surface of the picture plane (see page 32).

Gallatin's promotion of abstract art in the United States was buttressed by support from George L. K. Morris, an artist and critic known as one of the "Park Avenue Cubists." Morris was an avid proselytizer for abstraction and fought against the provincialism of the American regionalists, "art that was stuck fast in the mire of realism to an extent never before anticipated." He used two journals that he published, the *Miscellany* and *Plastique*, as vehicles for the transmission of transatlantic ideas around abstract art, and he served as an editor, art critic, and patron of *Partisan Review* when the journal was relaunched in 1937. Wealthy and well connected, Morris also kept the channels for communication with European artists open through his involvement with Abstraction-Création: Art non-figuratif, an international group of abstract artists founded in 1931 who issued an annual journal until 1936. The upheavals of fascism and forcing of artists into exile meant that the alliance only survived for five years. When Abstraction-Création folded, Morris became a founding member and chief spokesperson of the AAA group. His personal circle of acquaintance brought such European artists as Léger (with whom he studied in Paris), Mondrian, and Hélion into the group's orbit. The AAA's first exhibition in New York in 1937 comprised the works of some forty artists whose aesthetic was marked by hard-edged geometry infused with irregular amorphous forms. The assimilation of free-floating shapes set against the spatial armature of the grid indexes the joint influences of the surrealism of Arp and Miró with the neoplasticism of Mondrian. This hybrid abstract vocabulary also evinces the impact of Hélion, whom Davis counted among the "best artists" working in the United States. Hélion admired the FAP and believed that wall painting offered

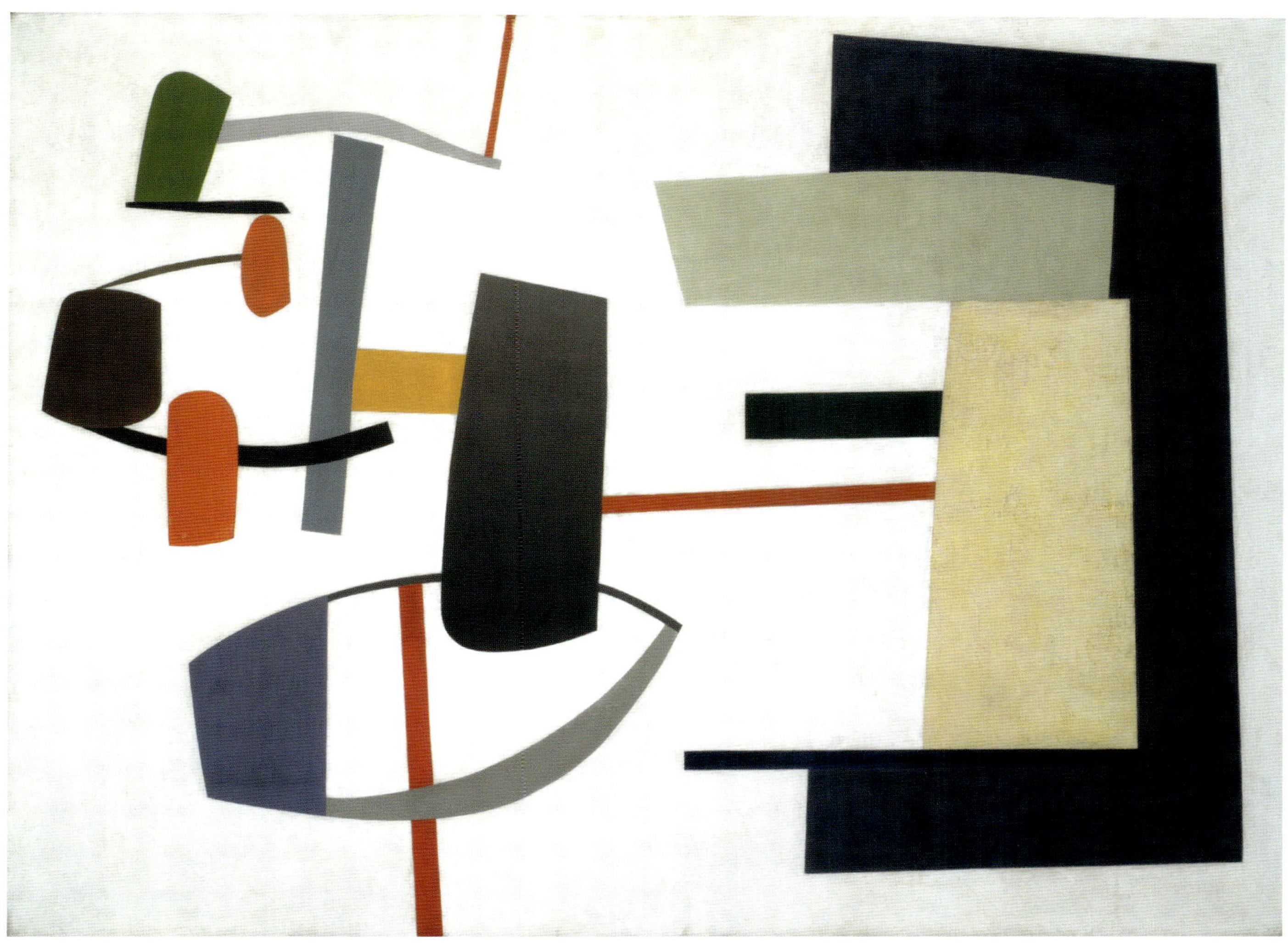

Jean Hélion, *Equilibrium,* 1933–34
Oil on canvas, 38⅜ × 51⅝ in. (97.8 × 130.8 cm). The Solomon R. Guggenheim Foundation, Peggy Guggenheim Collection, Venice 1976, 76.2553 PG44.

"the best chances for popularization of abstract painting." His *Equilibrium* series, many works of which were scaled to mural size, provided an accomplished model of the rapprochement between linear and organic elements that proved so influential within the AAA group. The Williamsburg murals of Ilya Bolotowsky and Albert Swinden are characterized by this stylistic amalgam (see pages 72–73, 122–23), as are several preparatory works for unrealized commissions, including Harry Bowden's *Suggestion for a Mural* (ca. 1936), McNeil's *Study for Williamsburg Mural* (1938), and Lee Krasner's *Untitled Mural Study* (1940). McNeil recalls this as an extraordinary moment in the history of American modernism: "There was a very cohesive group of modern artists in New York centered around the AAA, and also in relation to the Project. . . . And almost all of them were making murals." Even Morris, whose financial independence obviated against involvement with the FAP,

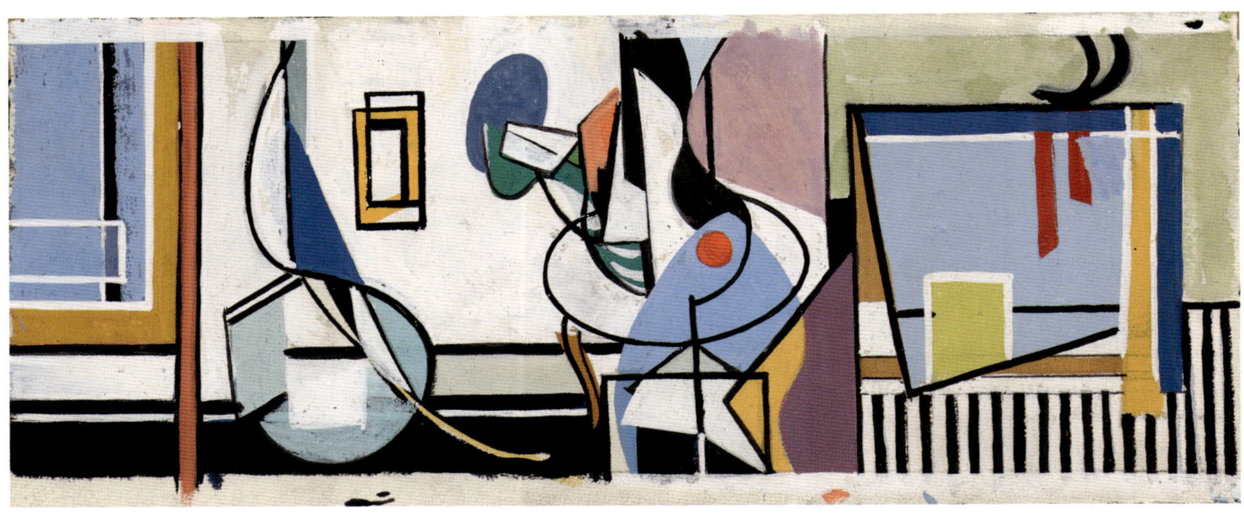

Harry Bowden, *Suggestion for a Mural (possible study for Williamsburg mural),* ca. 1936
Tempera or gouache and graphite on paper, 6½ × 15½ in. (16.5 × 39.4 cm). Harry Bowden Papers, Archives of American Art, Smithsonian Institution, Washington, DC.

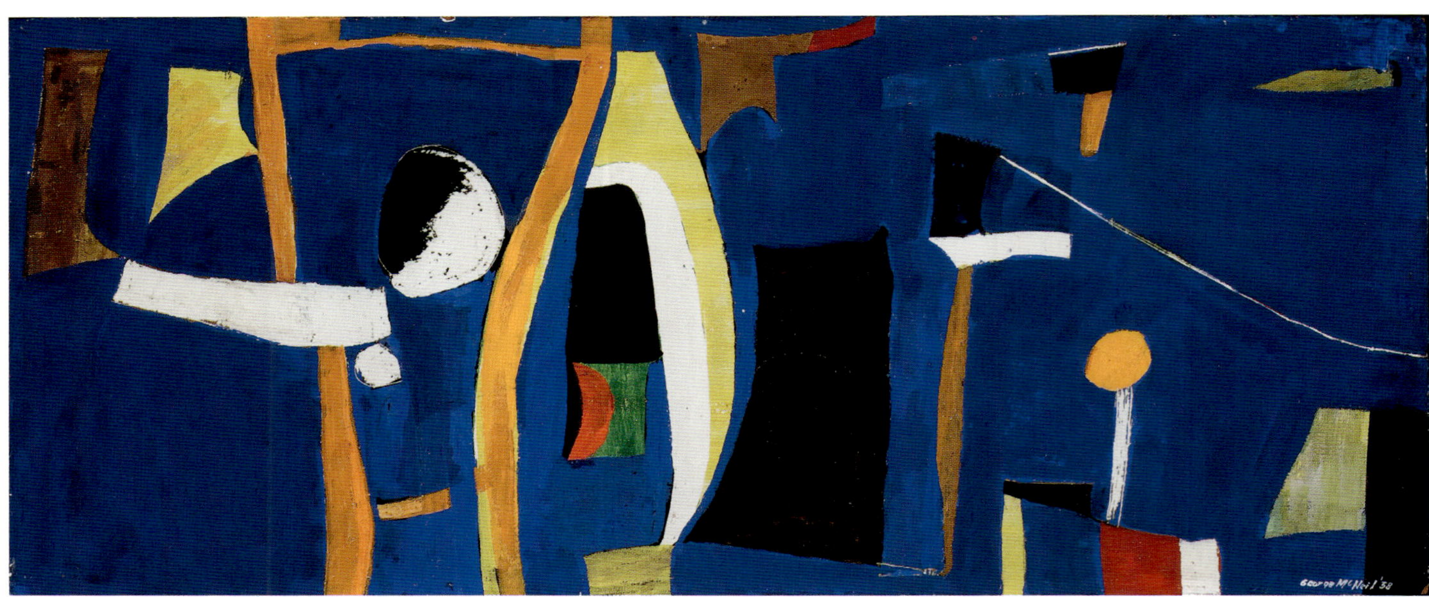

George McNeil, *Study for Williamsburg Mural,* 1938
Oil on board, 13 × 31¼ in. (33 × 79.4 cm). High Museum of Art, Atlanta. Gift of Jennifer and Terry Weiss in honor of Judy and Washington Falk, III, 2006.114.

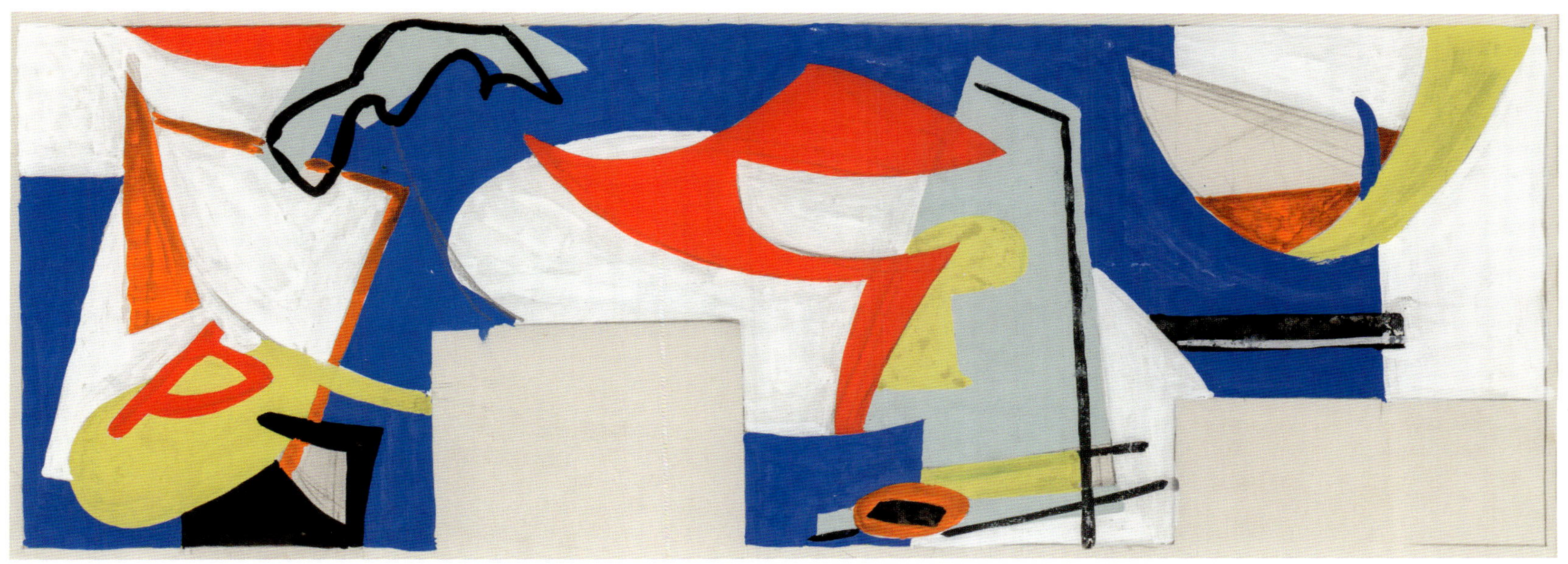

Lee Krasner, *Untitled Mural Study,* 1940
Gouache on paper, 17 × 22 in. (43.2 × 58.4 cm). © 2019 Pollock-Krasner Foundation / Artists Rights Society (ARS), NY.

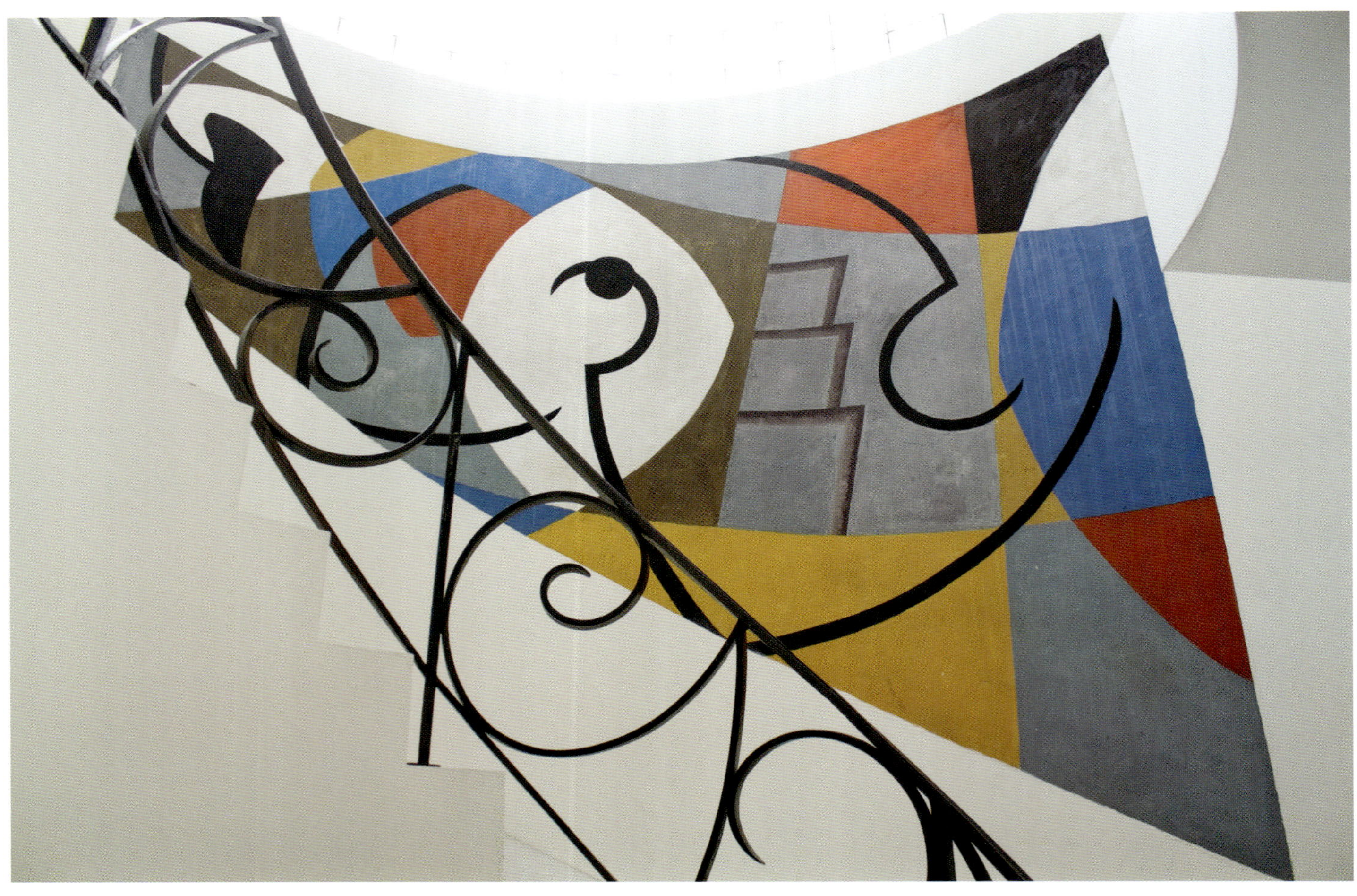

George L. K. Morris, *Mural,* 1940
Fresco, stairwell in foyer, Frelinghuysen Morris House & Studio, Lenox, Massachusetts. © Freylinghuysen Morris Foundation.

was concerned with translating his easel paintings into murals. He experimented with various ideas for wall paintings, eventually studying fresco at the Art Students League and executing murals at his home in Lennox, Massachusetts.[16]

Davis's commitment to the realism of abstraction put him at odds with the AAA's overarching focus on non-objectivity. Balcomb Greene, the first chairman of the group, held particularly strident views on the matter. He sought to expunge any trace of subjective expression or naturalistic description from his finished canvases. The meticulous surface of his Williamsburg mural was achieved by masking individual blocks of color with tape and applying paint with a spray gun. The emphatically flattened rectilinear planes and spare palette were in keeping with the austerity of his compositions of the 1930s, such as *Black Rectangle* (1937). Paul Kelpe, a personal friend of Greene's and founding member of the AAA, also espoused a strict non-objectivity. Kelpe's aesthetic was similarly characterized by disciplined formal clarity, though his palette was considerably brighter and more varied. He arrived in the United States from Germany in 1925 and was by then already fluent in the languages of European abstraction, demonstrating an

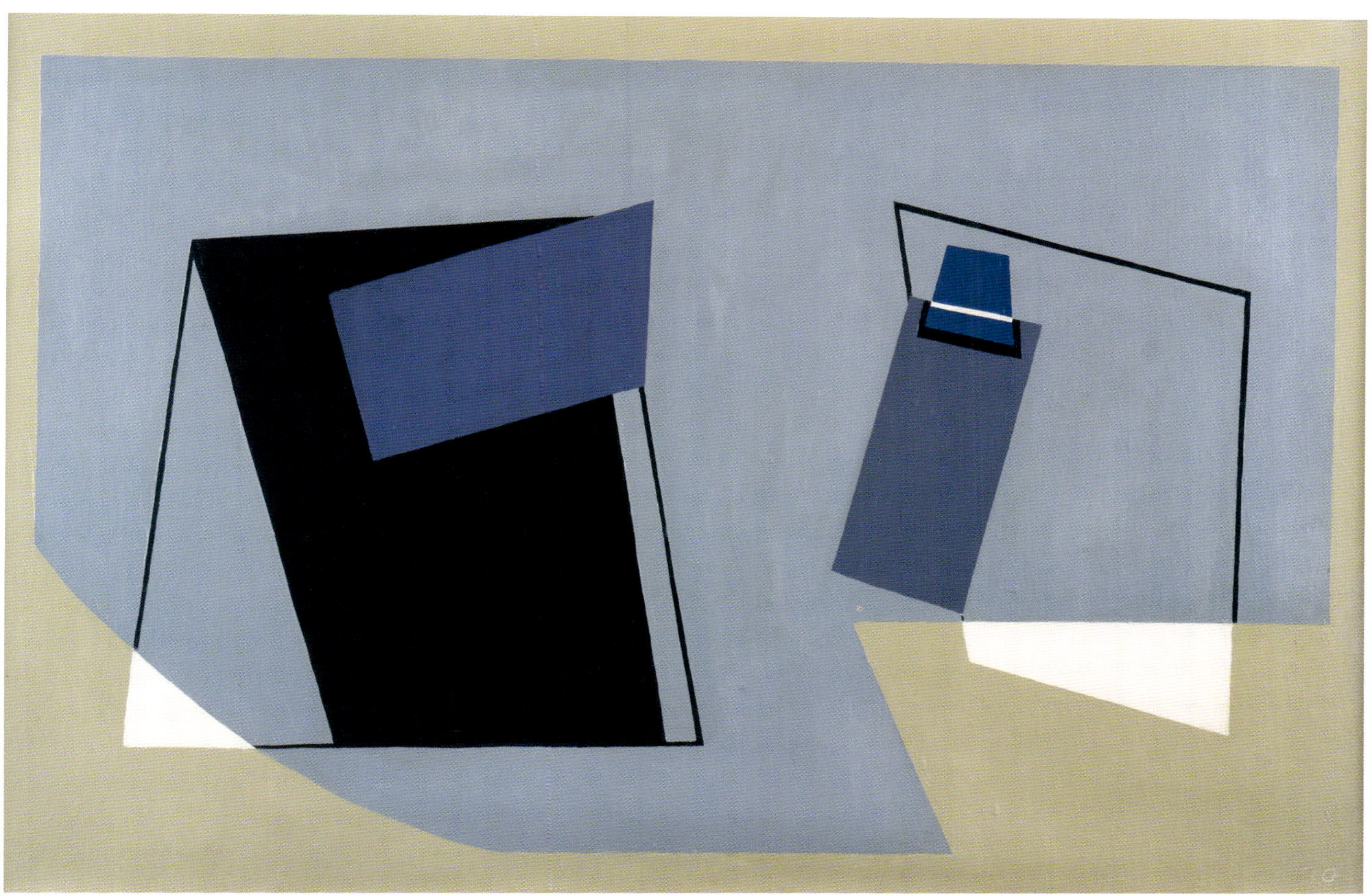

Balcomb Greene, *Black Rectangle,* 1937
Oil on canvas, 24 × 36 in. (61 × 91.4 cm). D. Wigmore Fine Art, New York. © The Estate of Balcomb and Terryn Greene.

affinity for the constructivism of Naum Gabo, László Moholy-Nagy, and Kurt Schwitters. His interest in the German and Russian avant-gardes brought him into the orbit of Katherine Dreier and her Société Anonyme, which she cofounded in 1920 to promote modern art in the United States. Drier purchased Kelpe's work for her collection and showed her own paintings alongside his in a traveling exhibition she organized in 1936. Initially settling in Chicago, Kelpe participated in the federal art initiatives of the 1930s but was frustrated by hostility toward non-objectivity on the part of local project administrators. The Chicago projects afforded him the opportunity to work on mural designs, and he was eager "to work on a larger scale and for a definite purpose." On learning that the New York Mural Division was open to varieties of abstraction, he moved to the city in 1935 and was hired by Diller to execute a commission for the Williamsburg Houses (see page 34). Kelpe's murals, which combine overlapping linear elements with shapes rotated in space, evince an increasing concern with achieving a synthesis between "the planar" and "the plastic," prompting members of the AAA to call for his resignation from the group because they deemed his paintings "three-dimensional realism and not abstract at all." Regardless of suggestions of volumetric space in his compositions, he did not conceive of his work as realist and sought instead for "an organization with an independent meaning of its own." For Kelpe, as for Greene, nature was never a point of departure for his abstractions.[17]

Although Kelpe and Greene attributed a social dimension to abstraction—with Greene participating in leftist initiatives of the period—they were unyielding in their resistance that art could perform a direct political function. As Greene put it, art "cannot sing the tune of home-soil nationalism or of prolitarian [*sic*] discontent." Greene's intractability on the "realism" issue was partly motivated by resentment of widespread demands on the part of both the Communist Party and the New Deal for "an art immediately comprehensible to the masses." In contrast to Davis's staunchly materialist perspective on artistic matters, Greene's aesthetic idealism and his stance on the need to protect art's autonomy brought his position closer to that espoused by Leon Trotsky, who argued that while art is a mode of production within the matrix of social and political relations, "a work of art, should in the first place, be judged by its own laws, that is, by the laws of art." Greene further chastised the hypocrisy of communists and fellow travelers who, with the shift to the Democratic Front, tempered their "attack on abstractionism by commending Hélion and Léger on their balance and their brushwork," or who were now willing to countenance Picasso following his apparent "lapse from individualism" with the painting of *Guernica*. Adopting a position that would subsequently attain cultural dominance—most conspicuously in the criticism of Clement Greenberg—Greene argued that only in pursuing his "remote ideal" could the non-objectivist ensure that art advanced in an inhospitable climate that sought to instrumentalize culture in the name of politics.[18]

As the decade came to close, appeals to restore to art its autonomy resonated more forcefully, but not all modernists heeded the call. "Too many have gained a safe retreat in non-objectivity," asserted Philip Evergood, "because they do not possess the mental equipment to be able to paint objectively in an interesting or profound way. It is easier to flee from life than to face it." Evergood was a figurative painter, but he recognized an affinity between his more expressionist works and Davis's vernacular cubism. Throughout the 1930s Evergood occupied leadership roles in many leftist organizations, and he grew to be "quite a good friend" of Davis when Davis was chairman of the American Artists' Congress against War and Fascism; they also worked together on the editorial board of *Art Front*. "We had many, many arguments," Evergood recalled, "many quite violent arguments about how deeply the artist should be involved in the social statement." But, he continued, "I always felt that my work in its vulgarity of color, we'll say, and its violence of color which I tried to get in many of my earlier paintings, I always felt that I had an affiliation with people like Stuart Davis."[19]

Head of the FAP's Easel Painting Division, Evergood was also a leading proponent of public muralism. Before the establishment of the projects, Evergood observed, painting was primarily a "precious" and "speculative" endeavor catering to a rich and select audience. The FAP brought painting out of the ivory tower—where Greene thought it should remain—and established a framework in which it "belongs to a people's audience." Federal support for muralism, he contended, had achieved more in a few years "for the closer understand-

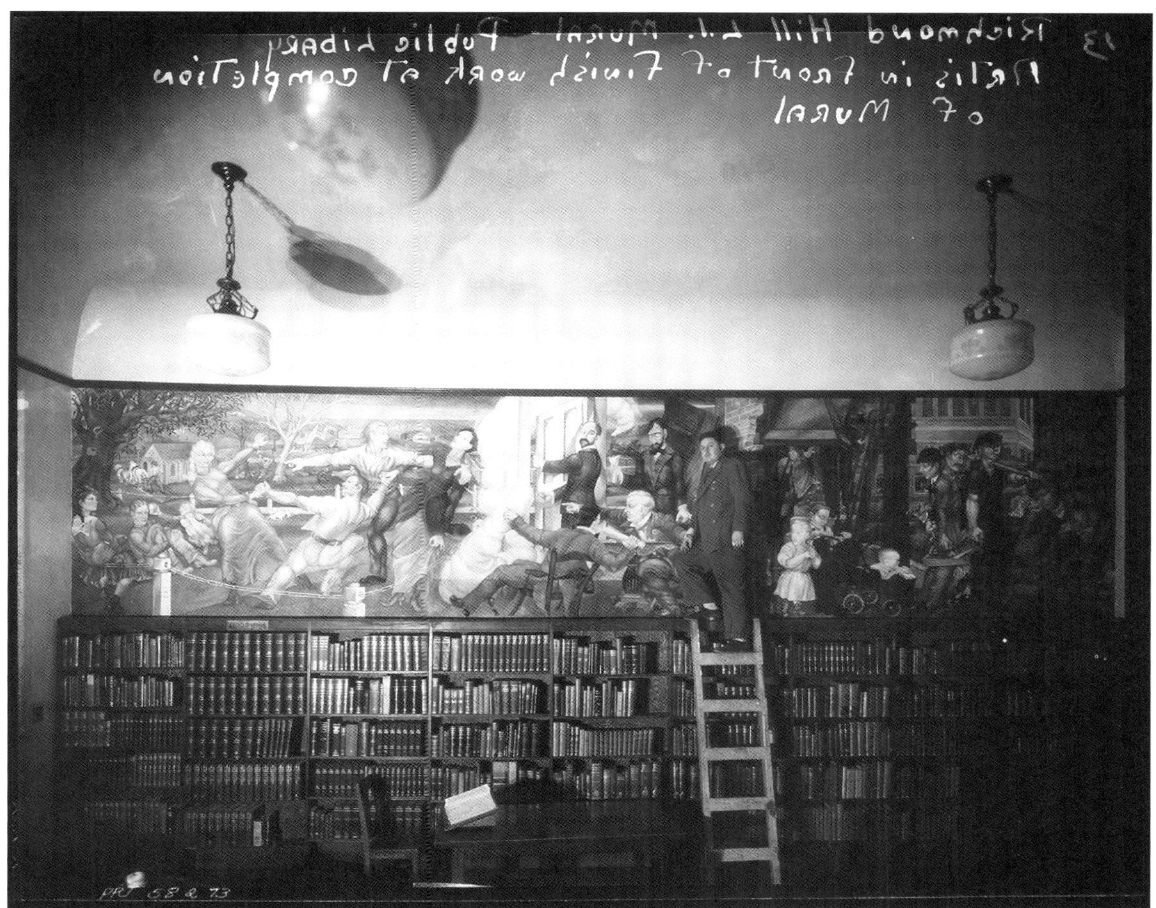

Peter A. Juley & Son, photographic firm, *Philip Evergood Standing in Front of "The Story of Richmond Hill," in the Richmond Hill Public Library, Richmond Hill, New York,* ca. 1938
Mural: oil on canvas, 1936–38, approx. 6 × 27 ft. (182.9 × 823 cm).

ing between the American artist and his public through the medium of the mural than any individual efforts could have achieved during a much longer period."[20] Evergood's mural *The Story of Richmond Hill,* completed in 1938 for the Richmond Hill branch of the Queens Borough Public Library, explores problems associated with contemporary urban life in contrast to the suburban alternative. The horizontal friezelike composition, which is installed above bookcases in one of the library's reading rooms, consists of a tripartite narrative that moves from the dark, dirty, and overcrowded city streets of lower Manhattan, through the enlightened planning of Richmond Hill by its founders, to the green expanses and blue skies afforded by relocation to the suburban oasis.

Garden communities were intended to hold out the utopian promise of better living conditions for all Americans. Evergood's mural, however, is more ambiguous on the subject of who had access to the good life. Reflecting the artist's communist political outlook and his concern for improving the quality of working-class life, the inhabitants of Richmond Hill pictured in his mural are shown with sufficient leisure time to pursue outdoor activities in the fresh air. Although Evergood's politics aligned with those of the social realists, his stylistic leanings did not. His figures, which verge on the grotesque, are hardly "ideal proletarian types," and his aesthetic owes more to the example of German expressionism, which had been widely shown in New York galleries since the mid-1920s. Efforts were made on the part of some artists and critics on the left to articulate a rationale for the use of expressionist devices, but uptake was limited. When Evergood's mural was unveiled, there were immediate calls for its removal. Richmond Hill residents and the library's board of directors were outraged that the artist's invocation of life in their community was neither "artistically [n]or historically correct." Disapproval was also voiced over the "repulsive" caricatures of gamboling human figures, who reminded local viewers of "Russian peasants of the worst sort." When the controversy erupted, Evergood was one of the leading social artists of the day, and infringement on freedom of expression incited a considerable backlash in his defense, with FAP administrators, the Artists Union, and even the more conservative National Society of Mural Painters decrying attempts at censorship within a democracy. The caricatured figures were not intended to insult viewers, Evergood explained; instead, "ugliness" and "deformation" were meant to be indicative of the cruelties and hardships of working-class life. "Our workers are the hope of America," he asserted, "but they bear on their faces and bodies and in their souls, the mark of social distortion to which they have been subjected." The mural remains in situ, and the hostility it elicited corroborates Evergood's claims for the revolutionary potential of expressionist techniques to arouse and disturb. His contorted bodies and lurid color combinations were fused with socially relevant content to heighten viewers' awareness of the degradations of working-class life.[21]

A rapprochement of figuration with modernist techniques also characterized the work of Francis Criss, whose mural for Williamsburg, *Sixth Avenue "L"* (1937–38), exemplifies his reinterpretation of the bold hues and two-dimensional planes of synthetic cubism to depict contemporary urban environments (see page 85). Criss was born in England but grew up in Philadelphia, where he trained at the Pennsylvania Academy and the Barnes Foundation, subsequently working under Jan Matulka at the Art Students League. His pristine articulation of sharply delineated forms, which are devoid of modeling or atmospheric effects, aligns his work with precisionism. At the same time, his mysterious, often unpeopled, cityscapes spark a tension between reality and fantasy that suggests the enigmatic quality of much social surrealism, an American aesthetic developed by modernists on the left who wed the dreamscapes of the European surrealists with social content. During his training under Matulka, Criss continued to cultivate an interest in mural painting that may have developed during his first extended trip to Europe in 1926 and would have been furthered with the increasing profile of Mexican muralism in New York. His early *Mural Study* (ca. 1930) is a New York cityscape featuring a street vendor peddling his wares beside the entrance to a subway station; signs, advertisements, and a barber pole are collaged into the fragmented urban space. In 1934, following a stint on the PWAP, where he undertook preparatory mural designs, Criss was a awarded a Guggenheim Fellowship to study European fresco painting; on his return he intended to apply his research to "a scheme

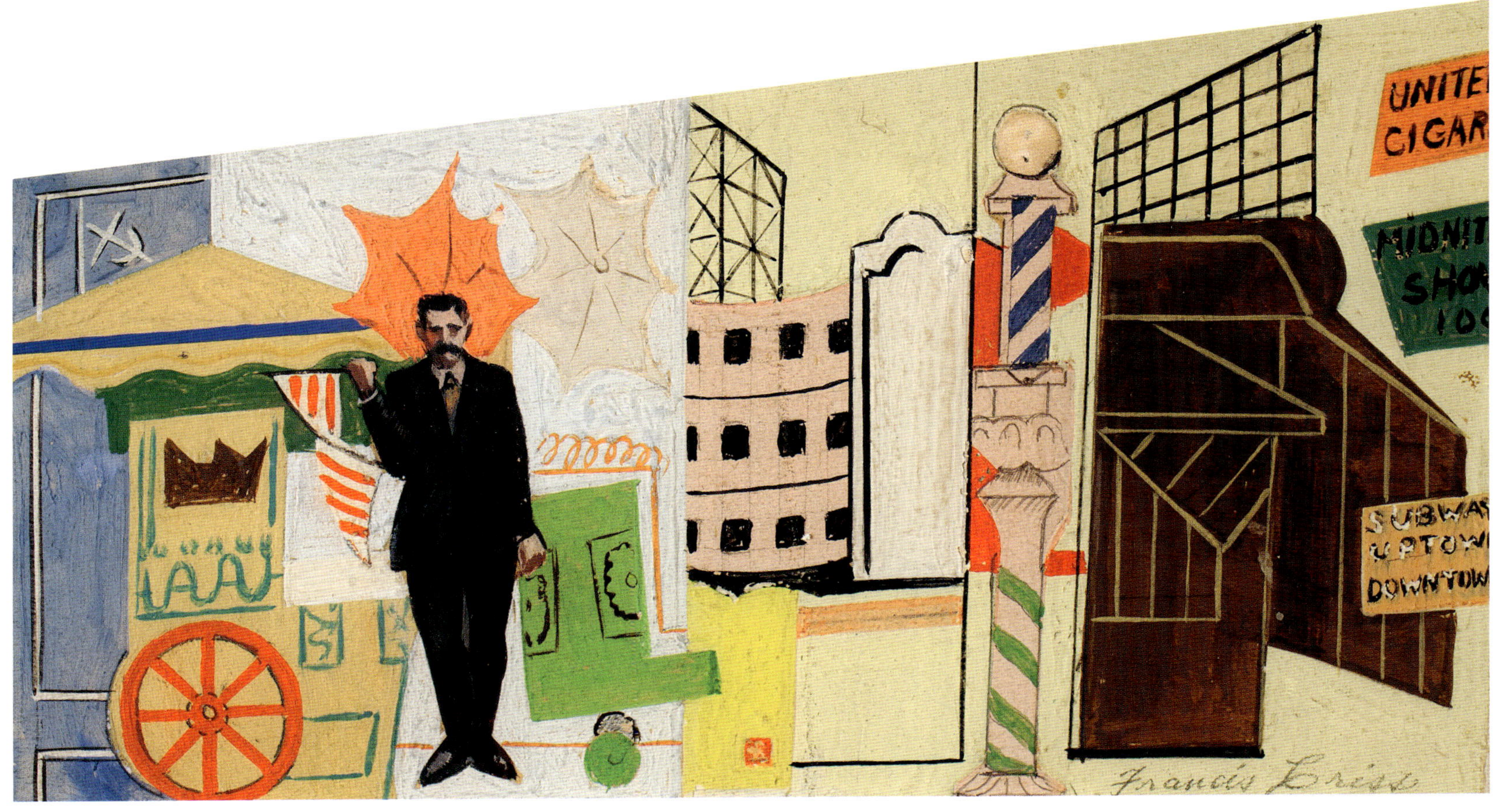

Francis Criss, *Mural Study,* ca. 1930
Oil on artist board, 4 × 7 in. (10.2 × 17.8 cm). Godel & Co., Inc., New York.

of contemporary American fresco." He often recycled his designs (as Davis did), and the unrealized *Mural Study* seems to have been repurposed for the easel painting *Columbus Circle,* completed in 1935. Similarly, his PWAP composition *City Landscape* (1934) was based on an earlier version of the painting entitled *Cityscape* (ca. 1932); the 1934 composition was then included unaltered in his layout as one of the multiple panels he intended to execute for Williamsburg (see pages 80–81).[22]

Criss's engagement with late cubism, fused with careful observation of the real world, brought his "semi-abstractionist" style close to that of Davis. The two artists frequently chose similar subject matter, such as the el station, and they both painted simplified objects stripped of extraneous detail that retained their identity as recognizable motifs, though Davis's work is generally far more abstract. Criss and Davis also found common ground in leftist politics, but whereas Davis avoided overt references in his art practice, Criss's antifascist paintings of the period, such as his well-known *Fascism* (1934), conjure a nightmarish reality; moreover, the symbol appearing in the top left-hand corner of Criss's earlier *Mural Study* bears a not implausible resemblance to a hammer and sickle. During the 1930s, Criss was recognized for deploying modernist techniques to create "powerful social documents," and he eschewed the ivory tower elitism of Greene. As Criss commented, artists "choose to live in the midst of life—not apart from it." Though only one of Criss's panels for Williamsburg was completed and was not installed, Diller praised the artist as "being among the country's leading abstract painters," and critics noted his "beautiful regard for architectural values." Criss's "exquisite development of purely abstract design," which combined elements of figuration and fantasy, recommended itself to the modern mural form.[23]

The Broad and Open Way

During the 1930s public muralism enabled modern artists to exceed the more circumscribed ambitions of the formalist project. Artists such as Davis engaged modernist vocabularies while maintaining a commitment to the human, the material, and the real. Such was the disorienting power of the Depression that it brought together struggling New York artists with government administrators, members of the East Coast elite, and prominent international modernists, many of whom dedicated their energies to making the most advanced modern art accessible to a broad audience. Retrospective assessments of murals such as *Swing Landscape* can, however, still be led astray by lingering ties binding modernism to the general rhetorical temper of formalism. Addressing the need for a more expansive understanding of modernism if we are to come to terms with all of its messy complexity, Marshall Berman observes: "If we think of modernism as a struggle to make ourselves at home in a constantly changing world, we will realize that no mode of modernism can ever be definitive." He proposes a more inclusive approach that insists on the reciprocal interplay of artistic and political priorities as part of the dynamic processes that sustain and create culture. This "broad and open way," as Berman conceives it, would allow for a return to the polyglot modernisms of the Depression era to recuperate the remarkable range of strategies modernists devised to meet the challenges of making an aesthetically sophisticated art that engaged social issues for a popular audience.[24]

1. Watson, "Personal Note," 195; oral history interview with George McNeil, January 9–May 21, 1968, Archives of American Art.

2. July 1937, Stuart Davis Papers, Harvard University; Davis applauds *Guernica* again in his notes in an undated passage from 1939 and later delivered a paper entitled "Guernica–Picasso" for a symposium at the Museum of Modern Art, New York, in November 1947, reprinted in Kelder, *Stuart Davis: Art and Art Theory*, 176–78. On the "moralizing" of easel painting during the 1930s, see Kiesler, "Between Murals without Walls and Walls without Murals," 10–12.

3. Susman, *Culture as History*, 154.

4. For characteristic usage of this phrase, see Stuart Davis, "Abstract Painting Today," in O'Connor, *Art for the Millions*, 127.

5. Von Wiegand, "Mural Painting in America," 793.

6. See Hemingway, "Cultural Democracy by Default"; and de Hart Mathews, "Arts and the People."

7. Cahill and Barr, *Art in America in Modern Times*, 43–44; on Cahill, see Jeffers, "Holger Cahill and American Art."

8. Davis, "What about Modern Art and Democracy?" 22.

9. David Alfaro Siqueiros, "Toward a Transformation of the Plastic Arts," in Anreus, Greeley, and Folgarait, *Mexican Muralism*, 333–34; see also Indych-López, *Muralism without Walls*.

10. "Foreword," *Murals for the Community*, n.p., mimeographed copy of pamphlet for an exhibition at the Federal Art Gallery, New York, May 24 to June 15, 1938, RG 69, National Archive and Records Administration; Golan, *Muralnomad*, 1; Sironi, "Manifesto of Mural Painting," 425.

11. Greene, "American Perspective," 14; Davis, "What about Modern Art and Democracy?" 21–22; Fernand Léger quoted in Fry, *Functions of Painting*, 115; Davis, "What about Modern Art and Democracy?" 17. On muralism in Popular Front France, see Ory, *Belle Illusion;* for Léger and America, see Lanchner, "Fernand Léger: American Connections," in *Fernand Léger*, 15–70; and Simon Willmoth, "Léger and America," in Serota, *Fernand Léger: The Later Years*, 43–54.

12. Davis, "Why an Artists' Congress?" in Baigell and Williams, *Artists against War and Fascism*, 66; see also Monroe, "Artists as Militant Trade Union Workers," 7–10.

13. See Wood, "Realism and Realities," 254–64. For Léger and realism, see Fry, *Functions of Painting*, 109–17. Davis began arguing for the realism of his work as early as 1927; see Davis to Edith Halpert, August 11, 1927, Downtown Gallery Records, Archives of American Art.

14. Kainen, "Abstract Art Exhibit Barely Comprehensible."

15. Von Wiegand, "Fine Arts," *New Masses* 24, no. 3 (July 13, 1937): 28; von Wiegand, "Fine Arts," *New Masses* 23, no. 13 (June 22, 1937): 29.

16. Davis, "What about Modern Art and Democracy?" 18; Jean Hélion quoted in Morris, "Art Chronicle: Interview with Jean Hélion," 36. On Hélion in the United States, see Schipper, *Jean Hélion: The Abstract Years*, esp. 175–239; and Balken, "Jean Hélion's American Connections," 44–50. McNeil oral history interview.

17. Van de Guchte and Manthorne, *Paul Kelpe*, 8, 10, 12.

18. Greene, "American Perspective," 12–14.

19. Evergood, "Sure, I'm a Social Painter," 257; oral history interview with Philip Evergood, December 3, 1968, Archives of American Art.

20. Philip Evergood, "Concerning Mural Painting," in O'Connor, *Art for the Millions*, 49.

21. "In WPA Mural You Can't See Richmond for the Pioneers," *New York World-Telegram*, May 4, 1938; Evergood, "Should Art Prettify Heroes?" On capitalist abuses of the mural, see Alexander, "Mural Painting in America," 28.

22. Stavitsky, *Restructured Reality*, 13.

23. Coates, "Art Galleries"; Boswell, *Modern American Painting*, 62; Stavitsky, *Restructured Reality*, 19; Burgoyne Diller, "Abstract Murals," in O'Connor, *Art for the Millions*, 69; Genauer, "Younger Painters in the East."

24. Berman, *All That's Solid Melts into Air*, 5–6, 14.

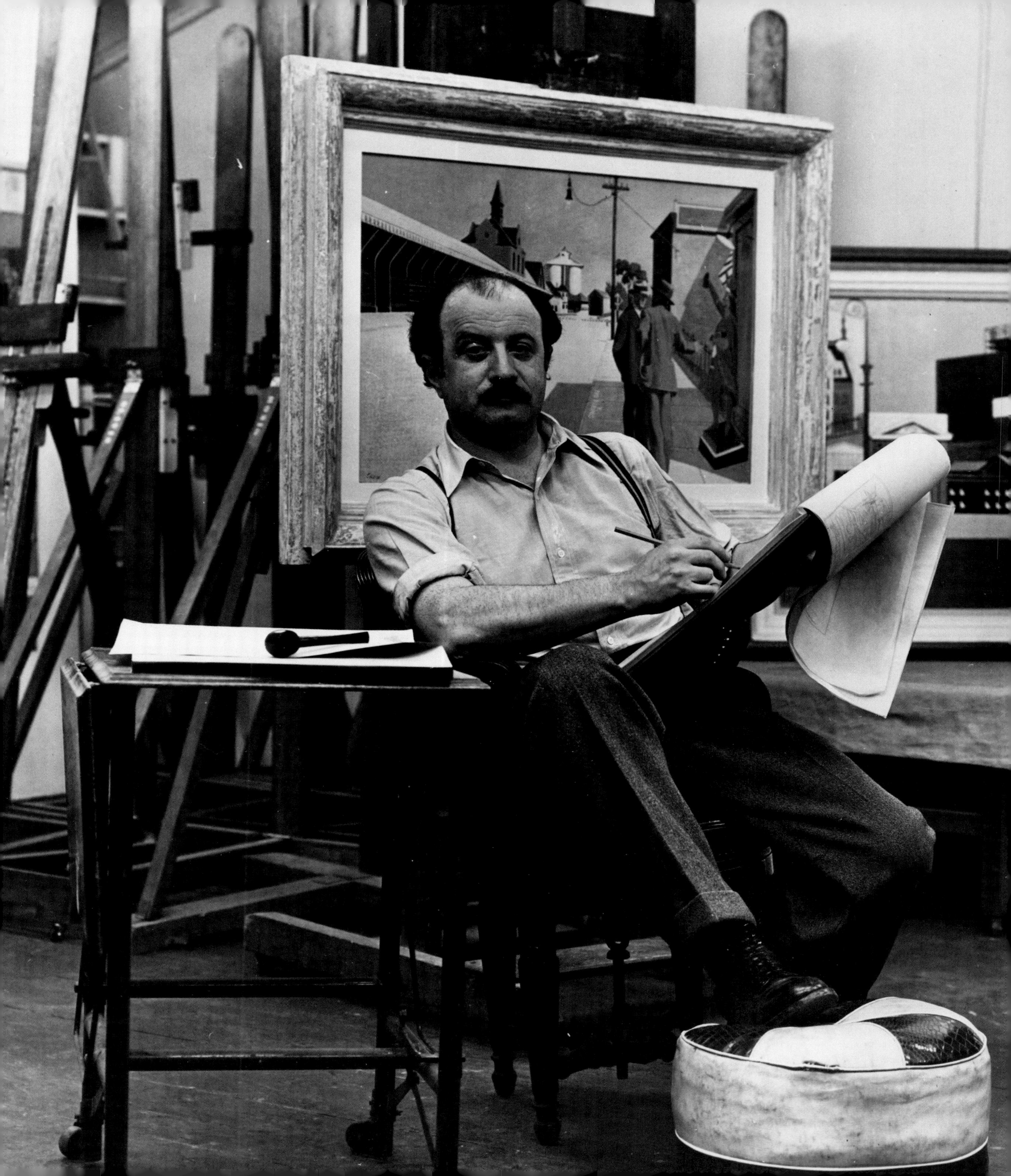

The Williamsburg Public Art Project

A Visual Compendium

Jennifer McComas

Swing Landscape evolved within the highly ambitious artistic program envisioned for the Williamsburg Housing Project. Burgoyne Diller, head of the Federal Art Project's Mural Division, and chief architect William Lescaze conceived of seventeen murals (designed by twelve painters) for the housing project's communal social rooms. They also planned for a program of relief sculptures to enhance the site. Intended to complement Lescaze's modernist architectural design, the program had a decidedly modernist—and primarily abstract—aesthetic orientation. As originally envisioned, the Williamsburg artistic program would have endowed the Brooklyn housing project with the largest collection of abstract public art in the United States—perhaps in the world. Unfortunately, for financial, political, and ideological reasons, the project was never fully realized. Ultimately, eight murals were painted, but only five (one each by Ilya Bolotowsky, Albert Swinden, Balcomb Greene, and a pair by Paul Kelpe) were installed. Of the other completed murals, those by Davis and Francis Criss entered museum collections (the Eskenazi Museum of Art and the Smithsonian American Art Museum, respectively). George McNeil's mural, known only from a documentary photograph, was lost. Because of the truncated nature of the project—and perhaps also owing to the marginal status of public housing in the United States—the Williamsburg murals have not received the attention they deserve. Indeed, the five murals installed in the housing project suffered vandalism and neglect and were eventually painted over before being rediscovered in the 1970s. Following extensive conservation treatment in the early 1990s, they were installed in the Brooklyn Museum, where they remain on long-term loan from the New York City Housing Authority.[1]

The artists whom Diller selected for the Williamsburg project were not a random assortment of modernists but rather a group that shared many common interests and experiences and participated in the same organizations and networks. Many of the Williamsburg artists received their artistic instruction at the Art Students League (where one of them, Jan Matulka, was a popular instructor) or with German émigré painter Hans Hofmann, who opened a school in New York in 1933. Five of them (Harry Bowden, Byron Browne, Willem de Kooning, Balcomb Greene, and George McNeil) had the opportunity to work directly with renowned French painter Fernand Léger on mural designs for the New York terminal of the French Line Shipping Company, a commission secured through the efforts of both Diller and Stuart Davis (but, unfortunately, never completed). And along with Burgoyne Diller, more than half of them were active as founding members of the American Abstract Artists, a group established in 1936. Diller turned to some of these artists (such as Bolotowsky, Davis, and Greene) repeatedly to design FAP murals. Leftist politics also commanded the attention of most, if not all, of the Williamsburg artists, who were involved in the antifascist and social justice activities of the Artists Union, the American Artists' Congress, and An American Group, among others. Finally, half of the Williamsburg artists shared the experience of immigration. Most of the others had traveled abroad to gain firsthand experience of European modernism. In an era when American culture is often perceived as inward facing and isolationist, the Williamsburg artists' international experiences shaped their identities not only as Americans but as citizens of the world and informed their approach to art-making.

The Williamsburg artists created numerous—perhaps hundreds of—sketches and studies during their work on the project. In the eighty years following the completion of the project, many of these studies have been lost or misidentified, and many are known only from photographs. This compendium draws on previous scholarship (especially the work of Nancy Troy, Greta Berman, and Jody Patterson), extensive archival research, and correspondence with several artists' estates or commercial representatives to provide the most complete visual documentation of the Williamsburg public art project to date.[2] The images illustrated here range from early conceptual sketches to completed murals. They are presented in chronological order, so that the evolution of each artist's mural (or sculpture) may be seen and insight may be gained into the process of creating a work of public art under the auspices of the Federal Art Project. It is my hope that this visual compendium will provide the impetus for further research into the Williamsburg project and additional identification of works associated with it.

Most of the black-and-white images in the compendium are photographs housed at the Archives of American Art, in the William Lescaze Papers at Syracuse University, or with the George McNeil Charitable Trust. With a few exceptions, the original sketches and studies they document are presumed to be no longer extant.

1. See London, *Legacy Regained*, 3; and Gallati, *Williamsburg Murals*.

2. Troy, *Williamsburg Housing Project*, 86–109; Berman, *Lost Years;* and Patterson, "Modernism for the Masses." Many Williamsburg mural studies are documented in FAP photographs, which can be accessed at the Archives of American Art. Several others were found in the papers of architect William Lescaze at the Syracuse University archives. Others are held by artists' estates, most notably in the case of George McNeil.

Ilya Bolotowsky

(born St. Petersburg, Russia, 1907; died New York, NY, 1981)

Bolotowsky was born to a prosperous Jewish family in Russia. Following the Russian Revolution, the family relocated to Istanbul before settling in New York in 1923. Bolotowsky spent the next six years studying at the National Academy of Design in New York and in 1932 returned to Europe for ten months to better acquaint himself with the latest trends in European modernist art. He was particularly influenced by cubism's flattening of space, but his works of the 1930s also reveal his interest in the biomorphic aesthetic of surrealism. Bolotowsky joined the Public Works of Art Program (PWAP) in 1934, painting works that conformed to the government's preference for "American Scene" subjects. But Bolotowsky is best known as an abstract painter. He was a founding member of the American Abstract Artists in 1937 and was one of the most prolific abstract muralists for the FAP. In addition to his mural for the Williamsburg Houses, Bolotowsky painted murals for New York's Hospital for Chronic Disease on Roosevelt Island (1937) and for the Hall of Medicine at the 1939–40 New York World's Fair. Bolotowsky's later work was heavily influenced by Piet Mondrian's neoplastic ideas and is characterized by geometric abstraction.

Bolotowsky produced many studies for his Williamsburg mural before arriving at the final design, which blends aspects of geometric and biomorphic abstraction. His completed mural was installed in 1938. It is now on view at the Brooklyn Museum.

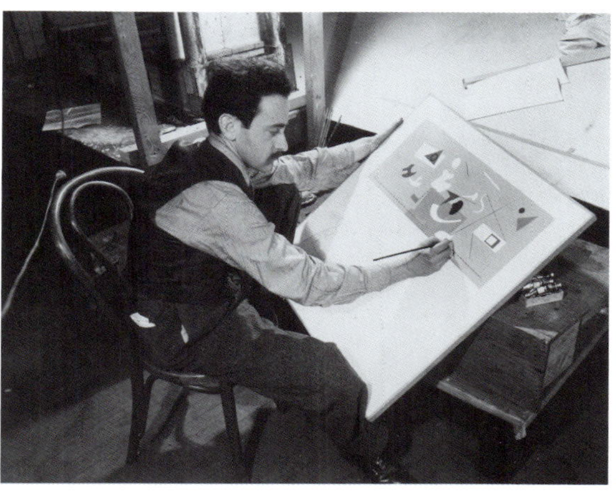

Ilya Bolotowsky, ca. 1939.

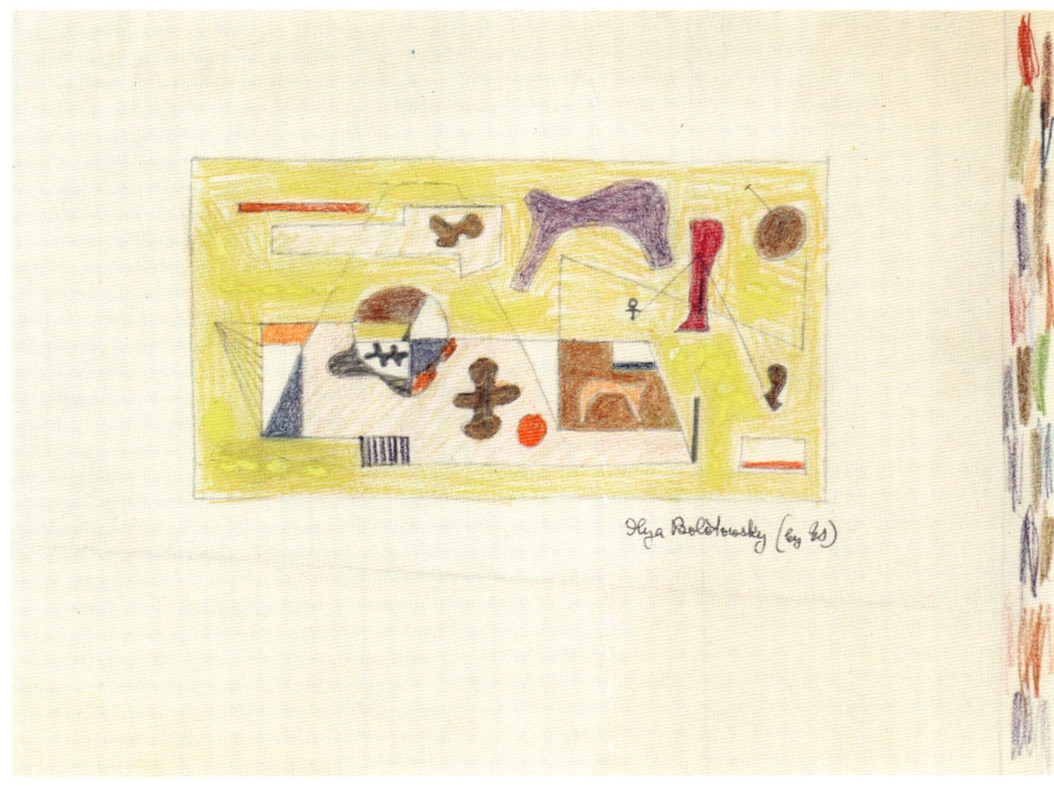

Ilya Bolotowsky, *Study for Williamsburg Housing Project Mural,* ca. 1936
Graphite, crayon, and gouache on paper, 8⅜ × 10⅞ in. (21.3 × 27.6 cm) (sheet).

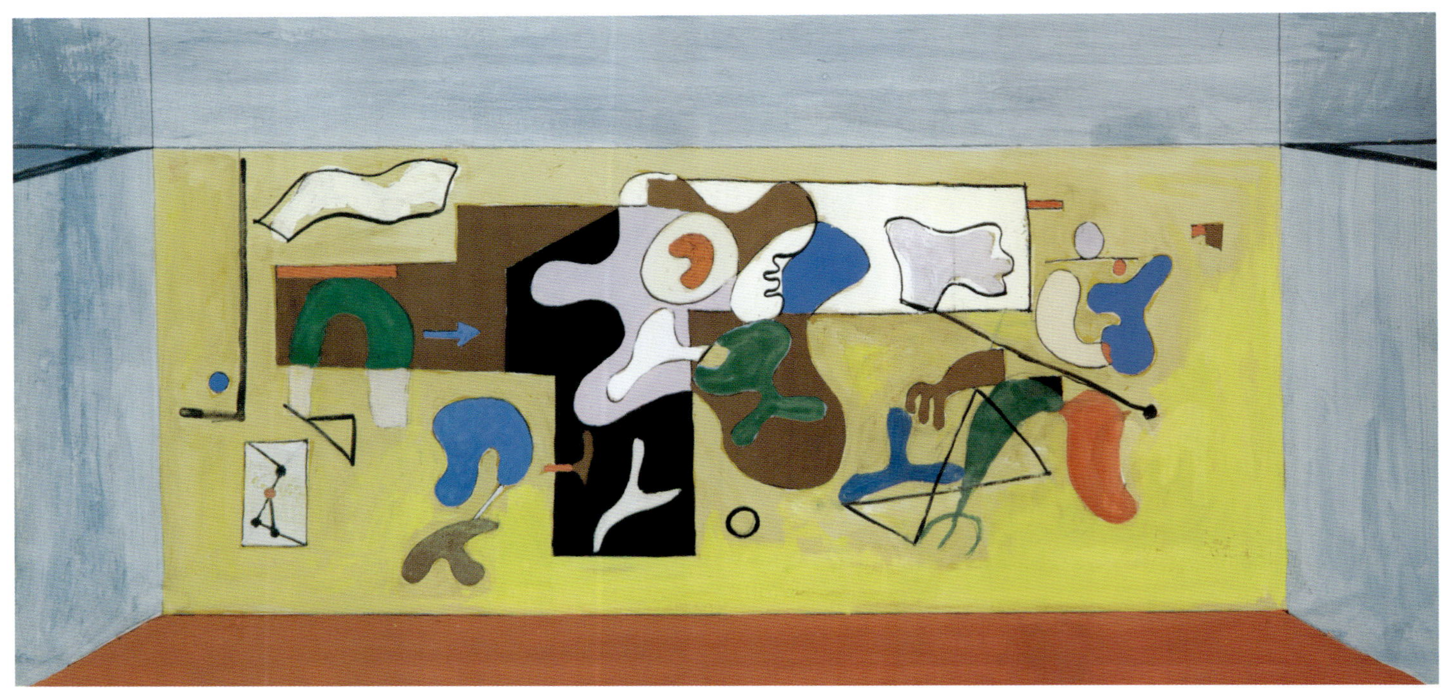

Ilya Bolotowsky, *Study for Williamsburg Housing Project Mural,* ca. 1936
Gouache on board, 6½ × 13¼ in. (16.5 × 33.7 cm). Current location unknown. The study was identified as a Williamsburg mural study by Doyle New York, which auctioned it on May 9, 2012.

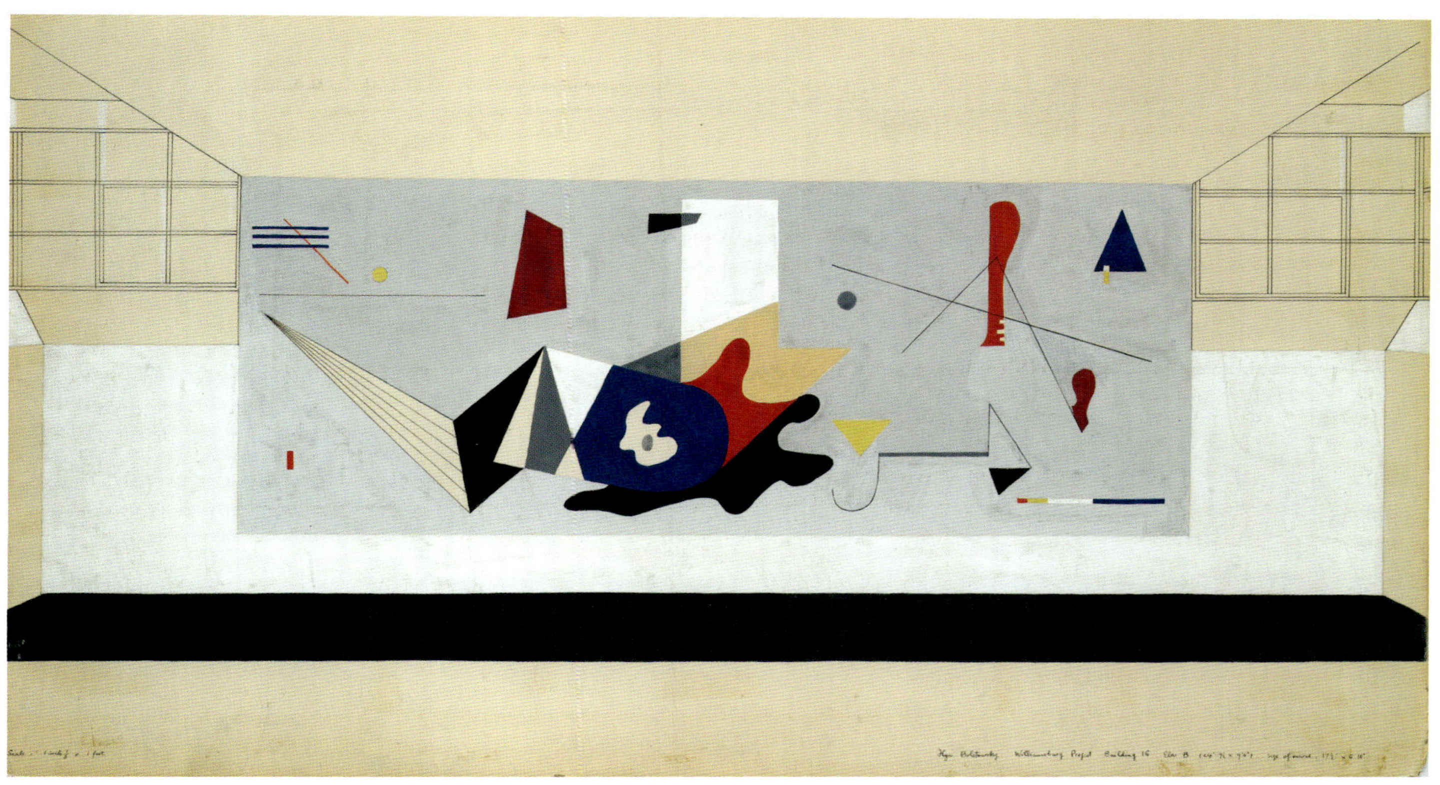

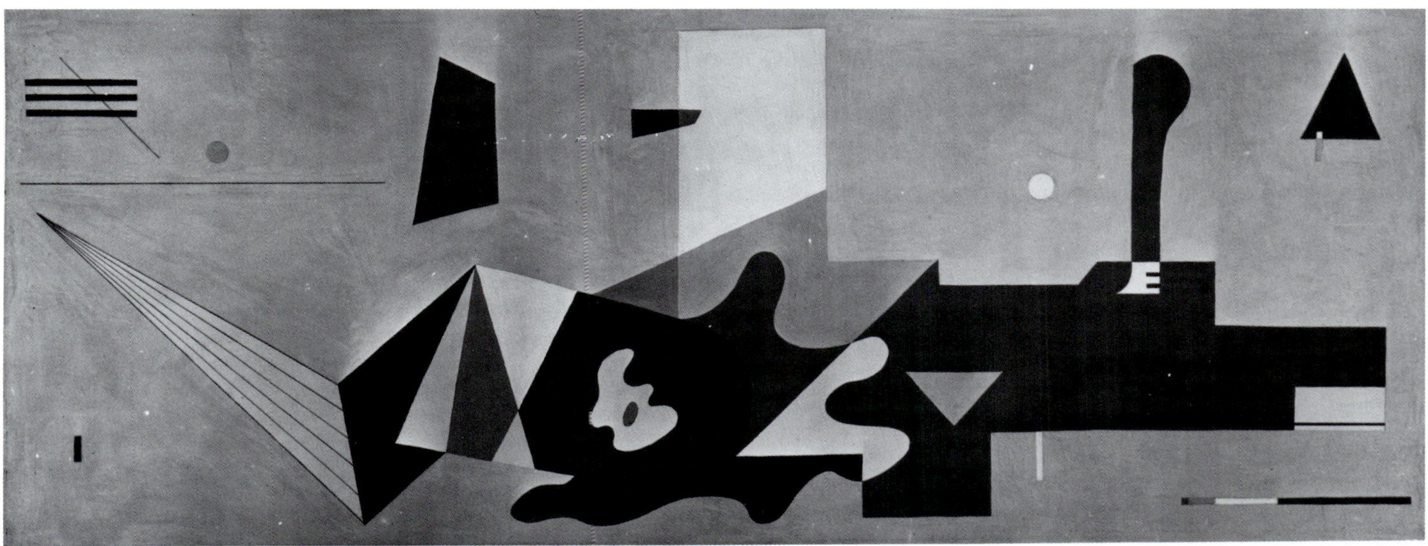

Ilya Bolotowsky, *Study for Mural for Williamsburg Housing Project, New York,* ca. 1936
Opaque watercolor and pen and ink on board, 16 × 30 in. (40.7 × 76.2 cm). Whitney Museum of American Art, 50th Anniversary Gift of the Edward R. Downe, Jr., Purchase Fund, Mr. and Mrs. William A. Marsteller and the National Endowment for the Arts, 80.4.

Ilya Bolotowsky, *Abstraction (Study for Williamsburg Housing Project Mural),* 1937
Oil on canvas, dimensions unknown. Current location unknown. This image may depict the finished mural now housed at the Brooklyn Museum.

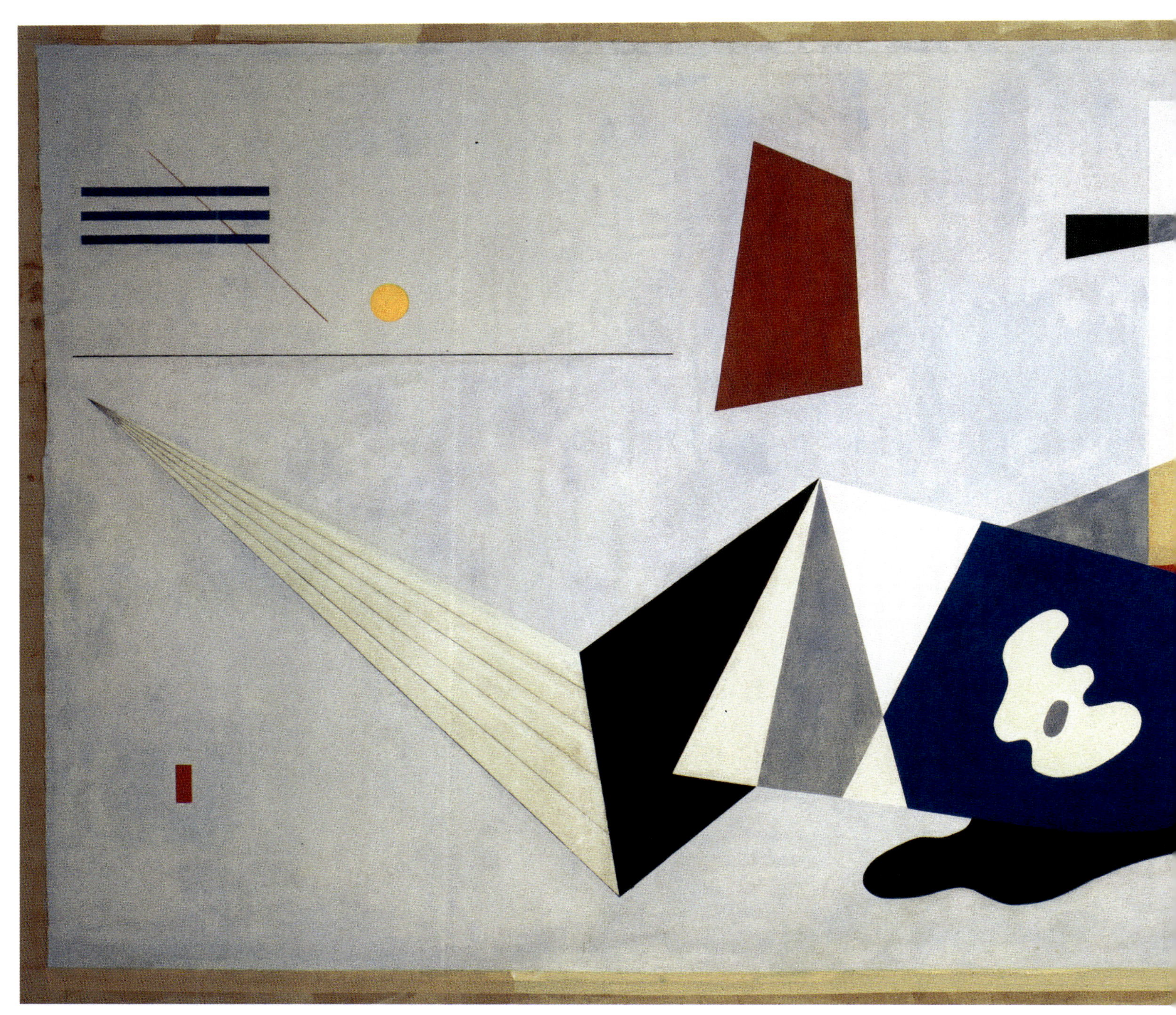

Ilya Bolotowsky, *Untitled, From the Williamsburg Housing Project Murals,* ca. 1938
Oil on canvas, 85 × 211 in. (215.9 × 535.9 cm). The Brooklyn Museum. On loan from the New York City Housing Authority, L1990.1.1.

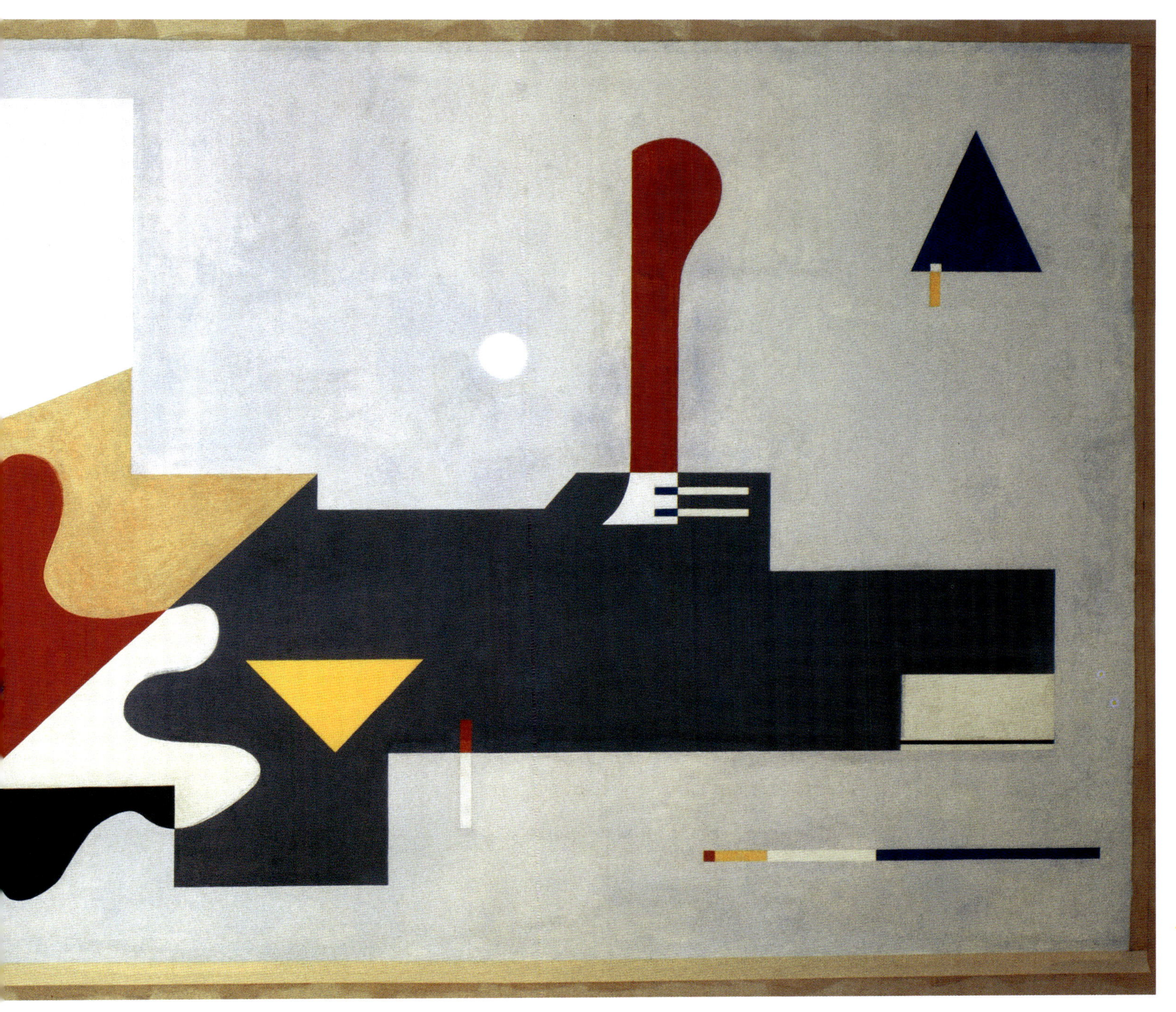

Harry Bowden

(born Los Angeles, CA, 1907; died Sausalito, CA, 1965)

In 1931, a summer class with renowned German émigré painter Hans Hofmann at the University of California, Berkeley, inspired Bowden to pursue an artistic career. In 1935, following his move to New York, he became one of Hofmann's assistants. He also worked with Fernand Léger on the French Line mural project. According to the catalogue for his memorial exhibition, Bowden painted "two large murals" for the Williamsburg Housing Project. If these murals were completed, they have since been lost, and no photographic evidence of their existence has come to light.[1] Bowden's studies for the Williamsburg mural project feature a biomorphic style.

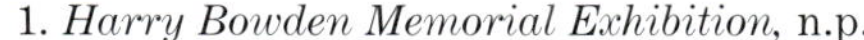

1. *Harry Bowden Memorial Exhibition*, n.p.

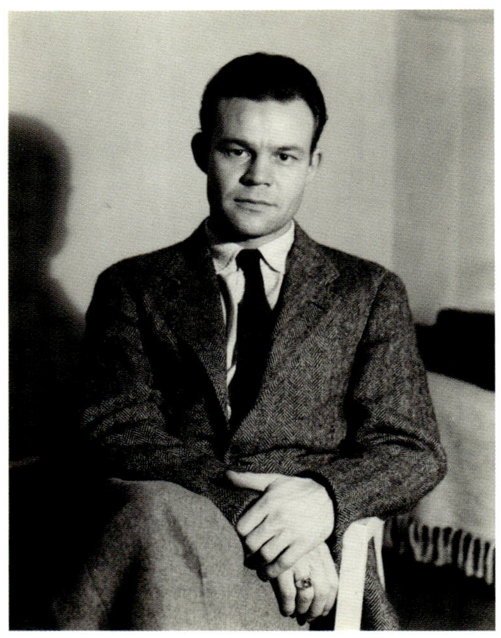

Harry Bowden, ca. 1930.

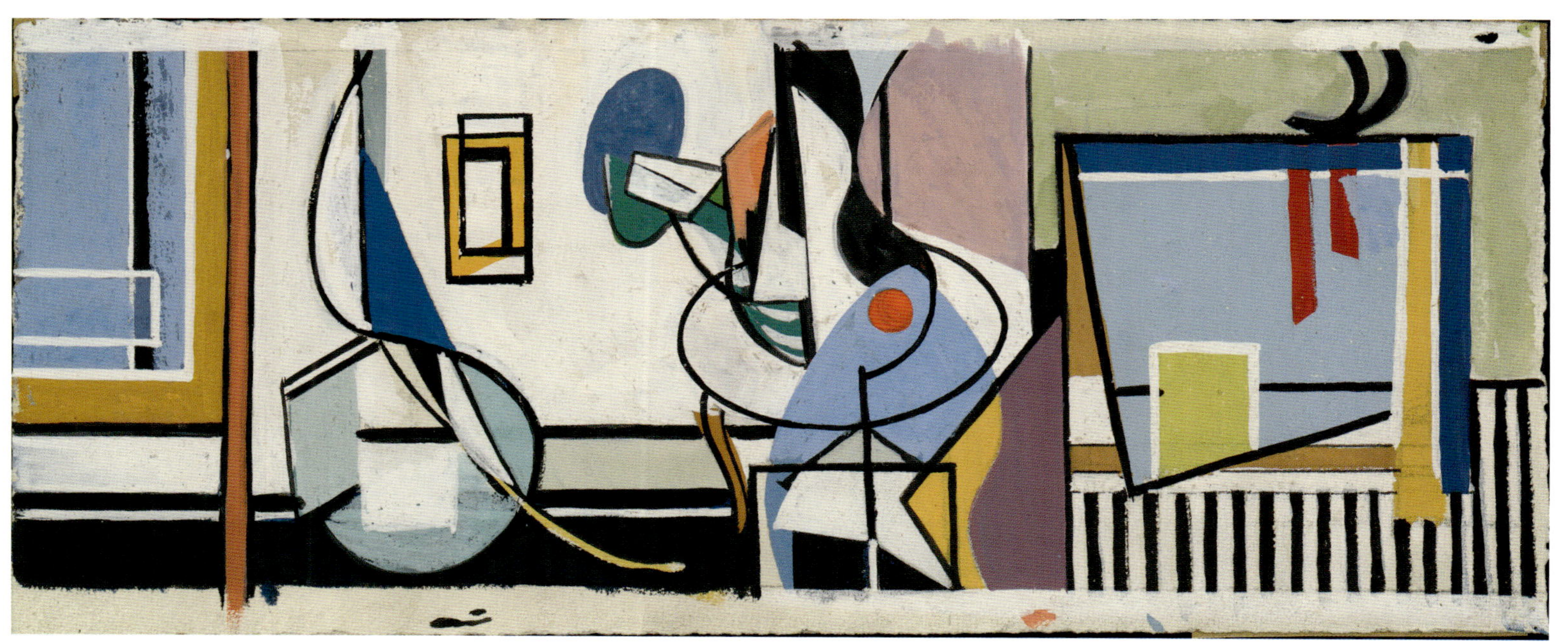

Harry Bowden, *Suggestion for a Mural (possible study for Williamsburg mural)*, ca. 1936
Tempera or gouache and graphite on paper, 6½ × 15½ in. (16.5 × 39.4 cm). Harry Bowden Papers, Archives of American Art, Smithsonian Institution, Washington, DC.

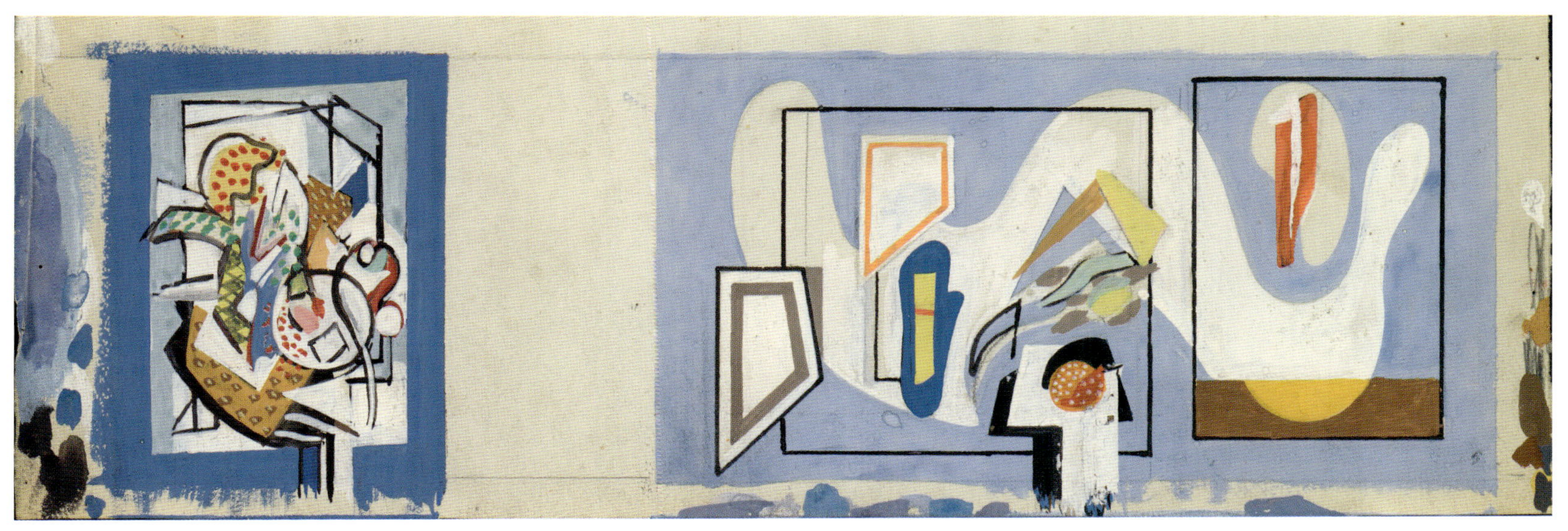

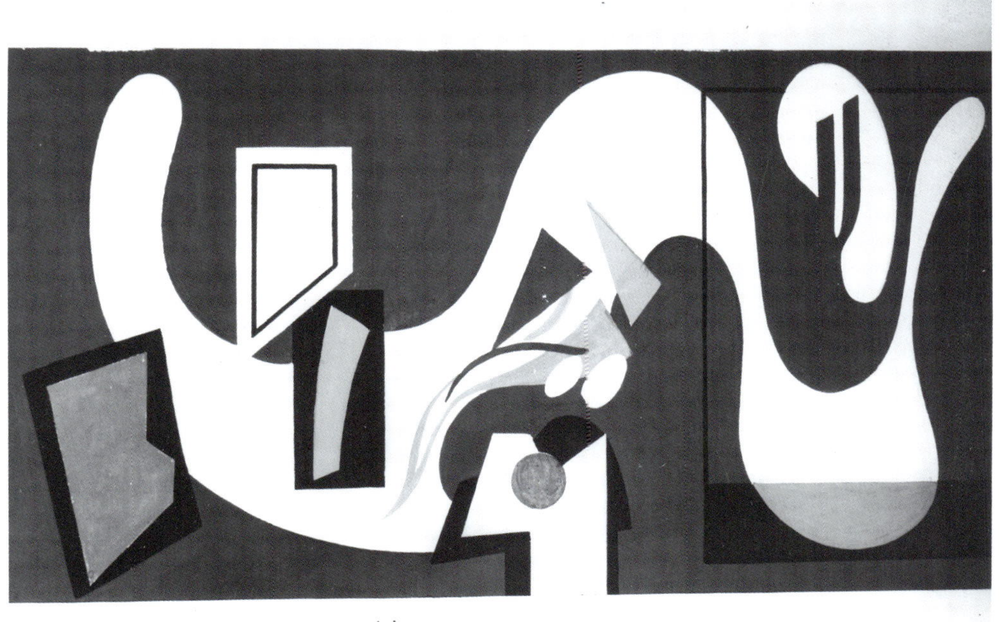

Harry Bowden, *Study for Williamsburg Mural,* ca. 1936
Tempera or gouache on paper, 4¾ × 14¾ in. (12.1 × 37.5 cm). Harry Bowden Papers, Archives of American Art, Smithsonian Institution, Washington, DC.

Harry Bowden, *Study for Williamsburg Mural,* 1936
Medium and dimensions unknown. Current location unknown (presumed lost).

Byron Browne

(born Yonkers, NY, 1907; died New York, NY, 1961)

Byron Browne was introduced to cubism and other modes of European modernism at Albert E. Gallatin's Gallery of Living Art at New York University in the late 1920s. He was active as an abstract muralist during the 1930s, painting murals for the United States Passport Office in Rockefeller Center, for the 1939 New York World's Fair, and for Studio D at Radio Station WNYC (1939). He also worked on a number of unrealized murals, including for the Williamsburg Houses, the Hospital for Chronic Disease, and the French Line terminal building. Browne was a vocal proponent of abstraction and was a founding member of the American Abstract Artists. An activist for artists' rights during the New Deal era, Browne joined the Artists Union in 1935 and participated in the American Artists' Congress.

Browne's studies for the Williamsburg project are known only through photographic documentation. Although his designs align with Burgoyne Diller's preference for geometric abstraction, Browne's work later became more gestural, and he worked alongside the abstract expressionists after World War II.[1]

1. Levin, "Byron Browne in the Context of Abstract Expressionism," 129.

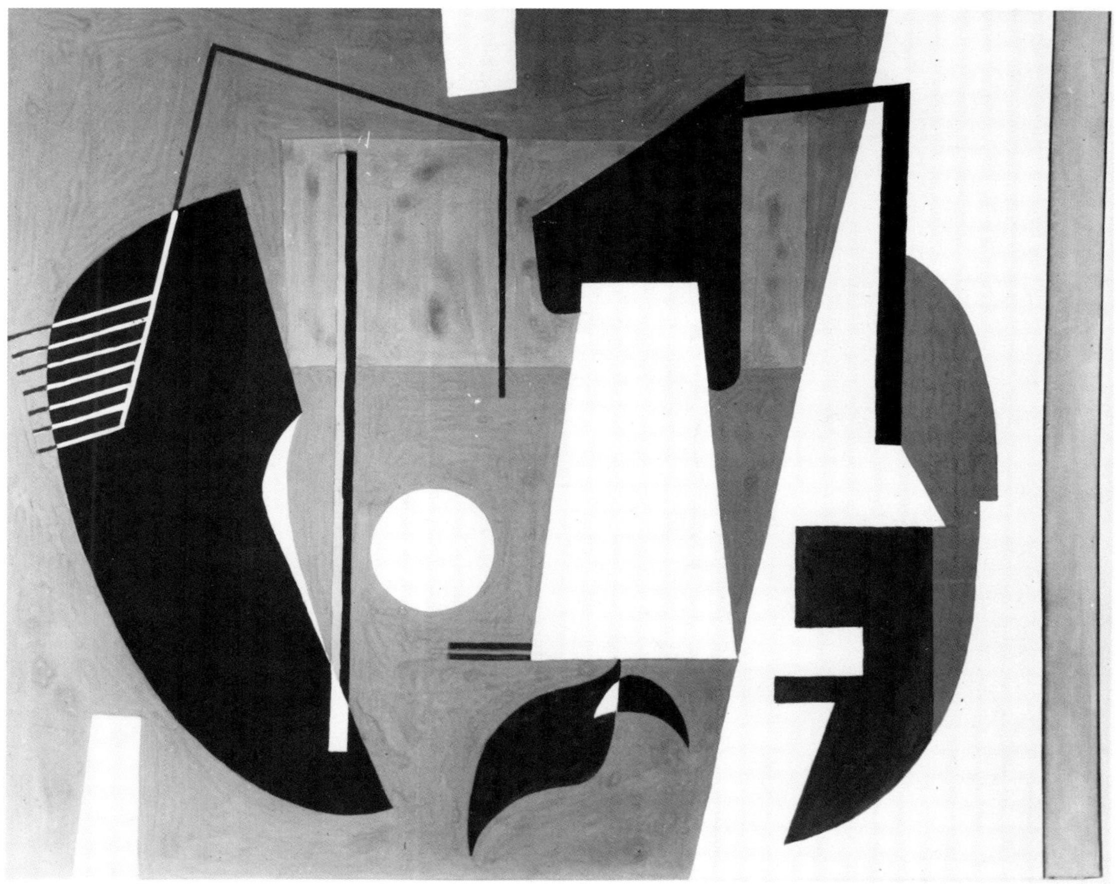

Byron Browne, *Study for Williamsburg Mural (for Social Room Block 2)*, 1936
Medium and dimensions unknown. Current location unknown (presumed lost).

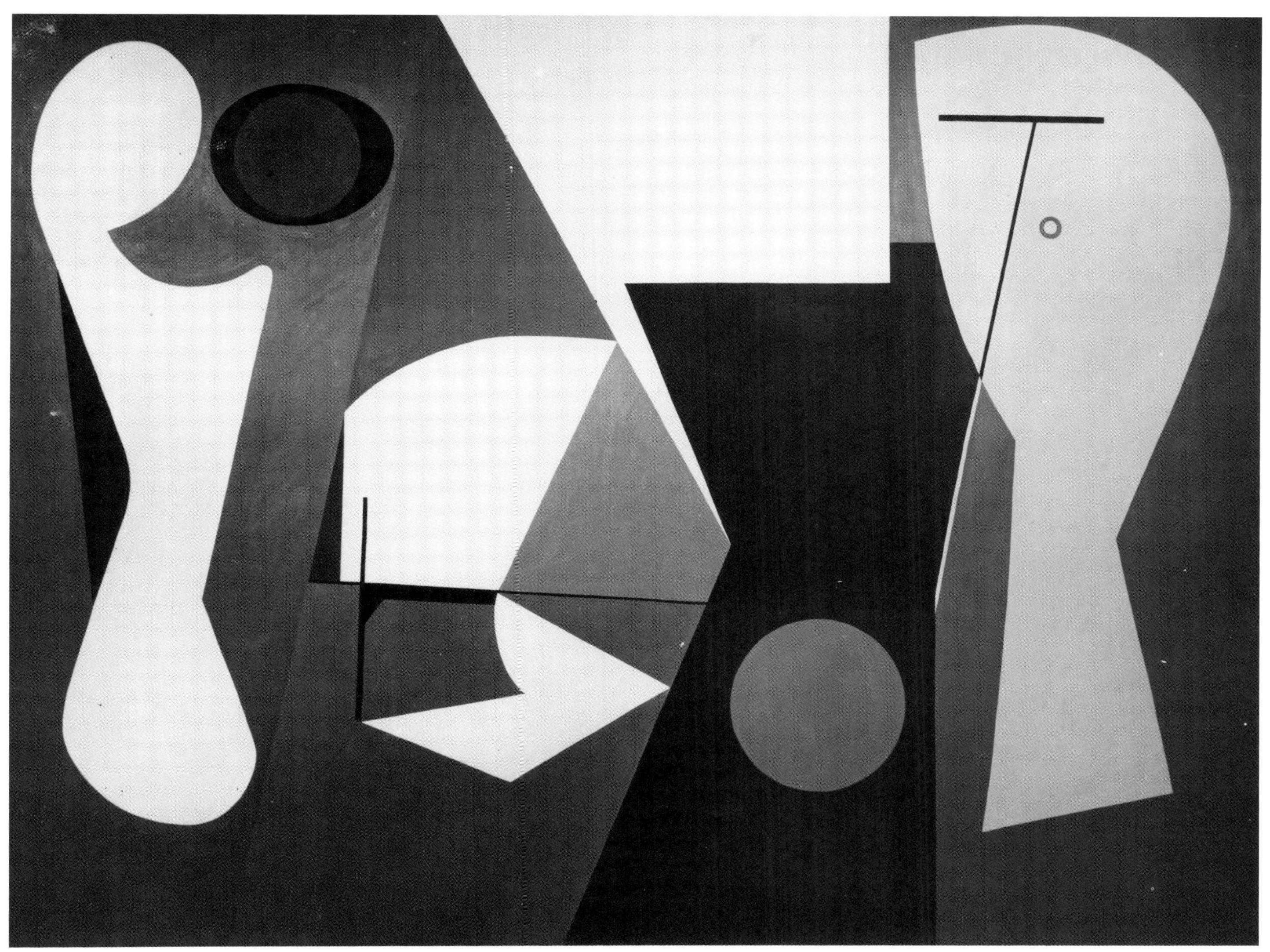

Byron Browne, *Abstraction (Study for Williamsburg Mural)*, 1937
Oil on canvas, dimensions unknown.
Current location unknown
(presumed lost).

Martin Craig

(born Paterson, NJ, 1906; died ?)

Martin Craig was a primarily self-taught sculptor, having studied physics and chemistry at the City College of New York. As a sculptor for the FAP from 1935 to 1938, he worked on a "group of architectural panels for the Federal Housing Commission."[1] It is unclear whether this refers to his designs for the Williamsburg Houses or to another project. Craig's designs for sculptural reliefs for Williamsburg are known only through photographs. The reliefs feature biomorphic forms and appear to have been designed for installation in covered porchlike areas. They were never realized, most likely for financial reasons. Craig also contributed sculptural designs for the New York World's Fair in 1939–40.[2]

1. *Craig, Fornas, Speyer: New Talent Exhibition*, master checklist (New York: Museum of Modern Art, 1955), https://www.moma.org/documents/moma_master-checklist_326016.pdf.

2. *Craig, Fornas, Speyer.*

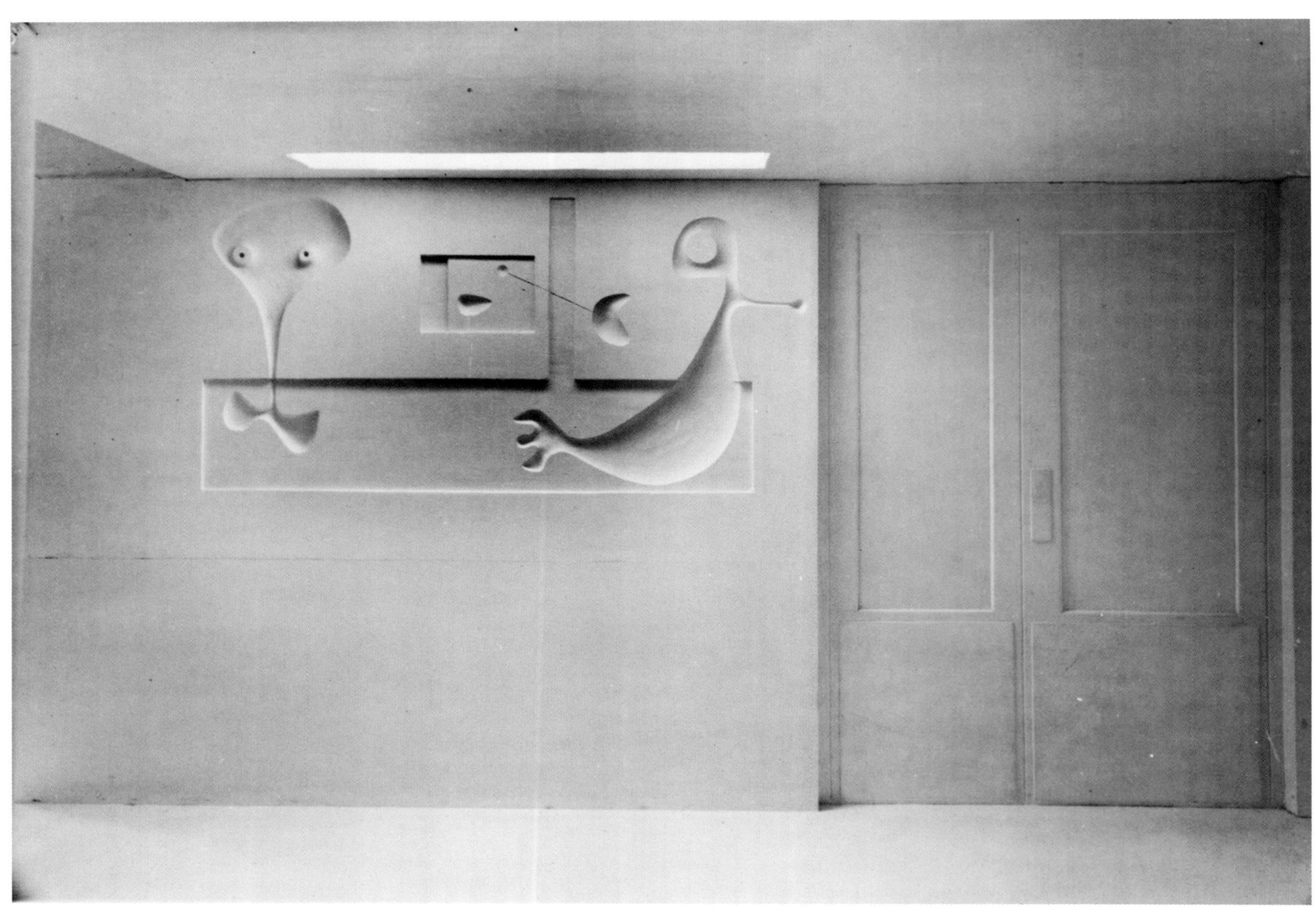

Martin Craig, *Abstraction (Study for Williamsburg Housing Project)*, 1937
Medium and dimensions unknown.
Current location unknown
(presumed lost).

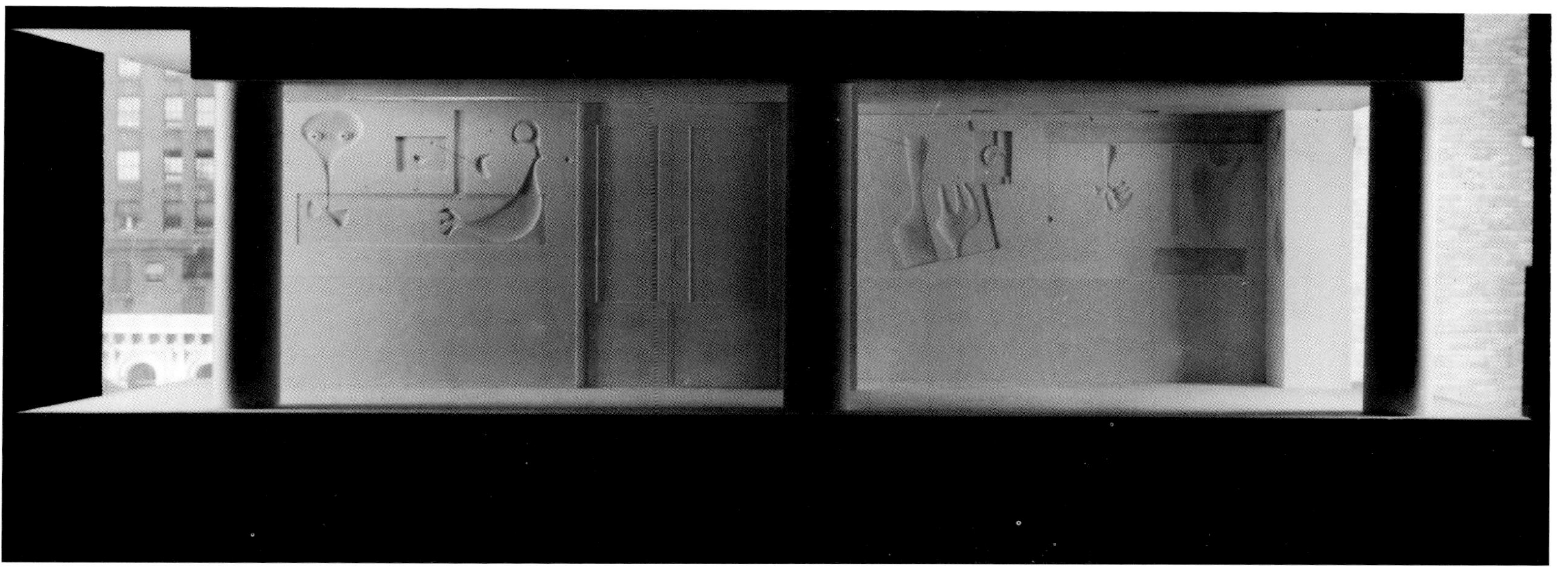

Martin Craig, *Abstract Scale Model for Williamsburg Housing Project,* 1937
Medium and dimensions unknown. Current location unknown (presumed lost).

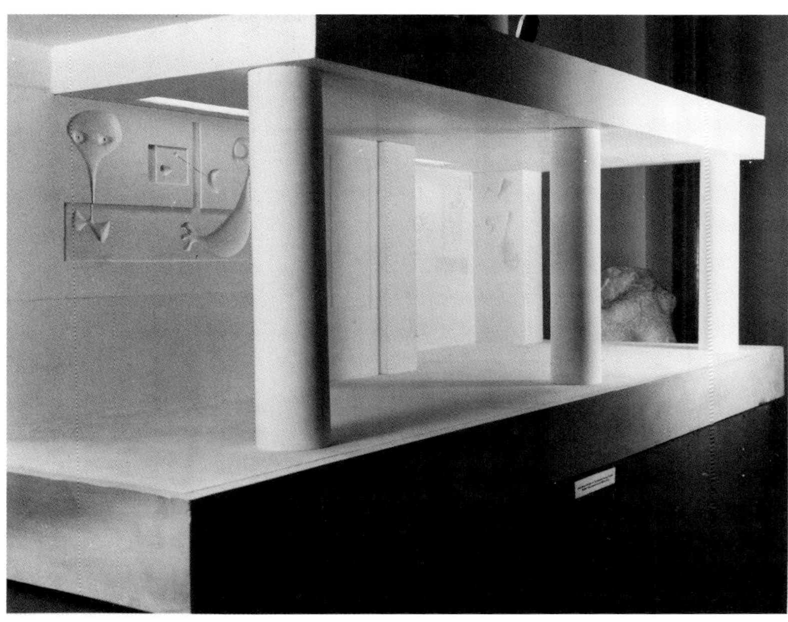

Martin Craig, *Abstraction (Study for Williamsburg Housing Project),* 1937
Medium and dimensions unknown. Current location unknown (presumed lost).

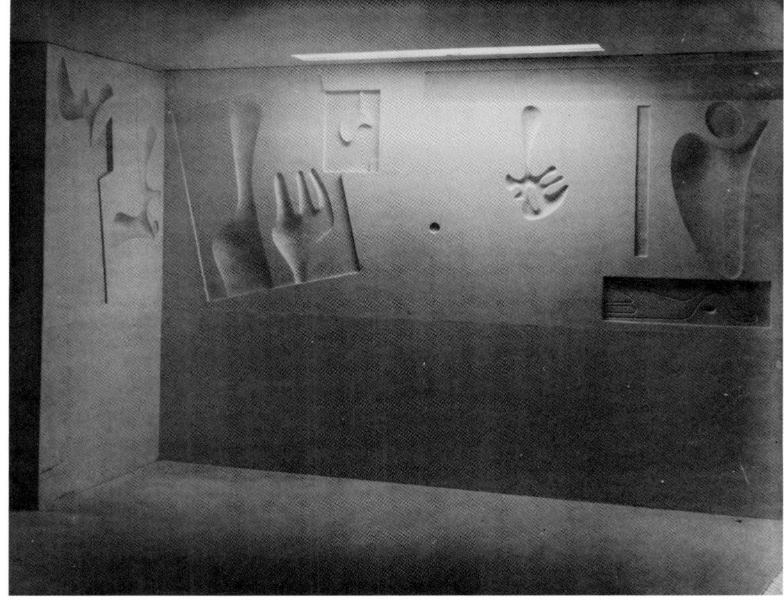

Martin Craig, *Abstraction (Study for Williamsburg Housing Project),* 1937
Medium and dimensions unknown. Current location unknown (presumed lost).

Francis Criss

(born London, England, 1901; died New York, NY, 1973)

When he was born in London, Francis Criss's parents were in the process of emigrating to the United States from Russia.[1] Arriving in 1904, the family settled in Philadelphia. Criss studied art at the Pennsylvania Academy of Fine Arts, at the Art Students League in New York, and privately with Jan Matulka. In 1934, he received a Guggenheim Fellowship, enabling him to study fresco painting in Italy. In Italy, he also studied the work of the surrealist Giorgio di Chirico, whose influence is also apparent in Criss's urban scenes. During the 1930s, Criss gained acclaim for his paintings of New York City streets, elevated trains, and subway stations. Reducing his subjects to their basic shapes and utilizing a simplified palette, these paintings show the influence of geometric abstraction, and more clearly of precisionism. During the Depression, Criss was active in leftist artists' groups, including the American Artists' Congress, the American Artists School, and An American Group, a cooperative that promoted social justice activities through art.[2] In addition to working on the Williamsburg Mural Project, he produced murals for Walter Reed Hospital in Washington, DC, under the auspices of the Federal Art Project.

Criss's Williamsburg mural designs reflect his preoccupation with New York cityscapes. Though they are highly stylized, their representational nature sets them apart from the nonobjective orientation of the larger Williamsburg project. Although he submitted designs for four murals, Criss completed only one, *Sixth Avenue El.* Like *Swing Landscape*, this mural was never installed in the housing project. It was acquired by the Smithsonian American Art Museum in 1966.

1. 1930 United States Federal Census. Census Place: Queens, NY. Ancestry.com online database.

2. Langa, *Radical Art*, 35.

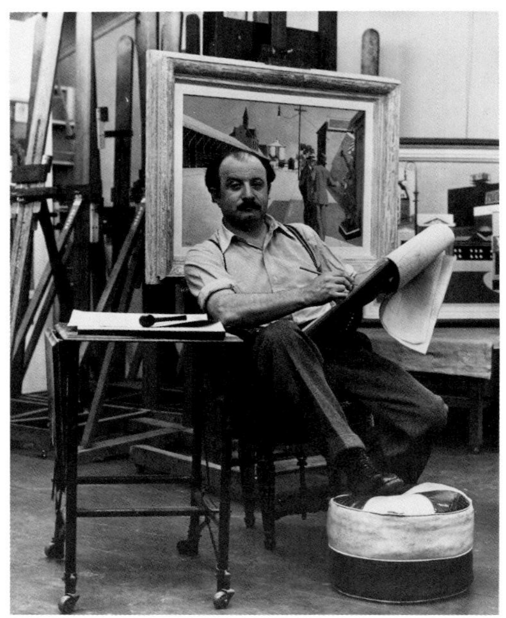

Francis Criss, October 1940.

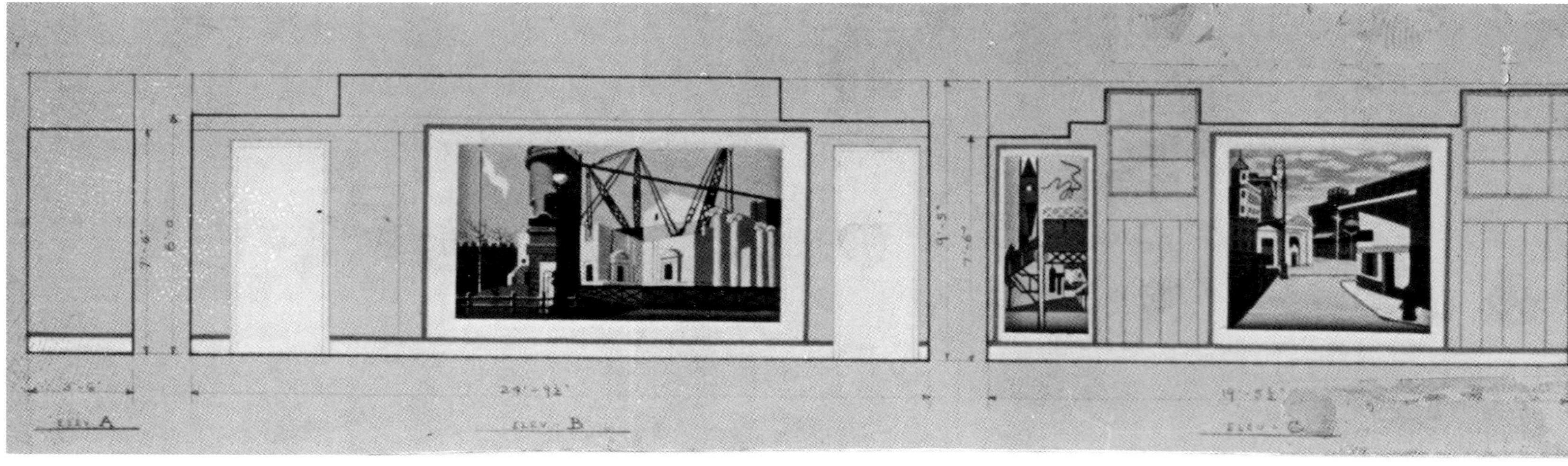

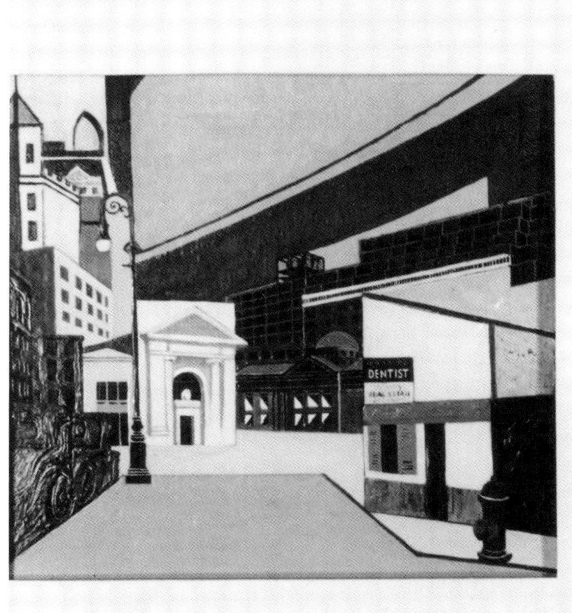

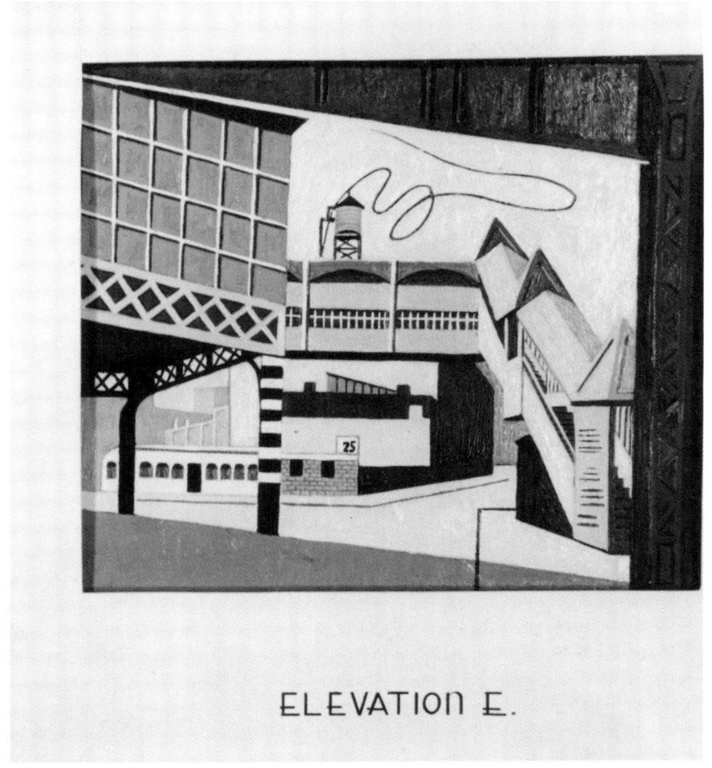

Francis Criss, *Elevation C and E for Williamsburg Social Room Block 4,* 1936
Gouache, dimensions unknown. Current location unknown (presumed lost).

Francis Criss, *Layout for Williamsburg Murals,* ca. 1937
Medium and dimensions unknown. Current location unknown (presumed lost).

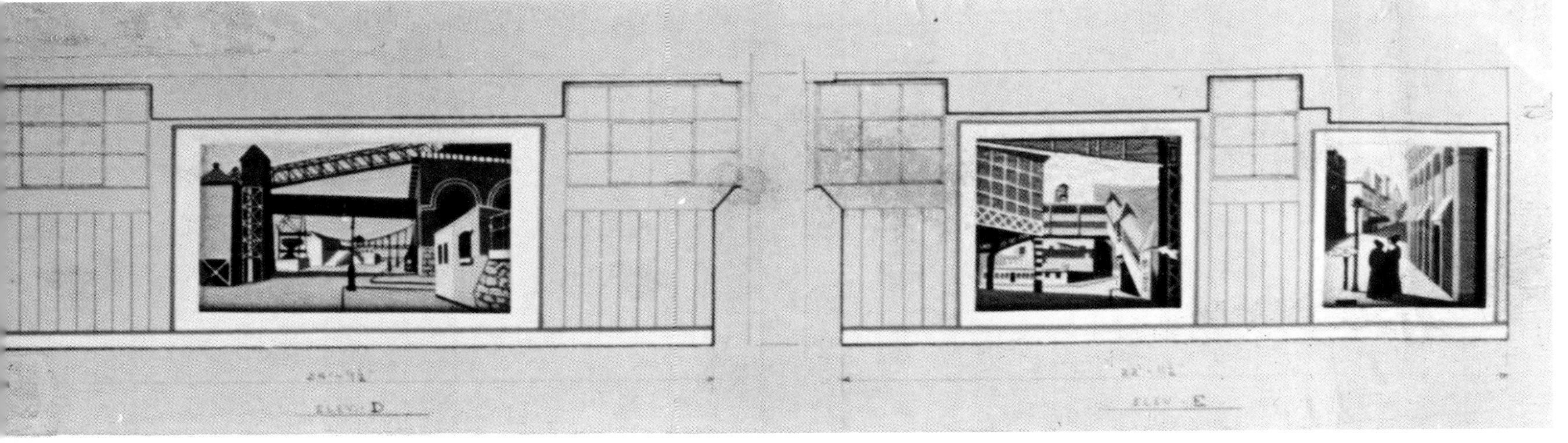

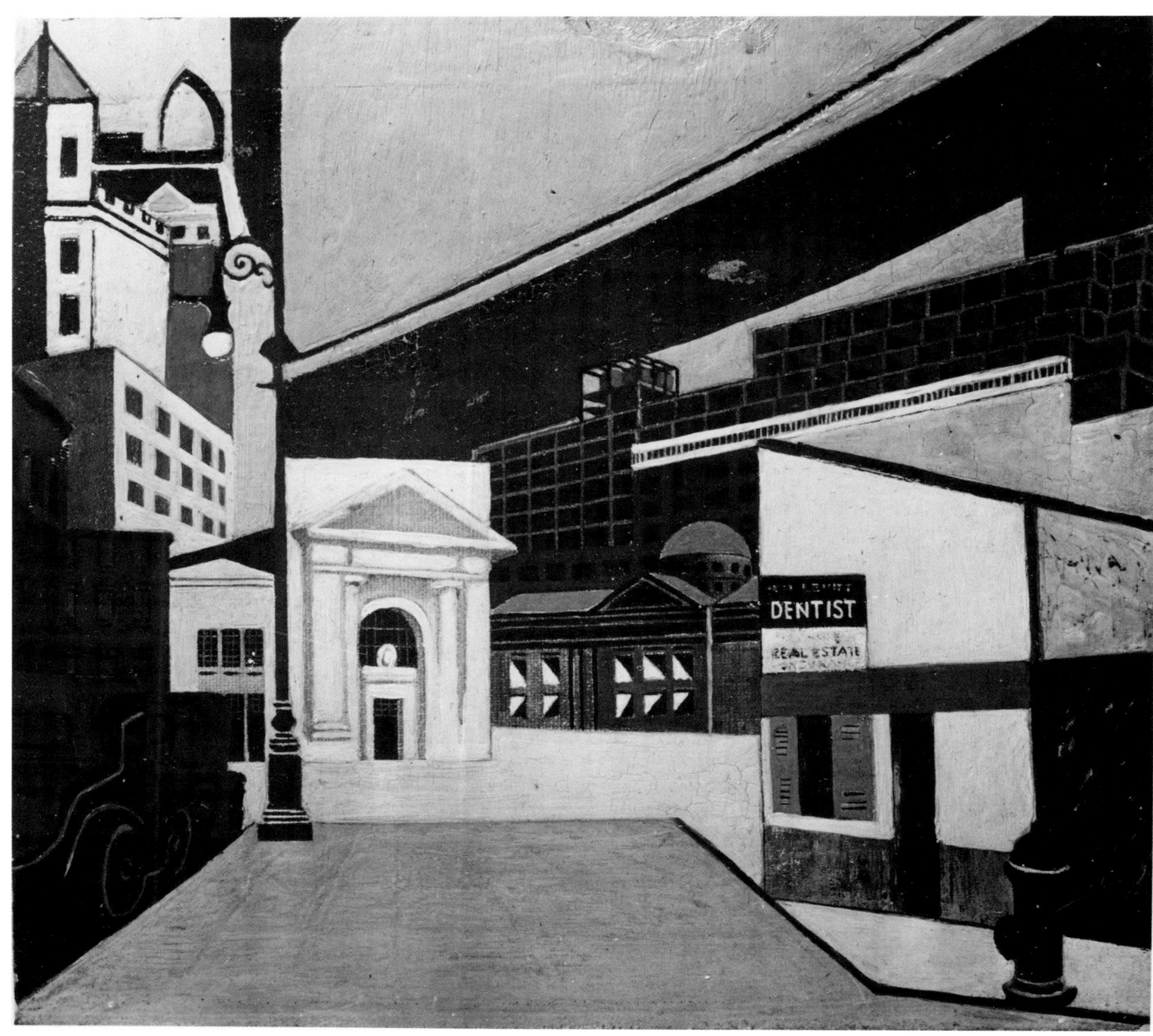

Francis Criss, *Study for Williamsburg Mural Project,* 1937
Oil on canvas, dimensions unknown. Current location unknown (presumed lost).

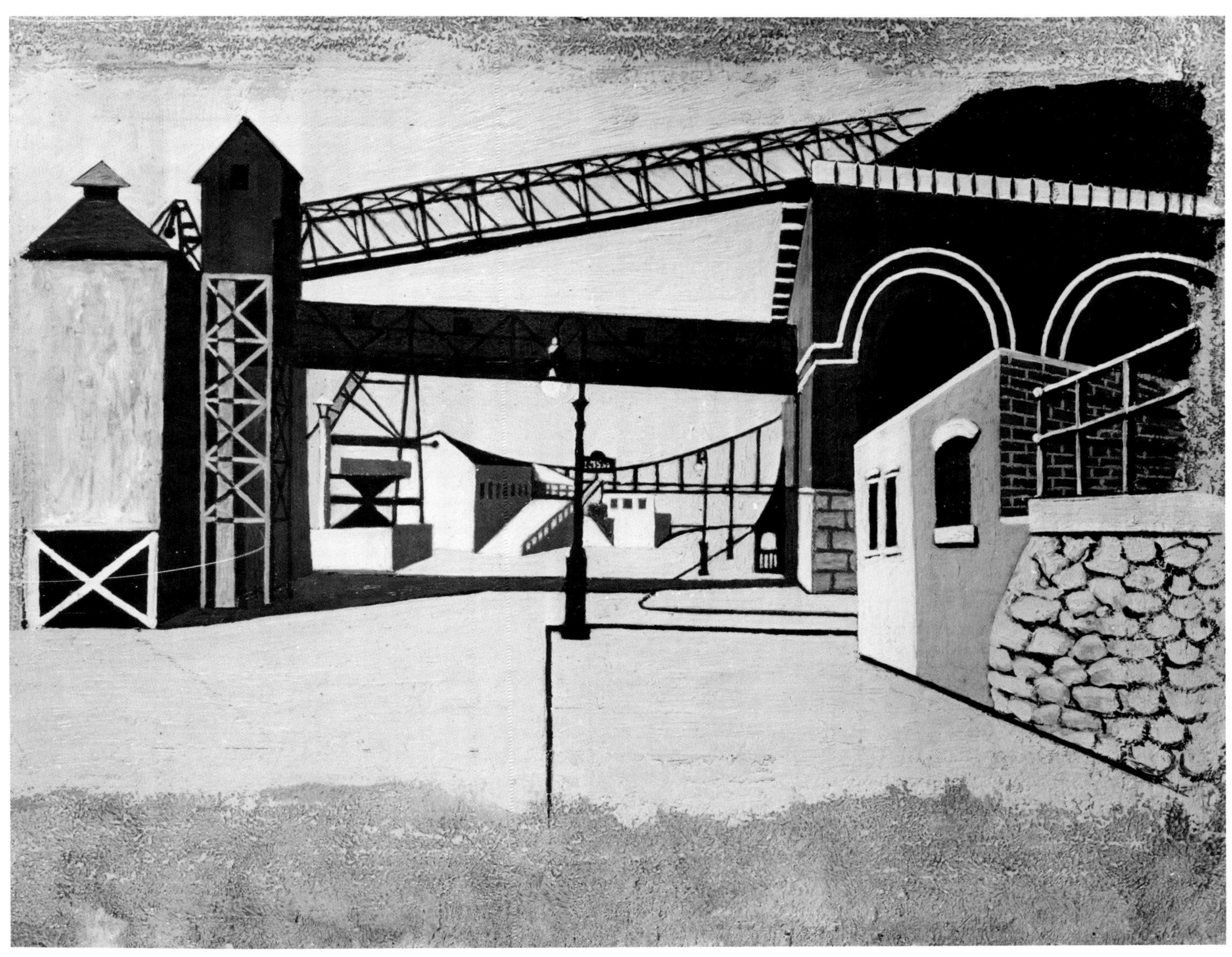

Francis Criss, *Study for Williamsburg Mural Project,* 1937
Oil on canvas, dimensions unknown. Current location unknown (presumed lost).

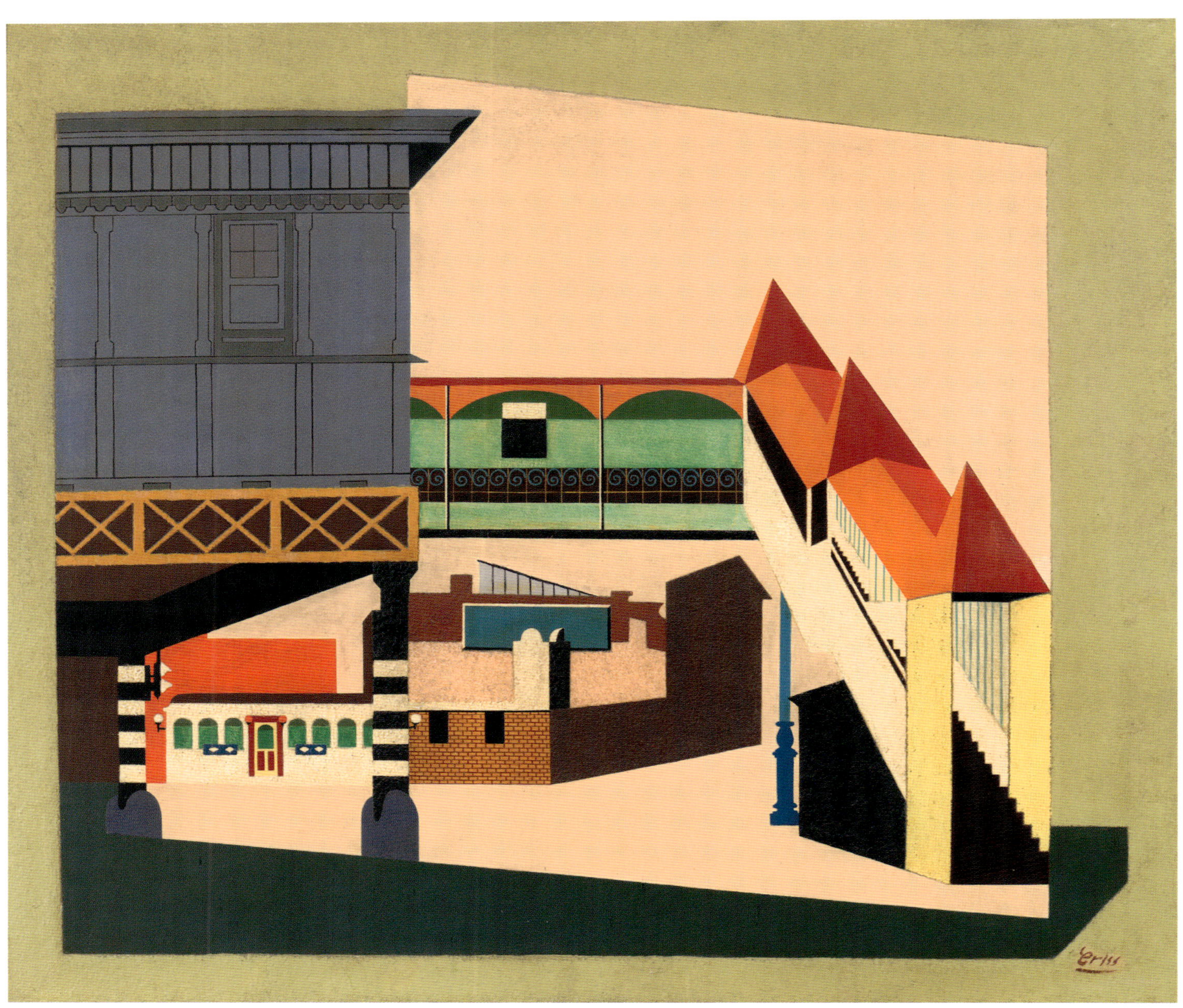

Francis Criss, *Sixth Avenue El,* ca. 1937
Oil on canvas, 36¼ × 41¹¹⁄₁₆ in. (92.1 × 105.9 cm). Whitney Museum of American Art, Purchase, with funds from the Felicia Meyer Marsh Purchase Fund, 82.1. This painting may have been one of Criss's final studies for his completed mural.

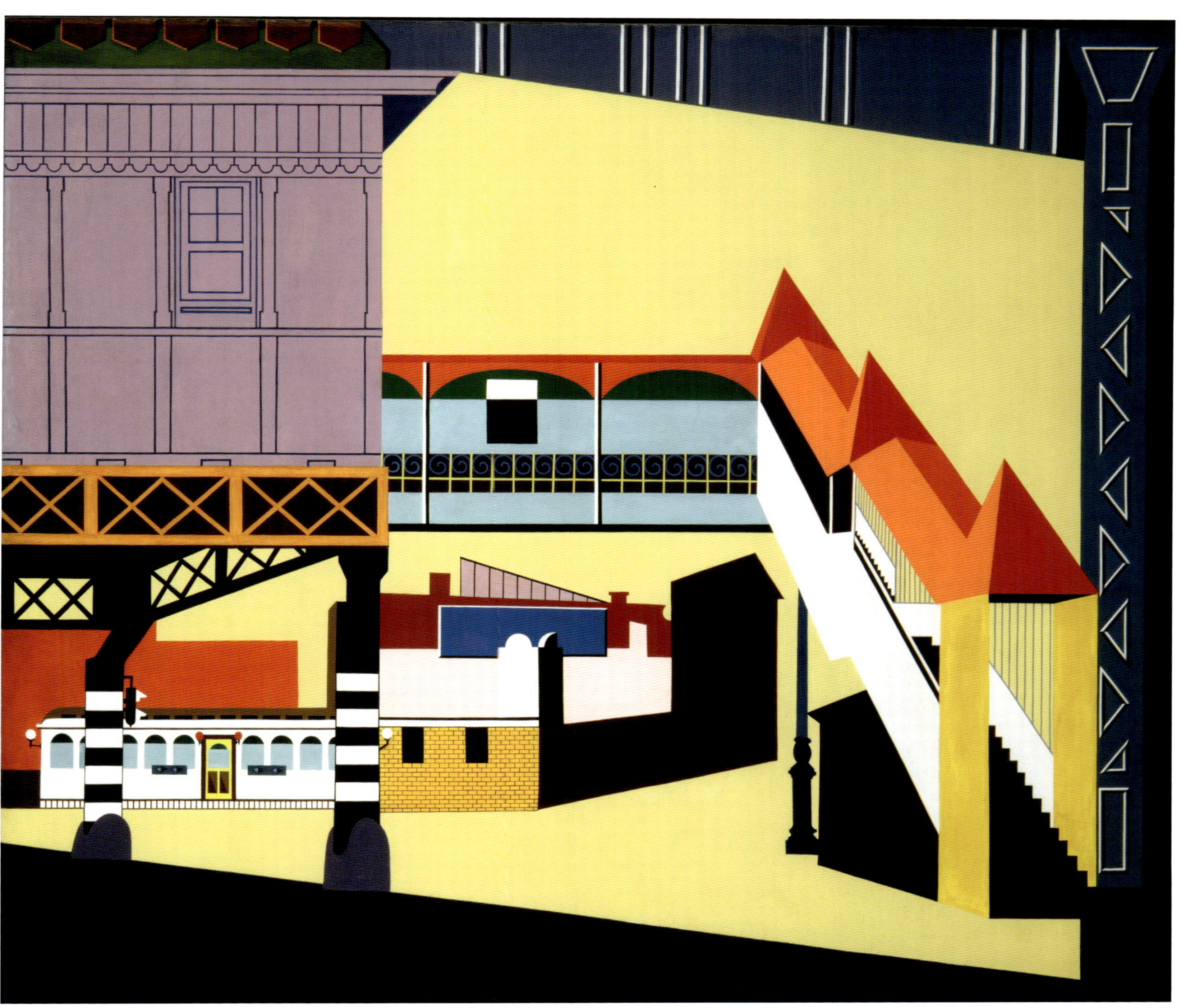

Francis Criss, *Sixth Avenue "L" (Mural, Williamsburg Housing Project, New York)*, 1937–38
Oil on canvas, 72 × 84 in. (182.9 × 213.4 cm). 1966.31.3, Smithsonian American Art Museum, Transfer from the Newark Museum.

Stuart Davis

(born Philadelphia, PA, 1892; died New York, NY, 1964)

Stuart Davis is widely recognized as one of the most innovative American artists of the twentieth century.[1] In 1913, the *International Exhibition of Modern Art* (better known as the Armory Show) served as Davis's introduction to European modernism. In the 1920s and 1930s he developed a unique approach to cubism in his series of *Egg Beater* paintings, and in his compositions based on the waterfront of Gloucester, Massachusetts, where he spent his summers. During the 1930s, however, he divided most of his time between artistic and social activism and mural painting. A tireless promoter of modernism, Davis served as the editor of (and contributor to) the Artists Union's magazine *Art Front* and as chair of the American Artists' Congress. *New York Mural,* his first mural, was commissioned by the Museum of Modern Art for the exhibition *Murals by American Painters and Photographers*. Davis also produced murals for Radio City Music Hall and, under the auspices of the FAP, for the Williamsburg Houses, Radio Station WNYC, and the New York World's Fair. Davis's studies for *Swing Landscape* show a continuous refinement of the composition's Gloucester-based imagery.

1. An extensive biographical timeline of Davis's life and work can be found in Barbara Haskell, "Stuart Davis: A Chronicle," in Haskell and Cooper, *Stuart Davis: In Full Swing,* 146–221.

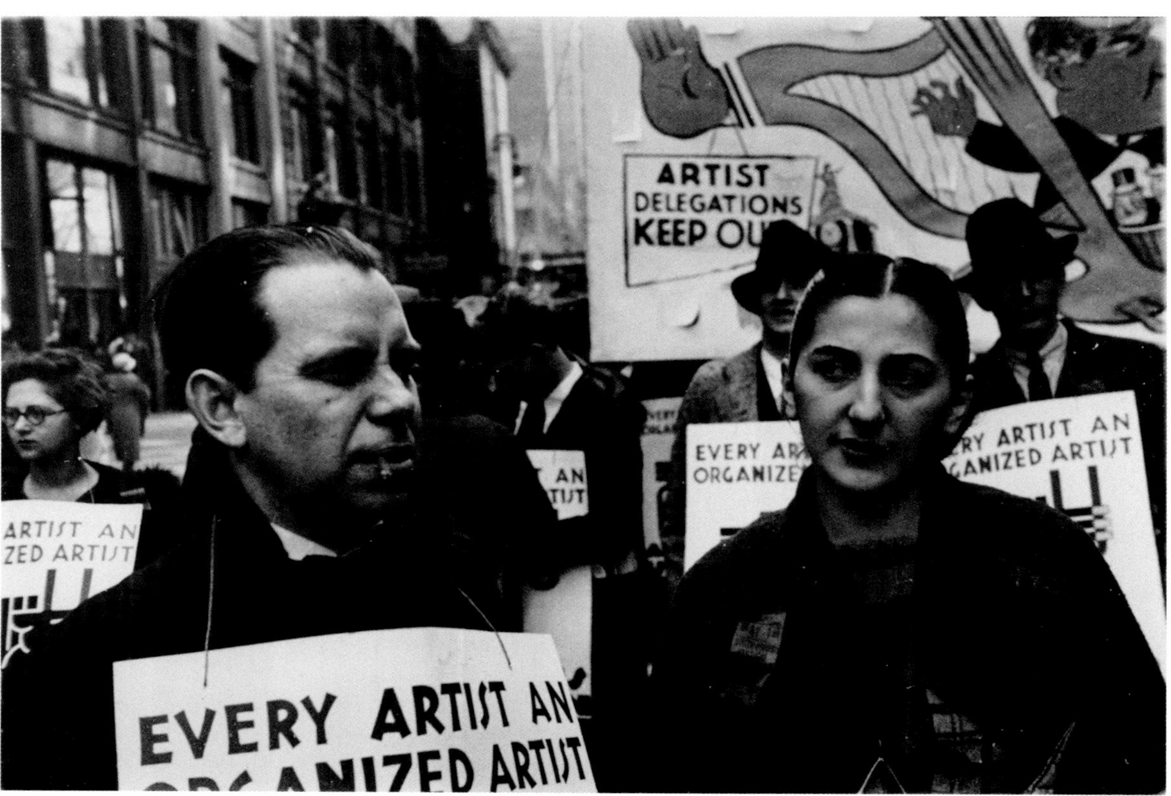

Ben Shahn, *Untitled (Stuart Davis and Roselle Springer among Artists' Union demonstrators, Division IX, May Day Parade, Communist Party route, Twenty-fifth Street between Fifth and Sixth Avenues, New York City),* May 1, 1935 (printed later)

Gelatin silver print. 8 1/16 × 10 1/16 in. (20.5 × 25.5 cm). Harvard Art Museums / Fogg Museum, Gift of Bernarda Bryson Shahn. Copyright © President and Fellows of Harvard College.

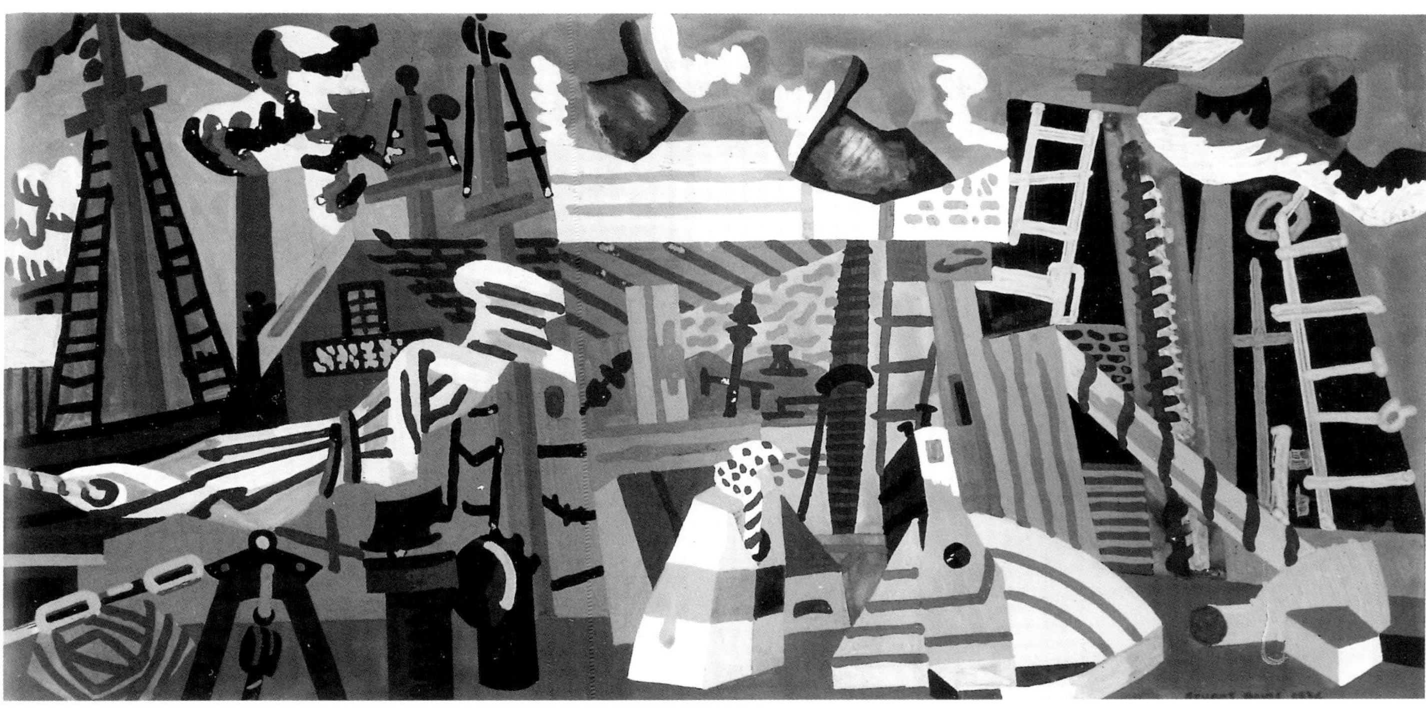

Stuart Davis, *Waterfront Forms (Study for Swing Landscape)*, 1936
Gouache on paper, 20 × 14 in. (50.8 × 35.6 cm). Current location unknown (presumed lost). According to the 2007 Davis catalogue raisonné, this was the sketch included in MoMA's 1936 exhibition *New Horizons in American Art.* An inscription on the photograph's verso reads: "Waterfront Forms by Stuart Davis Mural—executed 1938 ['8' crossed out] 6—placed 1940 Brooklyn College Academic Building Room 2147 Faculty Room Bedford Ave and Ave H." Because of this inscription, scholars once believed this was a sketch for a lost mural titled *Waterfront Forms.* Research conducted during the preparation of the catalogue raisonné led its authors to conclude, however, that *Waterfront Forms* was simply a variant title for *Swing Landscape* and that this gouache is one of Davis's early studies for his Williamsburg mural.

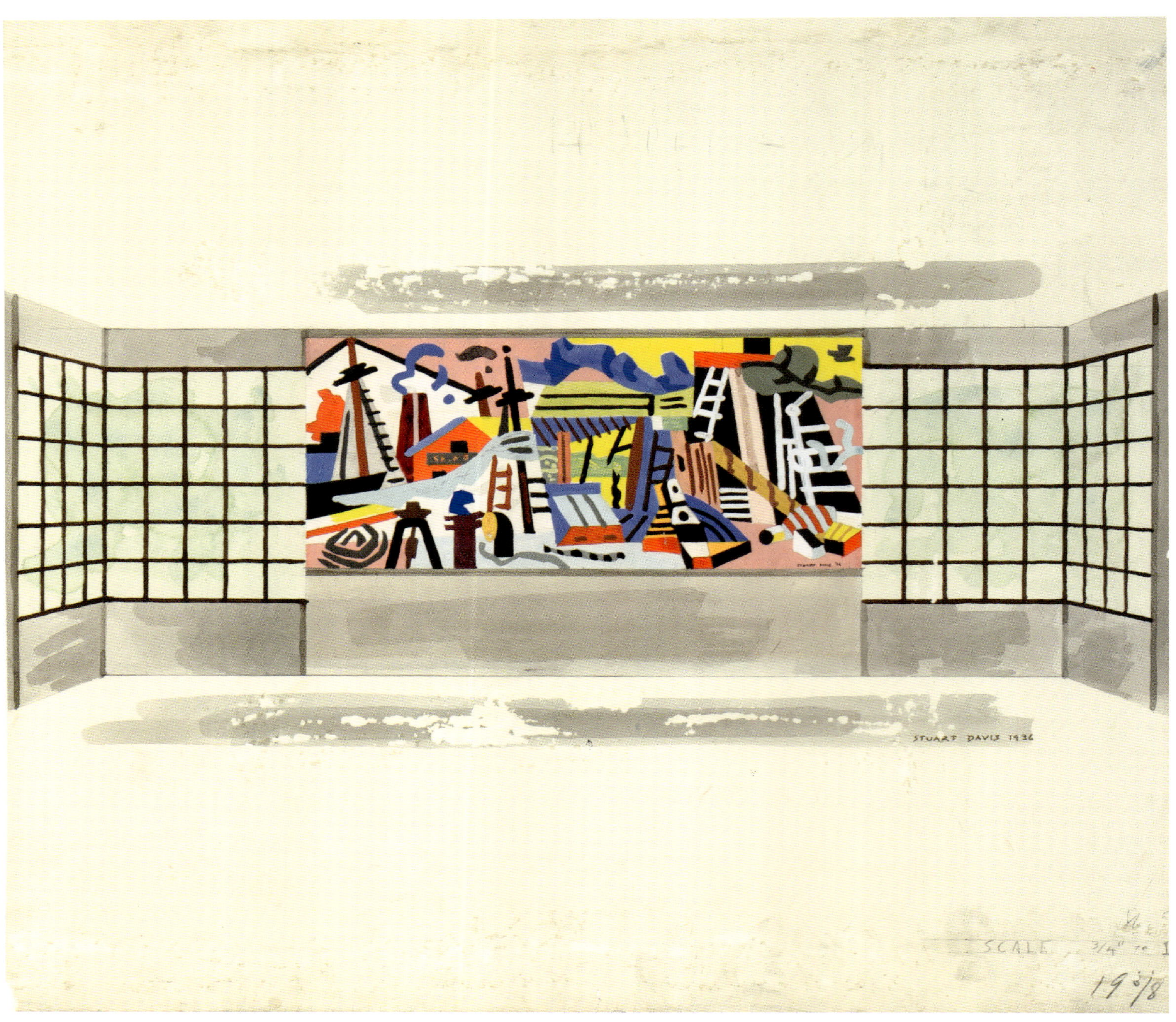

Stuart Davis, *Study for "Swing Landscape,"* 1936
Gouache and traces of graphite on paper, 19½ × 21⅞ in. (49.5 × 55.6 cm). Sheldon Museum of Art, University of Nebraska–Lincoln, Allocation of the U.S. Government, Federal Art Project of the Works Progress Administration, WPA-101.1943.

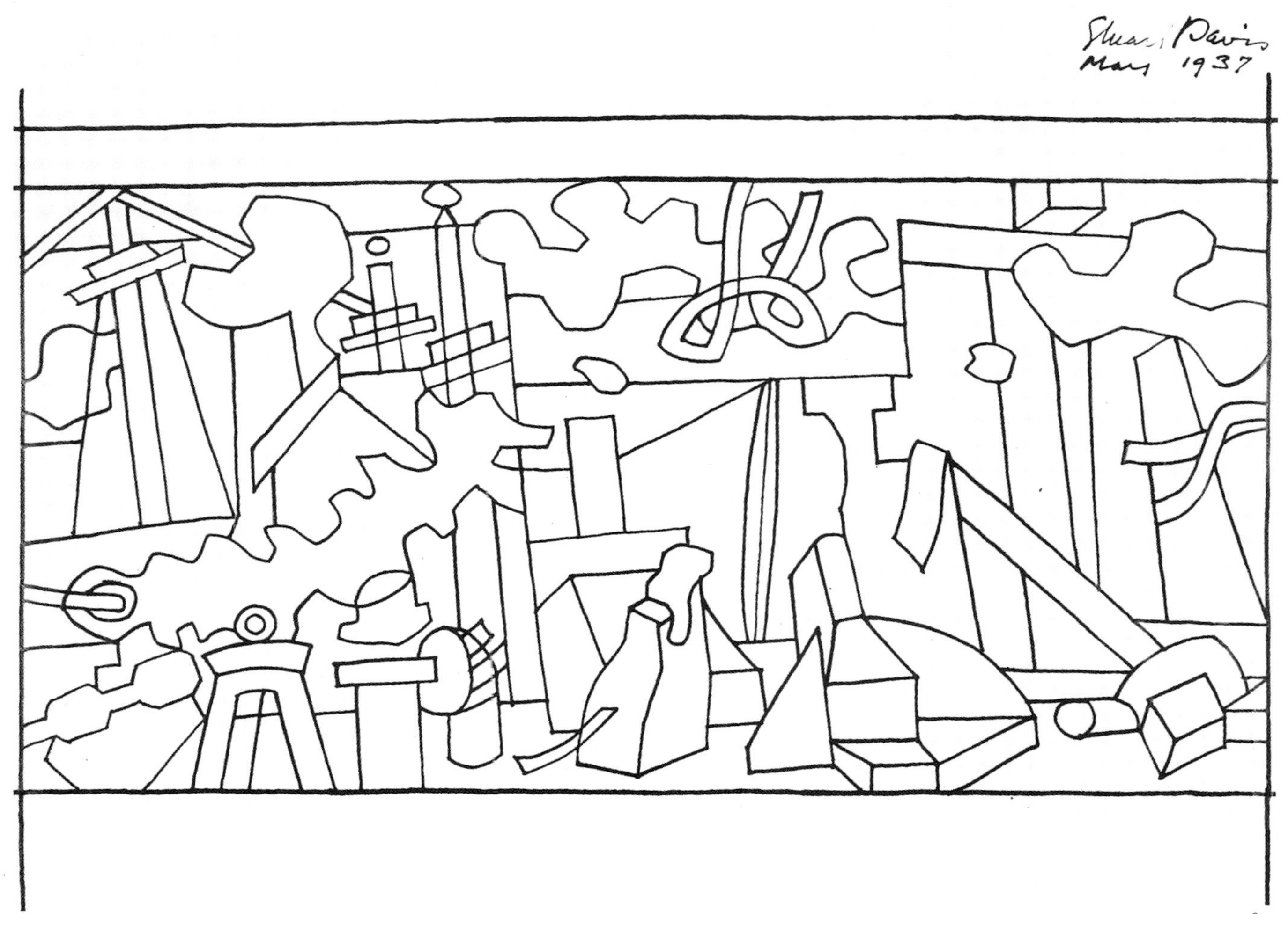

Stuart Davis, *Study for “Swing Landscape,”* 1937
Ink on architect’s tracing paper, 16 × 22 in. (40.6 × 55.9 cm). Private collection.

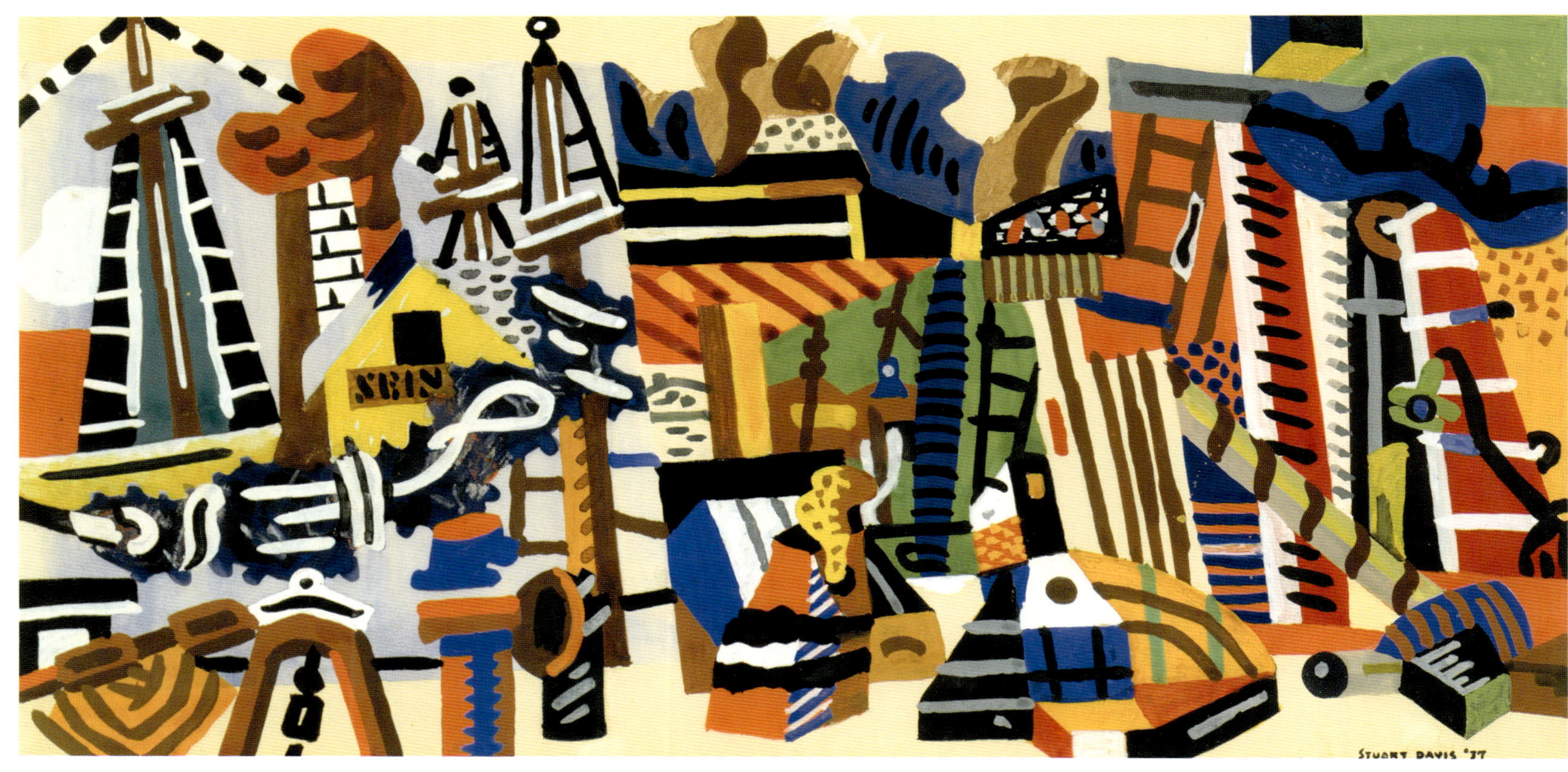

Stuart Davis, *Abstraction (Study for Swing Landscape)*, 1937
Gouache and watercolor on paper, 17⅞ × 23⅜ in. (27.6 × 59.4 cm). 1972.81, Smithsonian American Art Museum, Transfer from the General Services Administration.

Stuart Davis, *Abstraction (Study for Williamsburg Project)*, 1937
Oil on canvas, dimensions unknown.

Stuart Davis, *Study for Swing Landscape*, 1937–38
Oil on canvas, 22 × 28¾ in. (55.9 × 73 cm). Corcoran Collection (Museum Purchase and exchange through a gift given in memory of Edith Gregor Halpert by the Halpert Foundation and the William A. Clark Fund), National Gallery of Art, Washington, 2014.79.15. This painting is a fragment depicting only the left side of *Swing Landscape*.

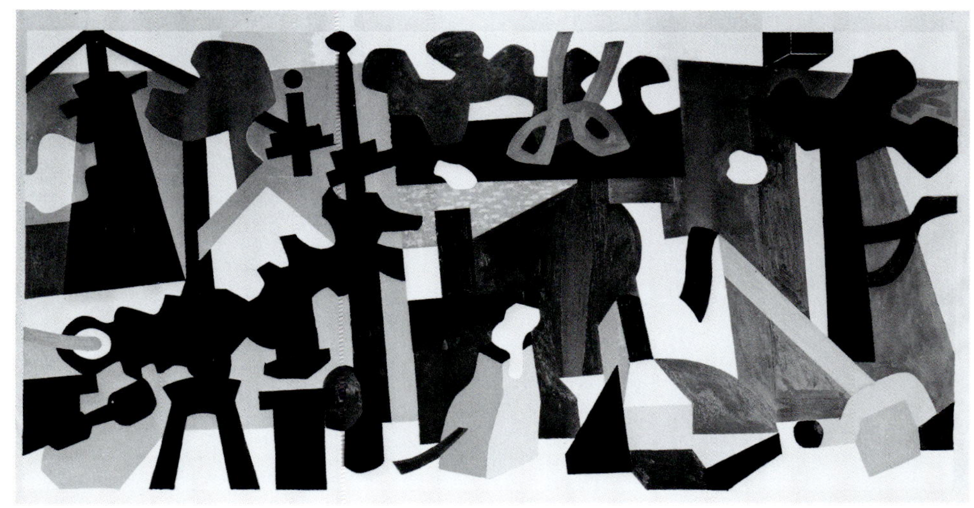

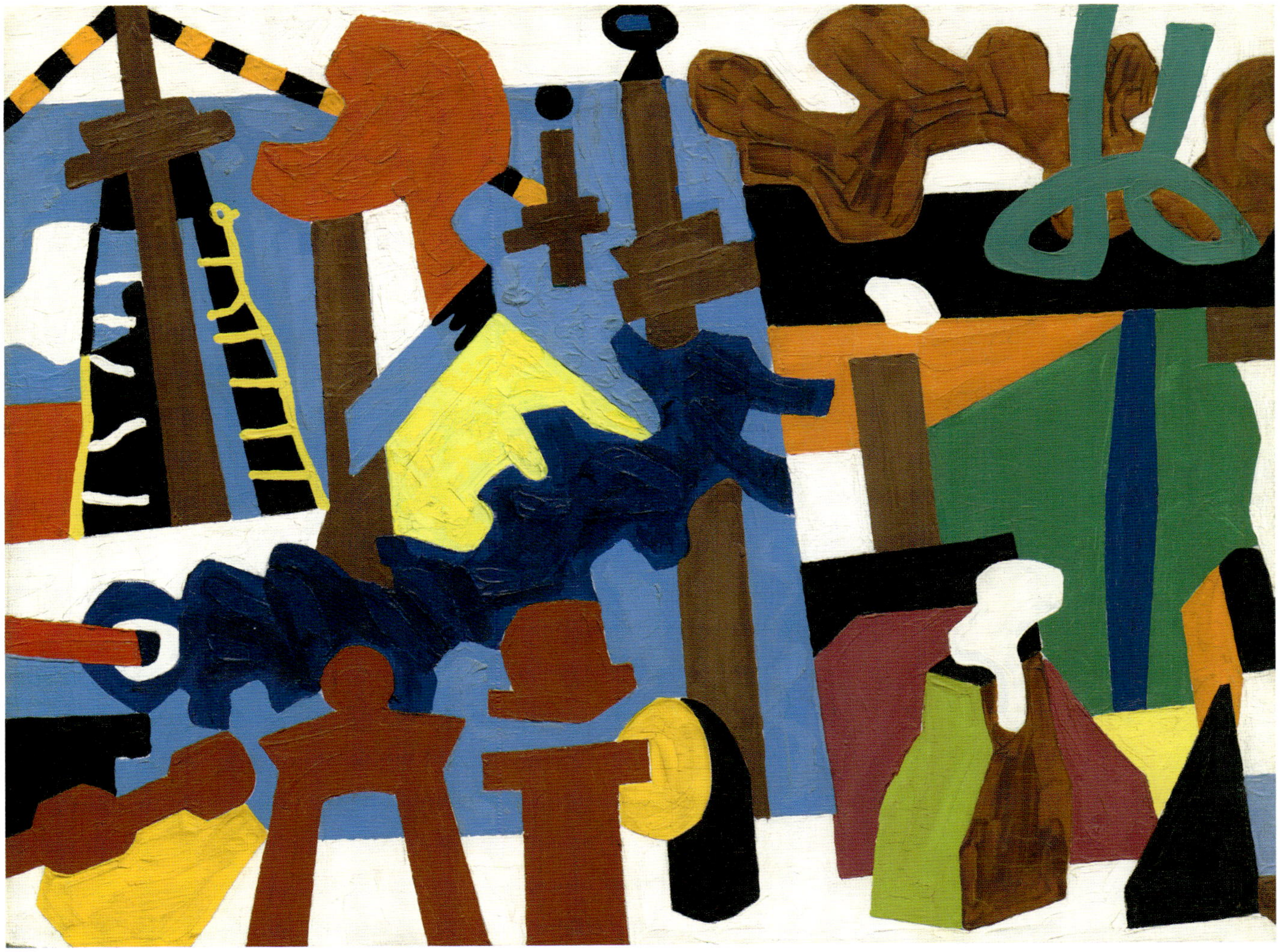

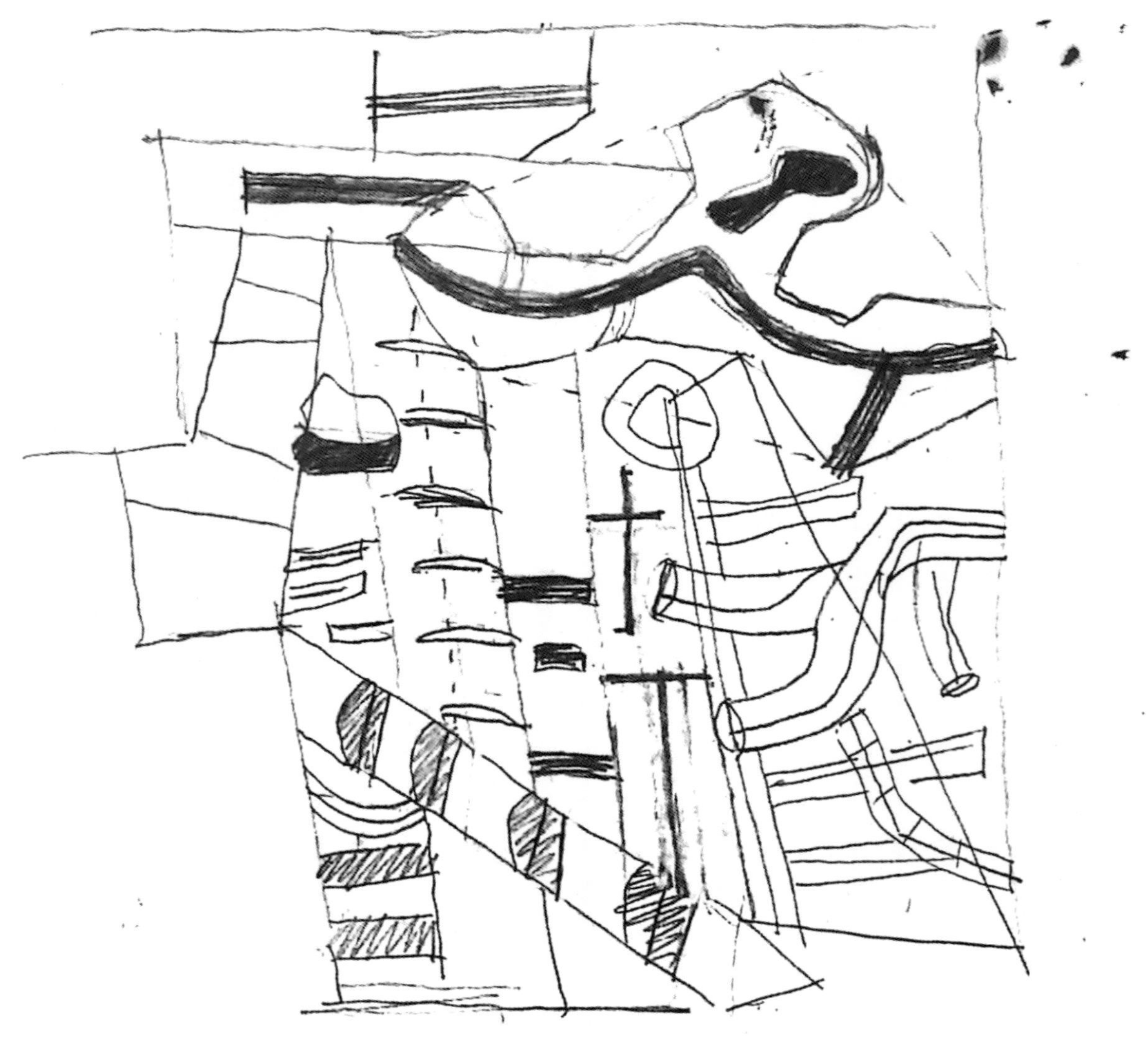

Stuart Davis, *Detail Study for "Swing Landscape,"* 1938
Pencil on paper, 8½ × 11 in. (21.6 × 27.9 cm). Estate of the artist. © 2019 Estate of Stuart Davis/Licensed by VAGA at Artists Rights Society (ARS), NY.

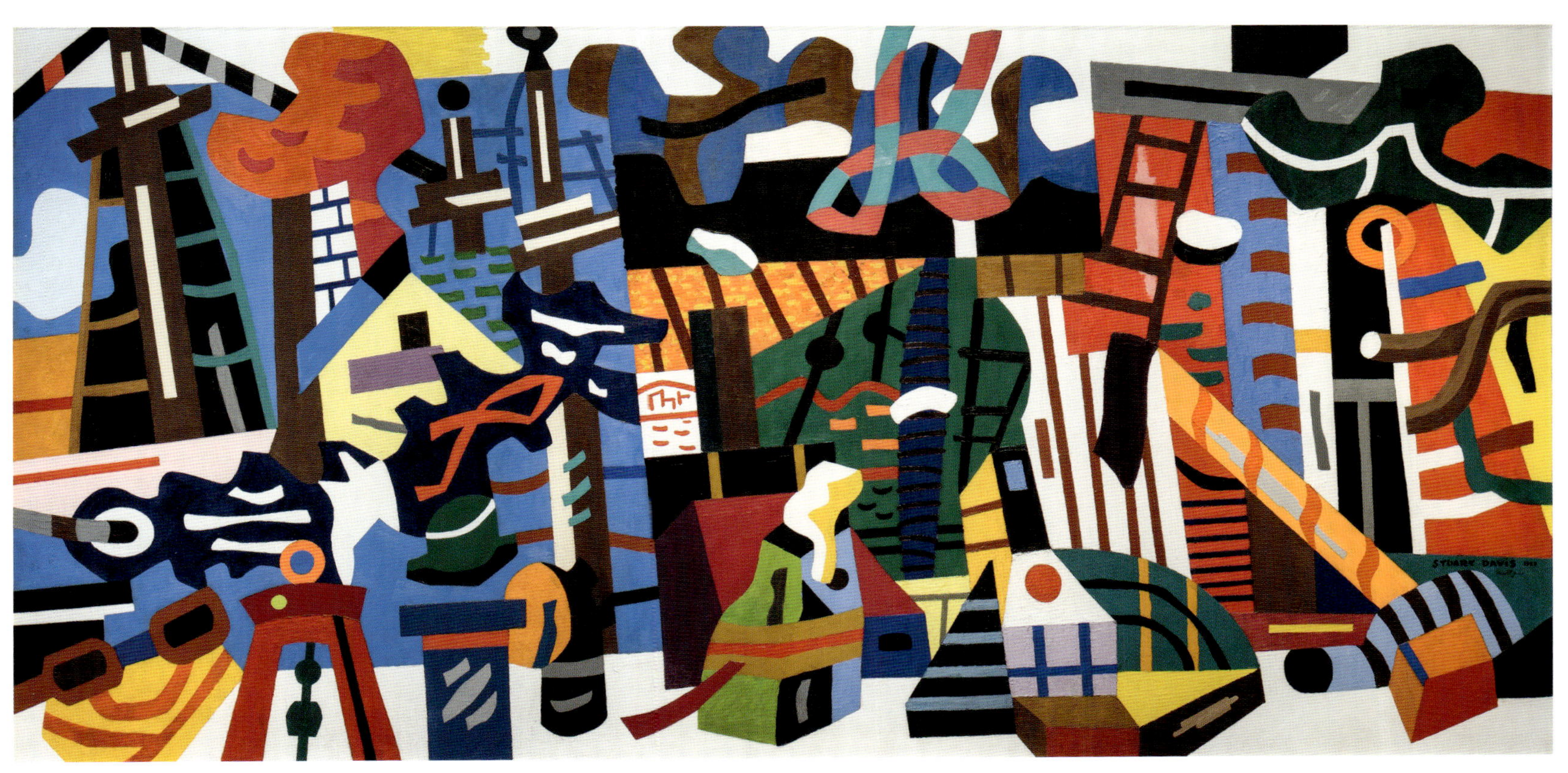

Stuart Davis, ***Swing Landscape,*** **1938**
Oil on canvas, $86\frac{3}{4} \times 173\frac{1}{8}$ in. (220.3×439.7 cm). Allocated by the U.S. Government, Commissioned through the New Deal Art Projects, Eskenazi Museum of Art, Indiana University, 42.1.

Balcomb Greene

(born Millville, NY, 1904; died Montauk Point, NY, 1990)

Balcomb Greene studied philosophy and psychology before embarking on an artistic career. In 1931 he and his wife, Gertrude (née Glass), spent a year in Paris, pursuing their interests in avant-garde art and literature. In 1937 he was elected as the first chairman of the American Abstract Artists. During the 1930s Greene developed an austere form of non-objectivity, which reached its full expression in the almost minimalist composition of his completed Williamsburg mural, which was installed there in 1938 (and is now at the Brooklyn Museum). Greene also worked on several other public art projects under the auspices of the FAP: a stained-glass window for the Bronx School of Arts and Sciences, a mural for the Hall of Medicine at the New York World's Fair, and a mural design for a chapel at the Rikers Island penitentiary. This design was rejected by the penitentiary's rabbi, who felt that one of the symbols in the composition too closely resembled a swastika—though this was surely not Greene's intention.[1]

Greene's one known Williamsburg mural study differs from the finished mural, though both reflect his austere version of neoplasticism.

1. Haskell, *Burgoyne Diller*, 67. It is unlikely that Greene, whose wife was Jewish, intended to include such an offensive symbol in the mural.

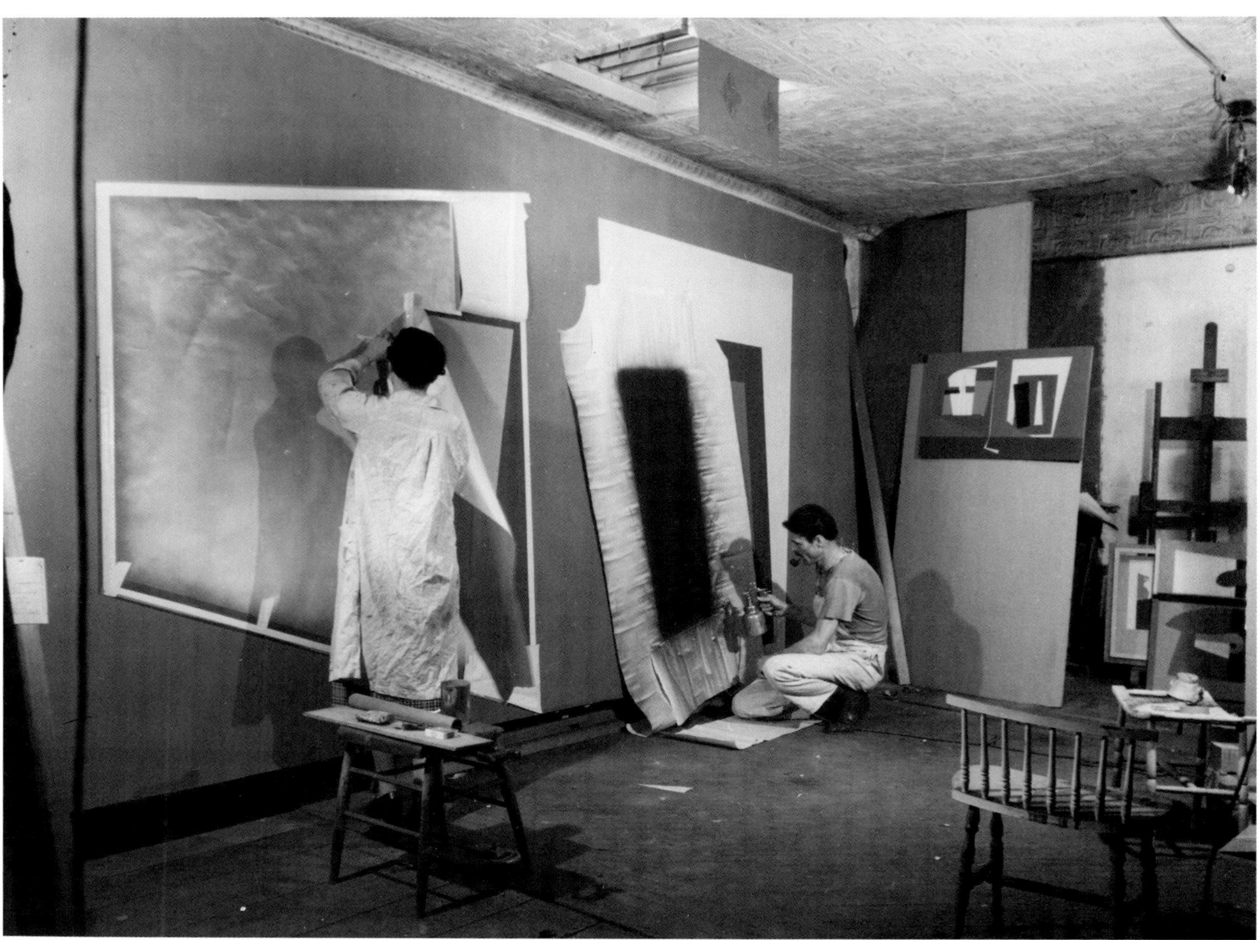

Balcomb Greene, 1939.

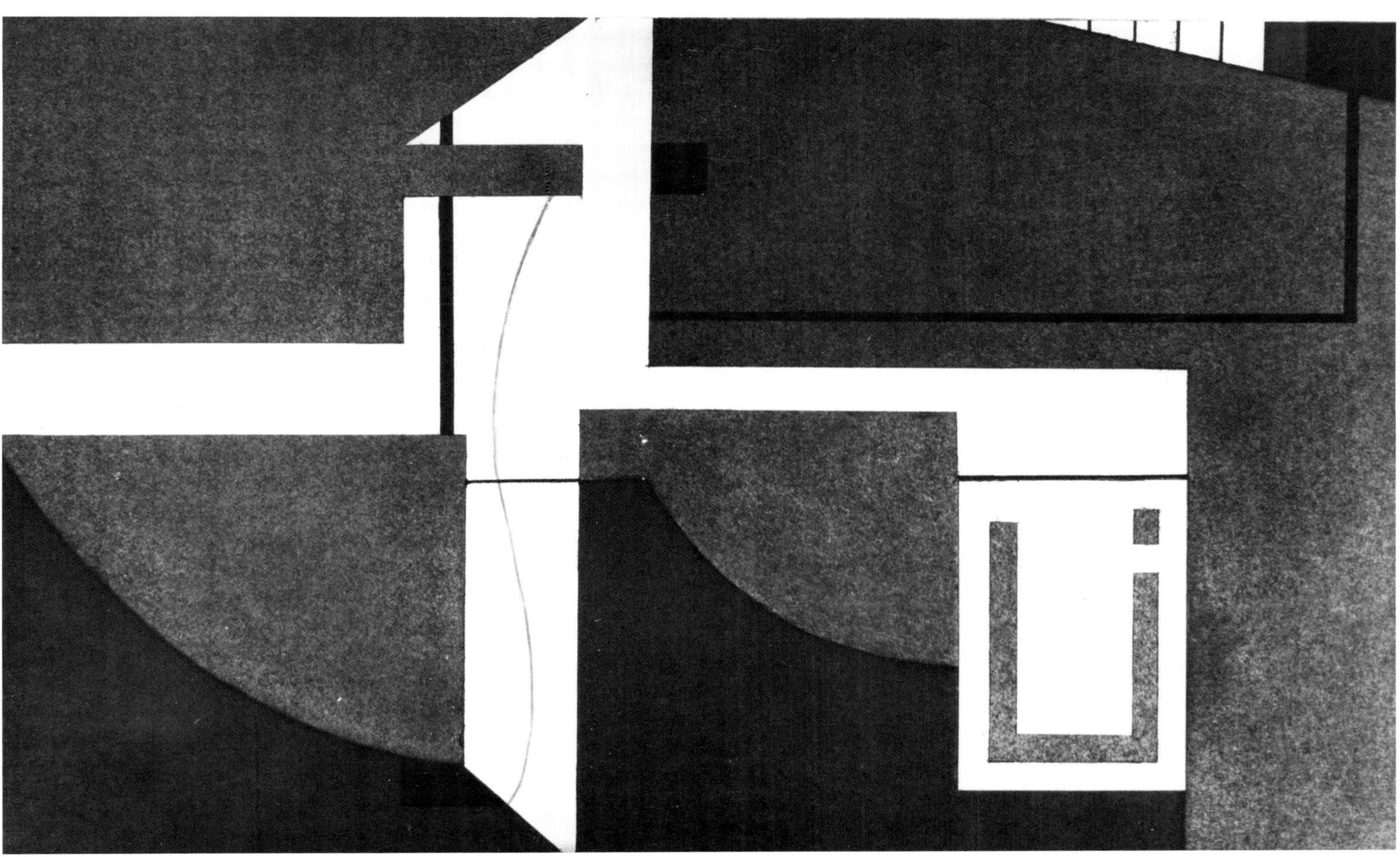

Balcomb Greene, *Study for Williamsburg Mural,* 1936
Medium and dimensions unknown. Current location unknown (presumed lost).

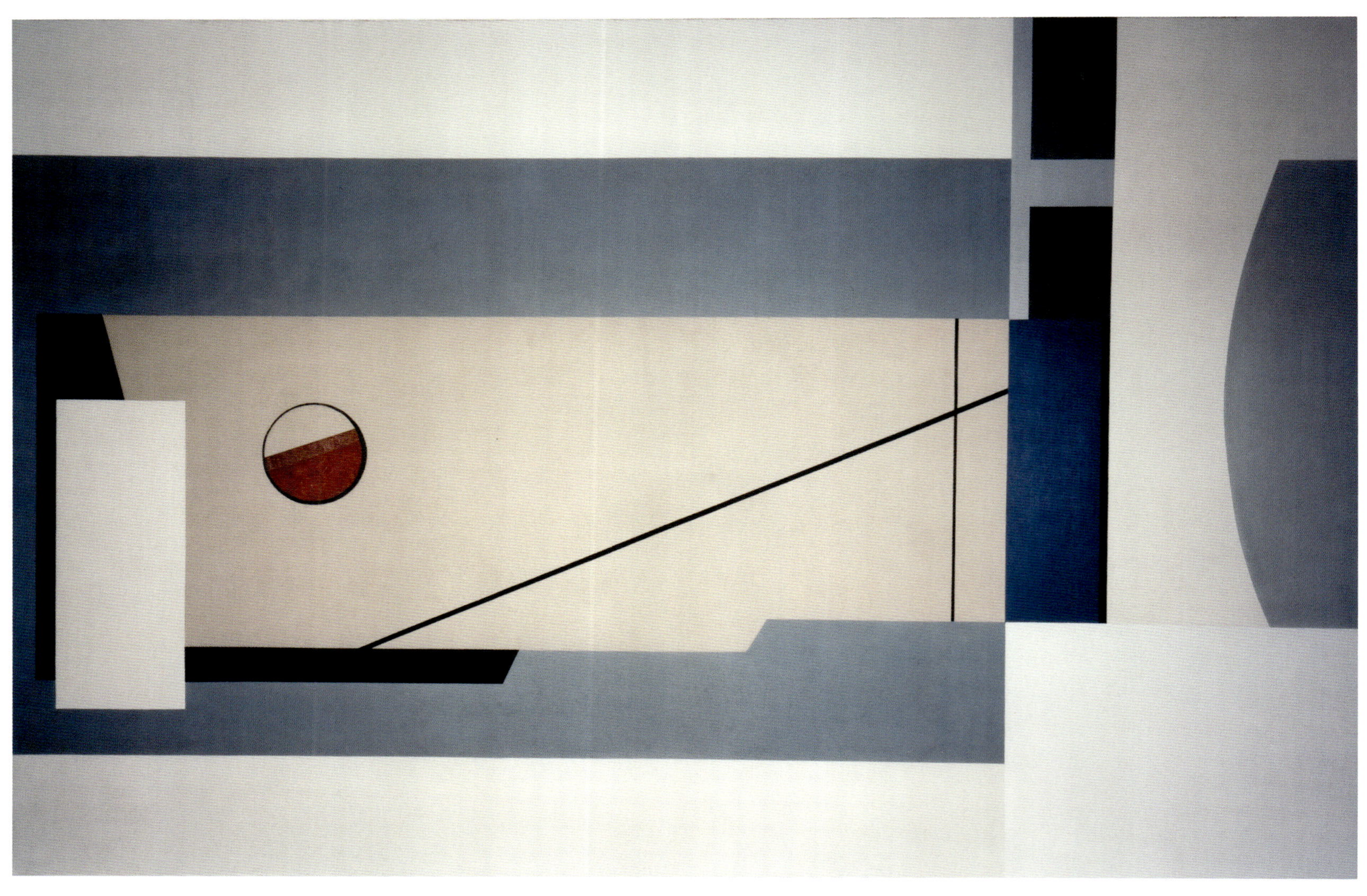

Balcomb Greene, *Untitled, From the Williamsburg Housing Project Murals,* ca. 1938
Oil on canvas, 91½ × 129¼ in. (232.4 × 328.3 cm). The Brooklyn Museum. On loan from the New York City Housing Authority, L1990.1.4.

Paul Kelpe

(born Minden, Germany, 1902; died Austin, TX, 1985)

Paul Kelpe grew up in Hanover, Germany, where he was introduced to the avant-garde work of Kurt Schwitters, Wassily Kandinsky, and the Russian constructivists through the collections of the city's Provinzialmuseum. After immigrating to the United States in 1925, Kelpe settled in Chicago. In 1935, he attempted to join that city's branch of the FAP, but its administrators preferred traditional styles and rejected his abstract sketches. Seeking an environment more receptive to his artistic interests, Kelpe moved to New York, where he found employment with the FAP's Mural Division from 1936 to 1939. Kelpe was also a founding member of the American Abstract Artists.

Originally, Kelpe's Williamsburg murals were to be installed alongside Davis's mural in one of the housing project's social rooms.[1] Possibly because of aesthetic disagreements between the artists, this plan was abandoned.[2] Kelpe ultimately completed two murals, which were both installed in the housing project in 1938 (and are now at the Brooklyn Museum). An early study reveals that his aesthetic ideas evolved dramatically during the mural project. Kelpe's Williamsburg murals are characterized by a tension between two- and three-dimensional space and a vivid palette of complementary colors.

1. A scale model showing murals by Kelpe and Davis in the Williamsburg Houses was included in MoMA's 1936 exhibition *New Horizons in American Art.*

2. Citing correspondence between Kelpe and the collector Katherine Dreier, Jody Patterson notes that "although [Kelpe] was initially assigned to collaborate with Davis on a joint mural, conflicts immediately arose and individual commissions were arranged" (*"Modernism for the Masses,"* 210).

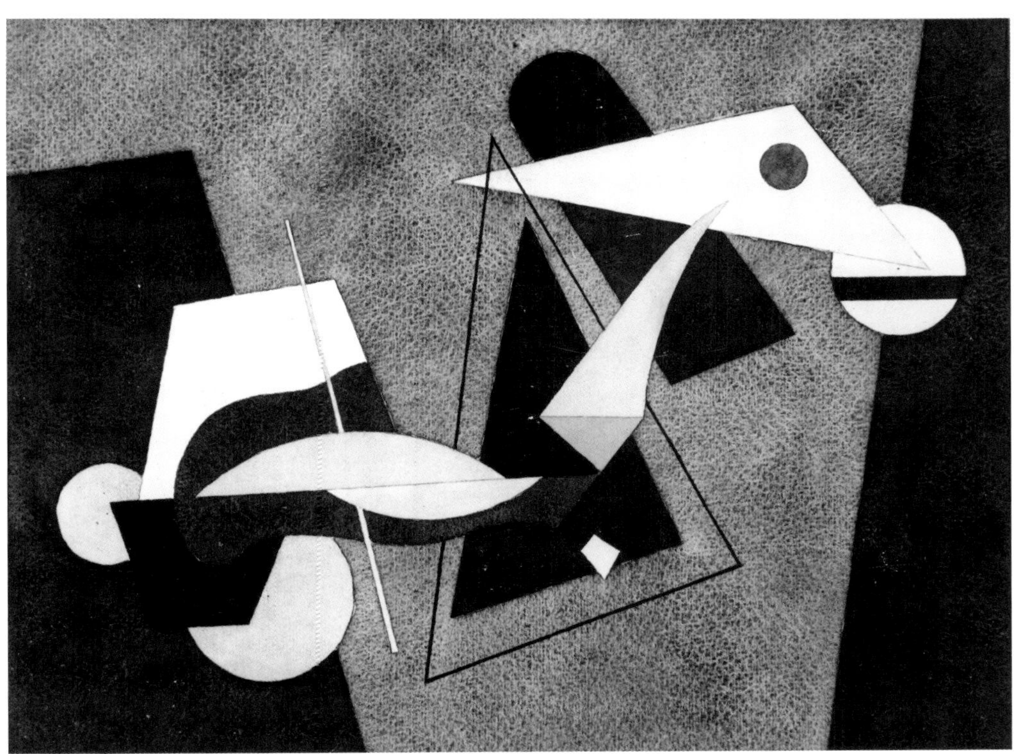

Paul Kelpe, *Study for Williamsburg Housing Project, Social Room Block 3,* 1936
Gouache, dimensions unknown.
Current location unknown (presumed lost).

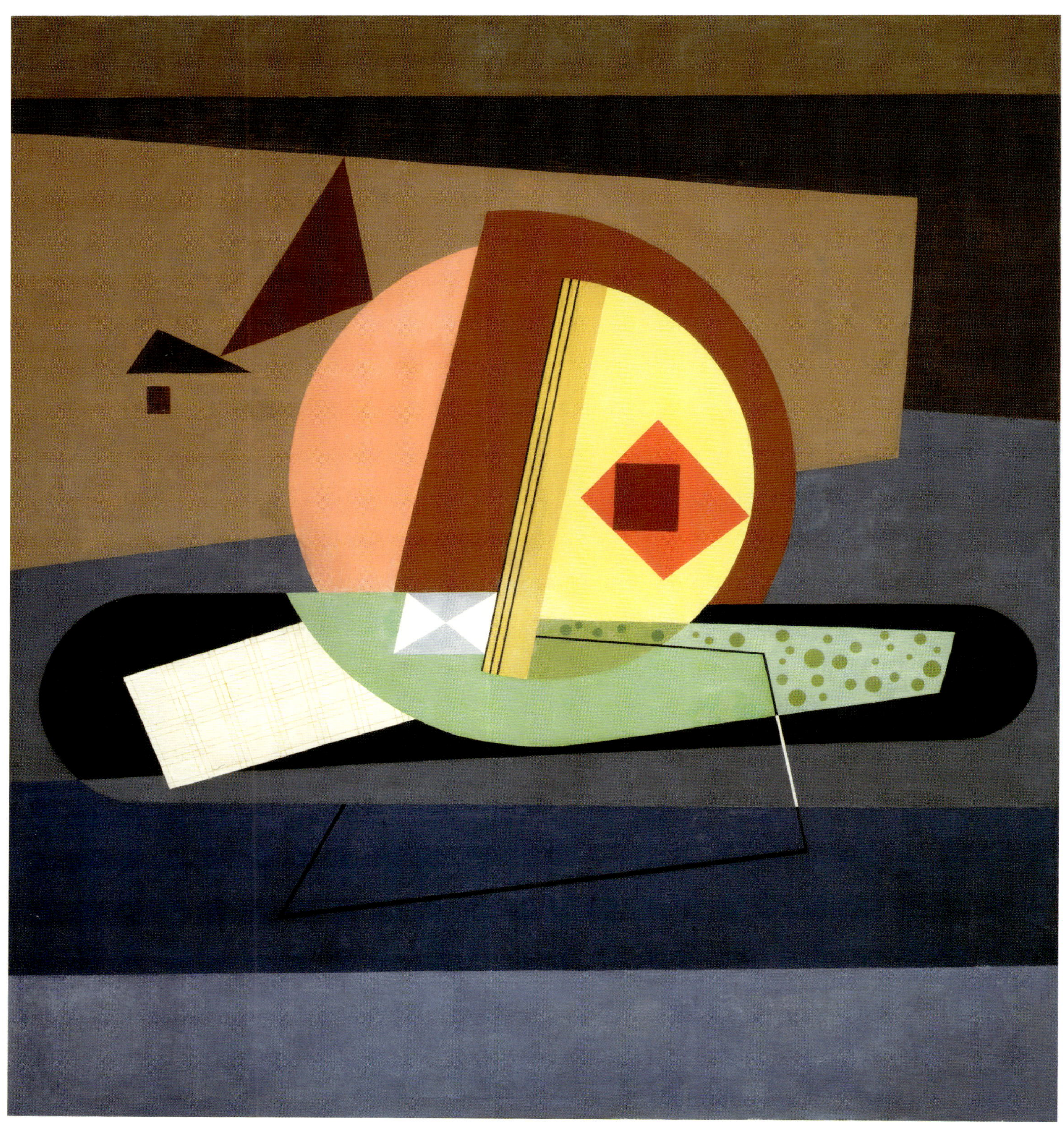

Paul Kelpe, *Untitled (left panel of a pair), from the Williamsburg Housing Project Murals,* ca. 1938
Oil on canvas, 98¼ × 89½ in. (249.6 × 227.3 cm). The Brooklyn Museum. On loan from the New York City Housing Authority, L1990.1.2.

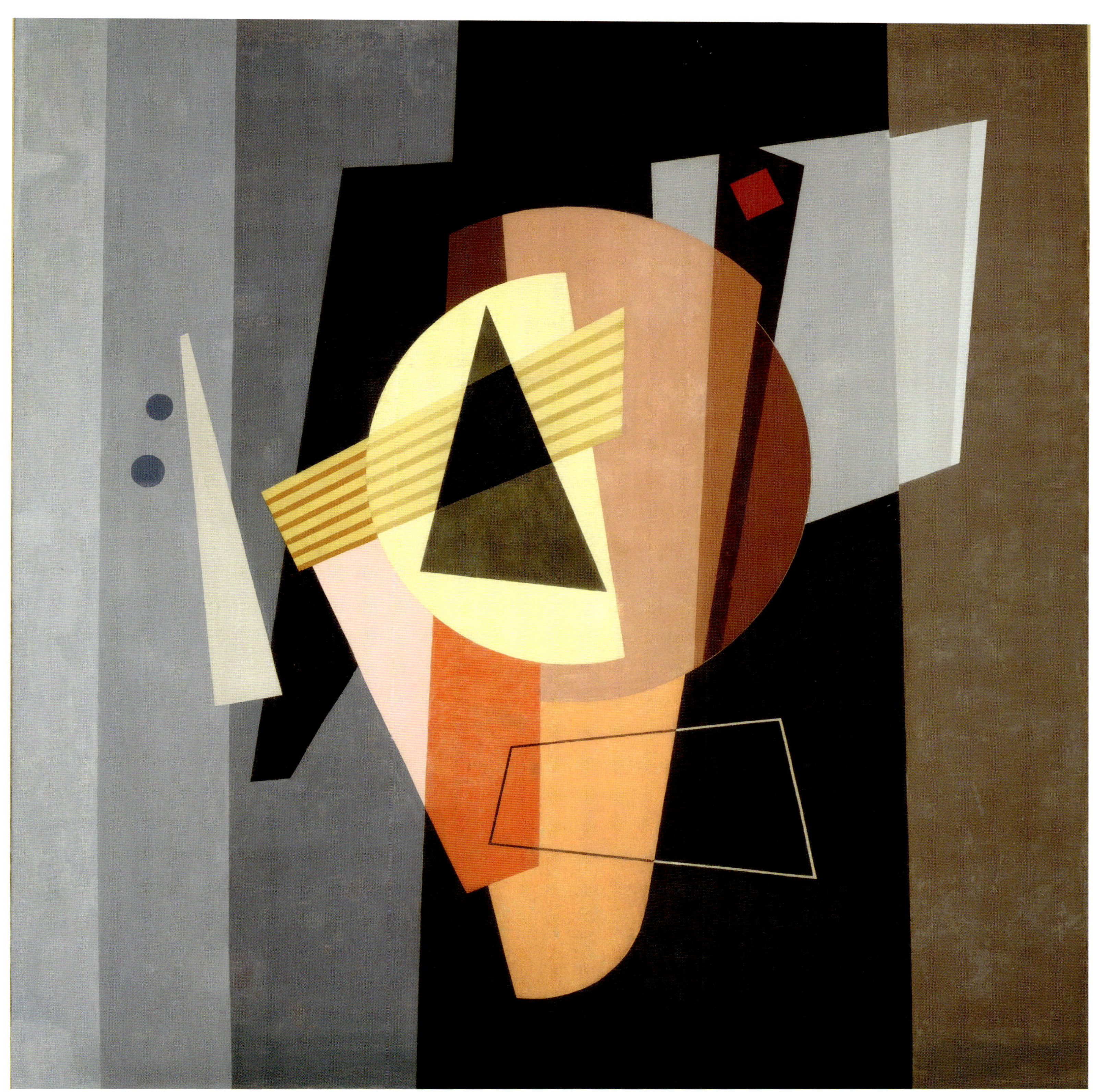

Paul Kelpe, *Untitled (right panel of a pair), from the Williamsburg Housing Project Murals,* ca. 1938
Oil on canvas, 98¾ × 96 in. (250.8 × 243.8 cm). The Brooklyn Museum. On loan from the New York City Housing Authority, L1990.1.3.

Willem de Kooning

(born Rotterdam, The Netherlands, 1904; died East Hampton, NY, 1997)

Best known for his postwar abstract expressionist paintings, Willem de Kooning arrived in the United State in 1926 to pursue a career as an illustrator. In 1930s New York, he became part of a circle of modernist artists that included Stuart Davis, John Graham, Arshile Gorky, and Jackson Pollock. In 1936, he worked with Fernand Léger on murals for the French Line Shipping Company's terminal in Manhattan, and in 1939, he received a commission to design a ninety-foot mural for the exterior of the Hall of Pharmacy at the New York World's Fair.[1] In 1935 he joined the FAP, enrolling first in the Easel Painting Division and then moving to the Mural Division. However, in mid-1937 he was dismissed from the WPA because of his citizenship status. Lacking immigration papers, he did not become an American citizen until 1961.

At the time of his dismissal from the FAP, de Kooning had completed at least three, and possibly four, studies for a Williamsburg mural; they are among his first experiments with abstracted biomorphic forms.[2] Burgoyne Diller may have assigned Lee Krasner to finish de Kooning's mural, but it was never completed.[3]

1. Elderfield, *De Kooning*, 71.

2. Elderfield, *De Kooning*, 69–70.

3. Landau, *Lee Krasner*, 64.

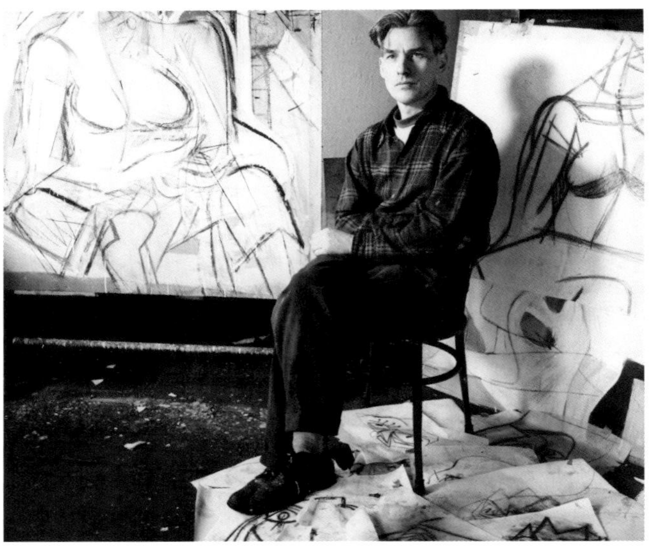

Willem de Kooning, April 1946. Photo: Harry Bowden.

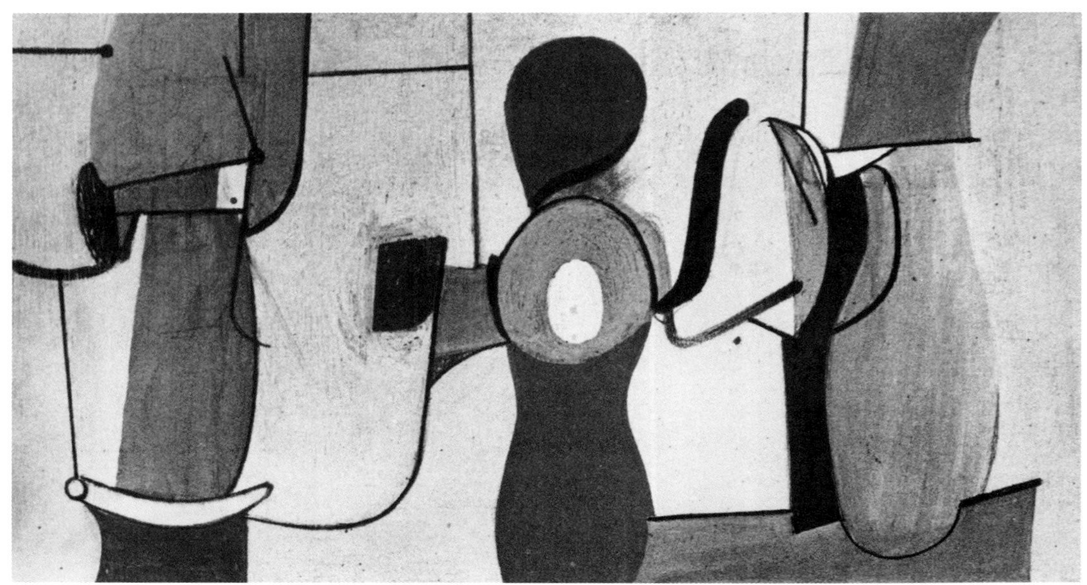

Willem de Kooning, *Study for Williamsburg Housing Project*, ca. 1936
Medium and dimensions unknown. Current location unknown (presumed lost). This study is reproduced in Thomas B. Hess's 1959 monograph on Willem de Kooning and in John Elderfield's 2011 retrospective catalogue; both identify it as a Williamsburg mural study.

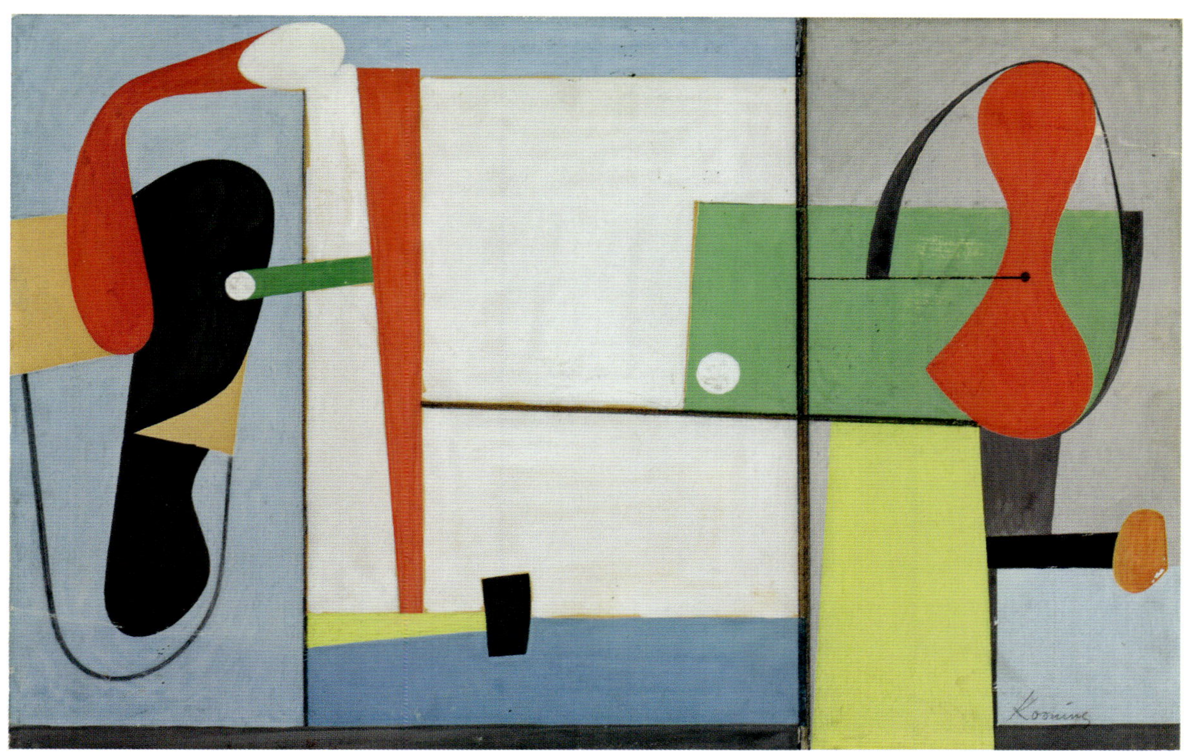

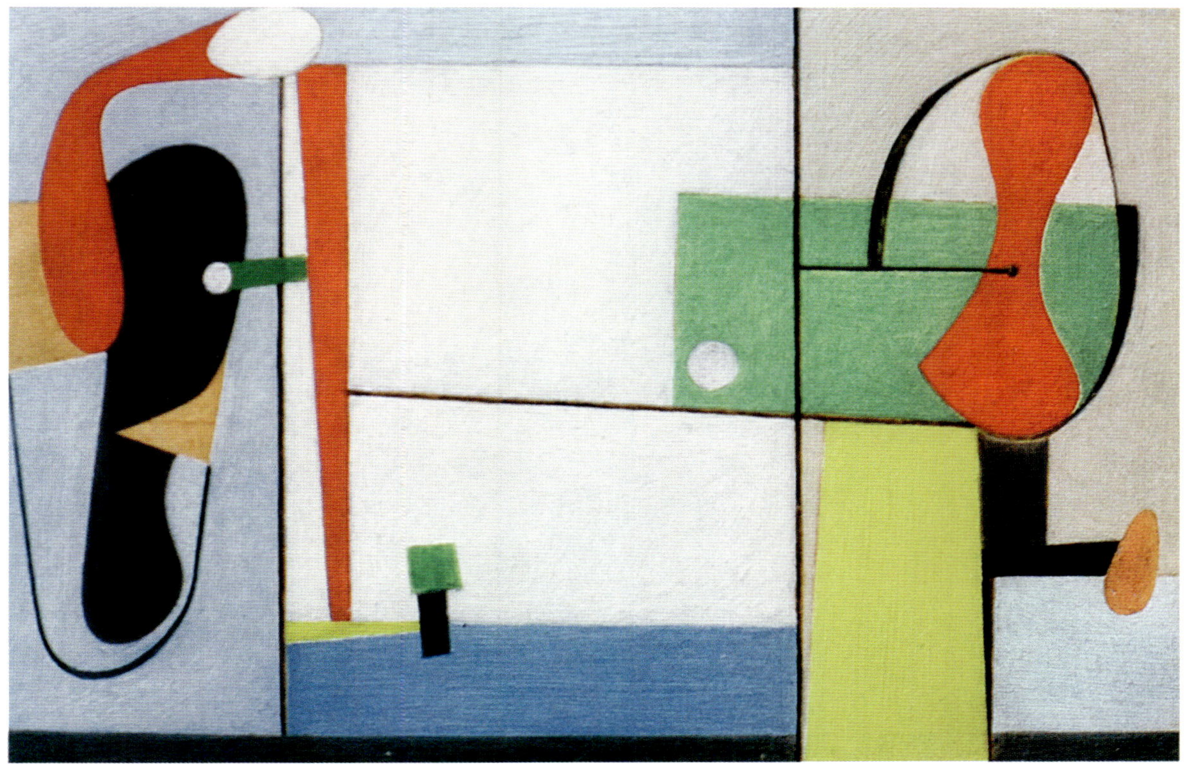

Willem de Kooning, *Study for the Williamsburg Project,* ca. 1936
Gouache and graphite on cardboard, $9\frac{5}{16} \times 14\frac{3}{8}$ in. (23.7×36.5 cm). Iris & B. Gerald Cantor Center for Visual Arts at Stanford University; Bequest of Dr. and Mrs. Harold C. Torbert, 1984.510.

Willem de Kooning, *Study for the Williamsburg Project,* ca. 1936
Medium and dimensions unknown. Current location unknown (presumed lost).

Jan Matulka

(born Vlachovo Březí, Bohemia [now Czech Republic], 1890; died New York, NY, 1972)

Jan Matulka studied art in Prague as a teenager before immigrating to the United States with his family at the age of seventeen. He received more training in traditional artistic techniques at the National Academy of Design in New York but also pursued his interests in modernism during frequent trips to Europe—especially to Paris, where he maintained a studio—in the 1920s and early 1930s. During this time, he also began teaching at the Art Students League in New York. Among his students were artists with whom he would work on the Williamsburg project, including Burgoyne Diller, George McNeil, and Francis Criss. Matulka was also friendly with Stuart Davis, and some of his work reveals Davis's influence. Like Davis, he spent several summers in Gloucester, Massachusetts, and he rented his Paris studio to Davis, who traveled to France in 1928–29. Matulka was involved in leftist politics and artistic activism during the 1930s, contributing drawings to leftist periodicals such as the *New Masses* and the Czech-language *Dělnick Kalendar*. In 1934 he joined the PWAP, and in 1935 he enrolled in the FAP's Mural Division. Matulka's career declined after the mid-1930s, partly because he never managed to establish a fruitful connection with an art dealer.[1]

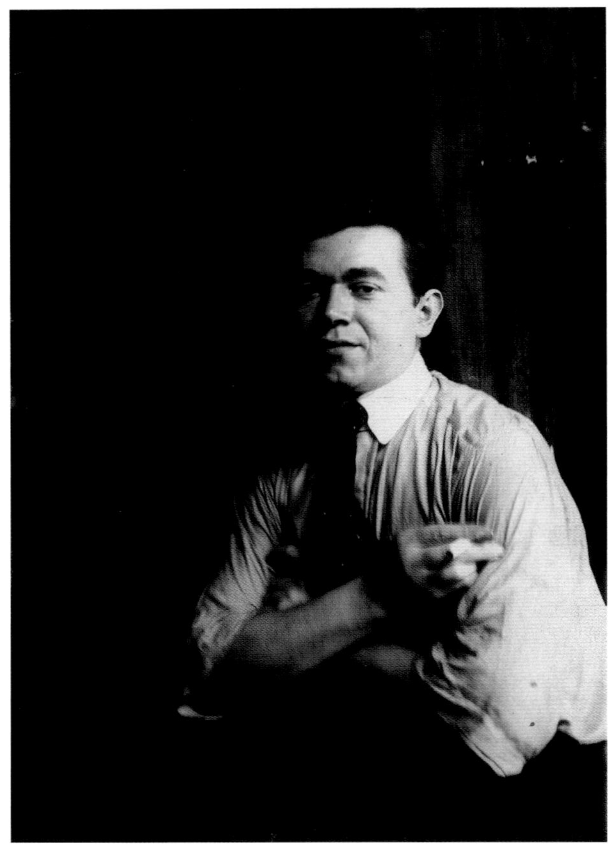

Jan Matulka, undated.

Matulka produced at least one study for a Williamsburg mural, known today only through a photograph located in the papers of William Lescaze. The design has a surrealist quality, featuring quasi-representational forms situated in an indeterminate perspectival space. Although he often painted abstract compositions, Matulka was less committed to abstraction than many of his fellow Williamsburg artists. He never joined the American Abstract Artists and continued to paint in a representational, even traditional, style, sometimes incorporating themes from Czech folklore, throughout his career.

1. For biographical information about Matulka, one of the least known of the Williamsburg artists, see Rugg, *Jan Matulka;* and Adams, *Jan Matulka.*

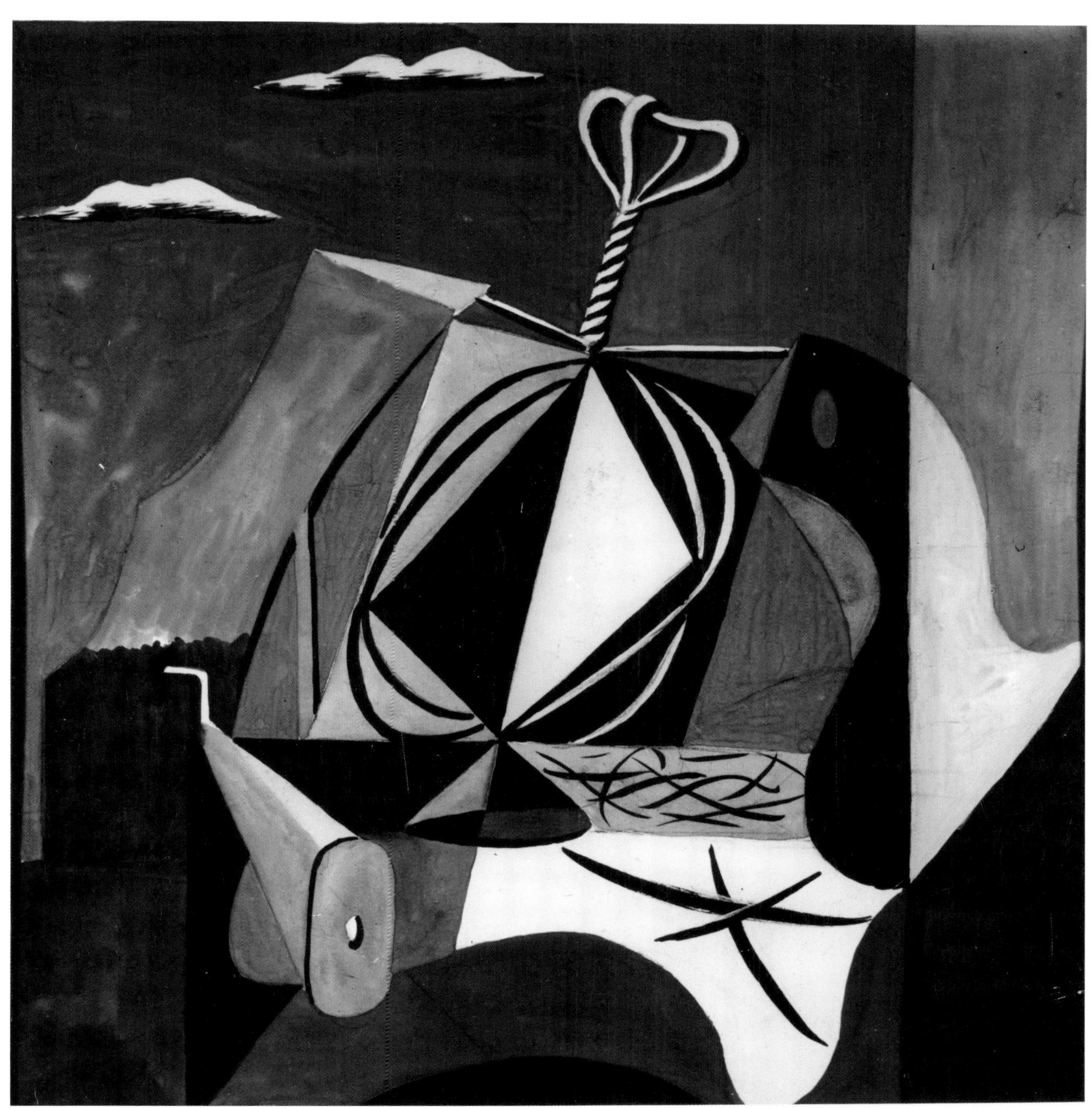

Jan Matulka, *Study for Williamsburg Mural,* 1936
Medium and dimensions unknown. Current location unknown (presumed lost).

George McNeil

(born New York, NY, 1908; died New York, NY, 1995)

George McNeil began his artistic studies at the Pratt Institute in Brooklyn before enrolling in classes at the Art Students League, where he studied with Jan Matulka and Hans Hofmann. Hofmann's mentorship was particularly important, leading McNeil to transition from a cubist-influenced style to a more painterly, expressive one, though he ultimately sought to reconcile both approaches in his work. He described his artistic approach in the 1930s as "a dialogue, not a conflict, between art freedom and control, between an intuitive, painterly evocation of images, and the thoughtful ordering of pictorial elements into abstract form."[1] McNeil joined the FAP in 1935 and was a founding member of the American Abstract Artists.

McNeil produced numerous studies—most reflecting a loose, biomorphic aesthetic but at least one conforming more closely to the hard-edge geometry preferred by Burgoyne Diller—for the Williamsburg project. McNeil's estate possesses a photograph of a complete (or nearly complete) mural believed to be his Williamsburg mural. However, the mural was never installed and has since been lost. In an oral history interview conducted by the Archives of American Art in 1968, McNeil described his working method and the scale of the now-lost mural (note that the estate's documentation suggests that the mural was approximately six by eighteen feet in size).[2]

> *I did this thing for the Williamsburg Housing Project on the WPA when I was on the Mural Project. It was never used. The canvas disappeared. But I tried to work the thing out logically. I made hundreds and hundreds of sketches and prior things. And I worked in a Neo-plastic manner. But then finally I had to make what amounted to a big easel painting, you know. I worked on a big painting, maybe two years. I don't know how big the painting was but it was maybe ten feel by twenty feet.*[3]

1. Quoted in McNeil artist biography, Smithsonian American Art Museum: https://americanart.si.edu/artist/george-mcneil-3243.

2. Memorandum from Helen McNeil-Ashton, August 20, 2019.

3. Oral history interview with George McNeil, January 9–May 21, 1968, Archives of American Art.

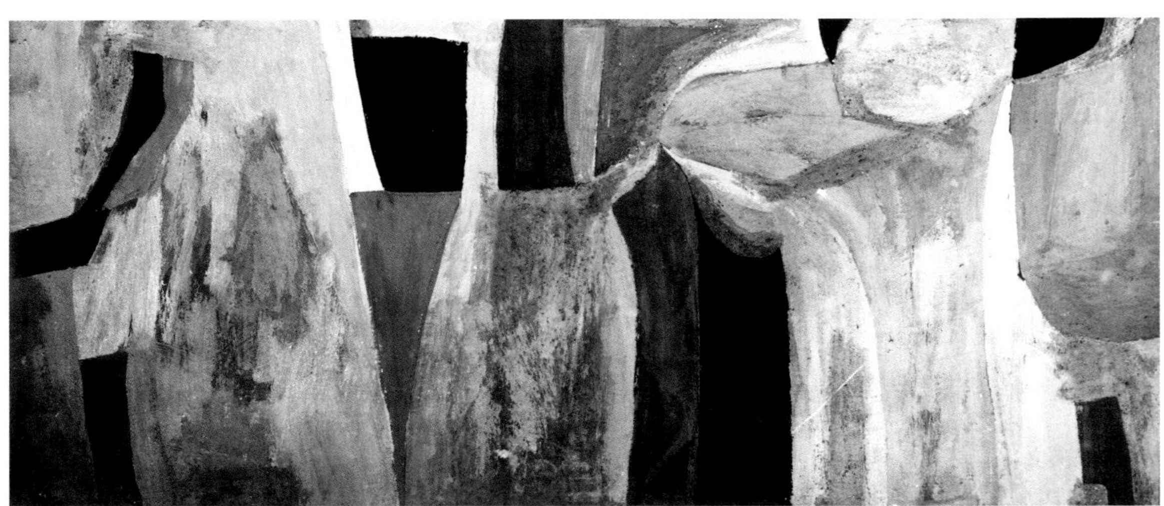

George McNeil, *Williamsburg Mural Study: Untitled IIIA*
Date, medium, and dimensions unknown. Current location unknown (presumed lost).

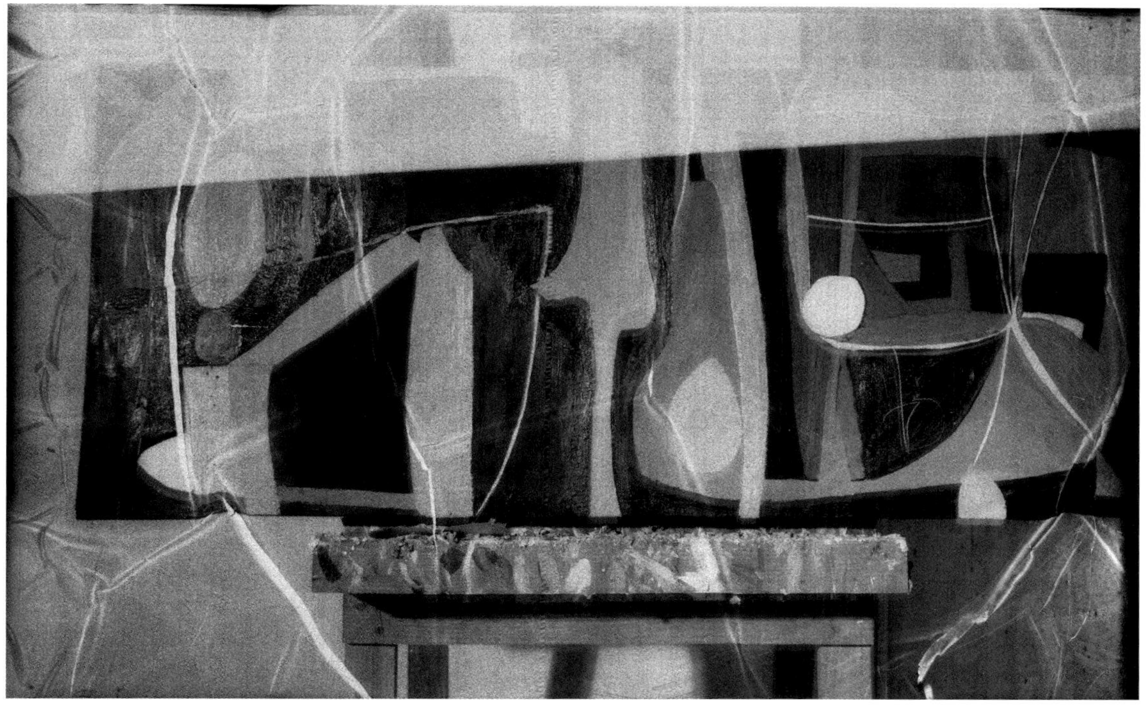

George McNeil,
Williamsburg Mural Study: Untitled IV
Date, medium, and dimensions unknown. Current location unknown (presumed lost).

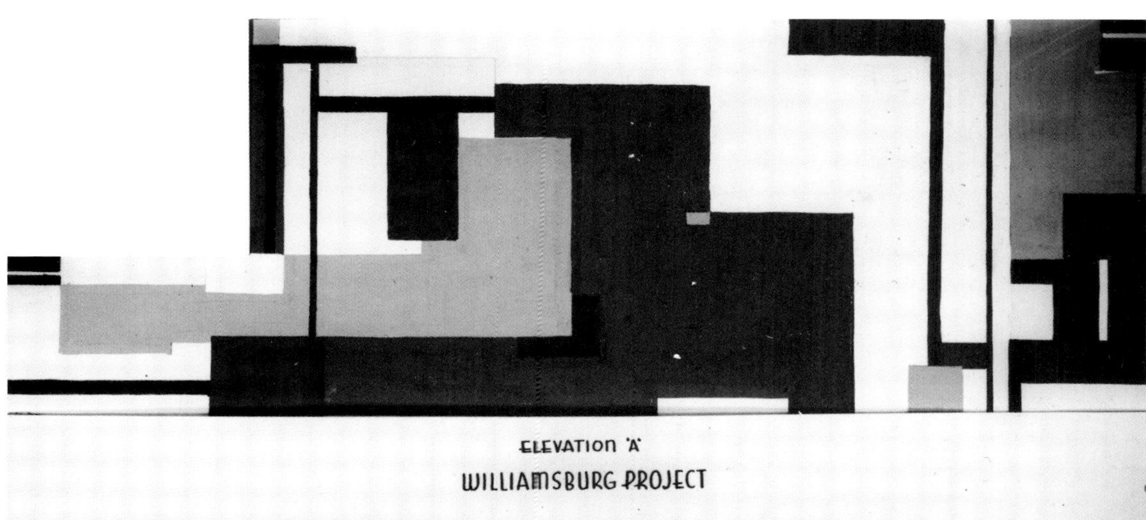

George McNeil, *Study for Williamsburg Project,* 1936–37
Medium and dimensions unknown. Current location unknown (presumed lost). Although this hard-edge, geometric composition appears quite different from McNeil's other identifiable Williamsburg mural studies, it reflects Burgoyne Diller's neoplastic preferences, cited by McNeil in his 1968 interview.

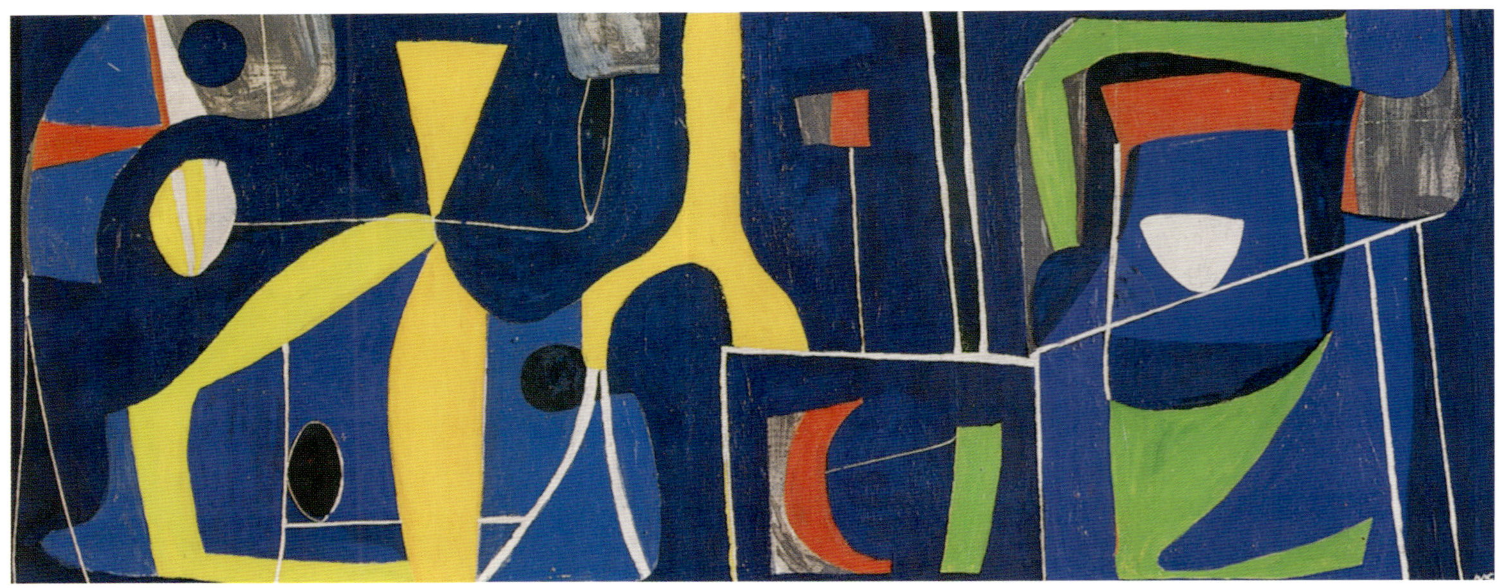

George McNeil, *Williamsburg Mural Sketch: Sinuous Composition* (also known as *Williamsburg Mural Study: Black-Yellow-Orange*), 1937
Tempera on board, 10 × 23¾ in. (25.4 × 60.3 cm). Current location unknown. Sold by Sid Deutsch Art Gallery to an unknown buyer in 1979. In 1998 it was in the collection of J. Donald Nichols of Nashville (Knott, *American Abstract Art of the 1930s and 1940s*, 81).

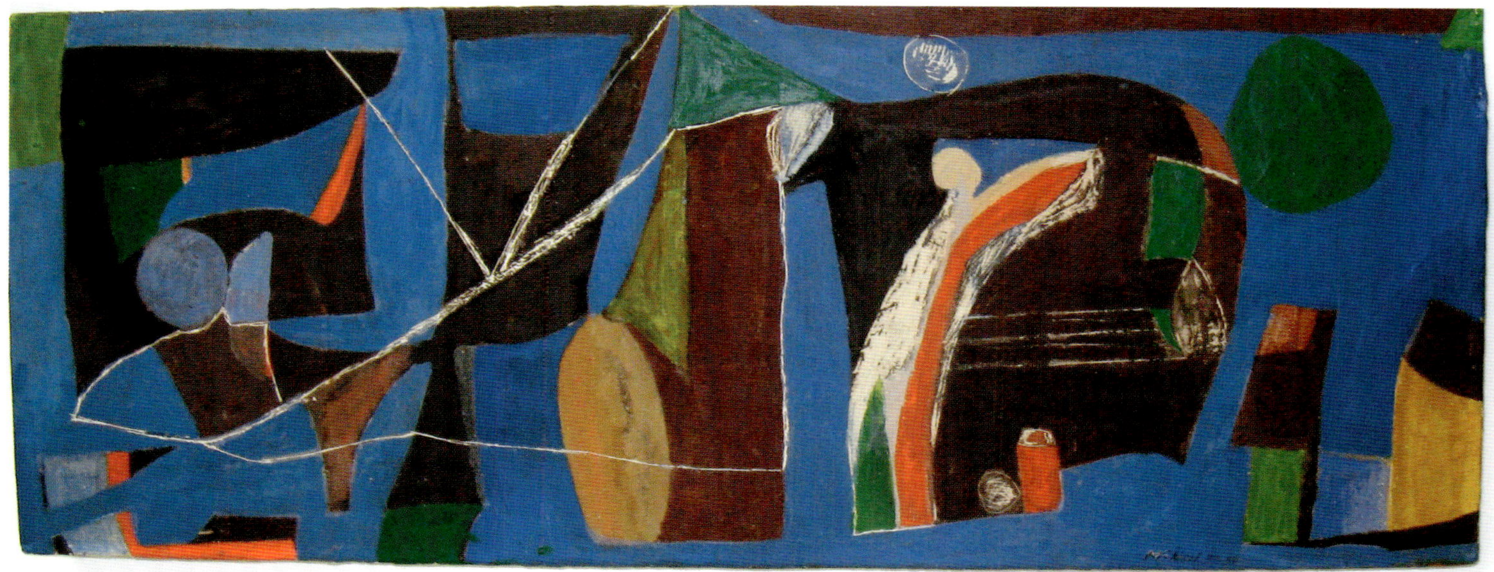

George McNeil, *Williamsburg Mural Study with Calligraphic Forms* (also known as *Williamsburg Mural Study with Calligraphic Shapes)*, 1937–38
Tempera on gesso board, 9½ × 24⅛ in. (24.1 × 61.3 cm). Estate of the Artist.

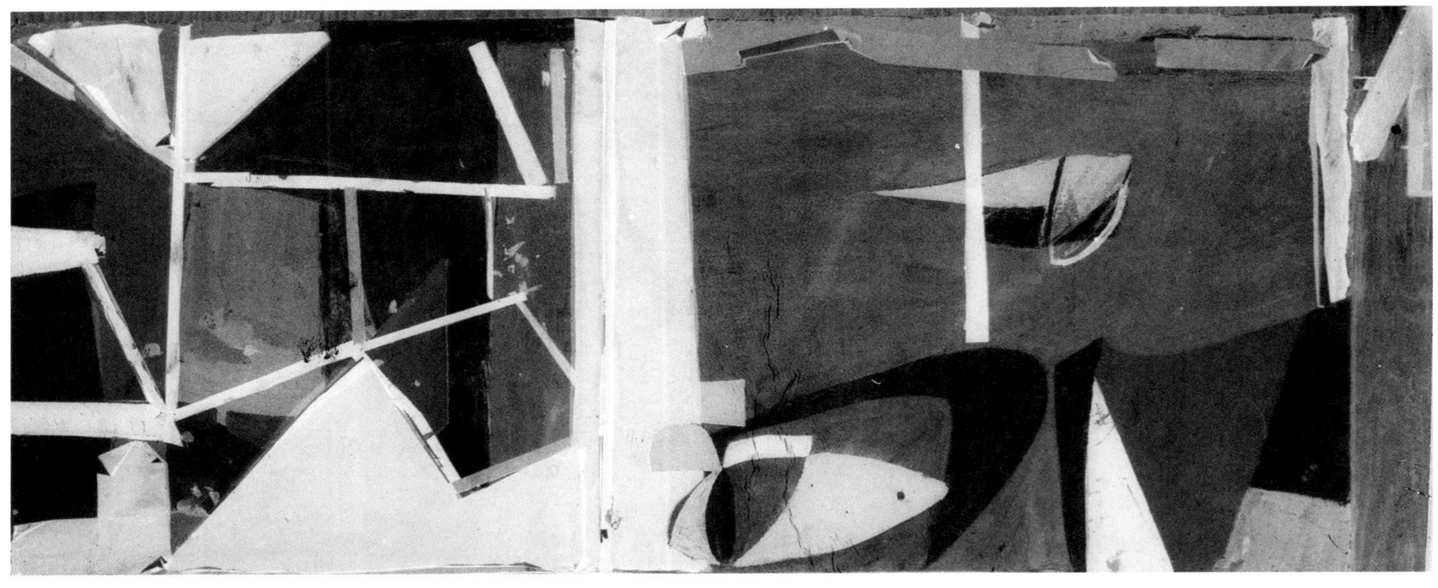

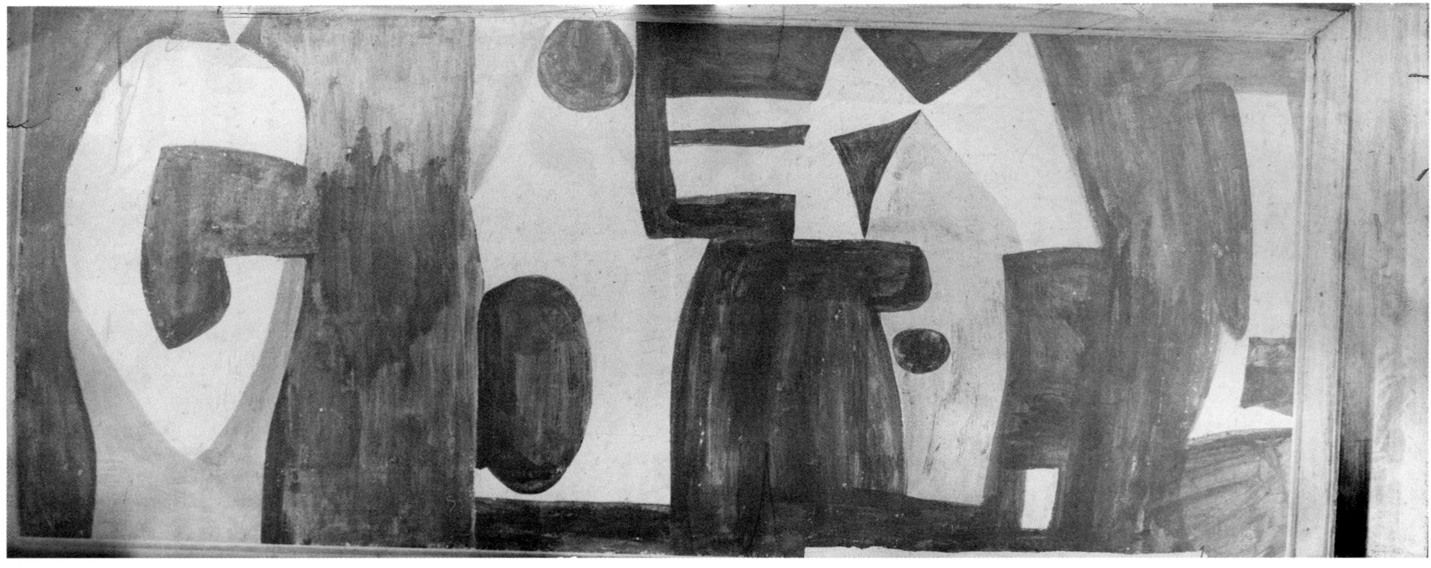

George McNeil, *Williamsburg Mural Study: Untitled I,* 1937–38
Medium and dimensions unknown. Current location unknown (presumed lost).

George McNeil, *Williamsburg Mural Sketch: Diamond Composition,* 1938
Tempera on board, 10 × 24 in. (25.4 × 61 cm). Current location unknown (presumed lost).

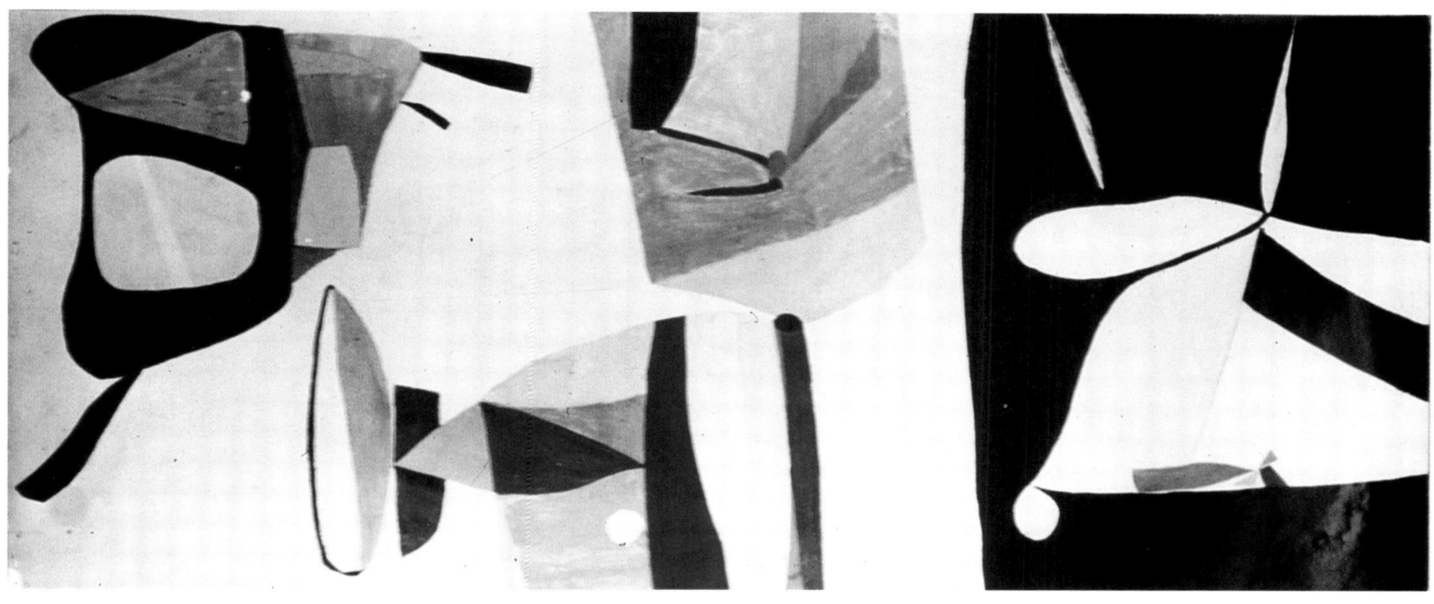

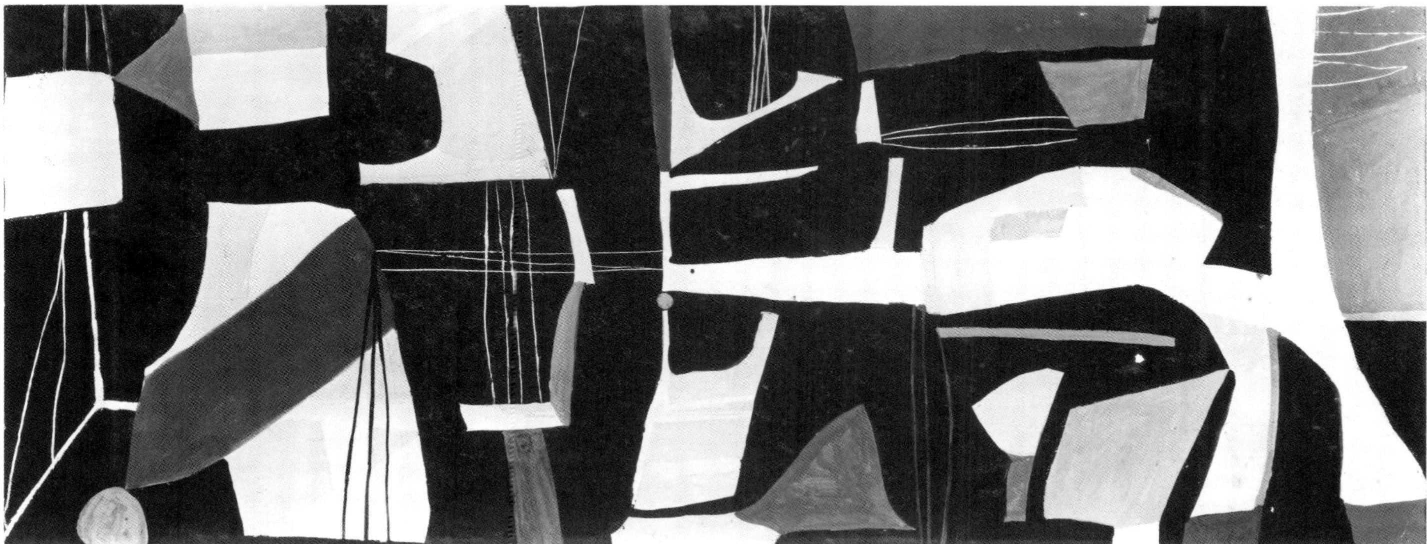

George McNeil, *Williamsburg Mural Study,* 1938
Casein on panel, 10 × 24 in. (25.4 × 61 cm). Current location unknown (presumed lost). In August 2019, Helen McNeil-Ashton, the artist's daughter, alerted the Eskenazi Museum of Art that the work had been sold through Olympia Galleries to a private collector in Atlanta in 1982.

George McNeil, *Williamsburg Mural Study: Composition in Black with Moving Forms,* 1938 (partially reworked by the artist in 1979)
Tempera on gesso board, 9½ × 23¾ in. (24.1 × 60.3 cm). Current location unknown. Sold through ACA Galleries to a private collector in San Francisco around 2000.

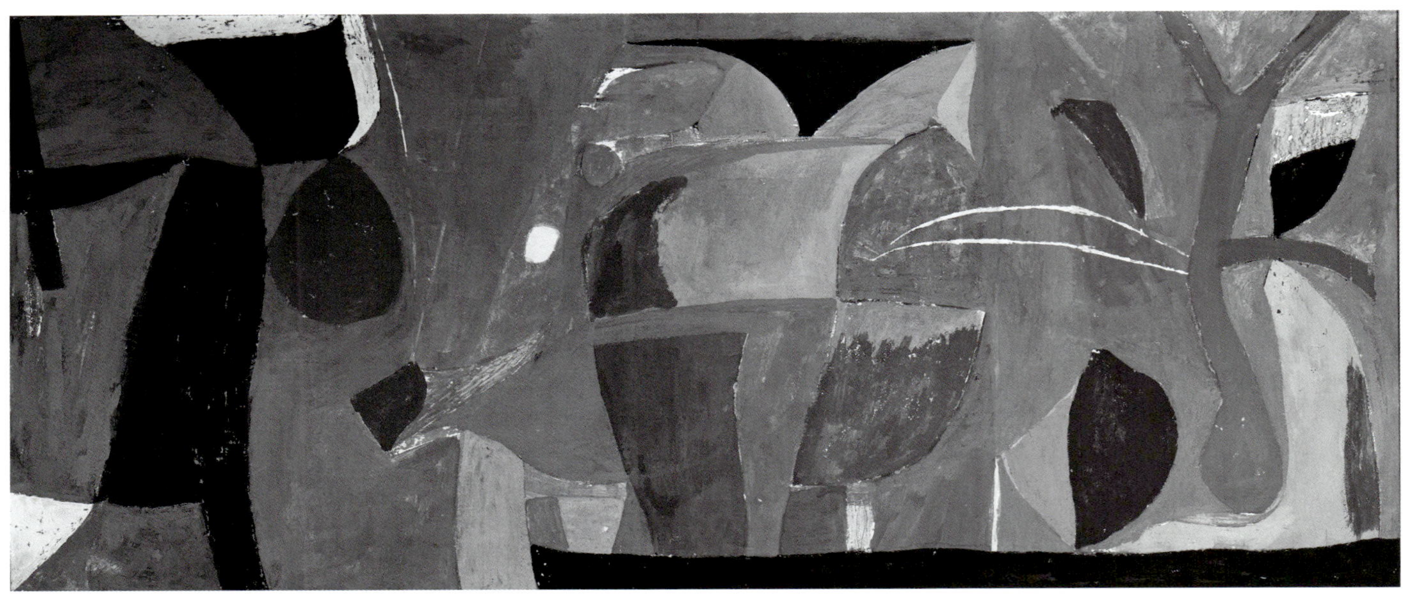

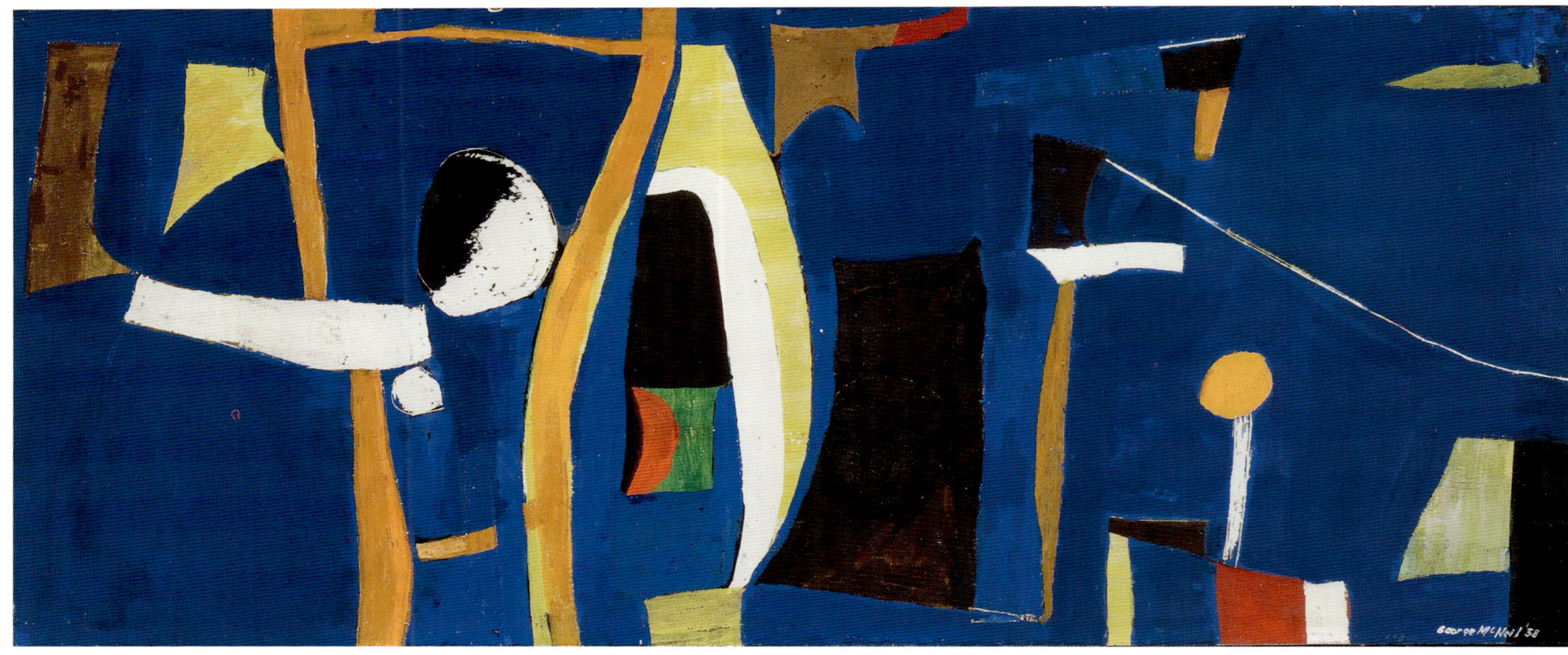

George McNeil, *Williamsburg Mural Study: Action Composition,* 1938
Medium unknown, 10 × 24 in. (25.4 × 61 cm). Current location unknown (presumed lost).

George McNeil, *Study for Williamsburg Mural,* 1938
Oil on board, 13 × 31¼ in. (33 × 79.4 cm). High Museum of Art, Atlanta, Gift of Jennifer and Terry Weiss in honor of Judy and Washington Falk, III, 2006.114.

This work had been incorrectly identified as a mural study for a project in Williamsport, Pennsylvania. In August 2019, Helen McNeil-Ashton, the artist's daughter, alerted the High Museum that it is a Williamsburg mural study.

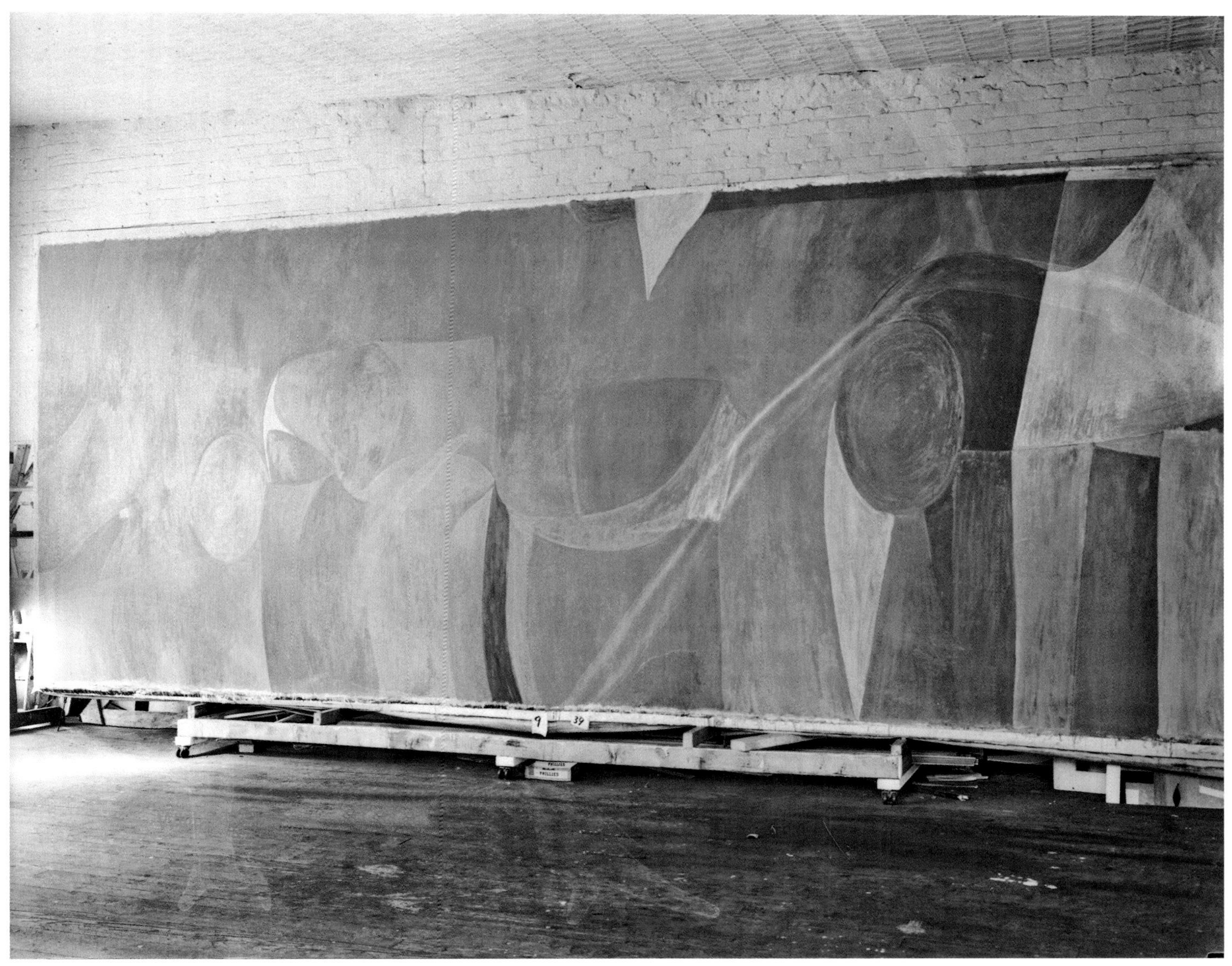

George McNeil, *Williamsburg Mural,* ca. 1938
Medium unknown, approx. 72 × 216 in. (182.9 × 548.6 cm). Current location unknown (presumed lost).

Eugene Morley

(born Scranton, PA, 1909; died New York, NY, 1953)

A printmaker and painter, Eugene Morley was very active in leftist political and artistic organizations during the 1930s. He contributed drawings to the *New Masses* and *Art Front* and was a member of the Artists Union. As an art instructor, he taught at the communist-affiliated John Reed Club School of Art and later at the American Artists School, which emphasized the social and didactic role of art.[1] In addition to his mural studies for the Williamsburg Housing Project, Morley produced a design for a porcelain enamel mural for a New York City subway station.[2] Although Morley's art generally aligned with the social realism preferred by most artists with Marxist or communist sympathies in the 1930s, his subway mural was strongly influenced by geometric abstraction.[3]

Because of his social realist inclinations, Morley's four mural studies differ considerably from the other Williamsburg artists' sketches and murals. Morley's portrayal of factory workers is also at odds with Burgoyne Diller's view that the Williamsburg tenants would find painted images of machines "neither interesting nor stimulating" after working for eight hours a day at factory jobs.[4] It is unsurprising, then, that none of Morley's sketches were included in MoMA's 1936 *New Horizons in American Art* exhibition, which featured studies by the other eleven muralists commissioned for the Williamsburg project.

1. Marquardt, "American Artists School," 21.

2. *Subway Art*, n.p.

3. Harrison, "Subway Art and the Public Use of Arts Committee," 65.

4. Berman, *Lost Years*, 142.

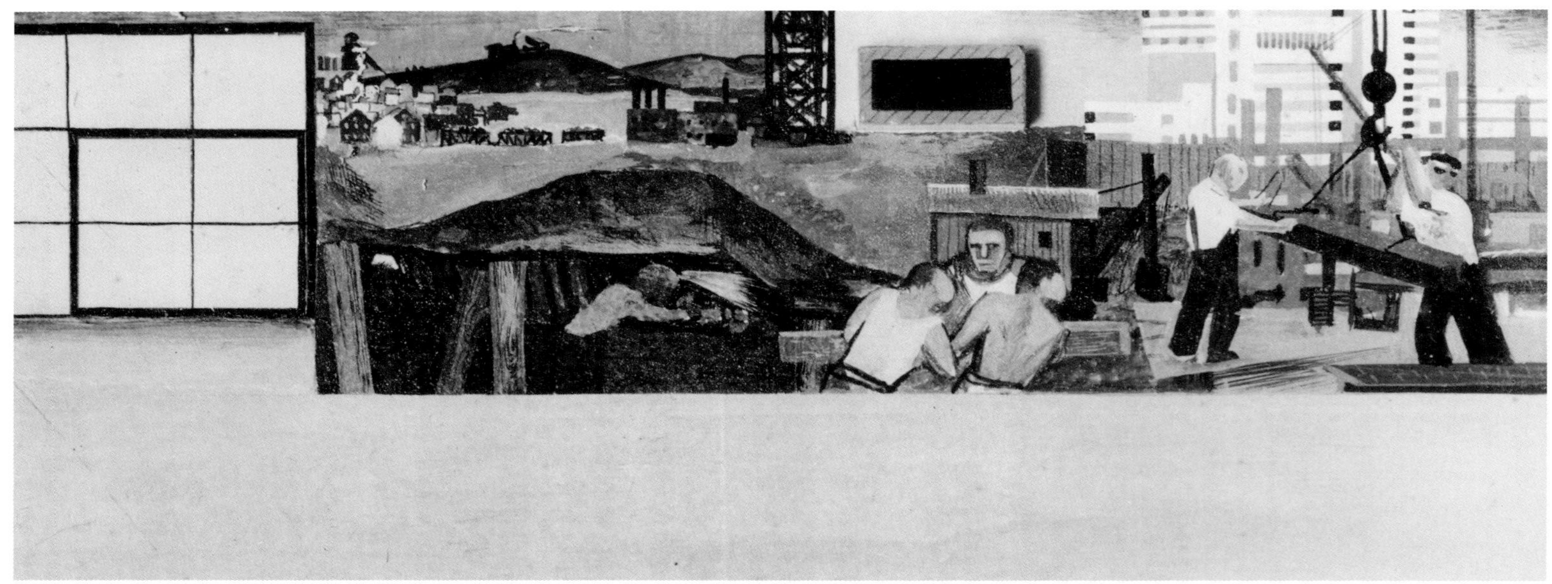

Eugene Morley, *Study for Williamsburg Project*, ca. 1936
Gouache, dimensions unknown.
Current location unknown
(presumed lost).

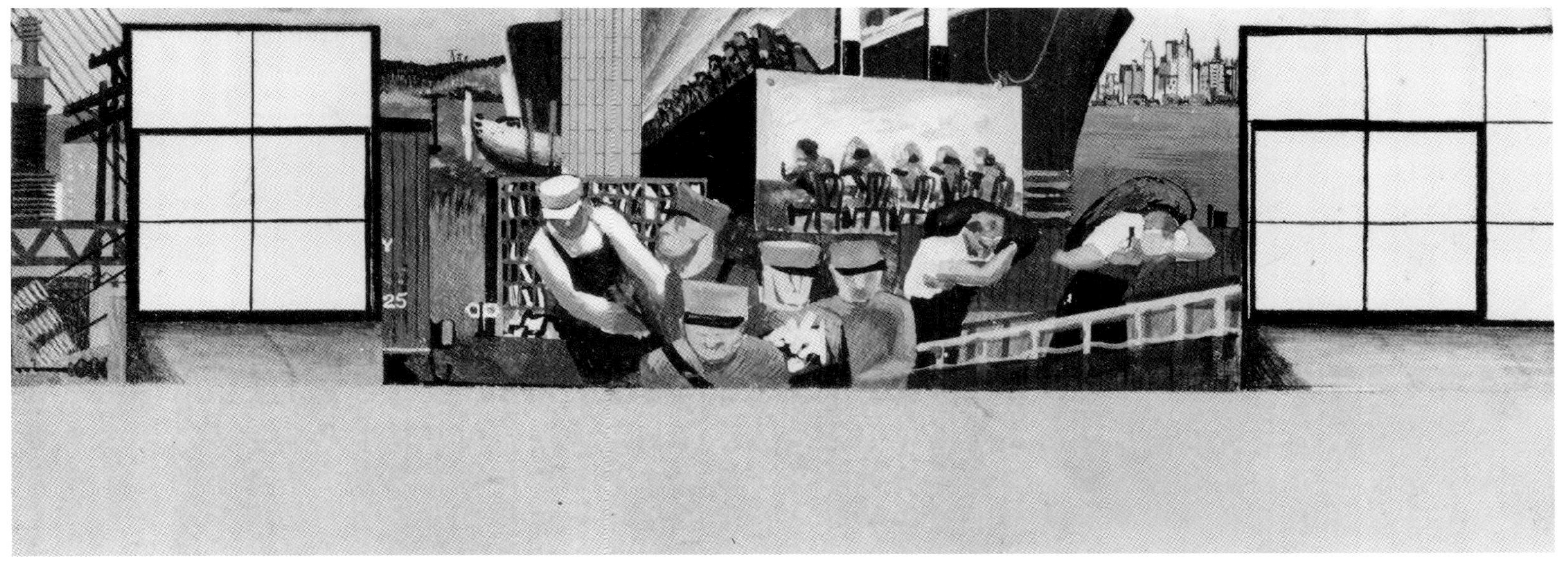

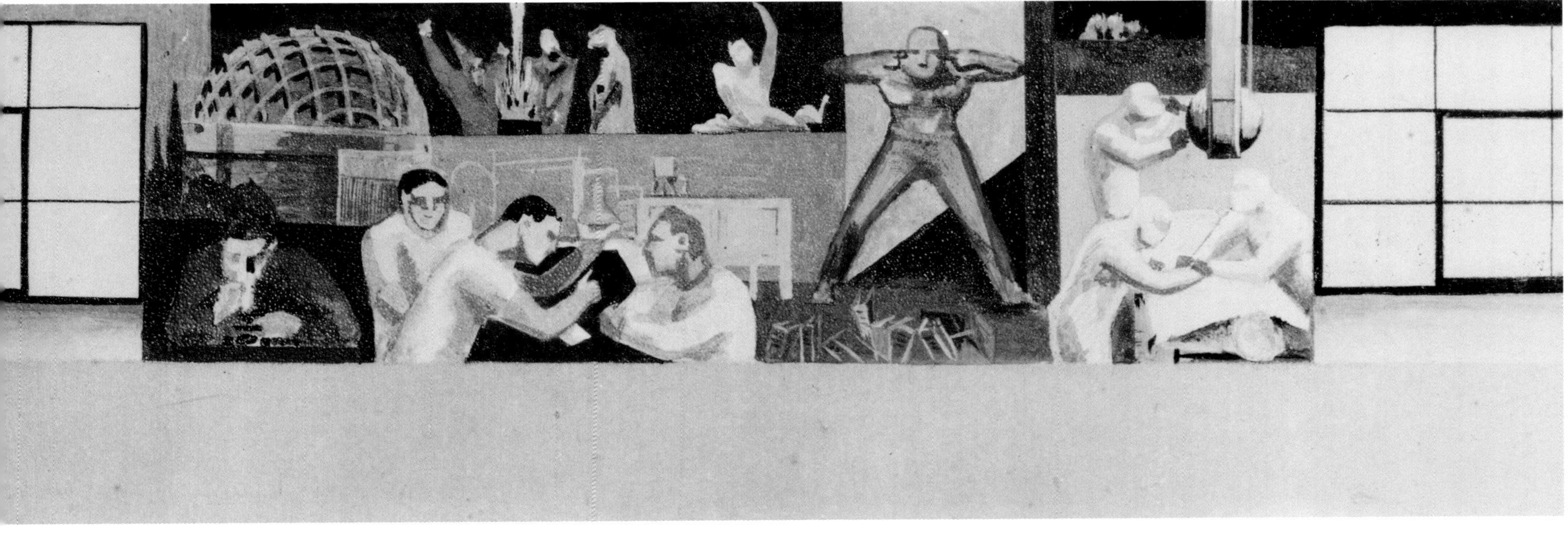

Eugene Morley, *Study for Williamsburg Project, Building 16, Block 4*, 1936
Gouache, dimensions unknown. Current location unknown (presumed lost).

Eugene Morley, *Study for Williamsburg Project, Building 16, Block 4*, 1936
Gouache, dimensions unknown. Current location unknown (presumed lost).

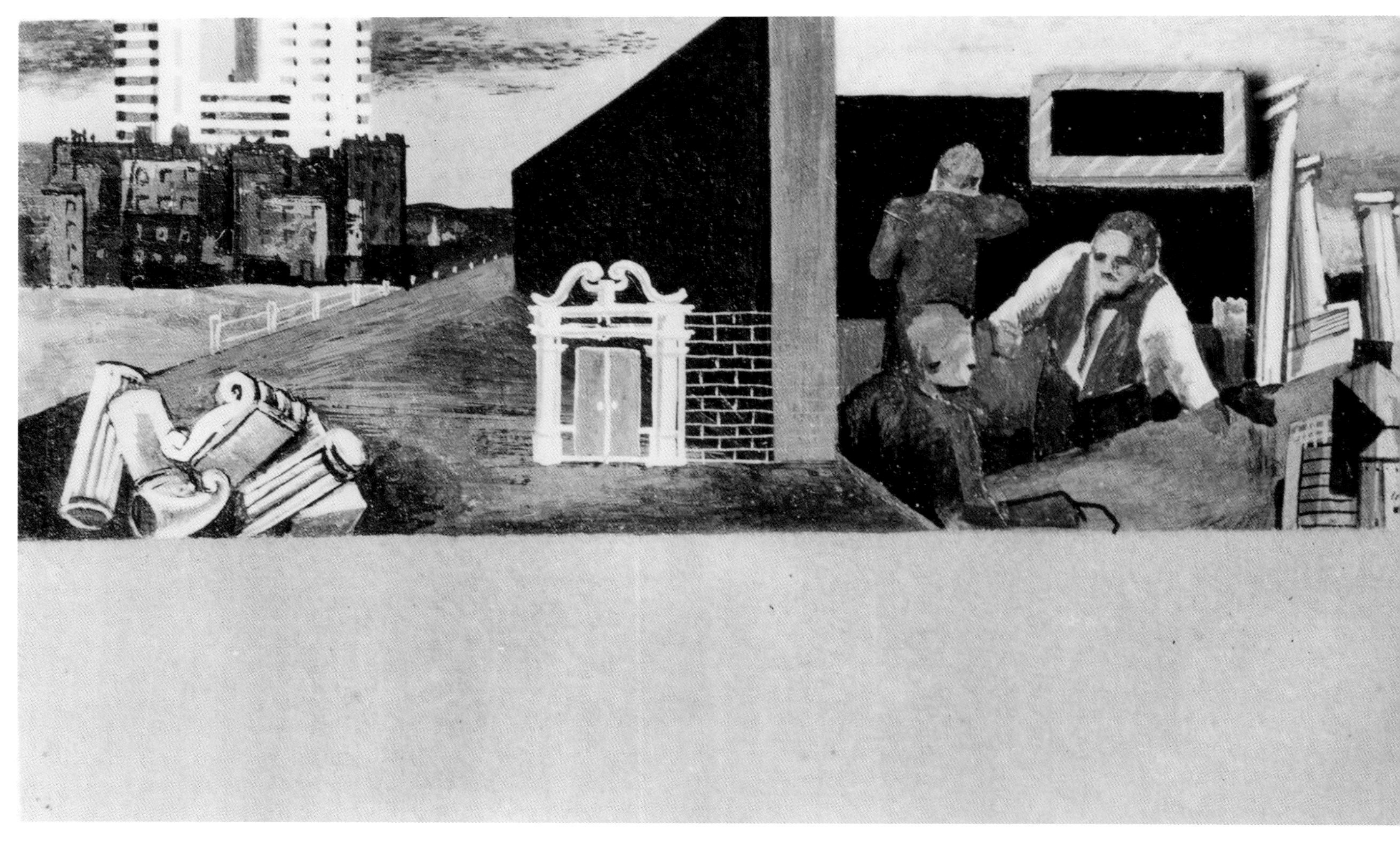

Eugene Morley, *Study for Williamsburg Project,* 1936
Gouache, dimensions unknown.
Current location unknown
(presumed lost).

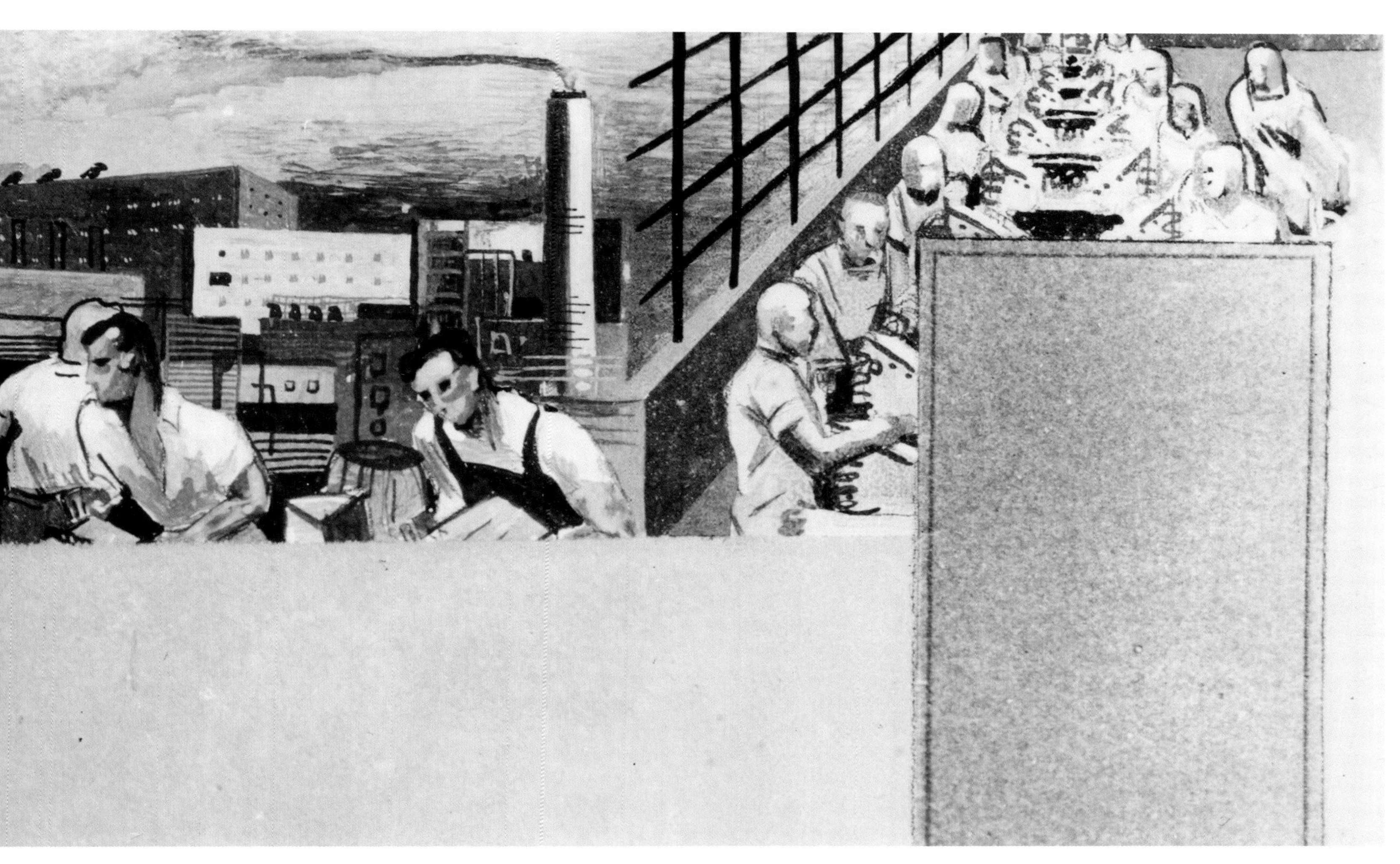

José Ruiz de Rivera

(born West Baton Rouge, LA, 1904; died New York, NY, 1985)

José Ruiz de Rivera began making sculptures in the early 1930s, later gaining national recognition for his work, which included commissions for the 1958 and 1964 World's Fairs in Brussels and New York, respectively. Though Rivera was known for curvilinear abstract metal sculptures, he experimented with other media and stylistic approaches in his early work, including *Composition* from 1936, thought to be a commission for the Williamsburg Housing Project. In her dissertation on FAP sculpture, Eleanor Carr states that Rivera carved a biomorphic abstract sculpture in white marble for the Williamsburg Houses.[1] A photograph of a sculpture matching Carr's description is housed in the FAP Photographic Division collection at the Archives of American Art. On the other hand, Rivera later recalled designing only one work for an FAP project—an aluminum sculpture for Newark Airport.[2] *Composition* is included in this compendium as a tentative Williamsburg-related work.

1. Carr, "New Deal and the Sculptor," 77.

2. Oral history interview with José Ruiz de Rivera, February 24, 1968, Archives of American Art: https://www.aaa.si.edu/collections/interviews/oral-history-interview-jos-de-rivera-12594#transcript.

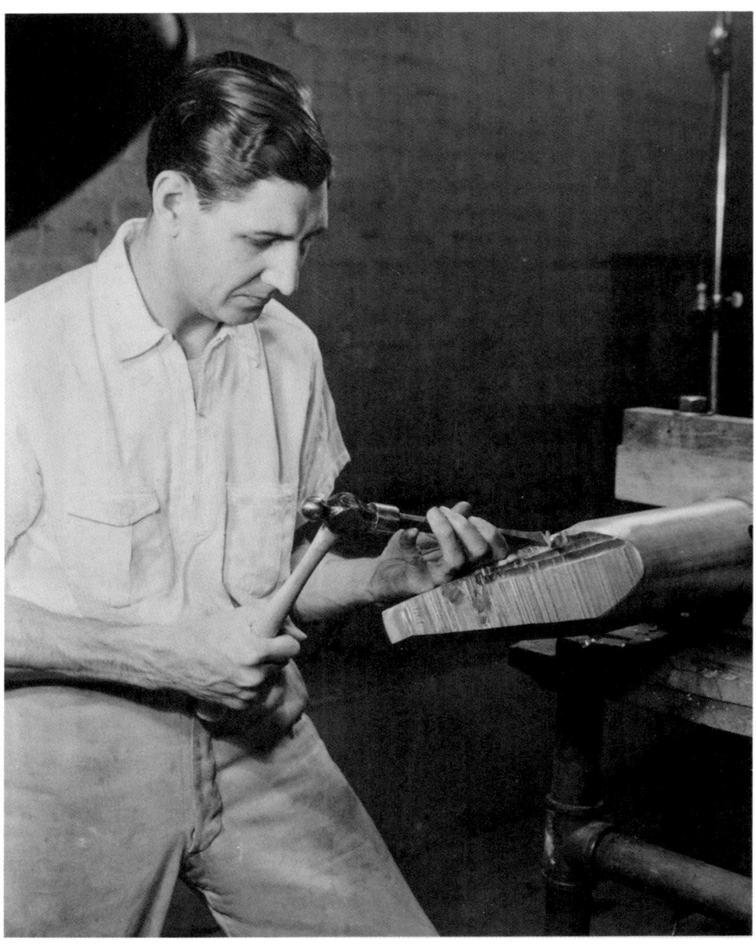

José Ruiz de Rivera at work, ca. 1937.

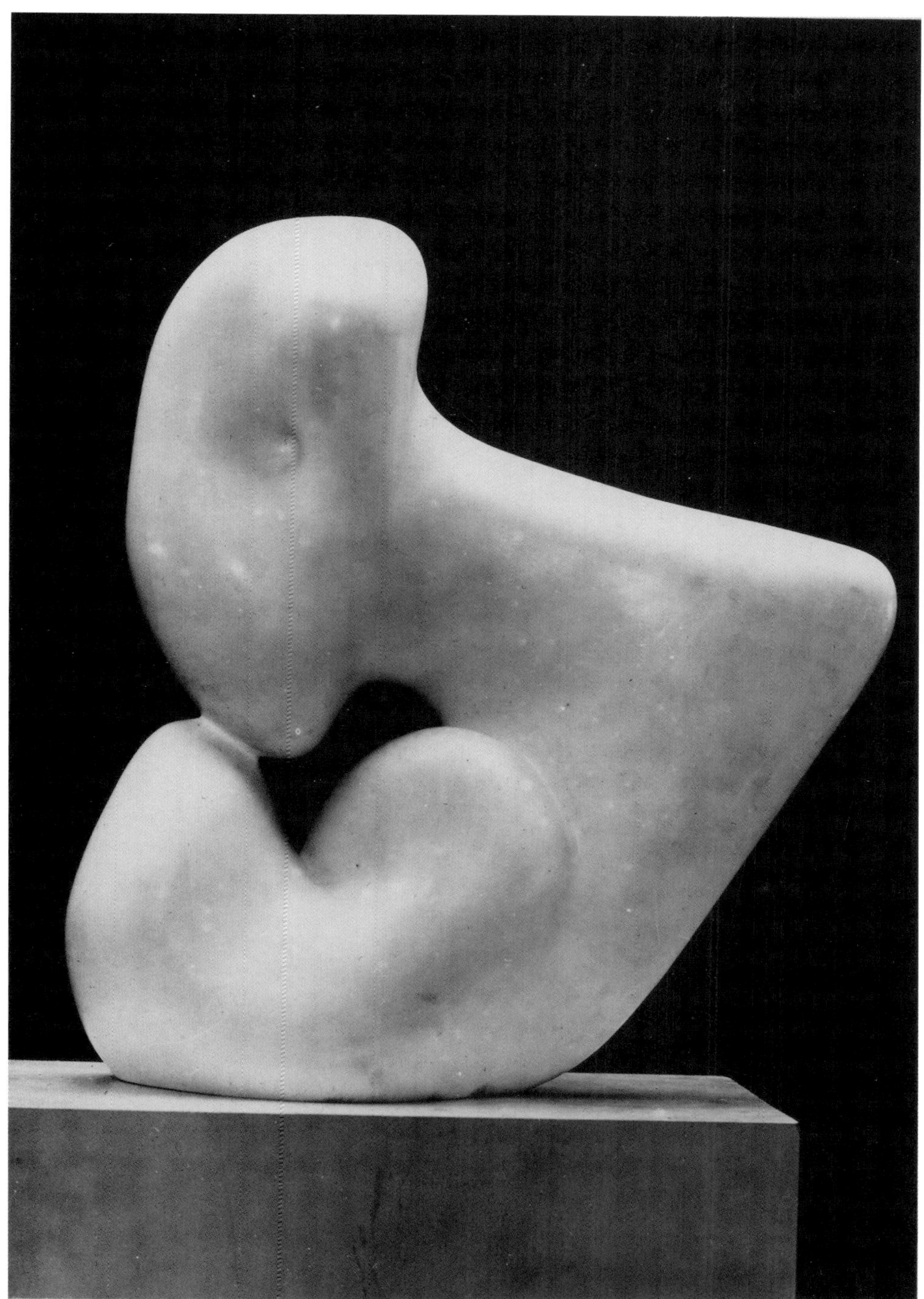

José Ruiz de Rivera,
***Composition,* 1936**
Marble, dimensions unknown.
Current location unknown
(presumed lost).

Albert Swinden

(born Birmingham, England, 1901; died New York, NY, 1961)

As a child, Albert Swinden moved from England to Canada with his parents. He immigrated to the United States in 1919. In New York, he studied at the National Academy of Design and the Art Students League. He began painting in a cubist-influenced abstract manner around 1930 and was a founding member of the American Abstract Artists. He was active within the FAP's Mural Division, painting murals for the Hospital for Chronic Disease on Roosevelt Island and the Chilean Pavilion at the New York World's Fair. His Williamsburg mural was installed in the housing project in 1938 (and is now on view at the Brooklyn Museum).

In 1938, Swinden described his philosophy of abstraction: "We are moved not only by particular, or individual forms, but by the relationship between the particular forms and their significance as a unity."[1] Although his Williamsburg mural is primarily geometric, Swinden incorporated several floating biomorphic shapes into the composition, giving it a playful sensibility. His mural studies all contain the same basic forms but reveal his experimentation with the placement and arrangement of the forms and with color selection.
In a 1991 brochure published in conjunction with the Brooklyn Museum's display of the Williamsburg murals, Barbara Dayer Gallati noted that Swinden's final mural includes compositional changes necessitated by the architecture of the social room in which it was installed. Most notably, he added a black horizontal strip of canvas to the top of the mural and a blue band at the right.[2]

1. Albert Swinden, "On Simplification," *American Abstract Artists Yearbook* (1938), cited in Gallati, *Williamsburg Murals*, n.p.

2. Gallati, *Williamsburg Murals*, n.p.

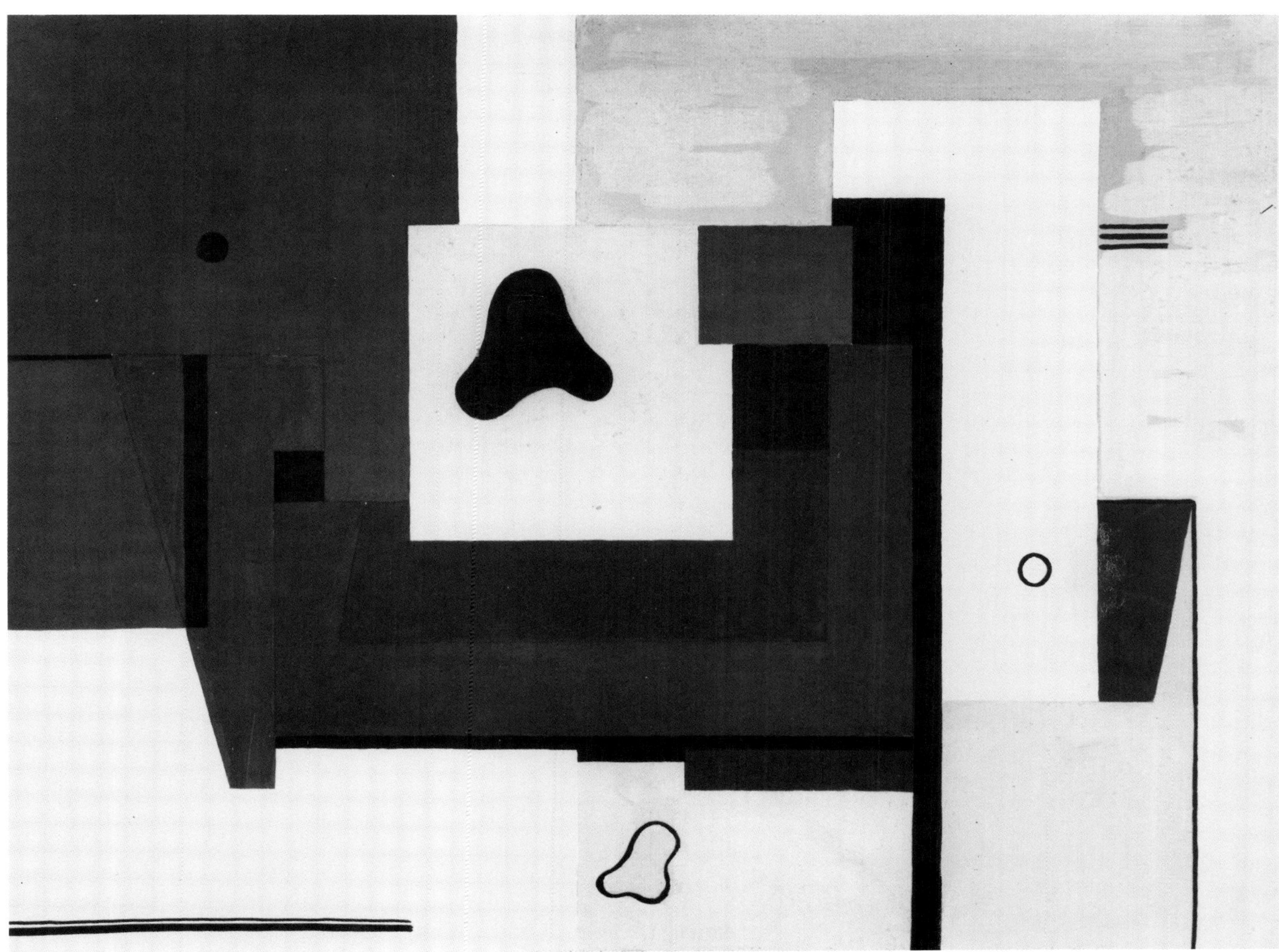

Albert Swinden, *Study for Williamsburg Project, Social Room, Block 3,* 1936
Gouache, dimensions unknown. Current location unknown (presumed lost). This photograph appears to document the gouache formerly in the collection of J. Donald Nichols (see page 120).

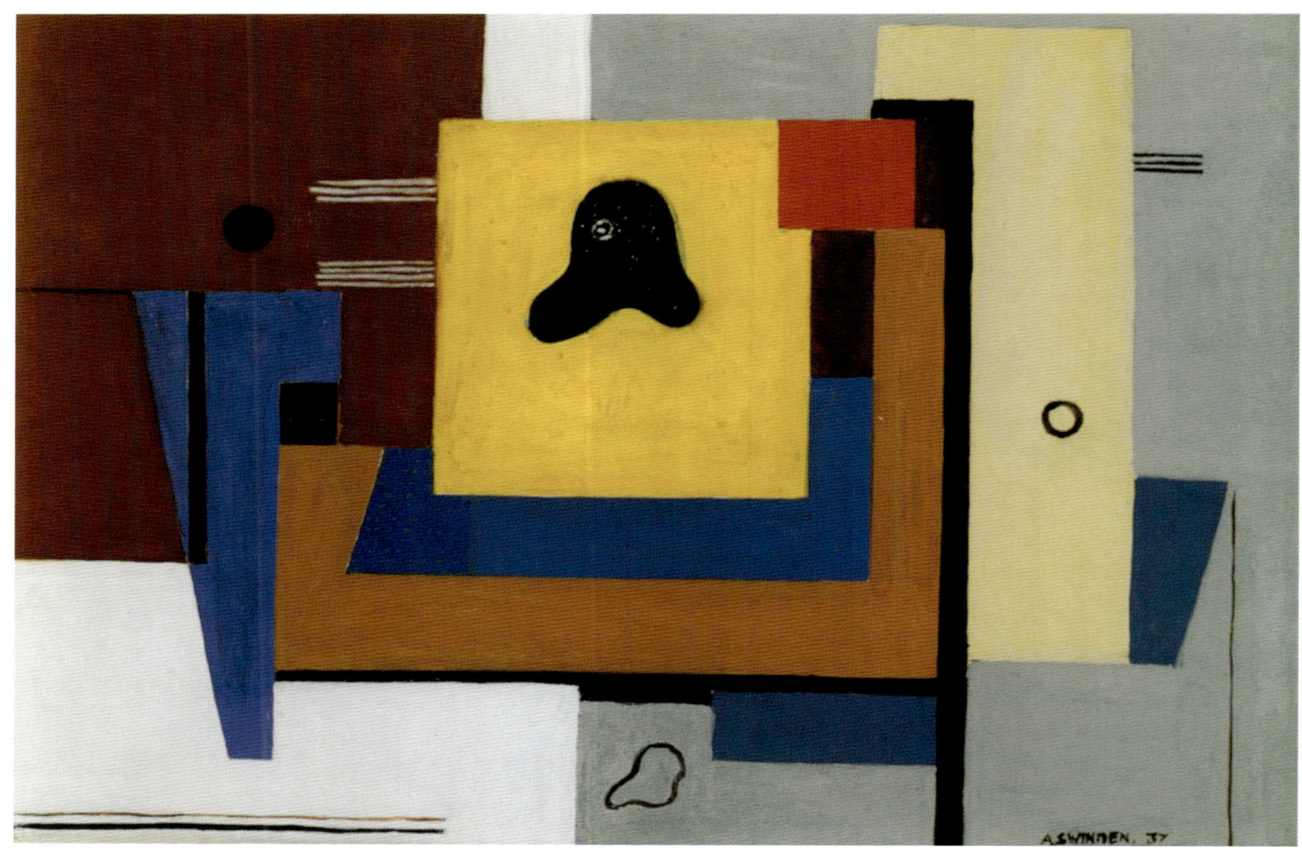

Albert Swinden, *Study for Williamsburg Project, Social Room, Block 3,* 1936–37

Casein on paper mounted on board, 8 × 11½ in. (20.3 × 29.2 cm). Current location unknown. This study was formerly in the collection of J. Donald Nichols, Nashville (Knott, *American Abstract Art of the 1930s and 1940s*, 99).

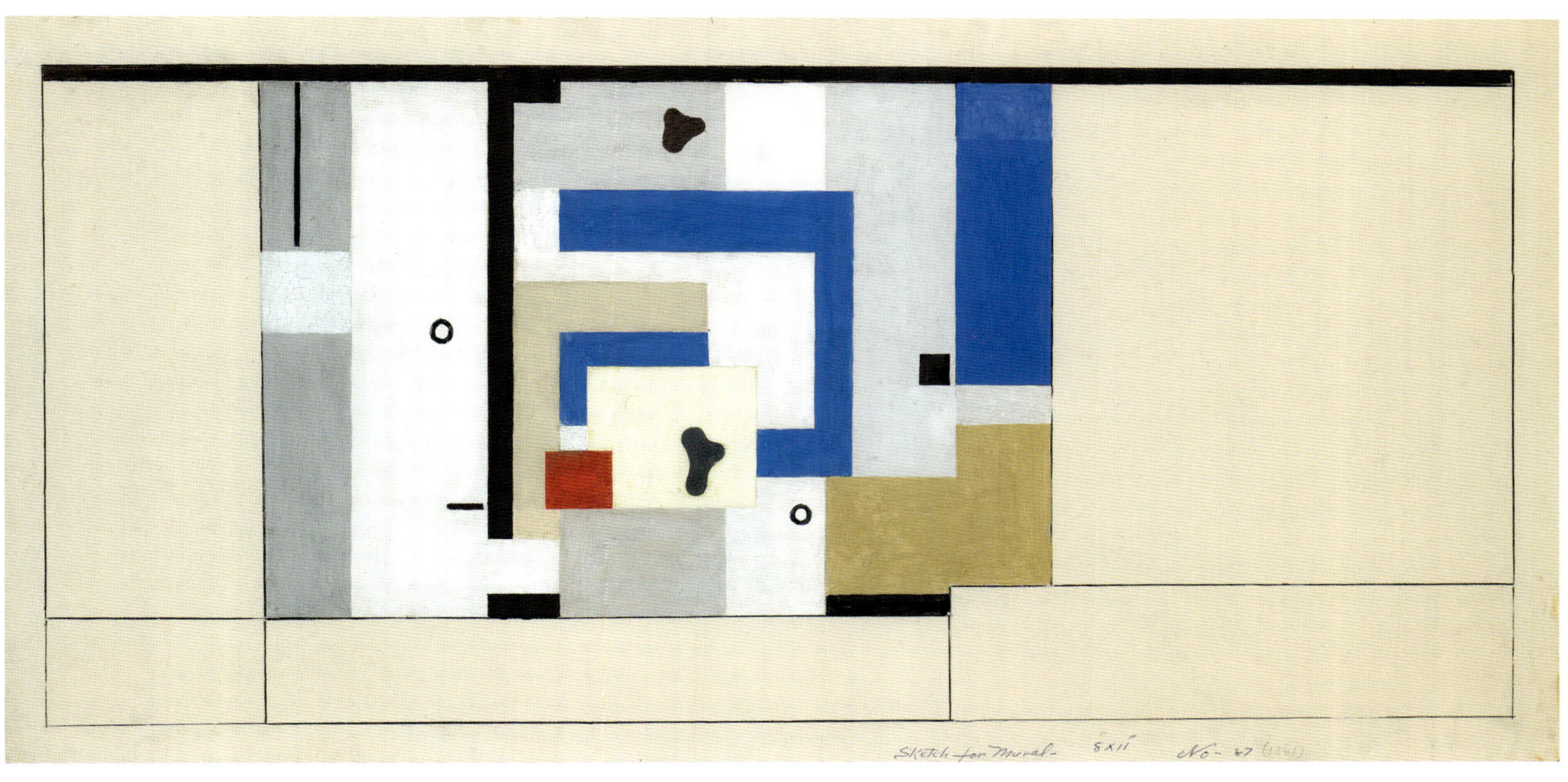

Albert Swinden, *Sketch for Mural, Williamsburg Housing Project,* ca. 1936–37
Opaque watercolor and pen and ink on board, 11 1/16 × 22 in. (28.1 × 55.9 cm). Whitney Museum of American Art, Purchase, with funds from the John I. H. Baur Purchase Fund and the M. Anthony Fisher Purchase Fund, 81.1.

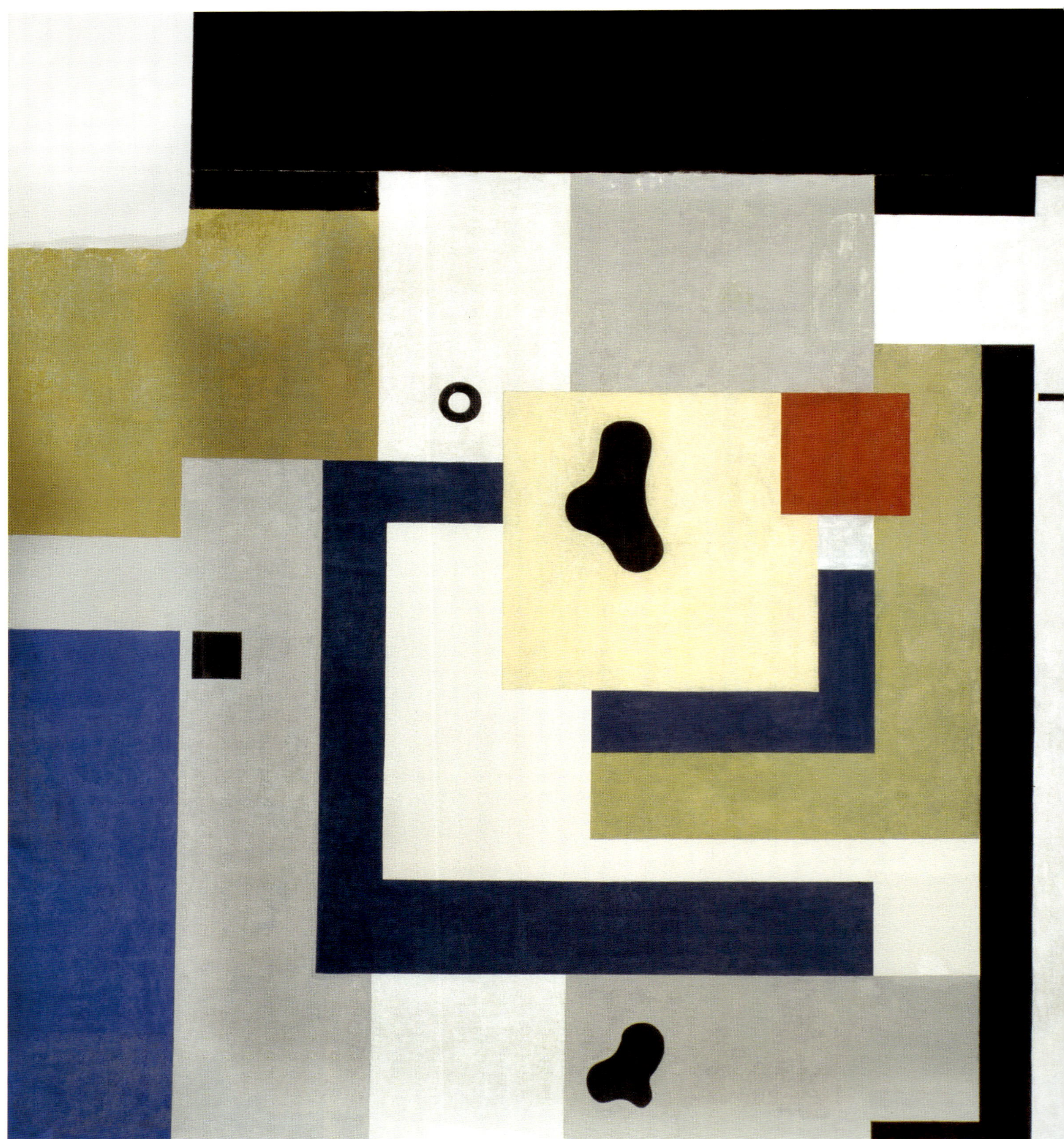

Albert Swinden, *Untitled, from the Williamsburg Housing Project Murals,* ca. 1938
Oil on canvas, 111¾ × 172⅜ in. (283.8 × 437.8 cm). The Brooklyn Museum. On loan from the New York City Housing Authority, L1990.1.5.

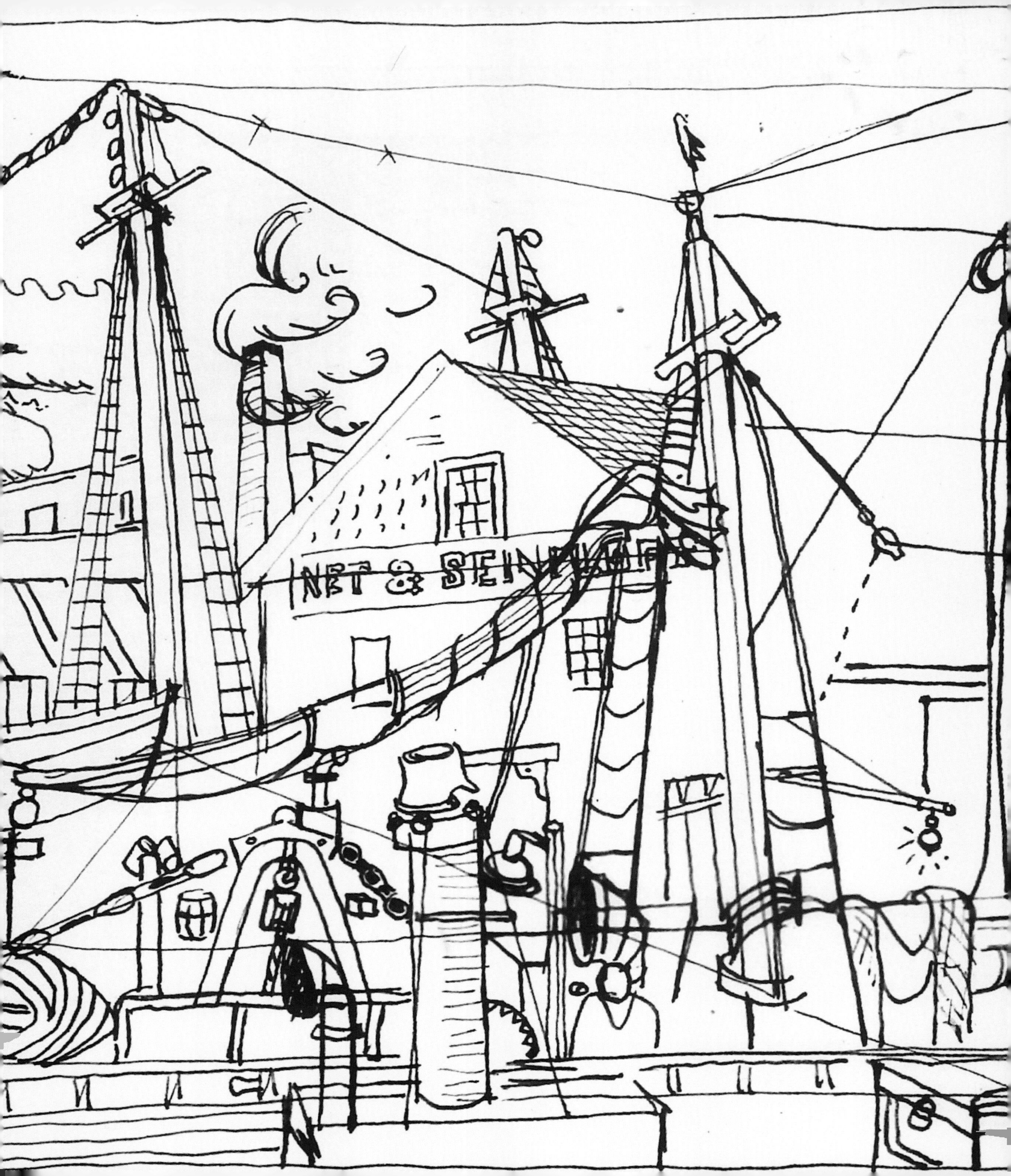
NET & SEIN

Checklist of the Exhibition

Swing Landscape

Stuart Davis
***Study for "Swing Landscape,"* 1936**

Gouache and traces of graphite on paper, 19½ × 21⅞ in. (49.5 × 55.6 cm)

Sheldon Museum of Art, University of Nebraska–Lincoln, Allocation of the U.S. Government, Federal Art Project of the Works Progress Administration, WPA-101.1943

See page 88

Stuart Davis
***Study for Swing Landscape,* 1937–38**

Oil on canvas, 22 × 28¾ in. (55.9 × 73 cm)

Corcoran Collection (Museum Purchase and exchange through a gift given in memory of Edith Gregor Halpert by the Halpert Foundation and the William A. Clark Fund), National Gallery of Art, Washington, 2014.79.15

See page 91

Stuart Davis
***Detail Study for "Swing Landscape,"* 1938**

Pencil on paper, 8½ × 11 in. (21.6 × 27.9 cm)

Estate of the Artist

See page 92

Stuart Davis
***Swing Landscape,* 1938**

Oil on canvas, 86¾ × 173⅛ in. (220.3 × 439.7 cm)

Allocated by the U.S. Government, Commissioned through the New Deal Art Projects, Eskenazi Museum of Art, Indiana University, 42.1

See page 93

Stuart Davis in Gloucester and New York

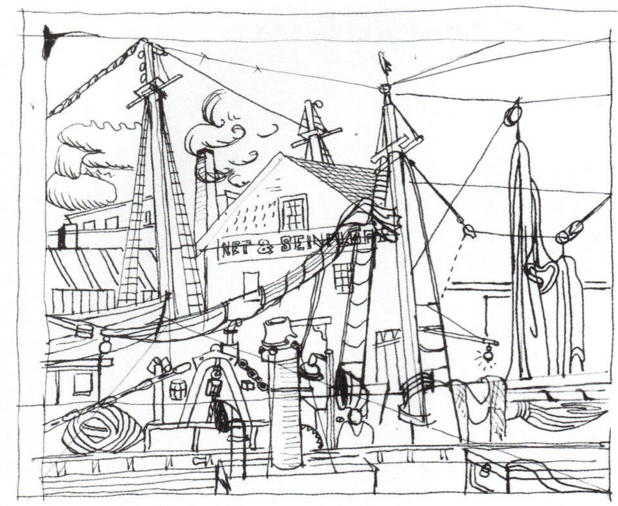

Stuart Davis
***From Sketchbook 3, Drawing for "Landscape with Drying Sails,"* 1931**

Ink on paper, 7⅝ × 9 in. (19.4 × 22.9 cm)

Estate of the Artist. © 2019 Estate of Stuart Davis / Licensed by VAGA at Artists Rights Society (ARS), NY

Stuart Davis
***Landscape with Drying Sails,* 1931–32**

Oil on canvas, 32 × 40 in. (81.3 × 101.6 cm)

Columbus Museum of Art, Ohio: Museum Purchase, Howald Fund II, 1981.012. © 2019 Estate of Stuart Davis / Licensed by VAGA at Artists Rights Society (ARS), NY

See page 19

Stuart Davis
***Red Cart,* 1932**

Oil on canvas, 32¼ × 50 in. (81.9 × 127 cm)

Addison Gallery of American Art, Andover, Massachusetts, museum purchase, 1946.15. © 2019 Estate of Stuart Davis / Licensed by VAGA at Artists Rights Society (ARS), NY

See page 18

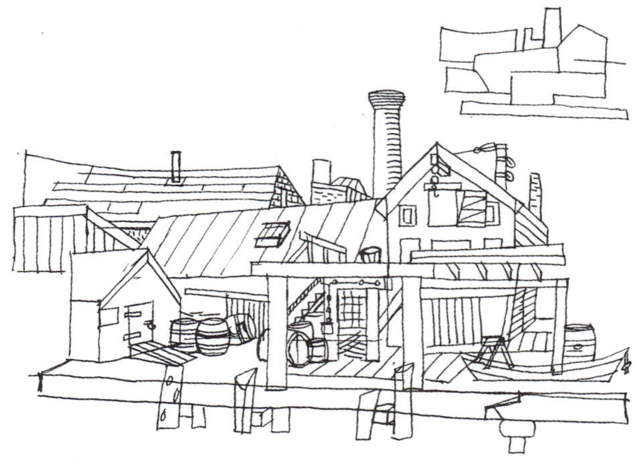

Stuart Davis
***Sketchbook 16–12 (Drawing for "Composite of Gloucester Docks"),* 1933**

Ink on paper, 8 × 10 in. (20.3 × 25.4 cm)

Estate of the Artist. © 2019 Estate of Stuart Davis / Licensed by VAGA at Artists Rights Society (ARS), NY

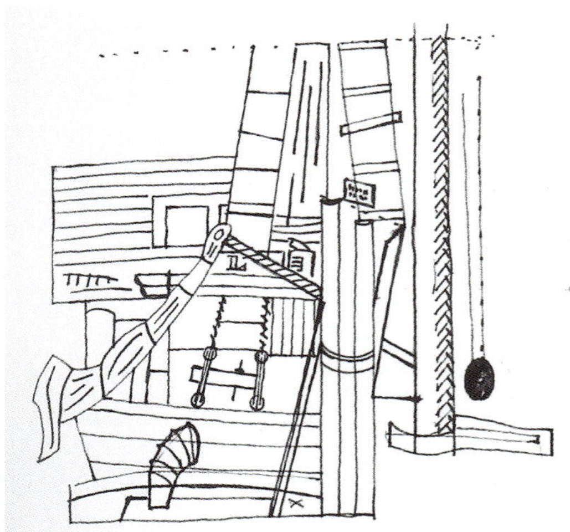

Stuart Davis
***Sketchbook 15–6 (Furled Sail, Drawing for "Analogical Emblem"),* 1933**

Ink on paper, 10 × 8 in. (25.4 × 20.3 cm)

Estate of the Artist. © 2019 Estate of Stuart Davis / Licensed by VAGA at Artists Rights Society (ARS), NY

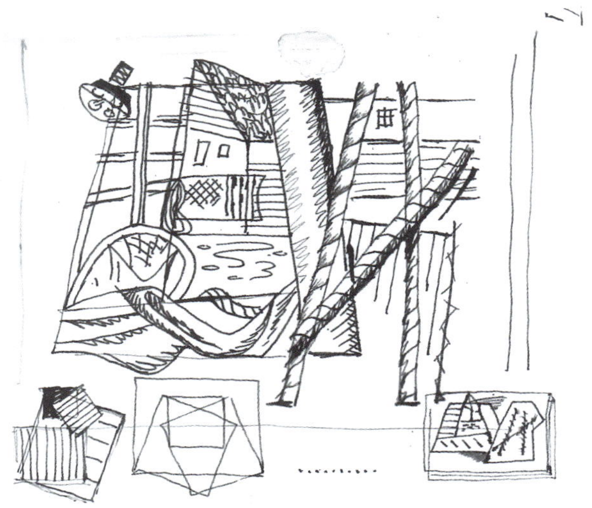

Stuart Davis
***Sketchbook 15–4 (Drawing for "Waterfront Landscape"),* 1933**

Ink and pencil on paper, 8 × 10 in. (20.3 × 25.4 cm)

Estate of the Artist. © 2019 Estate of Stuart Davis / Licensed by VAGA at Artists Rights Society (ARS), NY

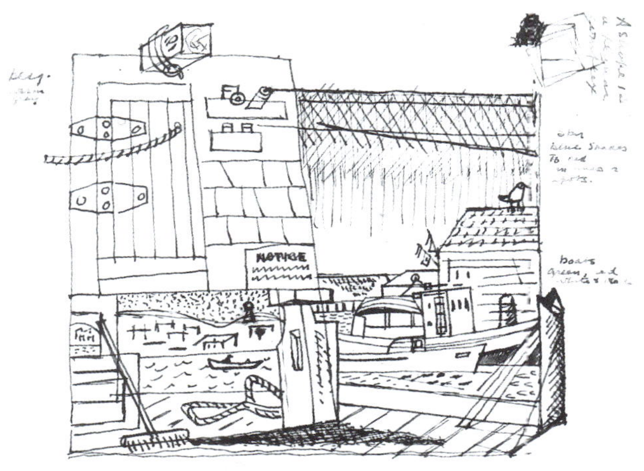

Stuart Davis
***Sketchbook 15–5 (Study for "Sail Loft"),* 1933**

Ink on paper, 8 × 10 in. (20.3 × 25.4 cm)

Estate of the Artist. © 2019 Estate of Stuart Davis / Licensed by VAGA at Artists Rights Society (ARS), NY

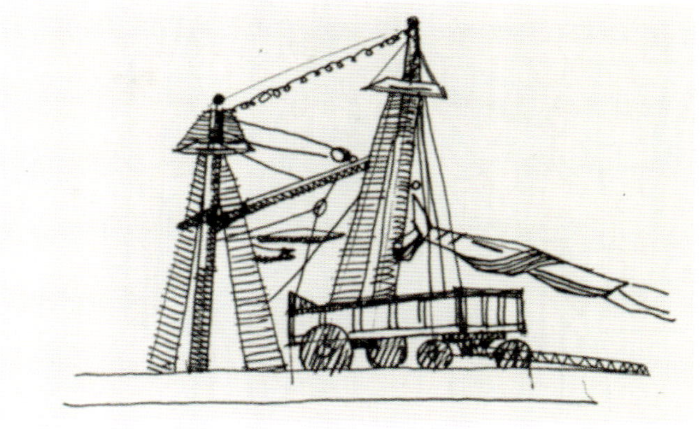

Stuart Davis
***Sketchbook 17–11 (Untitled),* 1936**

Ink on paper, 6 × 9 in. (15.2 × 22.9 cm)

Estate of the Artist. © 2019 Estate of Stuart Davis / Licensed by VAGA at Artists Rights Society (ARS), NY

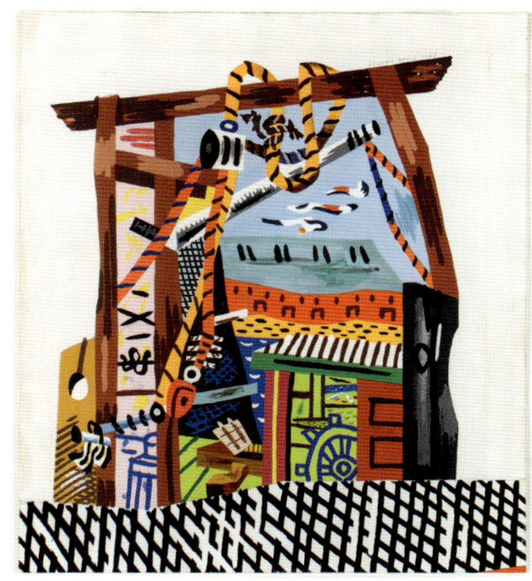

Stuart Davis
***Wheel House,* July 1937**

Gouache and graphite on illustration board, $18\frac{5}{16} \times 15\frac{15}{16}$ in. (48.1 × 40.5 cm)

Eskenazi Museum of Art, Indiana University, 41.1. © 2019 Estate of Stuart Davis / Licensed by VAGA at Artists Rights Society (ARS), NY

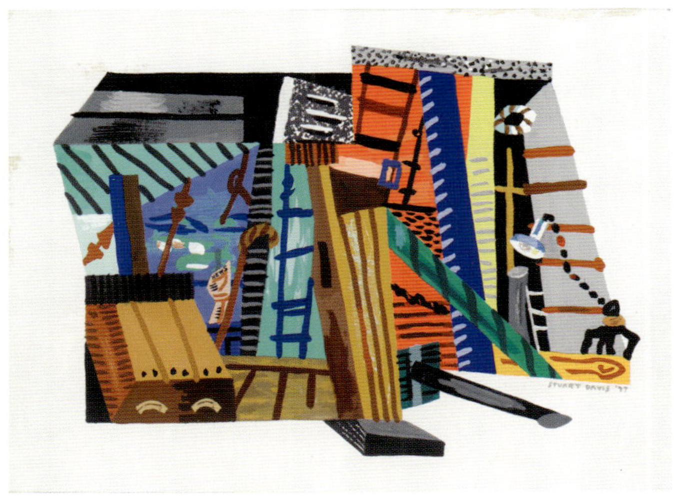

Stuart Davis
***Boats and Dock,* 1937**

Gouache and graphite on tan illustration board, prepared with white ground, 12$\frac{1}{16}$ × 15$\frac{15}{16}$ in. (30.7 × 40.5 cm)

Harvard Art Museums/Fogg Museum, Acquired through the Deknatel Purchase Fund and through the generosity of Sabatino Abate, Jr., Mr. and Mrs. Richard M. Bennett and Warren and Jane Shapleigh. © 2019 Estate of Stuart Davis / Licensed by VAGA at Artists Rights Society (ARS), NY

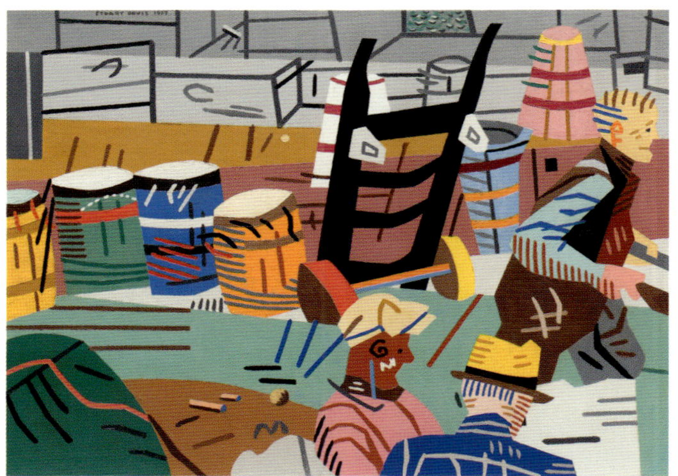

Stuart Davis
***The Terminal,* 1937**

Oil on canvas, 30⅛ × 40⅛ in. (76.5 × 101.9 cm)

Hirshhorn Museum and Sculpture Garden, Smithsonian Institution, Washington, DC, Gift of Joseph H. Hirshhorn, 1966, 66.1163. © 2019 Estate of Stuart Davis / Licensed by VAGA at Artists Rights Society (ARS), NY

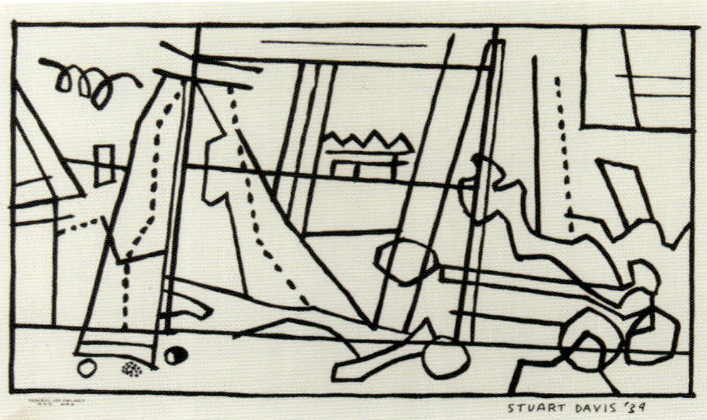

Stuart Davis
***Seine Cart,* 1939**

Lithograph on paper, 11½ × 16 in. (29.2 × 40.6 cm)

Allocated by the U.S. Government, Commissioned through the New Deal Art Projects, Eskenazi Museum of Art, Indiana University, 43.100

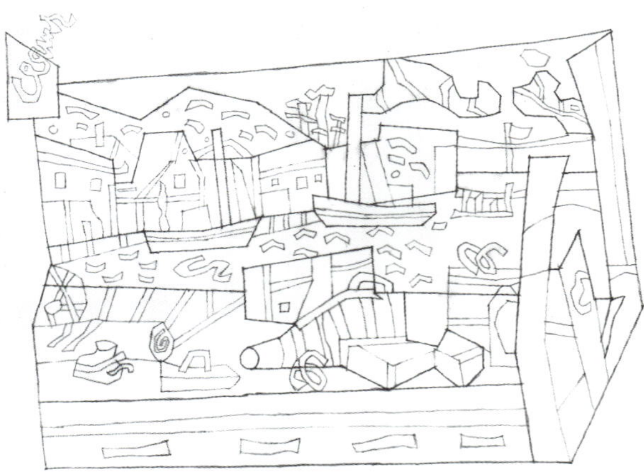

Stuart Davis
***Study for "Smith's Cove,"* ca. 1941**

Pencil on paper, 14½ × 19½ in. (36.8 × 49.5 cm)

Estate of the Artist. © 2019 Estate of Stuart Davis / Licensed by VAGA at Artists Rights Society (ARS), NY

Stuart Davis
***Ultra-Marine,* 1943**

Oil on canvas, 20 × 40⅛ in. (50.8 × 101.9 cm)

Pennsylvania Academy of the Fine Arts, Joseph E. Temple Fund, 1952.11. © 2019 Estate of Stuart Davis / Licensed by VAGA at Artists Rights Society (ARS), NY

See page 4

The Williamsburg Mural Project

Ilya Bolotowsky
***Study for Williamsburg Housing Project Mural,* ca. 1936**

Graphite, crayon, and gouache on paper, 8⅜ × 10⅞ in. (21.3 × 27.6 cm) (sheet)

Michael Rosenfeld Gallery, LLC, New York

See page 69

Ilya Bolotowsky
***Study for Mural for Williamsburg Housing Project, New York,* ca. 1936**

Opaque watercolor and pen and ink on board, 16 × 30 in. (40.7 × 76.2 cm)

Whitney Museum of American Art, 50th Anniversary Gift of the Edward R. Downe, Jr., Purchase Fund, Mr. and Mrs. William A. Marsteller and the National Endowment for the Arts, 80.4

See page 71

Harry Bowden
***Study for Williamsburg Mural,* ca. 1936**

Tempera or gouache on paper, 4¾ × 14¾ in. (12.1 × 37.5 cm)

Harry Bowden Papers, Archives of American Art, Smithsonian Institution, Washington, DC

See page 75

Harry Bowden
***Suggestion for a Mural (possible study for Williamsburg mural),* ca. 1936**

Tempera or gouache and graphite on paper, 6½ × 15½ in. (16.5 × 39.4 cm)

Harry Bowden Papers, Archives of American Art, Smithsonian Institution, Washington, DC

See page 74

Francis Criss
***Sixth Avenue El,* ca. 1937**

Oil on canvas, 36¼ × 41$^{11}/_{16}$ in. (92.1 × 105.9 cm)

Whitney Museum of American Art, Purchase, with funds from the Felicia Meyer Marsh Purchase Fund, 82.1

See page 84

Burgoyne Diller
***Composition,* 1943–44**

Oil on canvas, 42 × 42 in. (106.7 × 106.7 cm)

Davis Museum at Wellesley College, Gift of Theodore Racoosin, 1959.13. © 2019 Estate of Burgoyne Diller / Licensed by VAGA at Artists Rights Society (ARS), NY

See page 37

George McNeil
***Williamsburg Mural Study with Calligraphic Forms* (also known as *Williamsburg Mural Study with Calligraphic Shapes*), 1937–38**

Tempera on gesso board, 9½ × 24⅛ in. (24.1 × 61.3 cm)

Estate of the Artist

See page 107

George McNeil
***Study for Williamsburg Mural,* 1938**

Oil on board, 13 × 31¼ in. (33 × 79.4 cm)

High Museum of Art, Atlanta, Gift of Jennifer and Terry Weiss in honor of Judy and Washington Falk, III, 2006.114

See page 110

Albert Swinden
***Sketch for Mural, Williamsburg Housing Project,* ca. 1936–37**

Opaque watercolor and pen and ink on board, 11$^{1}/_{16}$ × 22 in. (28.1 × 55.9 cm)

Whitney Museum of American Art, Purchase, with funds from the John I. H. Baur Purchase Fund and the M. Anthony Fisher Purchase Fund, 81.1

See page 121

Abstract Murals between the World Wars

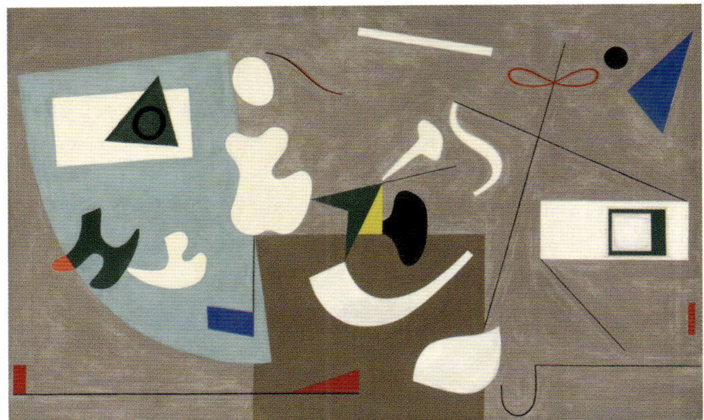

Ilya Bolotowsky
***Study for the Hall of Medical Sciences Mural at the 1939 World's Fair in New York*, 1938–39**

30 × 48 in. (76.2 × 121.9 cm)

Art Institute of Chicago, Wilson L. Mead Fund, 1977.1

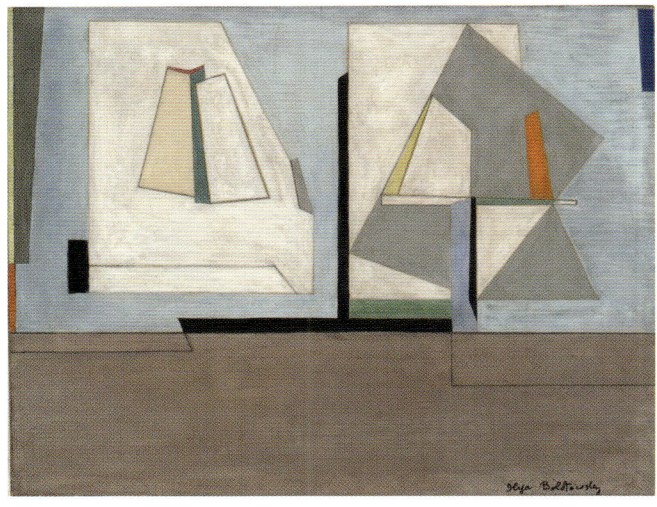

Ilya Bolotowsky
***Sailing (Study for Mural, Men's Day Room, Chronic Diseases Hospital, Welfare Island, New York)*, 1940**

Pencil and tempera on cardboard, 5¼ × 6¹¹⁄₁₆ in. (13.3 × 17 cm)

Yale University Art Gallery, Gift of the Estate of Katherine S. Dreier, 1953.6.167

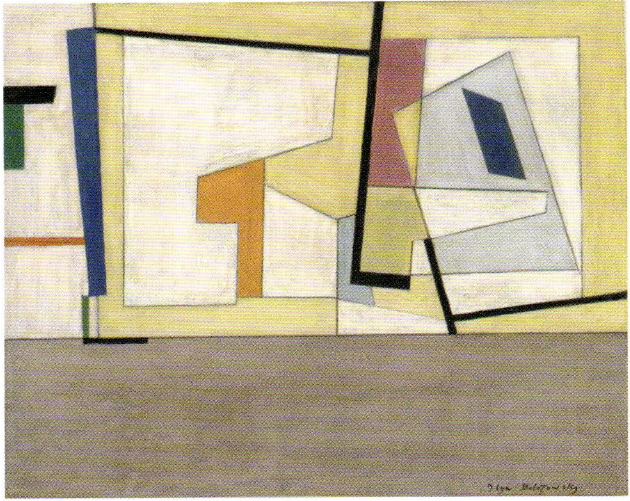

Ilya Bolotowsky
***Autumn (Study for Mural, Men's Day Room, Chronic Diseases Hospital, Welfare Island, New York)*, 1940**

Pencil and tempera on cardboard, 5¼ × 6¹¹⁄₁₆ in. (13.3 × 17 cm)

Yale University Art Gallery, Gift of the Estate of Katherine S. Dreier, 1953.6.168

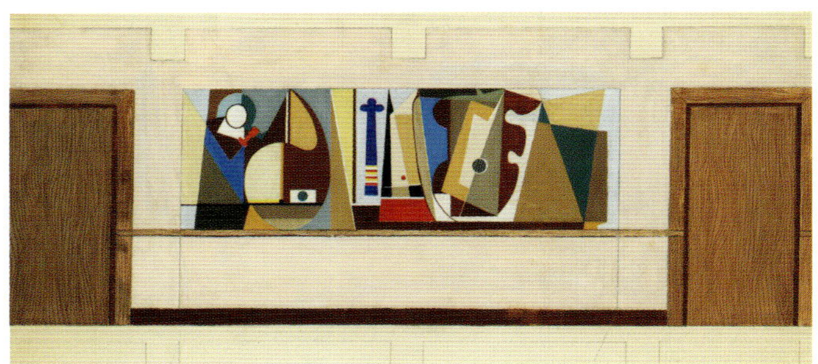

Rosalind Bengelsdorf Browne
***Mural Study in Environment (for Central Nurses Home, Welfare Island, New York)*, 1936–37**

Tempera, casein, colored pencil, and graphite pencil on paper mounted on cardboard, 14⁵⁄₁₆ × 30¹⁵⁄₁₆ in. (36.4 × 78.6 cm)

Whitney Museum of American Art, Gift of the Artist, 77.113

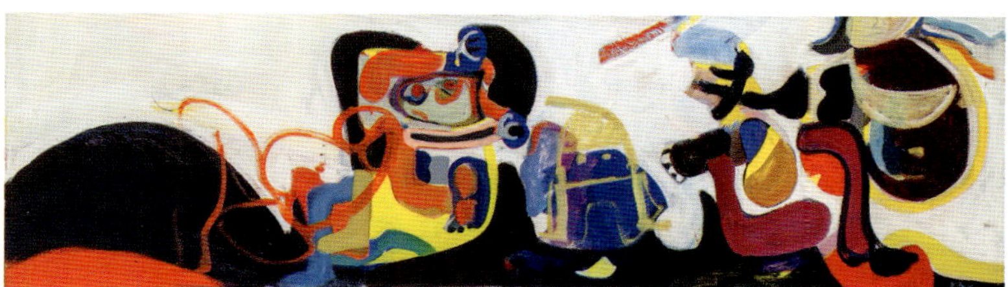

Peter Busa
***Mural Study for Children's Ward (probably Hospital for Chronic Diseases, the Bronx),* ca. 1940**

Oil on canvas, 24½ × 83¾ in. (62.2 × 212.7 cm)

Museum purchase with funds from the Clarence W. and Mildred Long Art Purchase Fund, Eskenazi Museum of Art, Indiana University, 2015.133

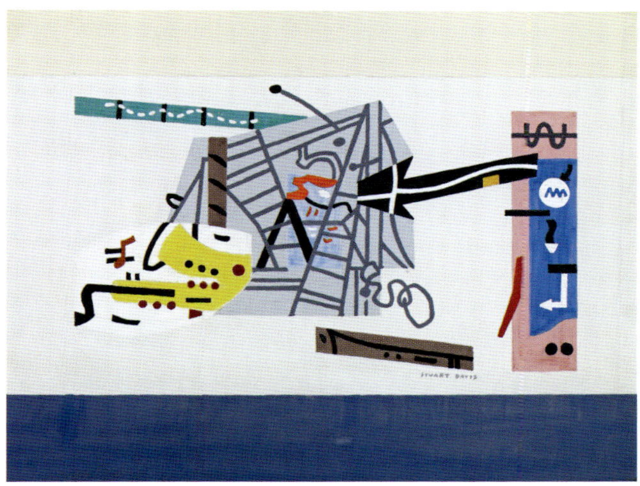

Stuart Davis
***Color Sketch for WNYC Mural,* 1938**

Gouache on board, 13¼ × 17⅝ in. (33.7 × 44.5 cm)

Promised Gift to Crystal Bridges Museum of American Art, Bentonville, Arkansas

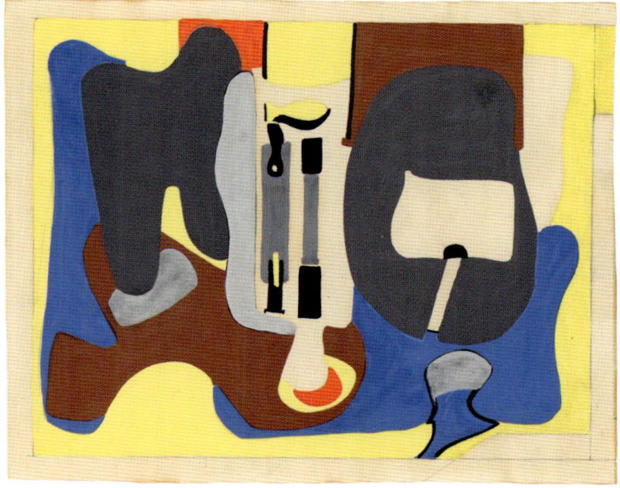

Arshile Gorky
***Study for "Mechanics of Flying," Newark Airport Aviation Murals,* 1936**

Opaque watercolor and graphite pencil on paper, 15 × 18¼ in. (38.1 × 46.4 cm)

Whitney Museum of American Art, 50th Anniversary Gift of Alan H. Temple, 80.16

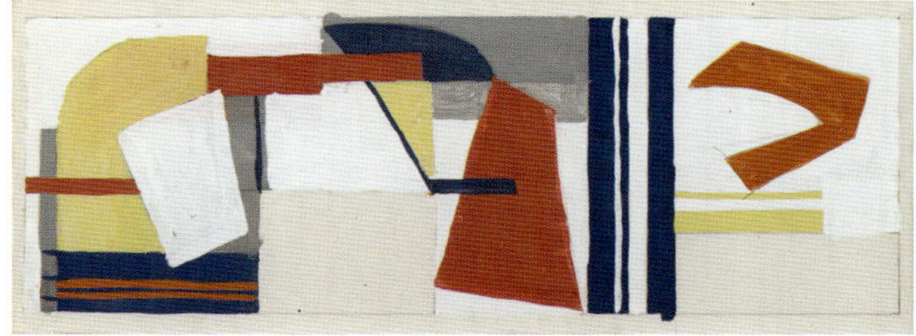

Lee Krasner
***Untitled Mural Study,* 1940**

Gouache on paper, 17 × 22 in. (43.2 × 55.9 cm)

Courtesy Kasmin Gallery, New York. © 2019 Pollock-Krasner Foundation / Artists Rights Society (ARS), NY

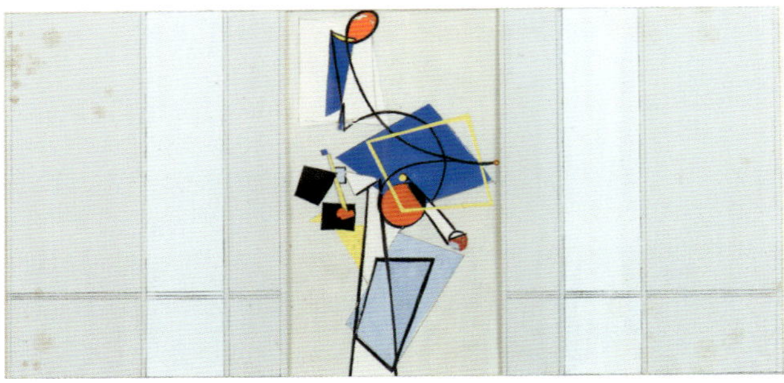

Lee Krasner
***Mural Study for Studio A, Radio Station WNYC,* 1941**

Gouache on paper, 19½ × 29 in. (49.6 × 73.7 cm)

Courtesy Kasmin Gallery, New York. © Pollock-Krasner Foundation / Artists Rights Society (ARS), NY

Fernand Léger
***Composition,* 1924**

Oil on canvas, 51½ × 39¾ in. (130.8 × 101 cm)

Jane and Roger Wolcott Memorial, Gift of Thomas T. Solley, Eskenazi Museum of Art, Indiana University, 75.41.1. © Artists Rights Society (ARS), NY / ADAGP, Paris

See page 16

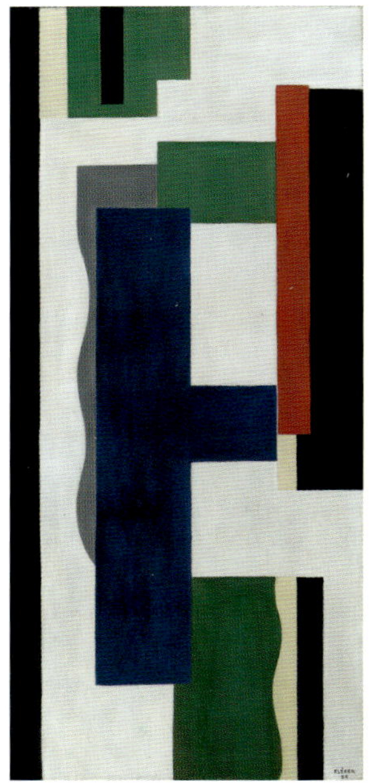

Fernand Léger
***Peinture Murale,* 1926**

Oil on canvas, 70⅞ × 31½ in. (180 × 80 cm)

Menil Collection CA63154. © Artists Rights Society (ARS), NY / ADAGP, Paris

Fernand Léger
***Study for a Cinematic Mural I,* 1938–39**

Gouache and pencil on board, 20 × 16 in. (50.7 × 40.5 cm)

Museum of Modern Art, Given anonymously, 738.1966. © Artists Rights Society (ARS), NY / ADAGP, Paris

See page 24

Fernand Léger
***Study for a Cinematic Mural II,* 1938–39**

Gouache and pencil on board, 19¾ × 15 in. (50.2 × 38 cm)

Museum of Modern Art, Given anonymously, 741.1966. © Artists Rights Society (ARS), NY / ADAGP, Paris

See page 24

Fernand Léger
***Study for a Cinematic Mural III,* 1938–39**

Gouache, ink, colored pencil, and pencil on board, 20 × 14⅞ in. (50.7 × 37.8 cm)

Museum of Modern Art, Given anonymously, 743.1966. © Artists Rights Society (ARS), NY / ADAGP, Paris

See page 25

Fernand Léger
***Study for a Cinematic Mural IV,* 1938–39**

Gouache and pencil on board, 20 × 15 in. (50.7 × 38 cm)

Museum of Modern Art, Given anonymously, 737.1966. © Artists Rights Society (ARS), NY / ADAGP, Paris

See page 25

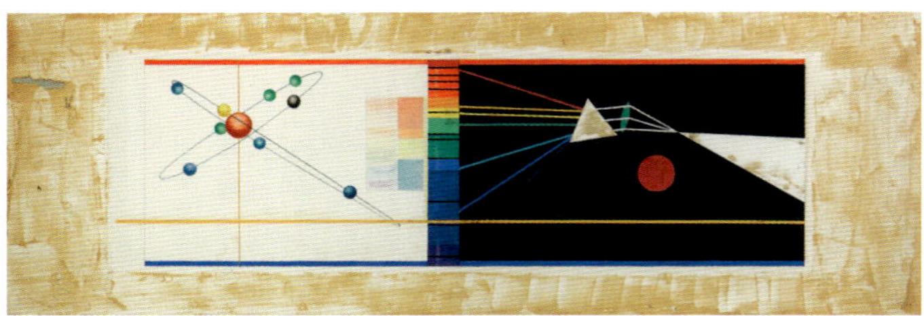

Eric Mose
***Mural Design for the Chemical and Plastics Building, New York World's Fair,* 1938**

Tempera on illustration board, 10 × 29½ in. (25.4 × 74.9 cm)

Museum of the City of New York, 41.44.103

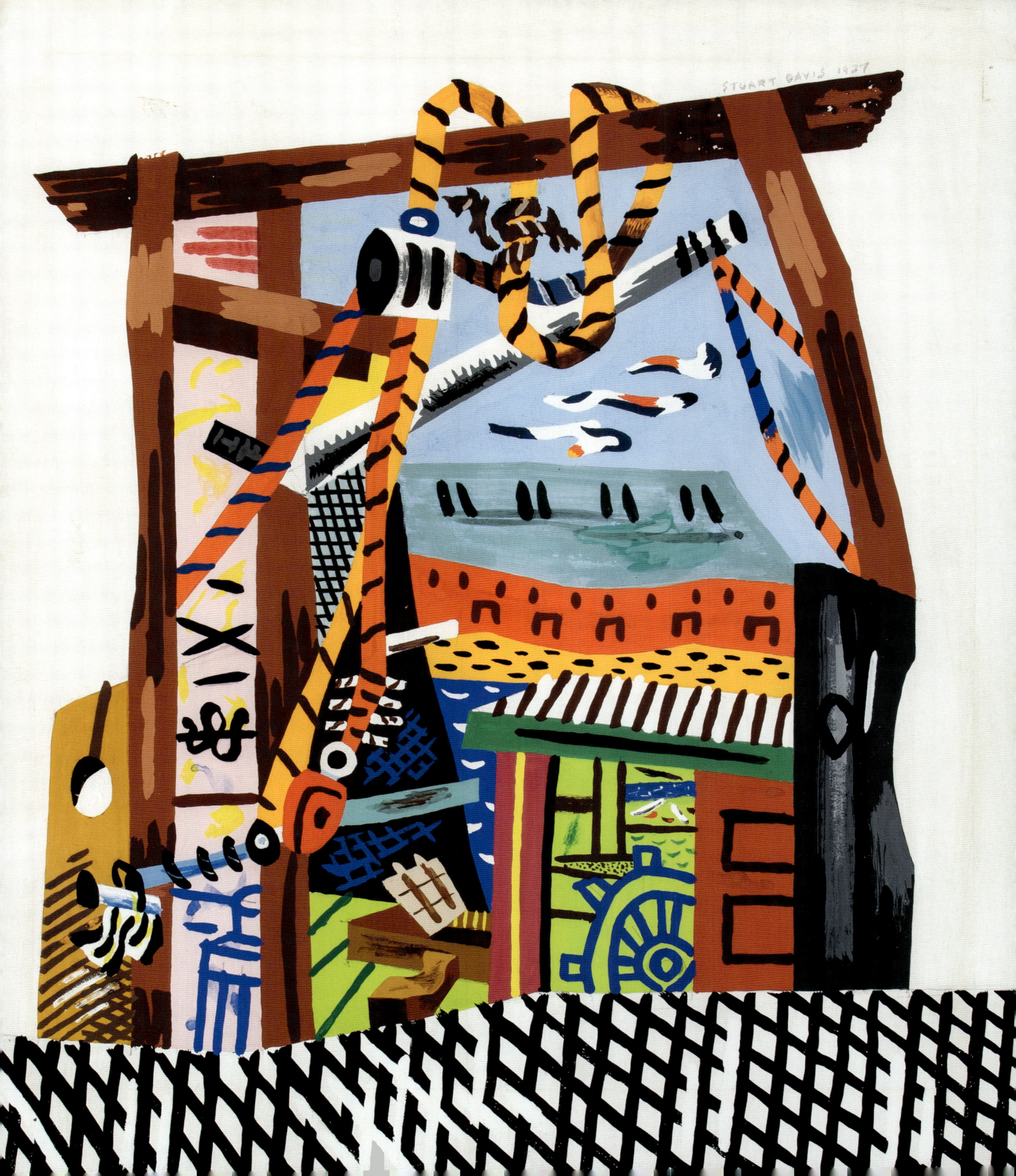
STUART DAVIS 1927

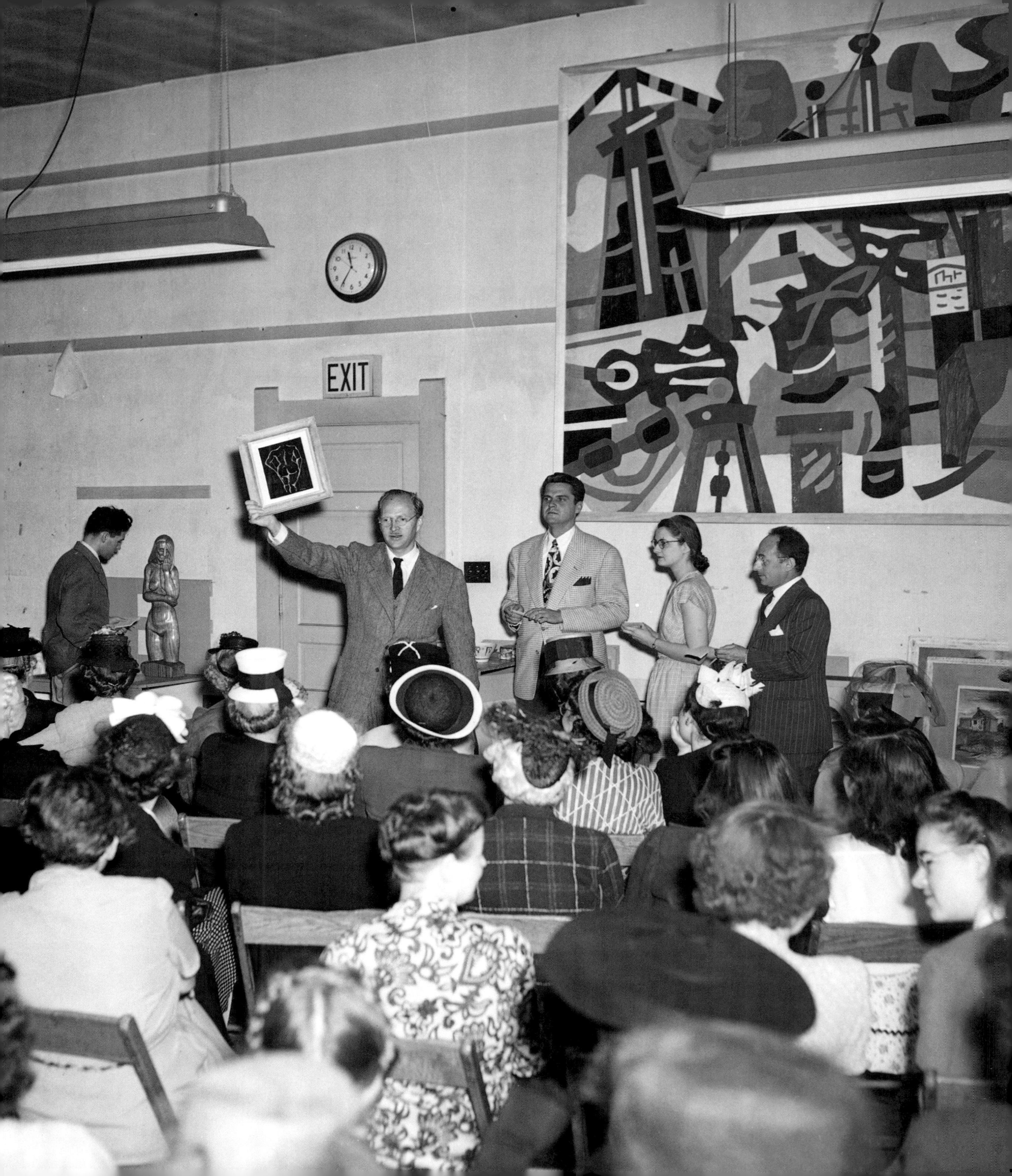
EXIT

Swing Landscape: A History

Jennifer McComas

1936

Stuart Davis, along with eleven other painters enrolled in the Works Progress Administration's Federal Art Project, is commissioned to paint a mural for the Williamsburg Housing Project in Brooklyn, New York. Under the guidance of the FAP Mural Division head, Burgoyne Diller, this project results in the first abstract murals produced in the United States. For more information on the Williamsburg mural program, see the *Visual Compendium* in this catalogue.

Davis produces a preliminary watercolor and pencil sketch for his Williamsburg mural. The mural design is superimposed on a grid showing its proposed placement within the architectural space (see page 83). He also paints a second study, possibly in gouache, now known only from a photograph in the artist's estate. A label on the photograph's verso titles it *Waterfront Forms.* Once thought to refer to a separate mural, the 2007 catalogue raisonné argues convincingly that *Waterfront Forms* was

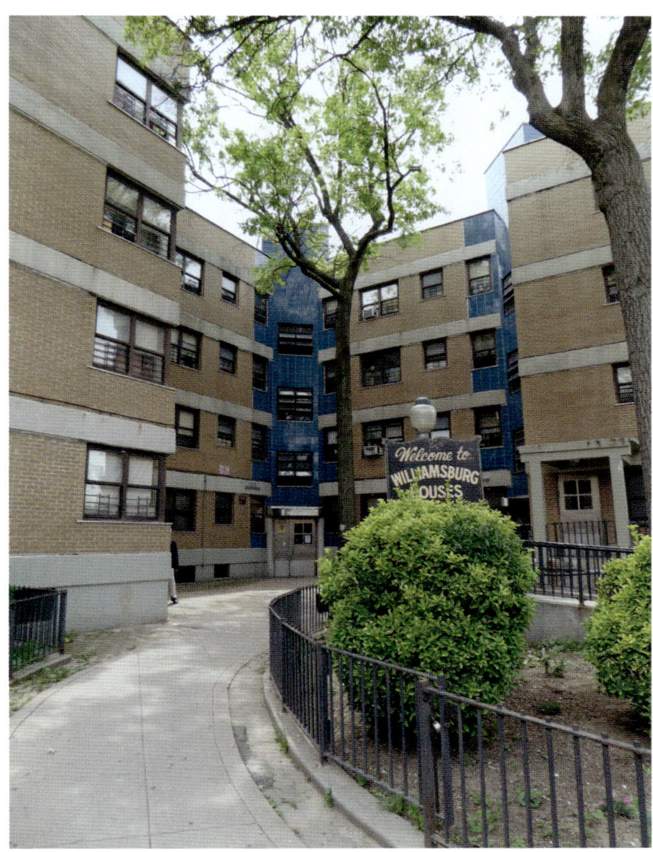

William Lescaze, architect. Williamsburg Houses, Brooklyn, 1938.

simply an early title for the mural later known as *Swing Landscape* (see page 87).[1]

Studies for eleven Williamsburg murals, including *Swing Landscape*, are featured in the exhibition *New Horizons in American Art* at the Museum of Modern Art, New York, on view from September 14 through October 12. A model of one of the Williamsburg Houses' social rooms with murals by Davis and Paul Kelpe is included in the exhibition.

On September 30, David C. Comstock, the WPA's color consultant, meets with William Lescaze, Burgoyne Diller, and Langdon Post, New York City Housing Authority chairman, to view the preliminary sketches for the Williamsburg murals. Comstock views the sketches favorably, having "no objection to the abstract designs in view of the present trends in decoration in NYC if color and composition are good." He recommends that approval be given for the artists to proceed with further studies.[2]

1937

Davis submits a more detailed watercolor study as well as an oil on canvas study for *Swing Landscape* for approval (see pages 90–91). On January 23, he records in his calendar that he "prepared canvas for 3" scale mural sketch." On March 18, he writes that the "mural for W.P.A. should be finished in 3" scale on canvas." On June 21, he notes giving the "mural sketch to B. Howitz to be approved in Washington."[3]

On February 25, Burgoyne Diller informs Langdon Post that the Mural Division has secured approval for acquiring the materials needed for the Williamsburg murals. According to Diller, "Many of the artists have now completed full-sized cartoons" and others have already begun painting the final murals.[4] Davis begins painting the final mural in his studio at 235 East Forty-Second Street, New York. On June 29, he records a disagreement with Diller over the mural's production. Diller rejects Davis's request for an assistant capable of conducting artistic research, which he believes is not necessary for an abstract composition. Diller also accuses Davis of having demanded special privileges, such as asking to paint his mural in tempera rather than oil, a request denied by the FAP. Davis counters that Diller has overstepped the sphere of his responsibilities by questioning Davis's artistic integrity.[5]

On July 27, H. A. Gray writes to Langdon Post that four panels by Francis Criss have been approved and that the sketches by Stuart Davis, Albert Swinden, and Ilya Bolotowsky are disapproved.[6] However, completed murals by Swinden and Bolotowsky are installed in the Williamsburg Houses the following year, and Criss completes only one mural, which is not installed. Davis, too, continues working on *Swing Landscape* until May 1938.

On August 26, Davis records a visit to the Williamsburg Housing Project site and the Brooklyn Navy Yard but writes that he "could not find material for sketching."[7] These notes suggest that the composition for *Swing Landscape* is still evolving, although the final mural hardly deviates from the watercolor sketches of 1936 and early 1937.

In October, Davis writes a memorandum titled "Synopsis on Abstract Art in Williamsburg Project." This unpublished text is his only known comment on the site for which he painted *Swing Landscape:*

> *Gov't housing program has as its purpose giving improved living conditions to people who are without them.*
>
> *Better living conditions mean changes in architecture. New building materials, more light, air, etc:*
>
> *Art is a historical product. The same age that has produced better houses has produced a better art, suited to [a] modern environment.*
>
> *This art reflects the colors and shapes of the time. It has a new sense of space and color which reflect the broader view and experience of modern man which modern technological advance has made possible.*
>
> *The train, auto, and airoplane* [sic], *have made a new sense of space and color.*

Abstract art reflects this new experience.

Abstract art has affected the design of all modern objects.

Everybody is familiar with the effect of abstract art on the shape and color of clothes, autos, cameras, airplanes, trains, cooking, utensils, etc:

They are not familiar with the art itself because it is too expensive.

But now the gov't has made a start in bringing this abstract art directly to the people in modern homes.[8]

1938

From May 24 to June 16, *Swing Landscape* is exhibited in *Murals for the Community* at the Federal Art Gallery, 225 West Fifty-Seventh Street, New York. *New York Times* critic Edward Alden Jewell expresses a sense of being overwhelmed by *Swing Landscape*'s chromatic vibrancy and visual energy in his review of the exhibition:

> *Stuart Davis, making the easel scream, supplies his public with seven-league boots: for in the very act of entering the long main gallery at the far end of which his landscape swings (the title is apt enough: "Swing Landscape"), already you are there. . . . This non-objective inebriant cancels everything else within range. The least that can be said for the mural, if mural it truly be (and I think Mr. Davis's decade-old "Eggbeater" series would magnify more convincingly), the least that can be said is that "Swing Landscape" deserves a room of its own or an entire housing project. And maybe the most that can be said for "Swing Landscape" is that, set up as a sign-board message to Mars on Mount Everest, it could decoy the cotillion of the spangled firmament.*[9]

Swing Landscape is rejected from the Williamsburg Houses, possibly around the time of the Federal Art Gallery exhibition. No documents providing a clear reason for the rejection have surfaced, but an aesthetic reason seems most plausible.[10] The style of the five murals ultimately installed in the Williamsburg Houses suggests that Diller and Lescaze deemed geometric abstraction most appropriate for the housing project. *Swing Landscape* is presumably warehoused at an undetermined location in New York City.

1940

On February 8, Davis's wife, Roselle, notes in her calendar that *Swing Landscape* was sent to Queens College, New York. The authors of the 2007 Davis catalogue raisonné propose that this "was likely a collection point or temporary installment site for WPA artwork."[11] Documentation in the artist's estate suggest that the mural was sent to Brooklyn College in 1940. This may also have been a temporary installation site or a storage facility for WPA art.[12]

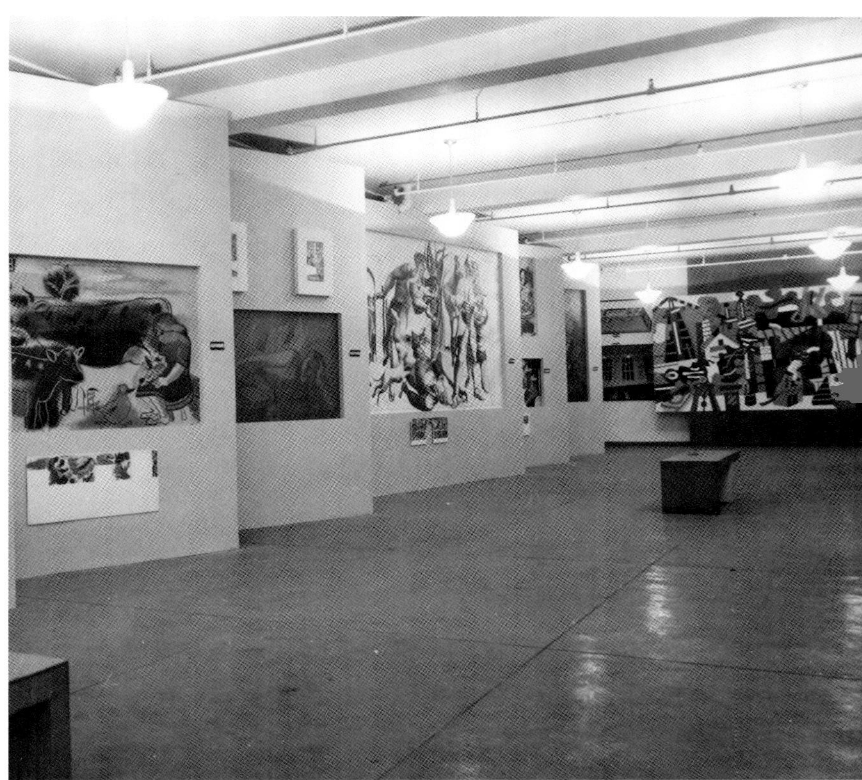

Installation photograph, *Murals for the Community*, Federal Art Gallery, New York, May 1938. *Swing Landscape* is hanging in the background.

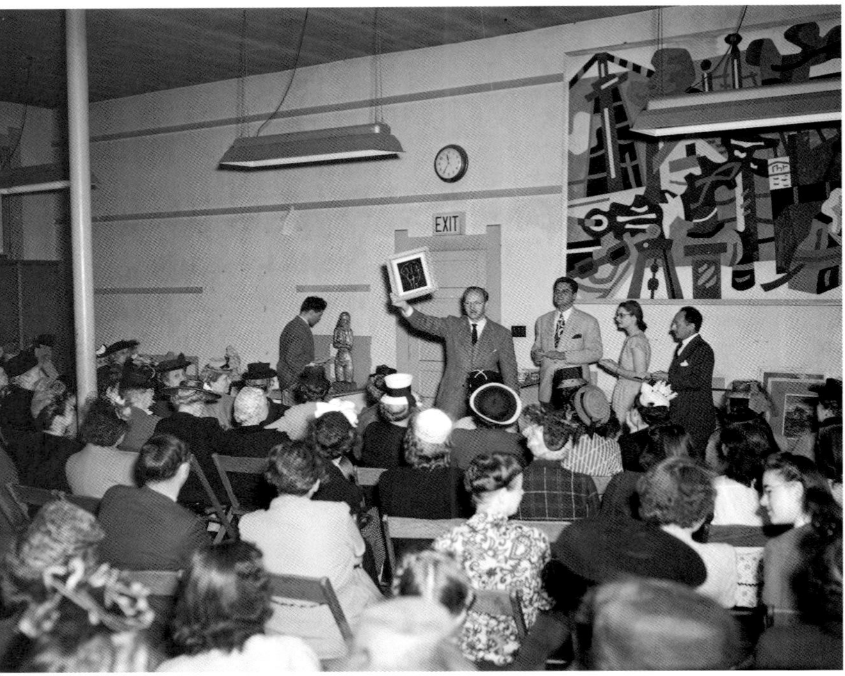

Auction of student artwork at Indiana University, with *Swing Landscape* hanging on the back wall, June 8, 1946.

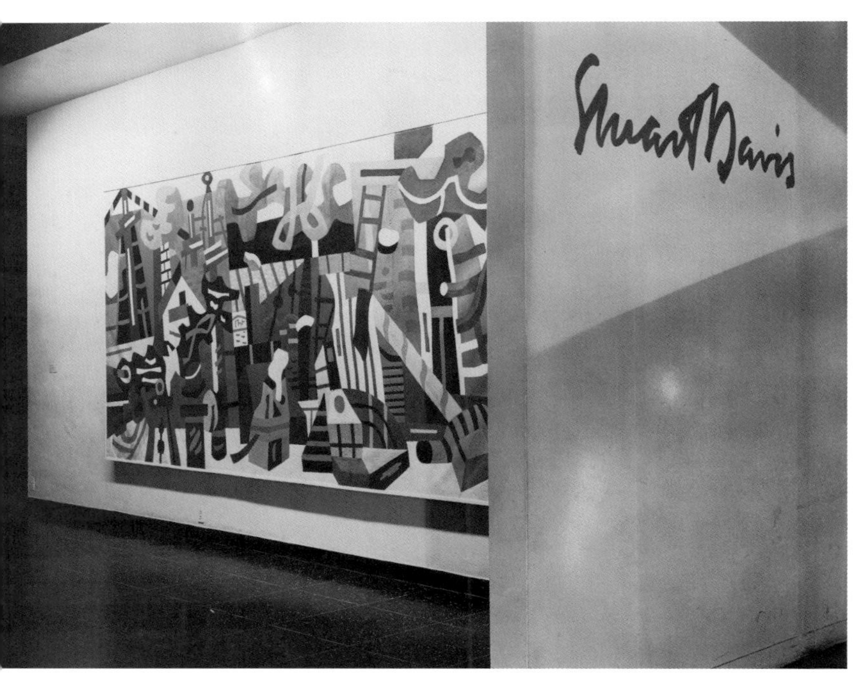

Soichi Sunami, installation view of the exhibition *Stuart Davis*, October 17, 1945–February 3, 1946. The Museum of Modern Art, New York. Photographic Archives, The Museum of Modern Art.

1941

In September, Davis inspects *Swing Landscape* in storage and notes cracking in the paint surface, which he attributes to the mural having been rolled and unrolled multiple times.[13] Repairs are made under the auspices of the FAP, and a stretcher is constructed for the mural at this time.[14]

In October, *Swing Landscape* is featured in the exhibition *Stuart Davis/Marsden Hartley* at the Cincinnati Modern Art Society, organized by Peggy Frank. A smaller version of this exhibition (not including *Swing Landscape*) travels in November to the Art Center Gallery at Indiana University, Bloomington.

Works produced under the auspices of the WPA could be acquired by tax-supported institutions through a process known as allocation. The Cincinnati Modern Art Society inquires about the conditions of acquiring *Swing Landscape* and is informed that the allocation would cost $1 per square foot, or $105.[15] The Cincinnati Modern Art Society declines to acquire *Swing Landscape*, and Henry Radford Hope, chair of Indiana University's fine arts department, subsequently expresses interest in acquiring the mural.[16]

1942

In early January, the WPA approves allocation of *Swing Landscape* to Indiana University. The mural arrives at Indiana University by early February. Until 1961, the university lacks a museum or adequate gallery space for displaying the mural, so it is frequently moved from one temporary location on campus to another.[17]

In April, Henry Hope informs Davis that the "allocation of 'Swing Landscape' has finally gone through." He mentions that the mural was unveiled at a dance "when it was hung as a back-drop for Tommy Dorsey's [swing] orchestra."[18]

1945–46

Swing Landscape is included in Stuart Davis's first major retrospective at the Museum of Modern Art, New York, on view from October 17, 1945, to February 3, 1946. The mural hangs adjacent to the title wall of the exhibition. At the close of the exhibition, curator James Johnson Sweeney writes to Henry Hope: "As you have undoubtedly heard, the exhibition has aroused exceptional interest from museum visitors and has been very well attended during the entire showing. Throughout the exhibition a great deal of attention was centered on your *Swing Landscape*. It fact it was a feature of the exhibition."[19] Sweeney also informs Hope that the drum on which the mural was rolled for transport was too small, resulting in additional cracking in the paint surface. MoMA calls in Davis to repaint the damaged areas.[20]

1957

John Lucas's article "The Fine Arts Jive of Stuart Davis," published in *Arts Magazine*, offers the first in-depth discussion of *Swing Landscape*'s visual parallels with jazz and swing music.[21]

1961

Swing Landscape undergoes major conservation treatment at the Intermuseum Conservation Association in Oberlin, Ohio. According to Thomas Solley, director of the Indiana University Art Museum from 1971 to 1986, "Many of the works created by Stuart Davis during the WPA period were not produced with the best possible materials, nor was the artist particularly concerned with the structural soundness of his technique. . . . By the early 1960's [our painting] had cracked, and paint was lifting in a way that threatened the future existence of the work."[22] The conservation work in Oberlin involves extensive consolidation and the construction of a new stretcher.

1962

The first dedicated facility for the Indiana University Art Museum opens on the Indiana University–Bloomington campus within a new fine arts building. *Swing Landscape* now has a permanent home.

1964

In a December 8 oral history interview conducted by curator and art historian William Agee for the Archives of American Art, the abstract artist Carl Holty reminisces about the FAP. He discusses *Swing Landscape*, speculating that Davis did not actually want the mural to be installed in the Williamsburg Houses. Although this suggestion seems farfetched, Holty's comments about *Swing Landscape*'s aesthetic incompatibility with the housing project are insightful, supporting the hypothesis that Davis's mural was rejected because a more streamlined, geometric aesthetic was ultimately preferred for the houses' social rooms:

> *In some instances, I don't know, I mean he's dead now [Davis died on June 24, 1964] and I think that Stuart Davis painted something, with willful intent not to have it go where it was to go. It was for a Williamsburg housing project, it's now a mural out at the University of Indiana. . . . I remember we would hear around the studios . . . that if a thing was too good it wasn't good enough. . . . Now Davis's picture was certainly the kind of picture that was too good, certainly too good to hang in the hallway of a new housing project and too loud, visually too loud and it was never put up there. And it was bought, I think, back from the WPA by Mrs. [inaudible] and was then sold to Indiana which is a very good and proper ending for it.*[23]

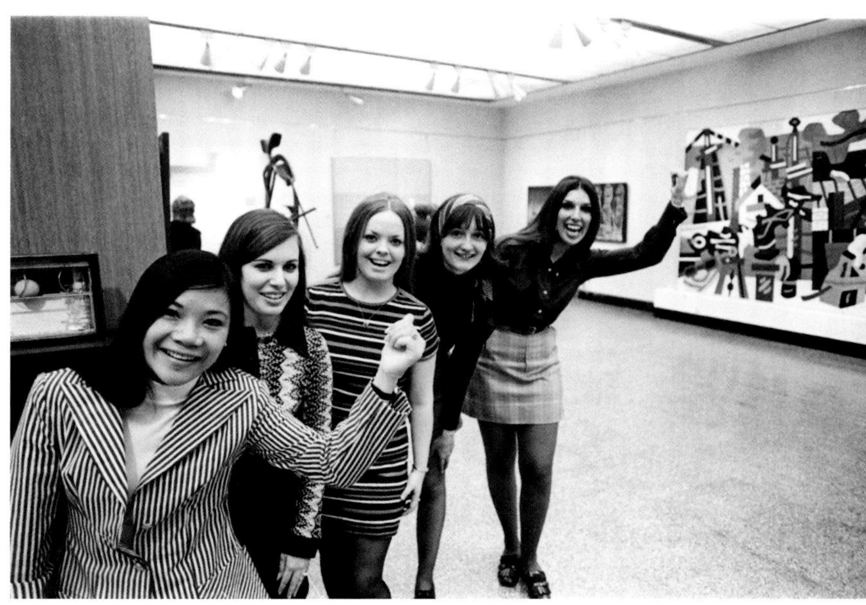

Women's Day Tour of Fine Arts Building, Indiana University. The students are in the original galleries of the Eskenazi Museum of Art, April 1972.

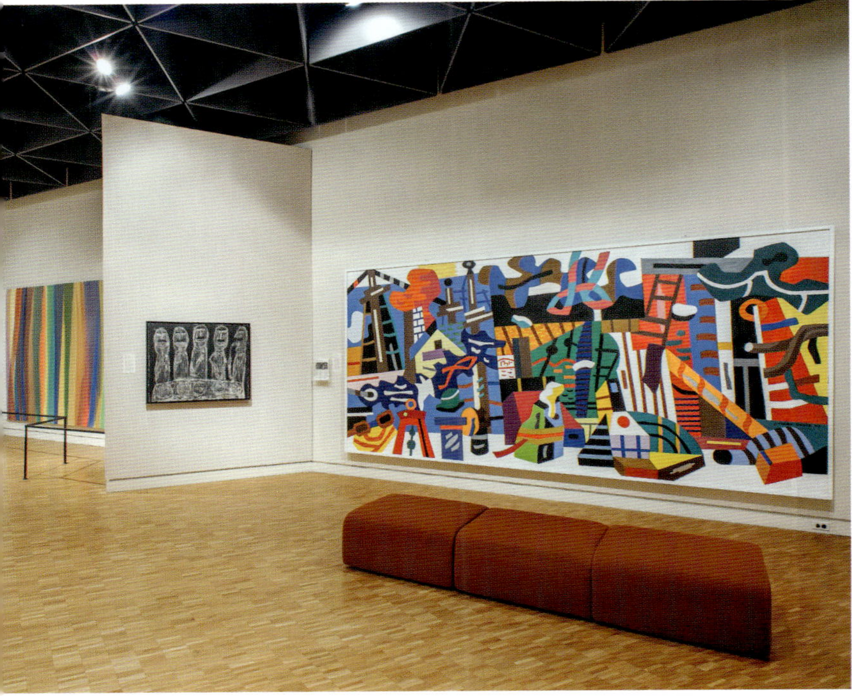

Swing Landscape on view in the Eskenazi Museum of Art's I. M. Pei Building (opened 1982), Indiana University.

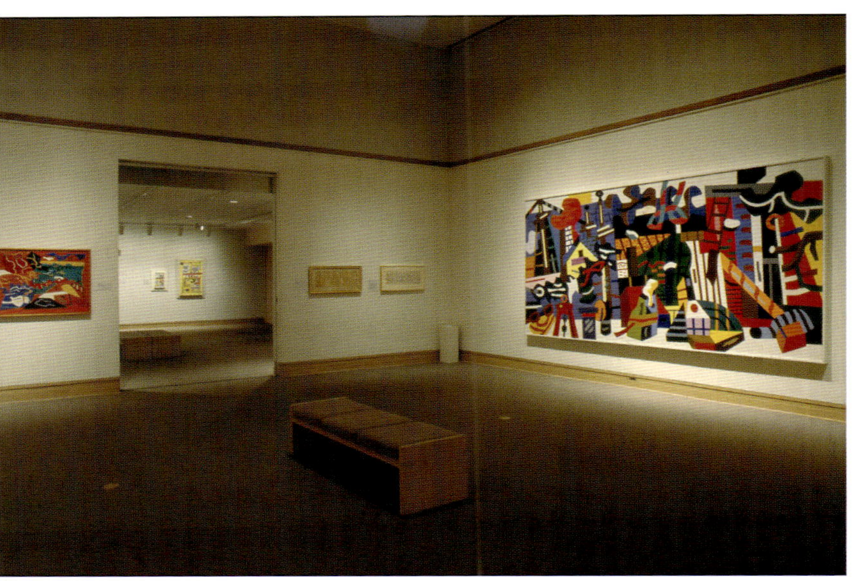

"Stuart Davis: American Painter," The Metropolitan Museum of Art, The Lila Acheson Wallace Wing, Twentieth Century Art Galleries, November 23, 1991–February 16, 1992.

1967

Swing Landscape, never in stable condition, has continued to deteriorate physically after its acquisition by Indiana University. From June to September, *Swing Landscape* undergoes another major conservation campaign at the Intermuseum Conservation Association in Oberlin, Ohio. The treatment involves removal of surface grime, discolored varnish, and oil overpaint; consolidation; and inpainting. The mural is relined and restretched on a new stretcher. A new strip frame is also constructed.[24] Conservator Richard D. Buck raises a question about Davis's materials: "The paint does not behave quite like an oil paint, nor like an oil paint mixed with varnish, and we wonder whether a casein paint may have been used in some parts, if not all, of the painting."[25] This query is intriguing in light of Davis's original request to paint the mural in tempera.[26] However, analysis of paint samples in 2003 confirms that Davis used only traditional oil paint in *Swing Landscape*.[27]

1968

Following complex negotiations regarding the mural's transport and condition, *Swing Landscape* is featured in William Agee's exhibition *The 1930s: Painting and Sculpture in America* at the Whitney Museum of American Art, New York. Agee describes *Swing Landscape* as one of the "greatest achievements" in the art of the 1930s.[28] The mural is prominently displayed in the museum's lobby.

1970

From April 6 to May 17, the mural is shown in the exhibition *The American Scene, 1900–1970*, at the Indiana University Art Museum.

1976

Swing Landscape is featured on the cover of a special issue of *Art in America* focusing on American art of the 1930s.[29]

1982

The Indiana University Art Museum moves into a new, modernist building designed by the firm of I. M. Pei. *Swing Landscape* forms an integral part of the reinstalled permanent collection.

1991

Conservation treatment is carried out by Martin Radecki, chief conservator at the Indianapolis Museum of Art. This treatment focuses on stabilization of the support and paint layer, as well as surface cleaning. A passive backing is constructed to stabilize the fabric support during transit.[30]

1991–92

Swing Landscape travels for the first time since 1968 to appear in *Stuart Davis: American Painter*, curated by Lowery Stokes Sims. The exhibition is on view at the Metropolitan Museum of Art, New York, from November 18, 1991, to February 6, 1992, and travels to the San Francisco Museum of Modern Art, where it is on view from March 26 through June 7, 1992. Although the exhibition receives mixed reviews, critic David Anfam writes that *Swing Landscape* "positively scintillates."[31]

1997

Swing Landscape is featured in a special issue of *Time* magazine focusing on American art. The issue is based on Robert Hughes's eight-part television series *American Visions*, which airs on PBS from May 28 to June 18, and publication of the same title.[32]

2003

Major conservation of *Swing Landscape*, funded by a grant from the National Endowment for the Arts, is again undertaken by the Intermuseum Conservation Association in Cleveland, Ohio.[33] Conservation is necessitated in part by aesthetic problems resulting from previous conservation campaigns. Areas of resin residue, deteriorated fills, and discolored retouching have become visible. The mural's structural instability has also continued to be a problem. The conservation team cleans the mural and removes varnish and wax resin from the 1967 treatment. Areas of paint lifting are consolidated, and several paint samples are analyzed.[34] The analysis shows that Davis painted *Swing Landscape* with traditional oil paints and not with casein or a commercial lacquer paint (such as Duco), as had been previously speculated.[35] According to Adelheid Gealt, director of the Indiana University Art Museum, "The visual reintegration of damaged areas and old repairs has restored the power of the image."[36]

2004–5

Swing Landscape travels for the first time to Europe, where it is included in the exhibition *Sounds and Lights: A History of Sound in the Art of the 20th Century* at the Musée National d'Art et de Culture, Centre Georges Pompidou, Paris, from September 22, 2004, through January 3, 2005.

2005

On returning from Paris, the mural forms the centerpiece of the small exhibition *Stuart Davis and American Abstraction: A Masterpiece in Focus* at the Philadelphia Museum of Art. On view from January 14 through April 17, 2005, the exhibition, curated by Kathleen Foster and

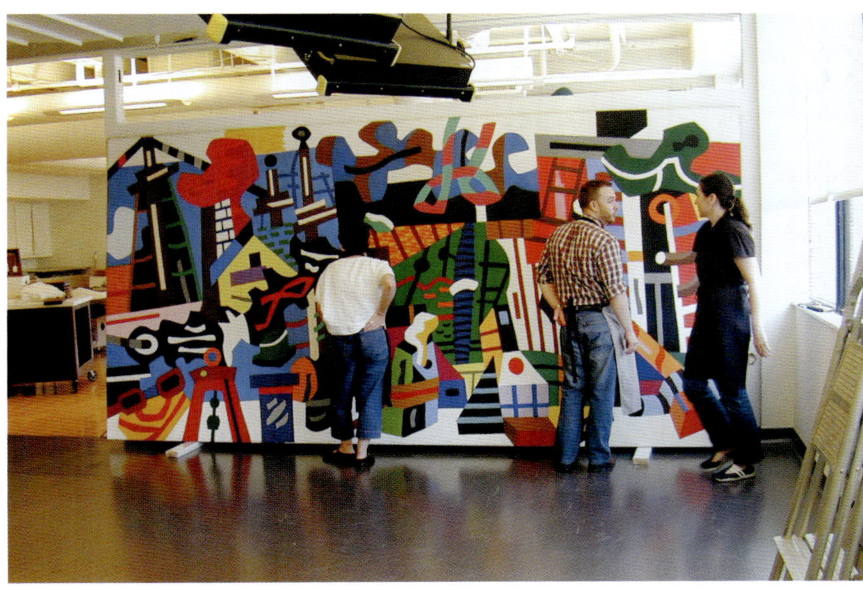

Swing Landscape undergoing major conservation treatment at the Intermuseum Conservation Association, Cleveland, Ohio, 2003.

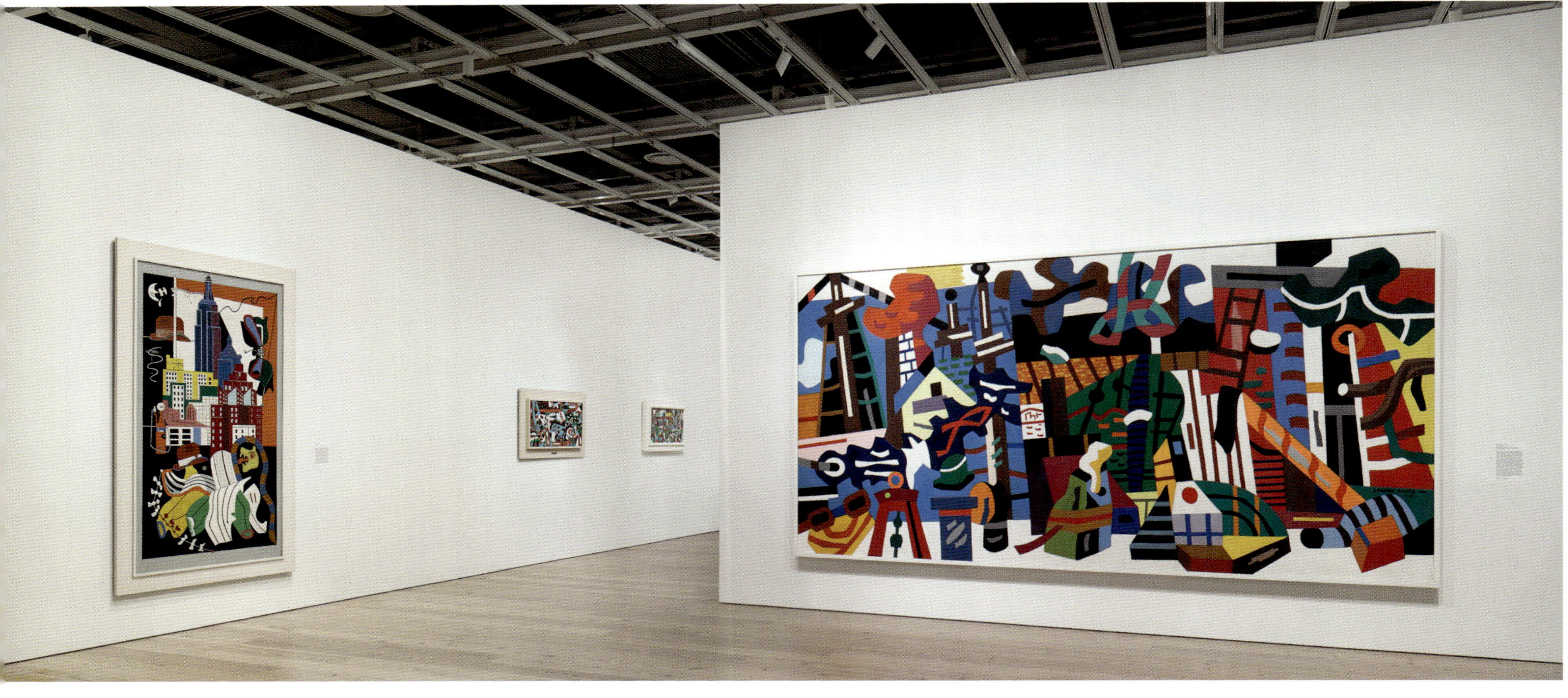

Installation view of *Stuart Davis: In Full Swing* (June 10–September 25, 2016). Whitney Museum of American Art, New York. Photo: Ron Amstutz.

Michael Taylor, juxtaposes the mural with paintings by nine other abstract painters of the 1930s. A review in the *Philadelphia Inquirer*, while expressing a cool attitude toward Davis's contemporaries, offers glowing praise for *Swing Landscape*: "*Swing Landscape*, one of [Davis's] most complex and spirited pictures, represents the apogee of his compositional style, which might be described as 'frozen animation.' The painting could easily stand for everything he contributed to American modernism."[37]

2007

A major catalogue raisonné of Stuart Davis's oeuvre is published by Yale University Art Gallery and Yale University Press.

2016–17

Swing Landscape is included in two of the venues hosting the third major Stuart Davis retrospective, *In Full Swing: The Art of Stuart Davis*, curated by Barbara Haskell and Harry Cooper. The mural is on view at the Whitney Museum of American Art, New York, from June 10 through September 26, 2016, and the National Gallery of Art, Washington, from November 20, 2016, through March 5, 2017. At the Whitney, it is centrally positioned among Davis's other murals from the 1930s. One reviewer enthuses that *Swing Landscape* is a "spectacular painting to see in person."[38]

In 2016, the Indiana University Art Museum is renamed the Eskenazi Museum of Art, following a major donation from Sidney and Lois Eskenazi of Indianapolis.

2018–19

While the Eskenazi Museum of Art is closed for major renovations, *Swing Landscape* is displayed at the Amon Carter Museum of American Art in Fort Worth, Texas.

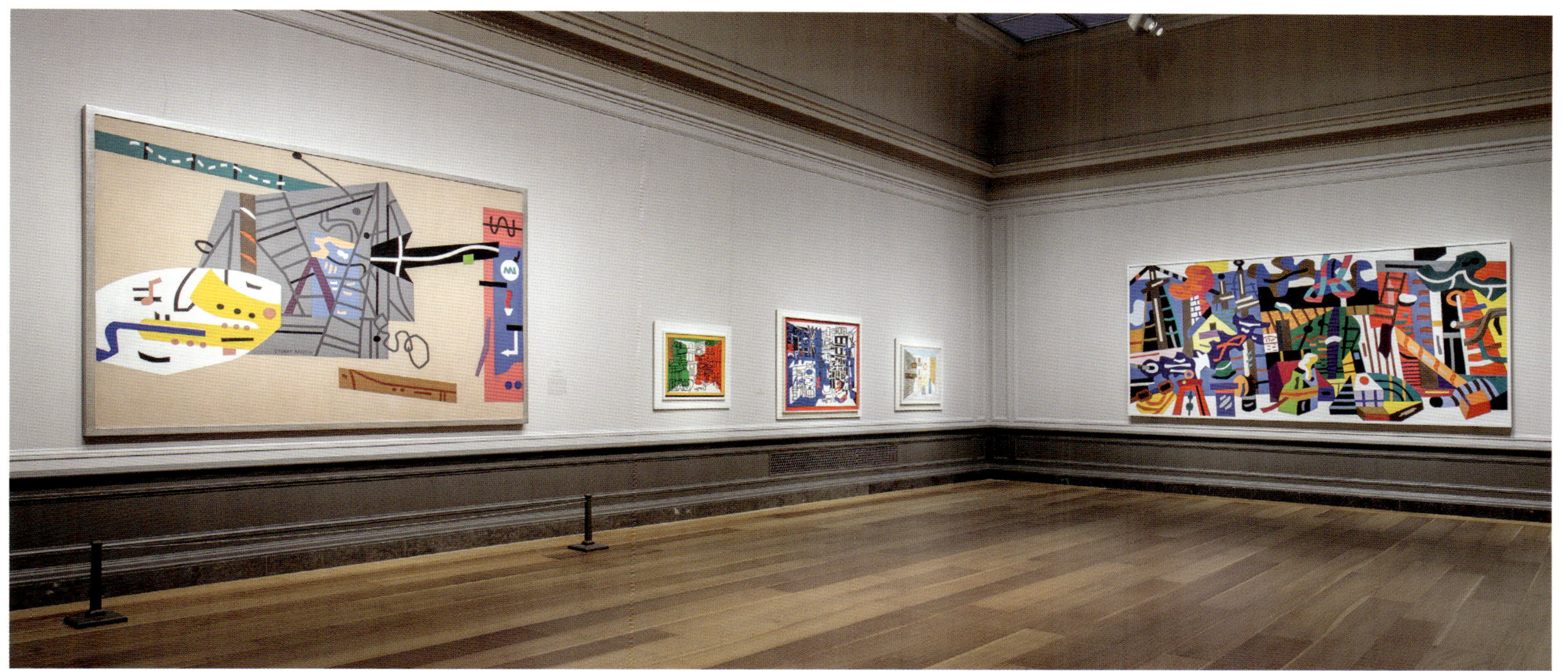

Installation photograph, *Stuart Davis: In Full Swing* (November 20, 2016–March 5, 2017), National Gallery of Art, Washington.

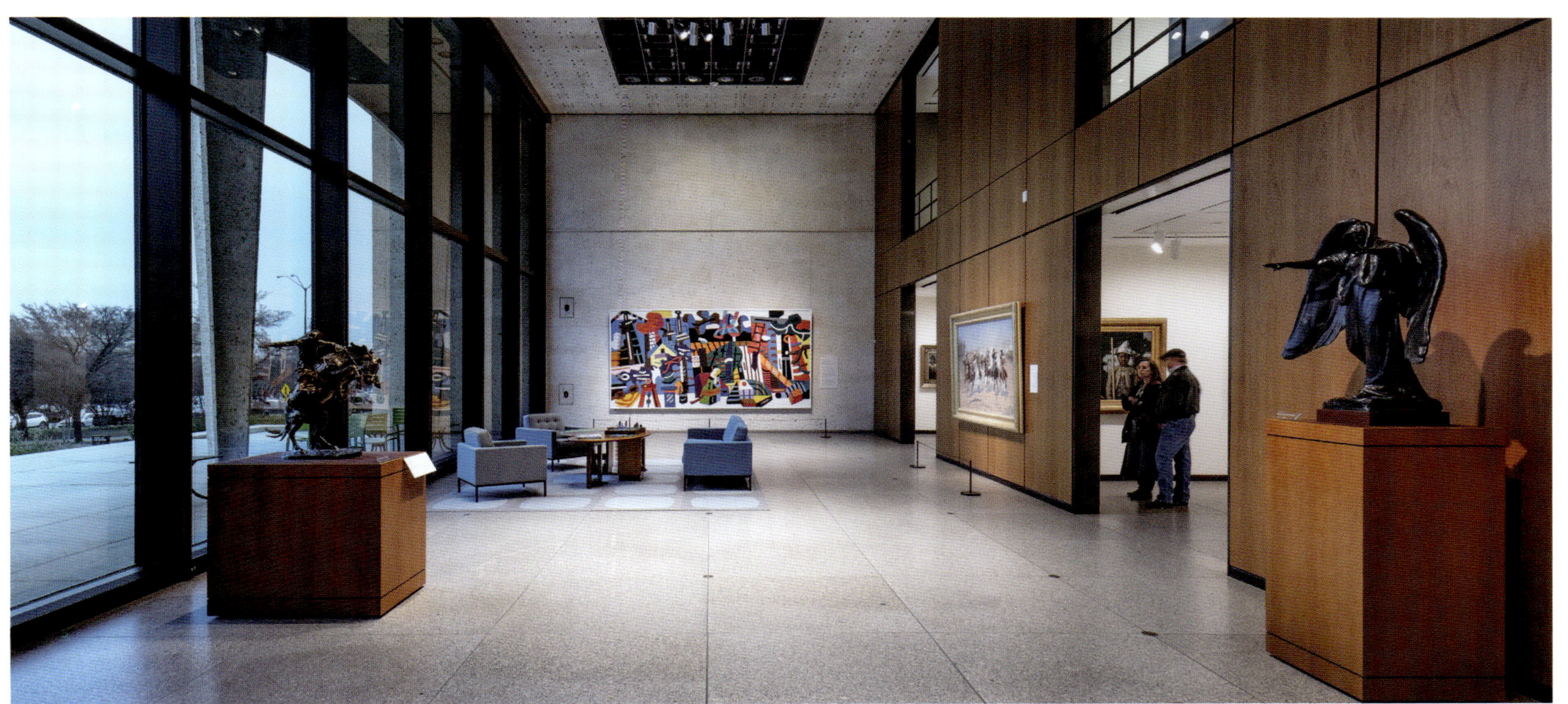

Swing Landscape on view at the Amon Carter Museum of American Art, Fort Worth, Texas, 2019.

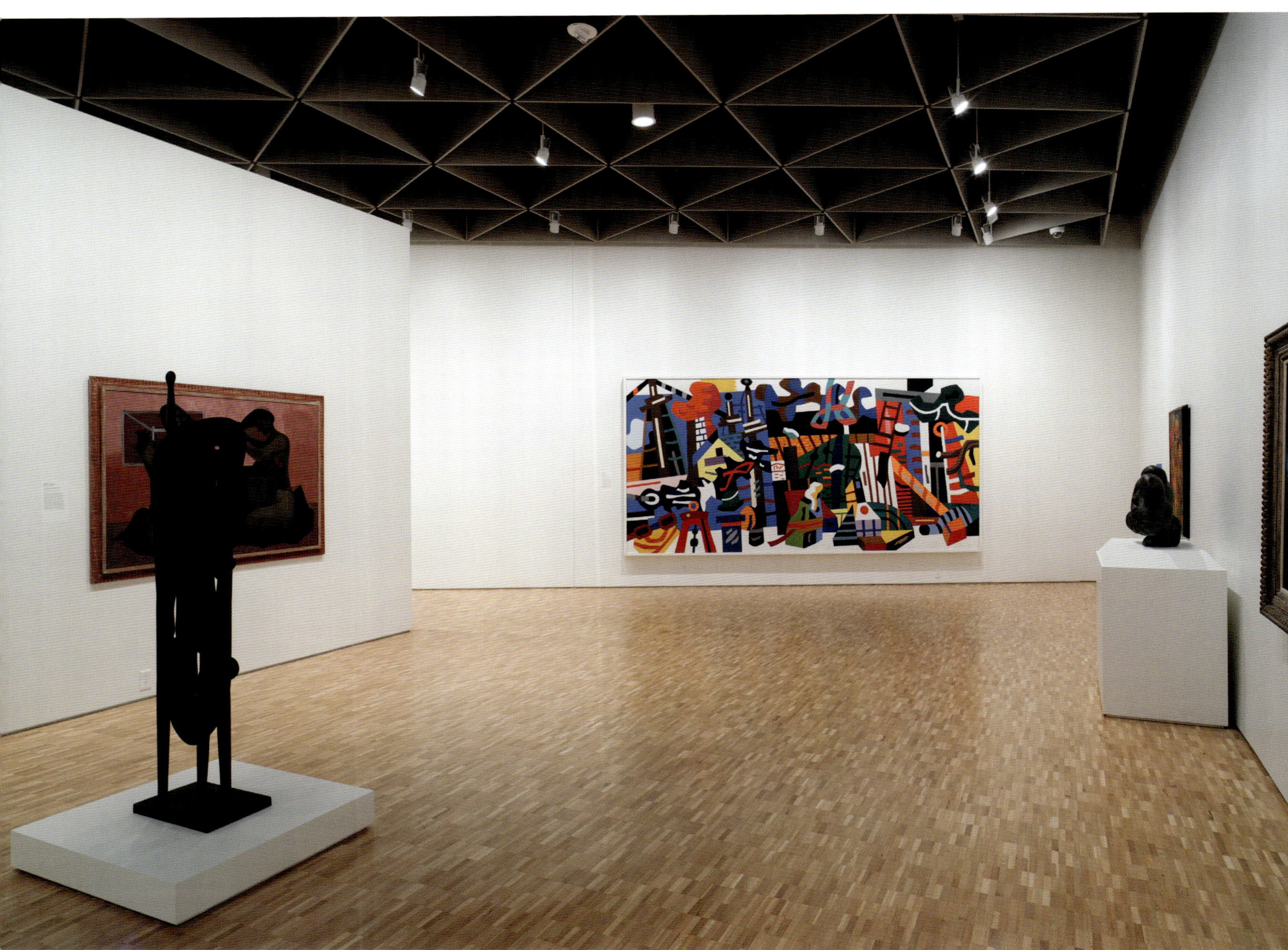

Swing Landscape on view in the newly reinstalled galleries of the Eskenazi Museum of Art, Indiana University, fall 2019.

2019

In November, the Eskenazi Museum of Art reopens to the public with fully reinstalled permanent collection galleries. *Swing Landscape* anchors a gallery devoted to the art of the Americas in the 1930s and 1940s.

1. Boyajian and Rutkowski, *Stuart Davis*, 2:625–26.

2. David C. Comstock to H. A. Gray, Director of Housing, Washington, DC, October 1, 1936, New York City Housing Authority (hereafter NYCHA) Papers, box 53B8, folder 11.

3. Cited in Boyajian and Rutkowski, *Stuart Davis*, 3:289.

4. Burgoyne Diller to Langdon Post, February 25, 1937, NYCHA Papers, box 53D, folder 15.

5. Memorandum, June 29, 1937, Stuart Davis Papers, "Writings re. American Artists Congress; FAP" folder, Archives of American Art.

6. Gray to Post, July 27, 1937, NYCHA Papers, box 53D1, folder 15.

7. Stuart Davis's calendar, August 26, 1937, cited in Boyajian and Rutkowski, *Stuart Davis*, 3:293.

8. Stuart Davis, "Synopsis on Abstract Art in Williamsburg Project," typescript, Stuart Davis Papers, microfilm reel 1, Houghton Library, Harvard University. Reproduced in full with permission from Earl Davis, Estate of Stuart Davis.

9. Jewell, "Commentary on Murals."

10. The Davis catalogue raisonné states that the mural was not installed because of architectural changes to the building, but it provides no citation. Boyajian and Rutkowski, *Stuart Davis*, 3:293.

11. Boyajian and Rutkowski, *Stuart Davis*, 3:293.

12. Boyajian and Rutkowski, *Stuart Davis*, 3:293.

13. Boyajian and Rutkowski, *Stuart Davis*, 3:293.

14. Stuart Davis to Peggy Frank, September 29, 1941, Cincinnati Modern Art Society Papers, University of Cincinnati Libraries, Archives and Rare Books Department. Copy in curatorial files, Eskenazi Museum of Art.

15. Davis to Frank, December 1, 1941; and V. Roger Wood, Chief Public Activities Programs Section, WPA, to Cincinnati Modern Art Society, December 4, 1941, Cincinnati Modern Art Society Papers. Copy in curatorial files, Eskenazi Museum of Art.

16. Frank to Wood, December 19, 1941, Cincinnati Modern Art Society Papers. Copy in curatorial files, Eskenazi Museum of Art.

17. Wood to Frank, January 12, 1942; Wood to Cincinnati Modern Art Society, January 26, 1942; and Mary Laura Sullivan to Henry Radford Hope, January 28, 1942, Cincinnati Modern Art Society Papers. Copy in curatorial file, Eskenazi Museum of Art.

18. Cited in Boyajian and Rutkowski, *Stuart Davis*, 3:293. The allocation paperwork for *Swing Landscape* has never been located, and some documents in the museum's files note that the WPA placed the mural with the university as a long-term loan of one hundred years. These documents are dated decades after the mural's allocation to the university and presumably reflect Hope's faulty memory (or his misunderstanding) of the WPA's allocation policy. Allocations were essentially donations (with certain stipulations) and did not have time limits.

19. James Johnson Sweeney to Hope, February 12, 1946, MoMA exhibition files, folder 298.2, MoMA Archives.

20. Sweeney to Hope, February 12, 1946, MoMA exhibition files, folder 298.2, MoMA Archives.

21. Lucas, "Fine Art Jive of Stuart Davis."

22. Thomas T. Solley to Michael Botwinick, director of the Brooklyn Museum, December 6, 1976, curatorial files, Eskenazi Museum of Art.

23. Oral history interview with Carl Holty, December 8, 1964, Archives of American Art.

24. Treatment Report from Intermuseum Conservation Association Laboratory, Oberlin, OH, September 1967, Conservation Files, Eskenazi Museum of Art.

25. Richard D. Buck to Mrs. Jack Gilfoy, June 10, 1967, Conservation Files, Eskenazi Museum of Art.

26. Memorandum, June 29, 1937, Stuart Davis Papers, box 1, "Writings, re. American Artists Congress FAP" folder, Archives of American Art.

27. Adelheid Gealt to David Bancroft, National Endowment for the Arts, November 30, 2004, Conservation Files, Eskenazi Museum of Art.

28. William C. Agee to Hope, July 26, 1968, Frances Mulhall Achilles Library, WMAA Exhibitions Archives, box 0045, folder 25, Whitney Museum of American Art.

29. *Art in America* 64, no. 5 (September–October 1976).

30. Martin J. Radecki to Gealt, November 8, 1991, Conservation Files, Eskenazi Museum of Art.

31. Anfam, "Stuart Davis. San Francisco."

32. Hughes, "American Visions," *Time*.

33. Funding was also sought, but not received, from the Getty Grant Program.

34. Treatment Summary from Intermuseum Conservation Association, 2003, Conservation Files, Eskenazi Museum of Art.

35. Radecki, Examination Report Addendum, 1991, Conservation Files, Eskenazi Museum of Art.

36. Gealt to Bancroft, National Endowment for the Arts, November 30, 2004, Conservation Files, Eskenazi Museum of Art.

37. Sozanski, "Jazzy Masterpiece on a Local Stage."

38. McGlyn, "Pops Standard."

Bibliography

Archives

Archives of American Art, Smithsonian Institution, Washington, DC
- Ilya Bolotowsky Papers
- Harry Bowden Papers
- Byron Browne Papers
- Holger Cahill Papers
- Francis Criss Papers
- Stuart Davis Papers
- Burgoyne Diller Papers
- Balcomb Greene Papers
- Jan Matulka Papers
- Federal Art Project Photographic Division Records
- Downtown Gallery Records

The Brooklyn Museum, New York
- Curatorial Files

Eskenazi Museum of Art, Bloomington, IN
- Curatorial Files
- Conservation Files
- Registrar's Files

Harvard Art Museums Archives, Cambridge, MA
- Stuart Davis Papers
- Paul J. Sachs Papers, HC 3

Houghton Library, Harvard University, Cambridge, MA
- Stuart Davis Papers

Indiana University Archives, Bloomington

LaGuardia & Wagner Archives, New York
- New York City Housing Authority (NYCHA) Papers

Museum of Modern Art Archives, New York
- Exhibition Files

National Archives and Records Administration (NARA), College Park, MD
- Records of the Works Projects Administration, RG 69

Syracuse University Archives, Syracuse, NY
- William Lescaze Papers

Whitney Museum of American Art, New York
- Exhibition Files

Published Sources

Adams, Henry. *Jan Matulka.* Exh. cat. Chicago: Thomas McCormick Gallery, 1999.

Agee, William C. *American Vanguards: Graham, Davis, Gorky, de Kooning, and Their Circle, 1927–1942.* Exh. cat. New Haven: Yale University Press, 2011.

——. *Modern Art in America, 1908–1968.* London: Phaidon, 2016.

Alexander, Stephen. "Mural Painting in America." *New Masses* 14, no. 9 (February 26, 1935): 26.

Anfam, David. "Stuart Davis. San Francisco." *Burlington Magazine* 134, no. 1068 (March 1992): 210.

Anreus, Alejandro, Robin Adèle Greeley, and Leonard Folgarait, eds. *Mexican Muralism: A Critical History.* Berkeley: University of California Press, 2012.

Architecture in Government Housing. Exh. cat. New York: Museum of Modern Art, 1936.

Baigell, Matthew, and Julia Williams, eds. *Artists against War and Fascism: Papers of the First American Artists' Congress.* New Brunswick, NJ: Rutgers University Press, 1986.

Bakan, Jonathon. "Jazz and the 'Popular Front': 'Swing' Musicians and the Left-Wing Movement of the 1930s–1940s." *Jazz Perspectives* 31, no. 1 (2009): 35–56.

Balken, Debra Bricker. "Jean Hélion's American Connections." In *Jean Hélion.* Exh. cat. Paris: Centre Georges Pompidou; London: Paul Holberton, 2004.

Barron, Stephanie, ed. *"Degenerate Art": The Fate of the Avant-Garde in Nazi Germany.* Exh. cat. Los Angeles: Los Angeles County Museum of Art, 1991.

Baudin, Katia, ed. *Fernand Léger: Painting in Space.* Exh. cat. Cologne: Museum Ludwig, 2016.

Bauer, Catherine. *Modern Housing.* Boston: Houghton Mifflin, 1934.

Berman, Greta. "Abstractions for Public Spaces, 1935–1943." *Arts Magazine* 56, no. 10 (June 1982): 82–84.

——. "The Lost Years: Mural Painting in New York City under the Works Progress Administration's Federal Art Project 1935–1943." PhD diss., Columbia University, 1975.

Berman, Marshall. *All That's Solid Melts into Air: The Experience of Modernity.* London: Penguin, 1998.

Blau, Eve. *The Architecture of Red Vienna, 1919–1934.* Cambridge, MA: MIT Press, 1999.

Blesh, Rudi. *Stuart Davis.* New York: Grove, 1960.

Bloom, Nicholas Dagen. *Public Housing That Worked: New York in the Twentieth Century.* Philadelphia: University of Pennsylvania Press, 2008.

Boswell, Peyton. *Modern American Painting.* New York: Dodd, Mead, 1940.

Bowman, Ruth. *Murals without Walls: Arshile Gorky's Aviation Murals Rediscovered.* Exh. cat. Newark, NJ: Newark Museum, 1978.

Boyajian, Ani, and Mark Rutkowski, eds. *Stuart Davis: A Catalogue Raisonné.* 3 vols. New Haven: Yale University Art Gallery, in association with Yale University Press, 2007.

Brace, Ernest. "An American Group, Inc." *Magazine of Art* 3, no. 5 (May 1938): 271–75.

Brock, H. I. "A Modernist Scans Our Skyline." *New York Times,* April 11, 1937.

Cahill, Holger. *New Horizons in American Art.* Exh. cat. New York: Museum of Modern Art, 1936.

Cahill, Holger, and Alfred H. Barr Jr., eds. *Art in America in Modern Times.* New York: Reynal and Hitchcock, 1934.

Carr, Eleanor. "The New Deal and the Sculptor: A Study of Federal Relief to the Sculptor on the New York City Federal Art Project of the Works Progress Administration, 1935–1945." PhD diss., New York University, 1969.

——. "New York Sculpture during the Federal Project." *Art Journal* 31, no. 4 (Summer 1972): 397–403.

Christ, John X. “Stuart Davis and the Politics of Experience.” *American Art* 22, no. 2 (Summer 2008): 42–63.

———. “Stuart Davis as Public Artist: American Painting and the Reconstruction of the Public Sphere.” *Art History* 33, no. 1 (February 2010): 65–82.

Coates, Robert. “The Art Galleries.” *New Yorker*, November 5, 1938.

Contreras, Belisario R. *Tradition and Innovation in New Deal Art.* London: Associated University Presses; Lewisburg, PA: Bucknell University Press, 1983.

Davis, Stuart. “The American Artists’ Congress.” *Art Front* 8 (December 1935): 8.

———. “The Cube Root.” *Art News* 41, no. 18 (February 1, 1943): 33–34.

———. “What about Modern Art and Democracy?” *Harper’s* (December 1943): 16–23.

de Hart Mathews, Jane. “Arts and the People: The New Deal Quest for a Cultural Democracy.” *Journal of American Aesthetics* 62, no. 2 (September 1975): 316–39.

Donnelly, Jennifer. “Myth, Modernity, and Mass Housing: The Development of Public Housing in Depression-Era Cleveland.” *Traditional Dwellings and Settlement Review* 25, no. 1 (Fall 2013): 55–68.

Dowes, Olin. “Art for Housing Tenants.” *Magazine of Art* (November 1938): 616–23, 662.

Elderfield, John. *De Kooning: A Retrospective.* Exh. cat. New York: Museum of Modern Art, 2011.

Erenberg, Lewis A. *Swingin’ the Dream: Big Band Jazz and the Rebirth of American Culture.* Chicago: University of Chicago Press, 1998.

Evergood, Philip. “Should Art Prettify Heroes?” *Daily Worker*, November 2, 1942.

———. “Sure, I’m a Social Painter.” *Magazine of Art* 36 (October 1943): 254–59.

Federal Writers Project. *The WPA Guide to New York City* [1939]. New York: Pantheon, 1982.

Frank, Peggy. *Marsden Hartley, Stuart Davis.* Cincinnati, OH: Cincinnati Modern Art Society, 1941.

Gallati, Barbara Dayer. *The Williamsburg Murals: A Rediscovery.* Exh. brochure. New York: Brooklyn Museum, 1990.

Genauer, Emily. “Younger Painters in the East.” *Parnassus* 9, no. 4 (1937): 17–18.

Golan, Romy. *Muralnomad: The Paradox of Wall Painting, 1927–1957.* New Haven: Yale University Press, 2009.

Goossen, Eugene C. *Stuart Davis.* New York: G. Braziller, 1959.

Grad, Bonnie L. “Stuart Davis and Contemporary Culture.” *Artibus et Historiae* 12, no. 24 (1991): 165–91.

Green, Nancy E., and Keri Butler. *Revealed: WPA Murals from Roosevelt Island.* Exh. brochure. Ithaca, NY: Herbert F. Johnson Museum of Art, Cornell University, 2016.

Greene, Balcomb. “American Perspective.” *Plastique* 3 (Spring 1938): 12–14.

Guchte, Maarten van de, and Katherine Emma Manthorne. *Paul Kelpe: Abstractions and Constructions, 1925–1940.* Exh. cat. Champaign: Krannert Art Museum, University of Illinois at Urbana-Champaign, 1990.

Hardy, Charles O. *The Housing Program of the City of Vienna.* Washington, DC: Brookings Institution, 1934.

Harris, Jonathan. *Federal Art and National Culture: The Politics of Identity in New Deal America.* Cambridge: Cambridge University Press, 1996.

Harrison, Helen A. “Subway Art and the Public Use of Arts Committee.” *Archives of American Art Journal* 30, no. 1/4 (1990): 2–12.

Harry Bowden Memorial Exhibition. Exh. cat. New York: Twentieth Century Galleries, 1965.

Haskell, Barbara. *Burgoyne Diller.* Exh. cat. New York: Whitney Museum of American Art, 1990.

Haskell, Barbara, and Harry Cooper. *Stuart Davis: In Full Swing.* Exh. cat. Washington, DC: National Gallery of Art; New York: Whitney Museum of American Art, 2016.

Hemingway, Andrew. *Artists on the Left: American Artists and the Communist Movement, 1926–1956.* New Haven: Yale University Press, 2002.

——. "Cultural Democracy by Default: The Politics of the New Deal Art Programmes." *Oxford Art Journal* 30, no. 2 (2007): 269–87.

Hess, Thomas B. *Willem de Kooning.* New York: George Braziller, 1959.

Hills, Patricia. *Stuart Davis.* New York: Harry N. Abrams, in association with the National Museum of American Art, Smithsonian Institution, 1996.

Hughes, Robert. "American Visions." *Time,* special issue (Spring 1997).

——. *American Visions: The Epic History of Art in America.* New York: Alfred A. Knopf, 1997.

Indych-López, Anna. *Muralism without Walls: Rivera, Orozco, and Siqueiros in the United States, 1927–1940.* Pittsburgh: University of Pittsburgh Press, 2009.

Jeffers, Wendy. "Holger Cahill and American Art." *Archives of American Art Journal* 31, no. 4 (1991): 2–11.

Jewell, Edward Alden. "Commentary on Murals." *New York Times,* May 29, 1938.

Kainen, Jacob. "Abstract Art Exhibit Barely Comprehensible." *Daily Worker,* February 25, 1938.

Kelder, Diane. *Stuart Davis: Art and Art Theory, 1920–31.* Exh. cat. New York: The Pierpont Morgan Library, 2002.

——, ed. *Stuart Davis.* New York: Praeger, 1971.

Kiesler, Frederick, "Between Murals without Walls and Walls without Murals." *Architectural Record* 81, no. 2 (1937): 10–12.

Knott, Robert, and J. Donald Nichols. *American Abstract Art of the 1930s and 1940s: The J. Donald Nichols Collection.* Exh. cat. Winston-Salem, NC: Wake Forest University; New York: Abrams, 1998.

Lanchner, Carolyn, ed. *Fernand Léger.* Exh. cat. New York: Museum of Modern Art, 1998.

Landau, Ellen G. *Lee Krasner: A Catalogue Raisonné.* New York: Abrams, 1995.

Lane, John R. *Stuart Davis: Art and Art Theory.* Exh. cat. New York: Brooklyn Museum, 1978.

Lane, John R., and Susan C. Larsen, eds. *Abstract Painting and Sculpture in America, 1927– 1944.* Exh. cat. Pittsburgh, PA: Museum of Art, Carnegie Institute, in association with Abrams, 1983.

Langa, Helen. *Radical Art: Printmaking and the Left in 1930s New York.* Berkeley: University of California Press, 2004.

Lanmon, Ann Lorraine Welling. "The Role of William E. Lescaze in the Introduction of the International Style to the United States." PhD diss., University of Delaware, 1979.

Léger, Fernand. "The New Realism Goes On." *Art Front* (February 1937): 7–8.

——. "The Origins of Painting and Its Representational Value" [1913]. Translated and reprinted in *Functions of Painting,* ed. Edward F. Fry. New York: Viking, 1973.

Levin, Gail. "Byron Browne in the Context of Abstract Expressionism." *Arts Magazine* 59, no. 10 (Summer 1985): 129–33.

London, Michele. *A Legacy Regained: The Rediscovery and Restoration of the "Lost" WPA Murals.* New York: New York City Housing Authority, n.d. [ca. 1990].

Lucas, John. “The Fine Art Jive of Stuart Davis.” *Arts Magazine* 31, no. 10 (September 1957): 33–36.

Lukach, Joan M. *Hilla Rebay: In Search of the Spirit in Art.* New York: George Braziller, 1983.

Marquardt, Virginia Hagelstein. “The American Artists School: Radical Heritage and Social Content Art.” *Archives of American Art Journal* 26, no. 4 (1986): 17–23.

McComas, Jennifer. “Canonizing Hitler’s ‘Degenerate Art’ in Three American Exhibitions, 1938–1942.” In *Re-Envisioning the Contemporary Art Canon: Perspectives in a Global World*, ed. Ruth Iskin. London: Routledge, 2017.

——. “Public Art and the Perils of Canonization: The Case of *Swing Landscape* by Stuart Davis.” *Journal of Art Historiography* 19 (December 2018): https://arthistoriography.files.wordpress.com/2018/11/mccomas.pdf.

McGlyn, Tom. “Pops Standard: Stuart Davis *In Full Swing*.” *Brooklyn Rail*, July 11, 2016.

Miller, Barbara Lane. *Architecture and Politics in Germany, 1918–1945.* Cambridge, MA: Harvard University Press, 1968.

Monroe, Gerald M. “Artists as Militant Trade Union Workers during the Great Depression.” *Archives of American Art Journal* 14, no. 1 (1974): 7–10.

Morris, George L. K. “Art Chronicle: Interview with Jean Hélion.” *Partisan Review* 4, no. 5 (April 1938): 33–40.

Murals by American Painters and Photographers. Exh. cat. New York: Museum of Modern Art, 1932.

Murals for the Community. Exh. brochure. New York: Federal Art Gallery, 1938.

O’Connor, Francis V., ed. *Art for the Millions: Essays from the 1930s by Artists and Administrators of the WPA Federal Art Project.* Boston: New York Graphic Society, 1973.

Ory, Pascal. *La Belle Illusion: Culture et politique en France sous le signe du Front Populaire, 1935–1938.* Paris: Plon, 1994.

Park, Marlene, and Gerald E. Markowitz. *New Deal for Art: The Government Art Projects of the 1930s with Examples from New York City & State.* Exh. cat. Hamilton, NY: Gallery Association of New York State, 1977.

Patterson, Jody. “The Art of Swinging Left in the 1930s: Modernism, Realism, and the Politics of the Left in the Murals of Stuart Davis.” *Art History* 33, no. 1 (February 2010): 98–123.

——. “Modernism for the Masses: Painters, Politics, and Public Art in New Deal New York.” PhD diss., University College, London, 2009.

Pommer, Richard. “The Architecture of Urban Housing in the United States during the Early 1930s.” *Journal of the Society of Architectural Historians* 37, no. 4 (December 1978): 235–64.

Postal, Matthew A. *Landmarks Preservation Designation Report, LP-2135.* New York: Landmarks Preservation Commission, June 24, 2003. http://home2.nyc.gov/html/lpc/downloads/pdf/reports/willhouse.pdf.

“Proposed Housing Development.” *Architectural Forum* 56 (March 1932): 265–66.

Radford, Gail. *Modern Housing for America: Policy Struggles in the New Deal Era.* Chicago: University of Chicago Press, 1998.

Rodgers, Daniel T. *Atlantic Crossings: Social Politics in a Progressive Age.* Cambridge, MA: Belknap Press of Harvard University Press, 1998.

Rugg, Whitney. *Jan Matulka: The Global Modernist.* Exh. cat. Montclair, NJ: Montclair Art Museum, 2004.

Schapiro, Meyer. “Race, Nationality, and Art.” *Art Front* (March 1936): 10–12.

Schipper, Merle. *Jean Hélion: The Abstract Years, 1929–1939.* Ann Arbor, MI: UMI Research Press, 1974.

Scott, William B., and Peter M. Rutkoff. *New York Modern: The Arts and the City*. Baltimore: Johns Hopkins University Press, 1999.

Serota, Nicholas, ed. *Fernand Léger: The Later Years*. Exh. cat. London: Whitechapel Art Gallery, 1987.

Sims, Lowery Stokes. *Stuart Davis: American Painter*. Exh. cat. New York: Metropolitan Museum of Art, 1991.

Sironi, Mario. "Manifesto of Mural Painting." In *Art in Theory, 1900–2000: An Anthology of Changing Ideas*, ed. Charles Harrison and Paul Wood. Oxford: Blackwell, 2003.

Sozanski, Edward J. "Jazzy Masterpiece on a Local Stage." *Philadelphia Inquirer*, January 30, 2005.

Spencer, Suzanne. "'Housing on Trial': The Museum of Modern Art and the Campaign for Modern Housing in the United States, 1932–1952." PhD diss., Emory University, 2004.

Stavitsky, Gail. *Restructured Reality: The 1930s Paintings of Francis Criss*. Washington, DC: Corcoran Gallery of Art, 2001.

Stern, Robert A. M., Gregory Gilmartin, and Thomas Mellins. *New York, 1930: Architecture and Urbanism between the Two World Wars*. New York: Rizzoli, 1987.

Strickler, Susan E., and Elaine D. Gustafson. *The Second Wave: American Abstraction of the 1930s and 1940s; Selections from the Penny and Elton Yasuna Collection*. Exh. cat. Worcester, MA: Worcester Art Museum, 1991.

Subway Art. Exh. cat. New York: Museum of Modern Art, 1938.

Susman, Warren I. *Culture as History: The Transformation of American Society in the Twentieth Century*. New York: Pantheon, 1984.

Sweeney, James Johnson. *Stuart Davis*. Exh. cat. New York: Museum of Modern Art, 1945.

Troy, Nancy J. "The Williamsburg Housing Project and the Polemic of Abstraction in American Painting of the 1930s." MA thesis, Yale University, 1976.

Urdang, Beth. *Stuart Davis, Murals: An Exhibition of Related Studies, 1932–1957*. Exh. cat. New York: Zabriskie Gallery, 1976.

Vallye, Anna, ed. *Léger: Modern Art and the Metropolis*. Exh. cat. Philadelphia: Philadelphia Museum of Art, 2013.

von Wiegand, Charmion. "Fine Arts." *New Masses* 23, no. 13 (June 22, 1937): 29.

——. "Fine Arts." *New Masses* 24, no. 3 (July 13, 1937): 28.

——. "Mural Painting in America." *Yale Review* 23, no. 4 (June 1934): 788–99.

Watson, Forbes. "The Personal Note." *Magazine of Art* 32, no. 4 (April 1939).

Wiedenhoeft, Ronald. *Berlin's Housing Revolution: German Reform in the 1920s*. Ann Arbor, MI: UMI Research, 1985.

Whiting, Cécile. *Antifascism in American Art*. New Haven: Yale University Press, 1989.

Wilkin, Karen. *Stuart Davis*. New York: Abbeville, 1987.

——. *Stuart Davis in Gloucester*. Exh. cat. West Stockbridge, MA: Hard Press, 1999.

——. "Stuart Davis in Philadelphia." *New Criterion* (April 2005): 42–47.

Wilkin, Karen, and Lewis Kachur. *The Amazing Continuity: The Drawings of Stuart Davis*. Exh. cat. New York: American Federation of Arts, in association with Harry N. Abrams, 1993.

Wilson, William. *Stuart Davis's Abstract Argot*. San Francisco: Pomegranate Artbooks, 1993.

Wood, Paul. "Realism and Realities." In *Realism, Rationalism, Surrealism: Art between the Wars*, ed. Briony Fer, David Batchelor, and Paul Wood. New Haven: Yale University Press; London: Open University, 1993.

Wurster, Catherine Bauer. "The Social Front of Modern Architecture in the 1930s." *Journal of the Society of Architectural Historians* 24, no. 1 (March 1965): 48–52.

Illustration Credits

Works created under the auspices of the WPA/FAP are in the public domain, and copyright clearance was not sought for those specific images. Works from Ani Boyajian and Mark Rutkowski, eds., *Stuart Davis: A Catalogue Raisonné* (New Haven: Yale University Press, 2007) are cited as Boyajian and Rutkowski, *Stuart Davis.*

Addison Gallery of American Art, Phillips Academy, Andover, MA/Art Resource, NY: p. 18

Image courtesy Amon Carter Museum of American Art, Fort Worth, Texas: p. 143

The Art Institute of Chicago/Art Resource, NY: p. 130

Harry Bowden Papers, 1922–1972, Archives of American Art, Smithsonian Institution: pp. 56 (top), 74, 75 (top), 100

Boyajian and Rutkowski, *Stuart Davis*, vol. 3, 280, cat. no. 1603: p. 20

Boyajian and Rutkowski, *Stuart Davis*, vol. 2, 625, cat. no. 1225: p. 87

Boyajian and Rutkowski, *Stuart Davis*, vol. 2, 302, cat. no. 622: p. 89

Boyajian and Rutkowski, *Stuart Davis*, vol. 2, 302, cat. no. 623: p. 92

Boyajian and Rutkowski, *Stuart Davis*, vol. 2, 209, cat. no. 443: pp. 124 (detail), 126 (top left)

Boyajian and Rutkowski, *Stuart Davis*, vol. 2, 285, cat. no. 585: p. 126 (top right)

Boyajian and Rutkowski, *Stuart Davis*, vol. 2, 277, cat. no. 569: p. 126 (bottom right)

Boyajian and Rutkowski, *Stuart Davis*, vol. 2, 276, cat. no. 567: p. 127 (top left)

Boyajian and Rutkowski, *Stuart Davis*, vol. 2, 276, cat. no. 568: p. 127 (bottom left)

Boyajian and Rutkowski, *Stuart Davis*, vol. 2, 298, cat. no. 613: p. 127 (bottom right)

Boyajian and Rutkowski, *Stuart Davis*, vol. 3, 277, cat. no. 1599: p. 128 (bottom right)

bpk Bildagentur/Kunstbibliothek, Staatliche Museen, Berlin/Art Resource, NY: p. 31

Brooklyn Museum: pp. 72–73, 96, 98, 99, 122–23

Columbus Museum of Art: p. 19

Photo courtesy Katherine Criss: pp. 80–81

Crystal Bridges Museum of American Art: p. 131 (bottom left)

D. Wigmore Fine Art, New York: p. 59

Davis Museum at Wellesley College, Wellesley, MA: p. 37

Photo: Doyle New York: p. 70

John Elderfield, *De Kooning: A Retrospective*, exh. cat. (New York: Museum of Modern Art, 2011), 71, figs. 4 and 5: pp. 100, 101 (bottom)

Eskenazi Museum of Art, Indiana University. Photo: Kevin Montague: pp. 2–3, 16, 93, 127 (bottom right) 128 (top right), 131 (top left), 140

Eskenazi Museum of Art, Indiana University. Photo: Shanti Knight: p. 144

Fayez Sarofim Collection: p. 30

Federal Art Project, Photographic Division collection, circa 1920–1965, bulk 1935–1942. Archives of American Art, Smithsonian Institution: pp. 12, 14, 66, 69, 71 (bottom), 77, 78, 79, 80, 82, 83, 91 (top), 94, 116, 117, 119, 137

Photographic Division, Federal Art Project, Work Projects Administration. Courtesy National Archives, photo no. 69-ANM-51-P2938-1: p. 34

Frelinghuysen Morris House & Studio, Lenox, Massachusetts: p. 58

Courtesy of Godel & Co., Inc., New York: p. 63

Harvard Art Museums/Fogg Museum. © President and Fellows of Harvard College: pp. 86, 128 (top left)

High Museum of Art, Atlanta: pp. 56 (bottom), 110 (bottom)

Hirshhorn Museum and Sculpture Garden, Smithsonian Institution, Washington, DC: p. 128 (top left)

Copyright ICA–Art Conservation: p. 141

Iris & B. Gerald Cantor Center for Visual Arts at Stanford University: p. 101 (top)

Indiana University Archives: pp. 40, 134 (detail), 138 (top), 139

Image courtesy of Kasmin Gallery. Photo: Diego Flores: pp. 44 (detail), 57, 131 (bottom right), 132 (top left)

Robert Knott, *American Abstract Art of the 1930s and 1940s: The J. Donald Nichols Collection*, exh. cat. (Winston-Salem, NC: Wake Forest University, 1998), 81: p. 106

Robert Knott, *American Abstract Art of the 1930s and 1940s: The J. Donald Nichols Collection*, exh. cat. (Winston-Salem, NC: Wake Forest University, 1998), 99: p. 120

William Lescaze Papers, Special Collections Research Center, Syracuse University Libraries: pp. 75 (bottom), 76, 81, 95, 97, 103, 105 (bottom), 112, 113, 114–15

Library of Congress Prints and Photographs Division, Washington, DC. Photograph: https://www.loc.gov/item/2004672462/: p. 9

Jan Matulka Papers, 1923–1960, Archives of American Art, Smithsonian Institution: p. 102

Photo: Jennifer McComas: pp. 8, 11 (top and bottom), 135

Photograph by Helen McNeil-Ashton, reproduced by permission of The George McNeil Charitable Trust: pp. 104, 105 (top), 107, 108, 109, 110 (top), 111

The Menil Collection, Houston. Photo: Paul Hester: p. 132 (top left)

Image © The Metropolitan Museum of Art. Image source: Art Resource, NY: p. 140 (bottom)

Courtesy of Michael Rosenfeld Gallery LLC, New York: p. 69

Museo Nacional Centro de Arte Reina Sofia, Madrid: p. 50

Digital Image © The Museum of Modern Art/Licensed by SCALA/Art Resource, NY: pp. 24–25, 138

The Museum of the City of New York/Art Resource, NY: pp. 6, 132

National Gallery of Art, Washington: p. 91

National Gallery of Art, Washington, Gallery Archives. Photo: Rob Shelley: p. 143

New York City Housing Authority Papers, The La Guardia and Wagner Archives, La Guardia Community College/The City University of New York. Photo: Anna-Marie Kellen: p. 11

Courtesy Norton Museum of Art, West Palm Beach, FL: p. 27

Courtesy of the Pennsylvania Academy of the Fine Arts: p. 4

The Philadelphia Museum of Art/Art Resource, NY: p. 23

The Phillips Collection, Washington, DC: p. 39

Portland Museum of Art, Portland, ME: p. 21

Sapienza University of Rome: p. 49

Sheldon Museum of Art, University of Nebraska–Lincoln: p. 88

Smithsonian American Art Museum, Washington, DC: pp. 61, 85, 90

The Solomon R. Guggenheim Foundation: p. 55

University of Iowa, Stanley Museum of Art: p. 53

Whitney Museum of American Art: pp. 71 (top), 84, 121, 130 (bottom right), 131 (top right), 142

Yale University Art Gallery, New Haven, CT: p. 130